Global Europe: Legal and Policy Issues of the EU's External Action

Volume 7

The *Global Europe Book Series: Legal and Policy Issues of the EU's External Action Series* is a peer-reviewed book series that explores the legal and policy issues pertaining to the EU's global actorness. The editors of the book series welcome edited volumes as well as monographs exploring the EU's identity as an international actor. The coverage extends to submissions identifying the internal and external factors that may challenge the EU's capacity to exercise value-based global leadership on crucial issues affecting European citizens as well as those from other parts of the world; critically reflecting on whether the external projection of the EU as a virtuous normative power comports with its practice on the ground as well as addressing the descriptive, normative and conceptual challenges that complement the ever-expanding global reach of EU law.

Sara Poli · Madalina Moraru · Luca Paladini · Clara Portela

The EU's Response to the War in Ukraine and Its Impact on the EU Legal Order

ASSER PRESS

Springer

Sara Poli
Department of Political Science
University of Pisa
Pisa, Italy

Madalina Moraru
Department of Political and Social Sciences
University of Bologna
Bologna, Italy

Luca Paladini
Department of Humanities
University for Foreigners of Siena
Siena, Italy

Clara Portela
Faculty of Law, Department
of Constitutional Law and Political Science
University of Valencia
Valencia, Spain

ISSN 2666-4828 ISSN 2666-4836 (electronic)
Global Europe: Legal and Policy Issues of the EU's External Action
ISBN 978-94-6265-766-3 ISBN 978-94-6265-767-0 (eBook)
https://doi.org/10.1007/978-94-6265-767-0

Published by T.M.C. ASSER PRESS, The Hague, The Netherlands www.asserpress.nl
Produced and distributed for T.M.C. ASSER PRESS by Springer-Verlag Berlin Heidelberg

This T.M.C. ASSER PRESS imprint is published by the registered company Springer-Verlag GmbH, DE, part of Springer Nature.
The registered company address is: Heidelberger Platz 3, 14197 Berlin, Germany

Foreword

The impact of Russia's invasion of Ukraine can hardly be overestimated, and of course the war that this act of aggression prompted is still raging, now in its fifth year. Much may be said about that impact, ethically, geopolitically and legally and this book provides a welcome and multi-faceted examination, *in media res*, of one specific dimension: the EU's response and how that response has shaped the EU 'as a legal order and as an international actor'—in the authors' well-expressed phrase.

It is often said that it is in responding to crises, both internally and externally generated, that the EU, historically, has taken some of the most significant steps in its process of integration. We can certainly see such moments in the EU's response to (for example) the fall of the Berlin Wall, the terrorist attacks of 11 September 2001, the financial and sovereign debt crises of 2009–2018, Brexit, and Covid. Even in comparison to these major events, the direct and indirect impacts of the Russian invasion of Ukraine are both deep and far-ranging—for Ukraine and Russia itself certainly, but also for the EU, for which the conflict has been seen as a test of its ability to act to defend its neighbourhood and its values. This book offers some fascinating studies of the EU's response, and responsiveness; and as the comments above suggest, it is concerned not only with assessing its effectiveness, but also in the way in which the need to find appropriate and effective instruments has influenced the EU's own development.

What are those instruments? Since an EEC instrument was first used in 1982 to impose economic sanctions against the Soviet Union as a response to the imposition of martial law in Poland, restrictive measures have become a key EU foreign policy instrument, used now not only against specific countries and regimes but also against individuals. They have expanded from simple quantitative restrictions on goods to include sophisticated measures on investment, foreign media, arms embargoes, and targeted 'smart sanctions' such as asset freezes and visa bans. From the start they have prompted debate as to competence, appropriate legal basis, scope and type of measures, compliance with both international law and the EU's own fundamental rights protections, including access to justice, and—not least—their effectiveness. Restrictive measures have played a central role in the EU's response to the invasion of Ukraine, being—it can be argued—transformed as a foreign policy tool in process:

it is telling that five chapters of this book are, entirely justifiably, devoted to restrictive measures. We have seen an expansion of designation criteria to such an extent that the authors suggest a distinct move away from the focus on 'smart sanctions' targeting individuals identified as primarily responsible for the acts of aggression and destabilisation, towards a broader objective of undermining Russia's economy.

The freezing of the assets of the Russian Central Bank, largely held in Belgium, exemplifies this approach, and although the EU has made innovative use of a tax on the revenues from these investments to support Ukraine via the European Peace Facility, the possibility of confiscation of those assets has still not been resolved, either legally or politically. Moves have also been made to make the sanctions regime more effective, targeting circumvention, including third country operators as targets, and through the use of criminal penalties, a ground-breaking innovation at Union level. For the first time, too, sanctions have been imposed on media outlets operating within the EU, the Court accepting that the dissemination of Russian propaganda justified their objective in 'safeguard[ing] the Union's values, fundamental interests, security and integrity.'

If both restrictive measures and the use of the European Peace Facility demonstrate both the capacity for innovation within the framework of existing foreign policy instruments and considerable flexibility in the EU's institutional ability to adapt to policy divergence between Member States, through *inter alia* the use of constructive abstention, the EU's response also demonstrates some conspicuous failures, in particular the failure to activate the 'essential elements' clause in its Partnership and Cooperation Agreement with Russia. The story is by no means always positive.

Alongside specific instruments, this book engages with the way in which the EU's foreign policy objectives have been (re)shaped in response to the changed geopolitical environment. A changing perspective on solidarity within its neighbourhood is strikingly manifested in the context of migration and asylum (the Temporary Protection Directive) and enlargement. While enlargement has always possessed a foreign policy dimension, its reactivation in the post-invasion context underlines its strategic geopolitical role. The EU is nonetheless still struggling to manage the interaction between the 'high politics' of enlargement and its more technocratic procedures, and—no less difficult—to manage the expectations of both Ukraine and its Member States. At a number of points during the narrative, this book prompts us to take stock of how immediate responses triggered by admirable sentiments of solidarity can be consolidated and maintained in the longer-term and in face of intra-Member State divergence and imbalances.

No doubt, as this book argues, the significant developments in the EU's defence capability since 2022 and perhaps more significant altered awareness of the need for Europe (not just the EU) to develop greater defence autonomy are the result of a combination of factors, not least the recalibration of US foreign policy under President Trump. Nonetheless the broader impact of Putin's policies of aggression continues to pose challenges for the EU's ability to respond in both civilian and military crisis management. Above all, the war in Ukraine still continues and Ukraine's extraordinary resilience and courage is itself a challenge to us all. We can be sure that this story is not yet ended and that there will be further chapters to write in documenting the impact of that war on the EU and EU foreign policy.

Bristol, UK
March 2026

Prof. em. Marise Cremona
Department of Law
European University Institute
Fiesole, Italy

Contents

About the Authors

Madalina Moraru is Associate Professor of EU Law at the University of Bologna, Department of Political and Social Sciences, Italy, and Principal Investigator of the European Research Council Starting Grant project ACCESS—Gatekeepers to International Refugee Law? The Role of Courts in Shaping Access to Asylum (2023–2028). Her research focuses on EU migration and asylum law, EU citizenship, EU external relations, fundamental rights, and the role of courts and judicial dialogue in EU governance. Prior to joining the University of Bologna, she held academic positions at the European University Institute, Masaryk University, Brunel University London, and the University of Trento, and was a Visiting Fellow at the Court of Justice of the European Union. She regularly contributes to judicial training and research projects on EU fundamental rights, migration law, and the rule of law, and has coordinated several EU-funded research and training projects. She is the author of the monograph *Protecting (Unrepresented) EU Citizens in Third Countries* and co-editor of several volumes on judicial interaction and EU migration law. Her work has appeared in leading journals including the *Common Market Law Review*, *European Constitutional Law Review*, *European Journal of Migration and Law*, and the *Journal of Refugee Studies*.

Luca Paladini is Associate Professor of European Union Law at the University for Foreigners of Siena in Italy. He graduated and specialized at the University of Milan, and he holds a Ph.D. in EU Law from the University of Bologna. He was Jean Monnet Fellow (2008–2009) and then Visiting Fellow (2009–2011) at the European University Institute (Florence). His research interests include the EU external action, the human rights international protection, and the domestic legal order conformity with international law and EU Law. Luca Paladini is co-editor of two edited books, and he is author of a book and more than sixty contributions on EU Law and International Law. He is member of the editorial team of the Legal Journals "DPCEonline", "Giurisprudenza italiana", and "Revista Hispanoamericana de derechos humanos". Since 2022, he is the Rector's Delegate for "students' traineeships and job placement".

Sara Poli is Full Professor of European law at the University of Pisa, Italy, and Jean Monnet Chair on enlargement and the rule of law. She has been visiting professor at Luiss, Rome and at the European University Institute. In the past, she received a Jean Monnet Chair on good governance inside and outside the EU and has been part of two Jean Monnet networks. She has been Marie Curie Fellow at the European University Institute and Robert Schuman Fellow at the Robert Schuman Centre of the same institution. Sara has previously worked at the Universities of Rome 'Tor Vergata' and Trieste. She has been lecturer of European Law at the University of Southampton in the United Kingdom and teaching assistant at the College of Europe (law department) in Bruges, Belgium. She obtained her Master of legal studies degree at the College of Europe, and her Ph.D. from the Scuola Superiore S. Anna (Pisa) where she also did her undergraduate studies. Sara has published in leading EU law journals in several areas of EU law, including EU external relations. She has published on EU restrictive measures since 2016 in various Journals, including the *Common Market Law Review* and the *Yearbook of European Law*; she has also published a monograph in Italian on *Le misure restrittive autonome dell'Unione europea* in 2019.

Dr. Clara Portela teaches Political Science at the Law School of the University of Valencia in Spain, having previously served as a professor at Singapore Management University and as a research fellow with the EU Institute for Security Studies in Paris, France. She holds a Ph.D. from the European University Institute and an MA from the Free University of Berlin, Germany. She received the THESEUS Award for Promising Research on European Integration for her monograph 'European Union Sanctions and Foreign Policy', and was the inaugural Konrad Adenauer Visiting Scholar at Carleton University, Canada and HypoVereinsbank Visiting Professor at the University of Innsbruck, Austria. She was also a Visiting Professor at the College of Europe, and has advised the European Economic and Social Committee, the European Parliament, the European Commission, the Ministry of Foreign Affairs of Spain, the Office of the Prime Minister of Finland, the Ministry of International Trade and Industry of Japan, and civil society organisations.

Abbreviations

ACI	Anti-Coercion Instrument
AIDA	Asylum Information Database
AMMR	Asylum and Migration Management Regulation
ARIO	Articles on the Responsibility of International Organisations
ARSIWA	Articles on Responsibility of States for Internationally wrongul ACTS
BIPs	Beneficiaries of International Protection
CARD	Coordinated Annual Review on Defence
CBR	Central Bank of Russia
CEAS	Common European Asylum System
CFDP	Common Foreign and Defence Policy
CFSP	Common Foreign and Security Policy
CJEU	Court of Justice of the European Union
CSDs	Central Securities Depositiaries
CSDP	Common Security and Defence Policy
DCFTA	Deep and Comprehensive Free Trade Area
ECRE	European Council on Refugees and Exiles
ECFR	European Charter of Fundamental Rights
ECtHR	European Court of Human Rights
EDA	European Defence Agency
EDIP	European Defence Industry Programme
EDP	European Defence Policy
EIB	European Investments Bank
EPF	European Peace Facility
ESDP	European Security and Defence Policy
EU	European Union
EUAA	European Union Agency for Asylum
EUMAMM	European Union Military Assistance Mission
Eurofound	European Foundation for the Improvement of Living and Working Conditions
FAQs	Frequently Asked Questions

G7	Group of Seven
GC	General Court
GCM	Global Compact on Migration
GCR	Global Compact on Refugees
GDP	Gross Domestic Product
GNI	Gross National Income
HR	High Representative of the Union for Foreign Affairs and Security Policy
ICAO	International Civil Aviation Organization
IMO	International Maritime Organization
MFF	Multiannual Financial Framework
NIOC	National Iranian Oil Company
NATO	North Atlantic Treaty Organization
NGEU	NextGenerationEU
NGOs	Non-governmental Organization
PESCO	Permanent Structured Cooperation
RRF	Recovery and Resilience Facility
SAFE	Regulation on Security and Action For Europe
SGP	Stability and Growth Pact
SFDR	Sustainable Finance Disclosures Regulation
SPFS	System for Transfer of Financial Messages
SWIFT	Society for Worldwide Interbank Financial Telecommunication (SWIFT)
TCNs	Third-Country Nationals
TEU	Treaty on European Union
TFEU	Treaty on the Functioning of the European Union
TP	Temporary Protection
TPMs	Temporary Protection Mechanisms
TPD	Temporary Protection Directive
UAF	Ukrainian Armed Forces
ULCM	Ukraine Loan Cooperation Mechanism
UN	United Nations
UNGA	United Nations General Assembly
UNHCR	United Nations High Commissioner for Refugees
UNSC	United Nations Security Council

Chapter 1
The Response to Russia's Aggression of Ukraine and the Transformation of the EU Legal Order: An Overview

Sara Poli, Madalina Moraru, Luca Paladini and Clara Portela

Contents

Abstract Russia's full-scale invasion of Ukraine in February 2022 has acted as a catalyst for significant transformations in European Union governance. This introductory chapter situates the volume by analysing the Union's unprecedented response, encompassing the adoption of far-reaching restrictive measures, the mobilisation of financial and military assistance, and the reconfiguration of internal policies and institutions. It traces the evolution from the EU's more incremental reaction to the 2014 annexation of Crimea to the comprehensive sanctions regime and enhanced security engagement after 2022, highlighting in particular the strengthened role of the European Commission, the High Representative, and the Council in the design and enforcement of sanctions. The chapter also identifies the broader legal and policy consequences of the war: the provision of lethal assistance through the European Peace Facility, the renewed centrality of enlargement as a geopolitical instrument, and the first activation of the Temporary Protection Directive. These developments illustrate how the EU is undergoing both constitutional and geopolitical change, while also exposing enduring tensions between supranational and intergovernmental dynamics. By outlining these themes, the chapter provides the analytical framework for the contributions in this volume, which collectively assess how the war in Ukraine has reshaped the EU as a legal order and as an international actor.

Although the introduction to the volume is the result of a collective effort of the authors, Sara Poli wrote Sect. 1.2, Madalina Moraru is the author of Sect. 1.4, Luca Paladini wrote Sect. 1.1 and Clara Portela wrote Sect. 1.3.

S. Poli et al., *The EU's Response to the War in Ukraine and Its Impact on the EU Legal Order*, Global Europe: Legal and Policy Issues of the EU's External Action 7,
https://doi.org/10.1007/978-94-6265-767-0_1

Keywords Aggression · Restrictive measures · Russia · Ukraine · Territorial integrity · CFSP · Transformation of the EU · Enlargement · Temporary protection · Defence

1.1 Introduction

Russia's full-scale invasion of Ukraine in February 2022 has acted as a catalyst for profound transformations in European Union governance, attracting scholarly attention. This introductory chapter sets the scene to examine how the EU responded to Russia's aggression and its impact on selected aspects of the EU's legal order. By tracing the evolution from the EU's limited reaction to the 2014 annexation of Crimea to a wide in scope sanctions regime and enhanced security engagement after 2022, the chapter reflects on the various forms of the EU's response as well as on internal changes that occurred as a result of the war. It thus lays the analytical framework for the contributions in this volume, which collectively assess how the war in Ukraine has reshaped the EU as a legal order and as an international actor.

The book starts off with the EU's response to the war in the context of the Common Foreign and Security Policy ('CFSP'), which is the first 'natural' policy area to be affected by the outbreak of the war. In particular, the focus is on restrictive measures enacted by the Council, a form of coercive diplomacy on which the EU has extensively relied in practice. The book analyses in depth the evolving legal framework of sanctions, taking into consideration the case-law of the Court of Justice[1] and also the outer limits under which the EU operates in adopting restrictive measures, particularly with respect to international law.

The EU has also provided military, financial and humanitarian support to Ukraine and has encouraged the European aspirations of this country. Therefore, the book shows how the war has tested the EU's capacity for solidarity and has reconfigured some of the EU policies, such as the enlargement policy or its strategy *vis-à-vis* the mass influx of displaced persons.

The conflict that broke out in the Eastern neighbourhood has furthermore been at the basis of several EU internal transformations. In this sense, we end our analysis focusing on the shift of the EU's competence in the area of criminal law between the Union and the Member States, on the balance of powers between the Commission and the Council in the context of the EU's response to the conflict and on consensus-building in the context of the CFSP. We also examine the changes that have directly and indirectly affected the Common Security and Defence Policy ('CSDP'), since 2022 and up to the present, in particular with the advent of the Trump presidency in the US.

[1] Poli and Finelli 2025; Poli 2022.

1.2 From Crimea to Full-Scale Invasion: The EU's Evolving Response to Russia's Breaches of *Erga Omnes* Obligations and the Reaction of the International Community

The European Union's unprecedented response to Russia's full-scale invasion of Ukraine in 2022 cannot be understood without recalling the earlier event of 2014. In that year, Russia annexed Crimea, in breach of Article 2(4) of the United Nations (UN) Charter[2] and fuelled separatism in eastern Ukraine, marking the end of Russia's status as the EU's Strategic Partner, as stressed for the first time by the then High Representative of the Union for Foreign Affairs and Security Policy/Vice-President of the Commission ('HR').

At that time, the EU primarily relied on limited restrictive measures, targeting individuals and selected sectors, while making the lifting of sanctions conditional on compliance with the Minsk agreements.[3] The Union complemented these measures with diplomatic engagement, notably through support for the Normandy format in which France and Germany sought to mediate under the auspices of the Organisation for Security and Co-operation in Europe (OSCE). Yet the HR played only a limited role, and neither sanctions nor diplomacy succeeded in reversing Russia's annexation or stabilising eastern Ukraine.[1]

The escalation of tensions in late 2021 and early 2022 exposed the limitations of this earlier approach. The European Council repeatedly called on Russia to defuse tensions and return to dialogue with Ukraine, but in February 2022, President Putin recognised the so-called 'people's republics' of Donetsk and Luhansk. The EU immediately imposed restrictive measures on the 336 Russian Duma members who endorsed this step.[5] When Russian forces invaded Ukraine on 24 February, the HR, Josep Borrell, publicly condemned the act in the strongest possible terms, pledging a comprehensive response.[6] The following day, the Council adopted the first of a series of far-reaching packages of individual and sectoral sanctions.[7] Unlike in 2014, the

---

[2] UN General Assembly Resolution ES-11/4, 12 October 2022, 'Territorial integrity of Ukraine: defending the principles of the Charter of the United Nations', A/RES/ES-11/4.

[3] See First Minsk Protocol of 5 September 2014, https://www.osce.org/home/123257, and OSCE 'Memorandum of 19 September 2014', www.osce.org/home/123806 [accessed 10 November 2025]. For comments see Van Severen 2021.

[4] Christie 2016; Lonardo 2022.

[5] Members of the Duma also ratified the Treaty of Friendship, Cooperation and Mutual Assistance between the Russian Federation and the Donetsk People's Republic and between the Russian Federation and the Luhansk People's Republic. This step was taken to provide the formal legal conditions for Russia's military intervention in Ukraine.

[6] High Representative/Vice-President Josep Borrell, Statement on Russia's military aggression against Ukraine, 24 February 2022, available at https://www.eeas.europa.eu/eeas/russias-aggression-against-ukraine-press-statement-high-representativevice-president-josep-borrell_en.

[7] Council Decision (CFSP) 2022/338 of 28 February 2022 amending Decision 2014/145/CFSP concerning restrictive measures in respect of actions undermining or threatening the territorial integrity, sovereignty and independence of Ukraine, OJ L 57, 28.2.2022, p. 1.

Commission quickly became central to implementation and enforcement, working closely with the High Representative of the Union and the Council to coordinate the Union's collective response.[8]

By July 2025, the EU had adopted nineteen sanctions packages in response to Russia's breaches of *erga omnes* obligations. This made the Russia sanctions regime the most extensive in the Union's history. In contrast to the limited measures of 2014, the new sanctions cover a vastly expanded list of individuals and entities, impose restrictions concerning critical sectors of the Russian economy, and address the circumvention of EU measures. Council Decision 2014/145 has been amended more than ninety times, illustrating both the legal complexity and political dynamism of this sanctions regime.[9] At the same time, the EU coordinated its actions with G7 partners, while adopting parallel restrictive measures against Belarus in response to its material support for Russia's aggression.

Despite several resolutions by the UN General Assembly (UNGA) condemning Russia's aggression,[10] a number of States from different groups in the international community have not enacted any coercive measure in relation to Russia's illegal activities and often have supported the circumvention of restrictive measures, as documented by trade statistics.[11] On the contrary, China, the Democratic People's Republic of Korea (DPRK) and Iran have directly supported Russia's war efforts. Many countries condemned the aggression; however, most of them stopped short from adopting sanctions against the aggressor, including key regional and global actors like Armenia, Turkey, Kazakhstan, Kyrgyzstan, India and Brazil.[12]

Scholars have underlined that the Union's 2022–25 response represents a qualitative break with its earlier practice.[13] Not only did it move from incrementalism to comprehensiveness, but it also reconfigured institutional roles, enhanced the Commission's position, and highlighted the High Representative's capacity to

[8] Lepeu 2025; Korkea-aho and Lonardo 2025.

[9] Council Decision 2014/145/CFSP of 17 March 2014 concerning restrictive measures in respect of actions undermining or threatening the territorial integrity, sovereignty and independence of Ukraine, OJ L 78, 17.3.2014, p. 16, as amended.

[10] UN General Assembly Resolution ES-11/1, 2 March 2022, 'Aggression against Ukraine', A/RES/ES-11/1; UN General Assembly Resolution ES-11/4, 12 October 2022, 'Territorial integrity of Ukraine: defending the principles of the Charter of the United Nations', A/RES/ES-11/4.

[11] Mills 2025; Palestini and Portela 2025.

[12] It is worth noting that Brazil did not impose commercial sanctions on Russia; nevertheless, it granted Ukrainians access to a humanitarian visa, despite the fact that Ukrainian nationals do not require a visa to visit Brazil for up to 90 days (see https://help.unhcr.org/brazil/en/informativos-para/populacao-ucraniana/). In addition, Brazil recognized refugee status in a limited number of cases. The labelling of refugees constitutes a political act, Brazil's conduct towards Ukrainian nationals may be interpreted as an implicit condemnation of Russia's aggression. This suggestion is compelling, although from a strictly legal perspective humanitarian visas and the recognition of refugee status remain primarily acts of international protection for individuals and, more broadly, expressions of solidarity with a people.

[13] It also provided Ukraine with lethal and non-lethal material on the basis of a Decision which is attributable to the Union rather than to Member States.

mobilise consensus in the Council. This marks a significant development in the EU's evolution as both a sanctions sender and a geopolitical actor.

The EU has also deployed other CFSP instruments to react to Russia's serious breaches of Article 2(4) of the UN Charter. First of all, the European Peace Facility has financed assistance measures for the supply to the Ukrainian armed forces of military equipment and platforms designed to deliver lethal force since 2022.[14] Scholars have stressed that the Council's decision to supply weapons to the Ukrainian army can be regarded as a first attempt to amend customary law, in particular to allow international organisations to act in collective self-defence in certain limited cases.[15] Thus, the war in Ukraine has offered the EU the opportunity to develop international law. Second, the EU has also acted to make perpetrators of international crimes accountable before the International Criminal Court; the HR has declared its support for the investigations by the Prosecutor of this Court of crimes committed in Ukraine and has taken note of the decision of the International Criminal Court's Pre-Trial Chamber II to issue arrest warrants[16] against the President of the Russian Federation Vladimir Putin, and Commissioner for Children's Rights in the Office of the President Maria Lvova-Belova, in connection with alleged crimes of unlawful deportation and unlawful transfer of children in the context of the conflict in Ukraine.[17] At the same time, Hungary's withdrawal from the Rome Statute in May 2025 has serious implications for the EU. Indeed, the Union is bound to respect international law and to promote the development of its principles and has also concluded an agreement on cooperation and assistance with the International Criminal Court.[18]

1.3 Transformations in EU Governance and Policies as a Result of the War in Ukraine

The Union's response to the war in Ukraine has generated broader transformations in its governance, legal order, and policy priorities.[19] The war in Ukraine has offered the opportunity to alter the decision-making process leading to the adoption of sanctions,

---

[14] Council Decision (CFSP) 2022/338 of 28 February 2022 on an assistance measure under the European Peace Facility for the supply to the Ukrainian Armed Forces of military equipment, and platforms, designed to deliver lethal force, OJ L 61, 28.2.2022.

[15] Rasi 2024.

[16] ICC Pre-Trial Chamber II, Decision on the Prosecutor's Application for the issuance of arrest warrants against Vladimir Vladimirovich Putin and Maria Alekseyevna Lvova-Belova, ICC-01/22-01/22, 17 March 2023.

[17] See Press release of HR Borrell of 19 March 2023, available at https://www.eeas.europa.eu/eeas/russiaukraine-statement-high-representative-following-icc-decision-concerning-arrest-warrant-against_en, accessed 12 November 2025.

[18] Council Decision of 10 April 2006 concerning the conclusion of the Agreement between the International Criminal Court and the European Union on cooperation and assistance, https://eur-lex.europa.eu/eli/dec/2006/313(1)/oj/eng.

[19] Broadly, see Portela 2023.

as well as to their design. While recent changes concern only the sanctions package against Russia, and traditional practice persists in other sanctions regimes, it is likely that new habits and procedures introduced for the mentioned restrictive measures may be transferred to other sanctions regimes and eventually outlive the Ukraine war. Yet, the transformations extend well beyond the sector of sanctions and speak to the evolution of the EU as a political and legal actor in times of crisis. Three sets of changes stand out.

The war has redefined the institutional balance in the management of restrictive measures. Traditionally, the Council and the High Representative dominated sanctions design and adoption under the CFSP. Since 2022, however, the Commission has acquired a far more visible role in overseeing implementation, compliance, and enforcement. It has developed new monitoring practices, including the appointment of a Sanctions Implementation Envoy, to address persistent circumvention.[20] The designation criteria have also expanded significantly, encompassing enablers of sanctions evasion and even actors beyond Russia itself. Scholars note that these institutional and substantive innovations amount to a structural reconfiguration of the EU as a sanctions sender, with long-term implications for the balance of powers within the CFSP.

The Russian war against Ukraine has also led to questioning the compatibility of EU measures/initiatives with international law. The Council's decision to provide assistance to Ukraine through the European Peace Facility, financed outside the EU budget, has been described as a ground-breaking precedent that may contribute to reshaping the law of collective self-defence by recognising a more active role for international organisations. As far as the institutional set-up is concerned, the Commission's greater involvement in sanctions enforcement has been interpreted as evidence of the EU's essential transformation in external action.

The conflict has also reverberated across core internal policies, with energy policy standing out as a domain where legal and institutional innovation has been particularly pronounced. Member States were compelled to limit or sever their dependence on Russian fossil fuels by diversifying supply, leading to a sharp reduction in oil imports within just a few years.[21] The Commission seized this opportunity to accelerate the green transition through the REPowerEU plan.[22]

Crucially, the 2022 Gas Storage Regulation[23] constituted the first binding legal instrument to operationalise the principle of energy solidarity enshrined in Article 194(2) TFEU, requiring Member States to ensure minimum storage levels to safeguard security of supply.[24] Building on these steps, the Commission has recently

[20] Lepeu 2025.

[21] Goldthau and Youngs 2023.

[22] European Commission 2022.

[23] Regulation (EU) 2022/1032 of the European Parliament and of the Council of 29 June 2022 amending Regulations (EU) 2017/1938 and (EC) No 715/2009 with regard to gas storage, OJ L 173, 30.6.2022, p. 17.

[24] Marin 2024, p. 103, and Perdana S et al. 2022.

proposed a phased ban on Russian gas imports, signalling a longer-term restructuring of the Union's energy landscape.[25]

Beyond energy, enlargement has regained centrality, with Ukraine and Moldova granted candidate status and the Western Balkans repositioned at the forefront of the Union's geopolitical agenda.[26] A new forum of discussion to bring together Member States, candidate countries and other European States was created: the European Political Community (EPC).[27] Yet, at the moment it seems unlikely that this new creature will promote the coordination of efforts to support Ukraine.

It is noteworthy that the war has also triggered an expansion of EU competences in criminal law, particularly in the field of sanctions enforcement. Furthermore, migration management was transformed by the activation of the Temporary Protection Directive (TPD),[28] which tested both the Union's capacity for solidarity and its institutional limits and fundamentally reshaped the European Commission's approach under the New Pact on Migration and Asylum. In 2020, the Commission proposed repealing the TPD in favour of a new "immediate protection status".[29] Nevertheless, the Ukrainian displacement reaffirmed the TPD's value and influenced the broader direction of the Pact.[30] Yet these advances were accompanied by internal strains: Member States diverged over the scope of financial and military support for Ukraine, and the Union remained excluded from ceasefire negotiations, revealing the fragility of its role as a peace broker.

Taken together, these developments highlight the dual nature of the EU's transformation in the wake of the war in Ukraine. On the one hand, the Union has displayed remarkable adaptability, revising its legal frameworks, enhancing institutional capacities, and accelerating policy integration. On the other, these changes have exposed structural tensions between intergovernmental and supranational logics, raising fundamental questions about the trajectory of EU governance in an era of protracted conflict.

1.4 The Structure of the Book

Having outlined the book's research themes and the context of the war in Ukraine in 2022, it is now appropriate to turn to the structure of the volume. This collection of essays investigates how Russia's war against Ukraine has reshaped the European Union, not only in its external relations but also within its internal constitutional order.

---

[25] European Commission 2025.

[26] European Council Conclusions, 23–24 June 2022, EUCO 24/22, paras 9–10.

[27] De Witte 2025.

[28] Council Implementing Decision (EU) 2022/382 of 4 March 2022 establishing the existence of a mass influx of displaced persons from Ukraine within the meaning of Article 5 of Directive 2001/55/EC, and having the effect of introducing temporary protection, OJ L 71, 4.3.2022, p. 1.

[29] European Commission 2020.

[30] See more in Chap. 9.

The volume gathers contributions that examine these transformations across three interrelated dimensions, adopting a distinctly interdisciplinary perspective. Thanks to a multidisciplinary team of authors, the chapters combine legal and political analysis to illuminate the issues at stake.

The first dimension concerns the EU's unprecedented adoption of restrictive measures and the legal challenges raised by their personal and territorial scope, implementation, and enforcement and compliance with international law. These issues are explored in detail in the first part of the book, Chaps. 2, 3, 4 and 6. Chapter 5 focuses on the challenges posed by decision-making within the Council with respect to restrictive measures and on the use of constructive abstention in the context of the CSDP.

The second dimension has to do with the impact of the war on the EU legal order and is explored in detail in Chaps. 7, 8, 9 and 10, which form the second part of the book. These chapters concern the developments of new areas of EU competence in the field of criminal law, the renewed salience of enlargement, the activation of the TPD to host Ukrainian civilians fleeing from war and its influence in the New Pact on Migration and Asylum, and the development of the CSDP.

As a result of the war, the EU was compelled to make its restrictive measures more effective by expanding the competence of the EU in the area of criminal law. After the years of 'enlargement fatigue' following the last accession of 2013, the enlargement of the Union has re-emerged as a geopolitical tool. As a result, the accession prospects of Ukraine, Moldova, and the candidate countries of the Western Balkans have advanced. Montenegro is likely to be the first country amongst those in line to enter the Union in 2028. Finally, the first-ever activation of the TPD in response to the displacement of millions of Ukrainians tested both the resilience and the limitations of the EU's asylum framework. Turning to defence, Russia's aggression did prompt certain institutional innovations within the CSDP, most notably the adoption of the Strategic Compass[31] and the establishment of EUMAM Ukraine. Yet, as subsequent developments reveal, the war itself exerted only a limited influence on the trajectory of the EU defence policy, without prejudice to the Union's repeatedly renewed support for Ukraine. Far more decisive have been external factors—above all the so-called "Trump Effect" and the launch of Readiness 2030—which now stand as the principal drivers of the EU's pursuit of genuine military autonomy.

The third dimension emerges across all chapters: this is the EU's institutional and constitutional transformations of the EU indirectly resulting from the war. The latter has caused a change in the role of the Commission in sanctions governance, the growing involvement of the European Parliament in enlargement and migration debates, and the tensions among Member States over financial and military support for Ukraine.

[31] Council of the European Union, A Strategic Compass for Security and Defence—For a European Union that protects its citizens, values and interests and contributes to international peace and security, 7371/22, 21 March 2022.

Our reflections are not intended to be comprehensive in scope: for example, they omit the changes in the EU energy policy which are a direct consequence of the war in Ukraine, given that other scholars have already addressed this topic.

By integrating these three perspectives, the book provides a legal and political analysis of how the war in Ukraine has reshaped EU governance. Such analysis is timely at a juncture—over three years into the war—where the impact of the war in Ukraine on the EU and its enduring effects are becoming easier to ascertain. In our chapters, we demonstrate that the Union's response is not limited to crisis management but points to long-term structural changes in its legal and political order.

In conclusion, this volume is conceived as a working tool for all those who, whether with an academic or professional interest in European integration, migration and asylum, criminal law, enlargement, or defence policy, must confront the challenges posed by Russia's aggression and by the Union's evolving legal order. It is intended not only for scholars in the fields of EU law, international law, and human rights, but also for practitioners—judges, lawyers, diplomats—together with policy makers, civil society actors, and students who, for study or research purposes, seek a comprehensive monograph on the Union's multifaceted response to the war. More broadly, however, this book also addresses readers who wish to gain a deeper understanding of this grave international crisis, which constitutes both a crucial test for the international community and a measure of the Union's resilience and of the credibility of its founding values in contemporary geopolitics. Our hope is that, given its wide potential readership, the volume may contribute meaningfully to the ongoing debate and to constructive developments within the European project at a time of unprecedented strain.

In sending this volume to press, the co-editors wish to warmly thank the publisher and editorial staff, whose dedication and professionalism have accompanied the project from its inception to its completion.

References

Christie E H (2016) The Design and Impact of Western Economic Sanctions against Russia. The RUSI Journal 161: 52–64.

De Witte B (2025) The European Political Community and the future of the EU. In Govaere I, Garben S, Spaventa E (eds) The Impact of the War (in Ukraine) on the EU. Hart Publishing, Cambridge, pp. 101–105.

European Commission (2020) Proposal for a Regulation Addressing Situations of Crisis and Force Majeure in Migration and Asylum. COM(2020) 613 final. https://eur-lex.europa.eu/legal-content/EN/TXT/?uri=CELEX:52020PC0613. Accessed 8 September 2025.

European Commission (2022) Communication from the commission to the European Parliament, the European Council, the Council, the European Economic and Social Committee and the Committee of the regions, COM (2022) 230 final, Repower EU plan, https://eur-lex.europa.eu/legal-content/EN/TXT/?uri=COM%3A2022%3A230%3AFIN.

European Commission (2025) Proposal for a Regulation of the European Parliament and of the Council on phasing out Russian natural gas imports, improving monitoring of potential energy

dependencies and amending Regulation (EU) 2017/1938, COM/2025/828 final, https://eur-lex.europa.eu/legal-content/EN/TXT/?uri=celex:52025PC0828.
Falkner R (2023) Weaponised Energy and Climate Change: Assessing Europe's Response to the Ukraine War. LSE Public Policy Review.
Goldthau A C and Youngs R (2023) The EU Energy Crisis and a New Geopolitics of Climate Transition. JCMS: Journal of Common Market Studies, 61: 115–124.
Korkea-aho E, Lonardo L (2025) How Russia's War against Ukraine Changed EU Sanctions Decision-making. Journal of European Integration.
Lepeu J (2025) Ukraine, the De-targetisation of EU Sanctions, and the Rise of the European Commission as Architect of EU Foreign Policy. International Politics.
Lonardo L (2022) Russia's 2022 War Against Ukraine and the Foreign Policy Reaction of the EU: Context, Diplomacy, and Law. Palgrave, Houndmills.
Marin L (2024) Solidarity and crisis in the European Union—A constitutional principle in the pandemic and the energy crises. Cacucci, Bari.
Mills C (2025) Sanctions against countries supporting Russia's invasion of Ukraine. Research briefings, House of Commons Library, 17 January 2025, https://researchbriefings.files.parliament.uk/documents/CBP-10048/CBP-10048.pdf, available online.
Palestini S, Portela C (2025) The Global South and the Contestation of Unilateral Sanctions against Russia. Cooperation and Conflict.
Perdana S et al. (2022) European economic impacts of cutting energy imports from Russia. Energy Strategy Review.
Poli S (2022) Article 47 of the Charter of Fundamental Rights in the CFSP: does it afford an adequate protection of the right to effective judicial protection to private parties? In: Eliantonio M, Bonelli M, Gentile G (eds) Effective judicial protection in the EU: reality or illusion? Hart Publishing, Oxford, pp. 177–192.
Poli S, Finelli F (2025) La Corte di Giustizia dell'Unione Europea e le tendenze giurisprudenziali emergenti in materia di misure restrittive adottate in relazione all'aggressione russa all'Ucraina [The Court of Justice of the European Union and Emerging Jurisprudential Trends on Restrictive Measures Adopted in Response to Russia's Aggression against Ukraine]. In: Alì A (ed) Le sanzioni dell'UE nei confronti della Russia tra sicurezza internazionale e diritti umani [EU Sanctions against Russia between International Security and Human Rights]. Nomos, Giappichelli, Turin.
Portela C (2023) The war over Ukraine and the transformation of EU governance. European Papers 8: 1125–1130.
Rasi A (2024) Providing Weapons to Ukraine: The First Exercise of Collective Self-defence by the European Union? European Papers 9: 397–422.
Van Severen S (2021) The Minsk Agreements: Has the Glimmer of Hope Faded? In: Bossuyt F, Van Elsuwege P (eds) Principled Pragmatism in Practice: The EU's Policy towards Russia after Crimea, Studies in EU External Relations, vol. 19, Brill, pp. 17–39.

Part I
The Shape and the Limits of the EU's Response to Russia's Aggression

Chapter 2
The EU's Reaction to the War in Ukraine Through Sanctions: The Evolution of Designation Criteria

Clara Portela

Contents

Abstract The formulation of designation criteria is an aspect that defines sanctions regimes like no other: they delineate the circle of targets which can be subjected to a sanctions regime, authorising the application of bans to individuals or entities which meet the conditions of designation. The EU has traditionally embraced a practice of carefully targeting its sanctions, which has found faithful reflection in the designation criteria of relevant legislation. However, Brussels' targeted approach entered a period of relaxation over the past decade which was exacerbated in the response to the Russian aggression of Ukraine, resulting in broadly defined designation criteria which considerably enlarged the circle of potential designees. The present chapter analyses this evolution, examining the criteria for listing embedded in sanctions regimes related to the war in Ukraine and contrasting them to recently introduced sanctions regimes against Russia which are unconnected to the crisis. The purpose of this analysis is to identify the transformative effects that the adoption of these measures had on the EU.

Keywords Designation criteria · Blacklist · CFSP · Targeted sanctions · Russo-Ukrainian war · Sanctions against individuals · De-listings · Sectoral sanctions

S. Poli et al., *The EU's Response to the War in Ukraine and Its Impact on the EU Legal Order*, Global Europe: Legal and Policy Issues of the EU's External Action 7,
https://doi.org/10.1007/978-94-6265-767-0_2

2.1 The EU's Approach to Sanctions Design and Targeted Designations

The formulation of designation criteria, which set out the conditions that need to be met for any individual or entity to be listed under a sanctions regime, is a central aspect of CFSP Decisions instituting restrictive measures, the EU's term for sanctions.[1] Designation criteria are also closely connected to the rationale of sanctions. According to the traditional understanding, the main goal of sanctions is to coerce the target into adopting the policies desired by the sender. Yet, when applying sanctions, senders may pursue a variety of goals beyond eliciting compliance. They may seek to condemn publicly a pattern of behaviour, setting standards for acceptable conduct in international affairs, to deny key technology to a target in an attempt to reduce its military capacity, or to slow its economic performance.[2] Sanctions can also be used to empower certain international organisations, such as the United Nations.[3]

In the case of the EU, several rationales have been identified. The collective use of sanctions helps define the identity of the EU as an international actor by positioning it as an advocate of multilateralism, Human rights and democratic standards.[4] EU official statements reveal that sanctions routinely pursue several objectives. On the one hand, the Council's statement that its sanctions should have 'maximum impact on those whose behaviour we want to influence' indicates that the EU views its sanctions as an influence attempt.[5] For its part, the European Security Strategy (ESS) adopted by the Council in 2003 uses a less ambitious formulation when referring to objectionable behaviour by third actors: 'those who are unwilling to [rejoin the international community] should understand that there is a price to be paid, including in their relationship with the European Union'.[6] This excerpt suggests that the EU employs sanctions to impose a penalty on transgressors of international norms.[7] This motivation dovetails with peace researcher Johan Galtung's claim that sanctions are intended to punish the receivers by depriving them of some value.[8] This relegates to a secondary place whether they elicit a change in the behaviour of the target. At the same time, the expression of condemnation and the international isolation of the target may sometimes take precedence over behavioural impact.[9]

In its foreign policy practice, the EU has long embraced a policy of adopting targeted sanctions. Targeted or 'smart' sanctions were devised in reaction to the severe humanitarian impact produced by the UN embargo Iraq in the 1990s. In contrast to

---

[1] The terms 'sanctions' and 'restrictive measures' are used interchangeably in this chapter.

[2] Jones and Portela 2020.

[3] Hoffmann 1967.

[4] Blavoukos and Bourantonis 2014; Portela 2015.

[5] Council of the European Union 2004, p. 3.

[6] Council of the European Union 2003, p. 10.

[7] For a discussion on the nature and the purposes of restrictive measures in legal terms, see Chap. 5 in this volume.

[8] Galtung 1967, p. 409.

[9] Portela 2023.

comprehensive embargoes, which affect the entire economy of the country on which they are applied, targeted sanctions focus harm on the leadership or elites responsible for the condemned behaviour.[10] Since the mid-1990s, the entire autonomous sanctions practice of the EU consists of targeted sanctions. With the publication of the CFSP Principles for the use of sanctions, the EU outlined its policy, which embraces the notion of targeted sanctions, pledging to minimise humanitarian consequences: 'Sanctions should be targeted in a way that has maximum impact on those whose behaviour we want to influence. Targeting should reduce to the maximum extent possible any adverse humanitarian effects or unintended consequences for persons not targeted.'[11] From this information, we infer Brussels' approach to designation: we can expect the EU to focus on those individuals and entities which bear responsibility for the objectionable behaviour, while the population at large, and innocent bystanders, ought to be spared from the effect of sanctions. In the following sections, this chapter analyses the evolution of designation criteria prior to and after the invasion of Ukraine 2022. By contrasting designation criteria for natural persons with those embedded in the sanctions regimes against Russia which are unrelated to the Ukraine crises, and juxtaposing them to the definition of sectoral measures, the present chapter assesses both the extent to which the response to the war in Ukraine departs from standard sanctions practice and the impact that this has exerted on the EU.

2.2 The Evolution of Designation Criteria of Sanctions Against Individuals

One of the traits of CFSP sanctions regimes that have attracted less attention over the past decades has been the design of their designation criteria. And yet, it is one of the aspects that has suffered a most noticeable and consequential evolution. In the framework of targeted sanctions, designation criteria are established with the aim of respecting the distinction between those responsible for the violations condemned, and those who are not, particularly the civilian population.[12] By the beginning of the twenty-first century, the EU had developed a standard formula for designation criteria, which announced that those persons whose activities seriously undermine[d] democracy, respect for Human rights and the rule of law in the country at hand were eligible for blacklisting. This wording corresponds to the typical scenario that attracted sanctions by the EU: abrupt democratic backsliding, such as that witnessed in Zimbabwe at the time.[13] In justifying the sanctions wielded in response to the flawed elections in Belarus in 2006, then-Commissioner for External Relations and European Neighbourhood Policy Benita Ferrero highlighted that it was 'important that sanctions be

[10] Brzoska 2003.

[11] Council of the European Union 2004, p. 3.

[12] Brzoska 2003.

[13] Dipama and Dal 2015.

clearly focused, targeting precisely the individuals—including Mr. Lukashenko—responsible for the fraudulent elections'.[14] Shortly after, the criteria governing listings were expanded. The customary reference to persons whose activities seriously undermine democracy, Human rights and the rule of law evolved into 'those identified as responsible for the policies or actions that have prompted the EU decisions to impose restrictive measures and those benefiting from and supporting such policies and actions.'[15] This is illustrated by the sanctions regime against Syria, which defined its target group as 'persons responsible for the violent repression against the civilian population in Syria, persons benefiting from or supporting the regime, and persons associated with them.'[16] The inclusion of 'persons associated with' those 'responsible for the violent repression against the civilian population in Syria' and those 'benefiting from or supporting the regime' broadens the targeted group considerably while introducing a degree of definitional vagueness. These groups can be pictured as 'concentric circles', depending on their level of responsibility in the condemned actions. While the universe of those 'identified as responsible for condemned policies' can be defined narrowly as it entails individuals in leadership positions, the group of 'those benefiting from and supporting such policies and actions' is potentially open-ended. Since it encompasses not only those benefiting in a narrow sense but also supporters, this group could, in theory, extend to anyone in the target country who lends backing to the leadership's actions.[17] It remains unclear in what ways individuals or groups can be held to 'benefit from' and 'support' the regime, and how these can be told apart from those who do not. The trend towards the expansion of the circles of individuals susceptible of being targeted beyond those directly responsible for the misdeeds was observable in the sanctions regime addressing the embezzlement of Ukrainian state assets following the change of government of 2014, which announced the freezing of assets of persons identified as responsible for the misappropriation of Ukrainian state funds as well as their accomplices, mentioning 'persons subject to investigation by the Ukrainian authorities: for the misappropriation of Ukrainian public funds or assets, or being an accomplice thereto; or for the abuse of office as a public office-holder in order to procure an unjustified advantage for him- or herself or for a third party, and thereby causing a loss to Ukrainian public funds or assets, or being an accomplice thereto'.[18]

Alterations in designation criteria have not been motivated by a desire to determine more precisely the degree to which potential designees are associated with condemned policies. Instead, innovation has been driven by the legal challenges that often led the Court of Justice of the EU to annul designations.[19] The Court cannot

---

[14] Ferrero-Waldner 2006.

[15] Council of the European Union (2012) Guidelines on implementation and evaluation of restrictive measures (sanctions) in the framework of the EU Common Foreign and Security Policy, Doc. 11205/12, Brussels, 15 June 2012, p. 8.

[16] Council Decision (CFSP) 2013, p. 18.

[17] Portela 2016.

[18] Council Decision (CFSP) 2014a, p. 16.

[19] Calleja Crespo and Rollnert Pellicer 2025; see also Chap. 3.

interfere with the power of the Council to decide the scope *ratione personae* of restrictive measures or choose their designation criteria.[20] Yet, as a result of Lisbon Treaty, 'non-state entities have become not only official addressees of EU measures but also potential applicants in the context of annulment actions brought against sanctions, in accordance with the principle that the Union is based on the rule of law'.[21] Cognisant that its listings are subject to the scrutiny of the Court, the Council adopted a cautious approach to selecting targets. Tellingly, in the period from 2010 to 2014, cases concerning sanctions became the third most recurrent issue area among the cases heard by EU Courts, becoming the second by 2017.[22] As recognised by a senior official from the Council Legal Service, in the years that followed the Kadi case, the Council lost around two-thirds of the cases before it started to win: 'In 2012, 2013 and 2014 the Council was still losing twice as many cases as it won, while in 2015 that trend was reversed; the Council then won more than twice as many cases as it lost. The same applies for 2016'.[23] This reversal is due to the broadening of the designation criteria, accompanied by the Council's strengthened preparation of statement of reasons for the listings and improved gathering of evidence to support individual designations. Thanks to this extension, listing criteria became less vulnerable to legal challenges, although designations did not necessarily proliferate. The fact that the EU takes a longer time than the US to blacklist individuals and entities, and that the number of European designations is consistently and considerably lower than Washington's,[24] illustrates that Brussels faces legal constraints from which the US is free, and which could not be fully surmounted with recourse to the expansion of designation criteria or the strengthening of evidence packages that underpin the listings.

The reminder of this chapter examines how designation criteria have been adjusted in the sanctions regimes directed against Russia in response to the aggression and destabilisation actions in Ukraine, thanks to their flexible design. After an introduction of EU sanctions regimes concerning Russia's violations of international law in Sect. 2.3, Sect. 2.4 looks at the designation criteria affecting individuals and entities; Sect. 2.5 is devoted to designation criteria applicable to sectoral sanctions while Sect. 2.6 reflects on the evolution of designation criteria before Sect. 2.7 closes with some concluding remarks.

---

[20] Poli 2018, p. 297.

[21] Poli 2017, p. 167.

[22] Court of Justice of the European Union, Annual Report, Publications Office of the European Union, Luxembourg, 2017.

[23] House of Lords 2017.

[24] Borzyskowski and Portela 2018.

2.3 The Sanctions Regime Landscape

The current landscape of sanctions regimes directed at Russia presents a diverse picture, whose complexity makes a mapping exercise necessary before the formulation of designation criteria can be discussed. Firstly, a few sanctions regimes are categorised on the EU's website under the rubric 'Russia', while others appear under the rubric 'Ukraine'.[25] Confusingly, those sanctions regimes imposed in response to the aggression and destabilisation of Ukraine are scattered between both rubrics. The allocation of certain sanctions regimes to the rubric 'Ukraine', however, does not entail that Kyiv finds itself at the receiving end of sanctions on account of any instance of misbehaviour. Instead, this labelling is motivated by a policy of non-recognition of unlawfully annexed or occupied territory. Portions of land that have fallen under the control of Russian forces as a result of Moscow's aggression continue to be regarded as part of Ukraine, whose name is maintained in the rubric in deference to its sovereignty. To complicate things further, not all sanctions regimes under the rubric of 'Russia' are related to the invasion of Ukraine: one of them, simply alluding to the 'situation in Russia' in its title, focuses on Moscow's repression of the domestic political opposition. Lastly, certain designations of Russian targets are scattered throughout horizontal or thematic sanctions regimes.[26] Because such blacklists are unrelated to territorially defined crises and are only tangentially related to the invasion of Ukraine, the relevance of their listings to the war in Ukraine is often tenuous if not absent.

The following table (see Table 2.1) offers an overview of sanctions regimes classified under the three rubrics mentioned, highlighting those sanctions regimes that are part of the EU's response to Russia's aggression against Ukraine. Each entry features the code of the initial CFSP Decision that gave rise to the sanctions regime, alongside a keyword-type excerpt of the title, and in the case of the Russia- and Ukraine-focused regimes, a brief description of their rationale. Ukraine related sanctions regimes are marked in bold, while the remaining ones appear in italics.

A glance at this summary overview reveals that the EU sanctions imposed in response to the Russian aggression of Ukraine are disaggregated into four separate sanctions regimes, most of which originated in 2014.[27] These measures can be easily classified in two types:

- Two sanctions regimes address Russian actions to destabilise of Ukraine, through the imposition of individual sanctions (Council Decision (CFSP) 2014b)[28] and sectoral measures (Council Decision (CFSP) 2014/512).[29]

---

[25] See EU sanctions map at https://sanctionsmap.eu/#/main, accessed 4 September 2025.

[26] Council Decision (CFSP) 2018; Council Decision (CFSP) 2019; Council Decision (CFSP) 2020.

[27] All of them except for the Donetsk and Luhansk sanctions regime (Council Decision (CFSP) 2022a).

[28] The corresponding regulation to this CFSP act is Council Regulation (EU) 2014a.

[29] The corresponding regulation to this CFSP act is Council Regulation (EU) 2014c.

Table 2.1 Summary overview of sanctions regimes affecting Russia and Ukraine[30]

Russia	Ukraine	Horizontal
sanctions regime code: CFSP Decision 2024/1484 addressing: 'situation in Russia' • *systematic repression and deterioration of the human rights situation in Russia*	**sanctions regime code: CFSP Decision 2022/266 addressing: 'recognition of non-government controlled areas of Ukraine' (Donetsk and Luhansk)'** • **Russian recognition of the non-government controlled areas of Donetsk and Luhansk oblasts of Ukraine and dispatch of Russian troops into these areas**	*sanctions regime code: CFSP Decision 2018/1544 addressing: 'proliferation and use of chemical weapons'*
sanctions regime code: CFSP Decision 2024/2643 addressing: 'Russia's destabilising activities' • *Russian hybrid attacks threatening democracy, the rule of law, stability or security in the Union, its Member States and its partners*	**sanctions regime code: CFSP Decision 2014/145 addressing: 'actions undermining or threatening the territorial integrity, sovereignty and independence of Ukraine'** • **violation of Ukrainian sovereignty and territorial integrity by the Russian Federation**	*sanctions regime code: CFSP Decision 2019/797 addressing: 'cyber-attacks threatening the Union or its Member States'*
sanctions regime code: CFSP Decision 2014/512 addressing: 'Russia's actions destabilising the situation in Ukraine (sectoral restrictive measures)' • **illegal annexation of Crimea and the destabilisation of Ukraine**	**sanctions regime code: CFSP Decision 2014/386 addressing: 'restrictions on goods originating in Crimea or Sevastopol'** • **illegal annexation of Crimea to the Russian Federation**	*sanctions regime code: CFSP Decision 2020/1999 addressing: 'serious human rights violations and abuses'*
	sanctions regime code: CFSP Decision 2014/119 addressing: 'misappropriation of state funds of Ukraine' • *recovery of assets of persons responsible for the misappropriation of Ukrainian state funds and human rights violations*	

Source https://sanctionsmap.eu/#/main and own elaboration (regimes discussed in this chapter provided in bold)

[30] Full references to legislation are listed in the bibliography. Throughout this chapter, and for reasons of economy, only the initial acts of CFSP decisions are cited, unless otherwise indicated.

- Two additional sanctions regimes focus on the prohibition of commercial interaction with unlawfully annexed territories: Crimea and Sevastopol (Council Decision (CFSP) 2014/386)[31] (embargo on goods) and Donetsk and Luhansk (Council Decision (CFSP) 2022/266) (embargo on goods).[32]

Having clarified the complex, fragmented nature of the EU's sanctions regime in response to Russia's aggression of Ukraine, our analysis focuses mostly on the sanctions regimes directly relevant to the invasion, while the Crimea and Sevastopol and Donetsk and Luhansk regimes are discussed after the Council Decision (CFSP) 2014/512 regime as it focuses on sectoral bans.

2.4 Sanctions Regimes Imposed in Response to the Aggression in Ukraine

2.4.1 The CFSP Decision 2014/145 Regime

Most of the sanctions regimes in question originated with the 2014 annexation of Crimea and Sevastopol and destabilisation of Eastern Ukraine, and were speedily and substantially upgraded following the invasion of Ukraine in February 2022. Chronologically, the first regime to be enacted is CFSP Decision 2014/145, addressing the violation of Ukrainian sovereignty and territorial integrity by the Russian Federation. The initial legal act of March 2014 stipulates that travel restrictions and an asset freeze should be imposed against 'persons responsible for actions which undermine or threaten the territorial integrity, sovereignty and independence of Ukraine, including actions on the future status of any part of the territory which are contrary to the Ukrainian Constitution, and persons, entities or bodies associated with them.'[33] The designation criteria featured at the end of the preamble. The initial blacklist, adopted concurrently with the enactment of the sanctions regime, listed 21 individuals who had supported the military incursion into Ukraine, organised the unlawful referendum on the annexation of Crimea, or had accepted appointments in the new leadership of the peninsula.

In its current configuration, the designation criteria have acquired remarkable sophistication, multiplying the universe of individuals and entities susceptible of being listed in their annexes, as well as their length. There are no less than ten subsections in Article 1 of Council Decision (CFSP) 2014/145, which imposes a prohibition of entry for listed individuals, and read as follows:

> (a) natural persons responsible for, supporting or implementing actions or policies which undermine or threaten the territorial integrity, sovereignty and independence of Ukraine, or

---

[31] The corresponding regulation to this CFSP act is Council Regulation (EU) 2014b.

[32] The corresponding regulation to this CFSP act is Council Regulation (EU) 2022.

[33] Council Decision (CFSP) 2014b.

stability or security in Ukraine, or which obstruct the work of international organisations in Ukraine;

(b) natural persons supporting, materially or financially, or benefitting from Russian decision-makers responsible for the annexation of Crimea or the destabilisation of Ukraine;

(c) natural persons conducting transactions with the separatist groups in the Donbas region of Ukraine;

(d) natural persons supporting, materially or financially, or benefitting from the Government of the Russian Federation, which is responsible for the annexation of Crimea and the destabilisation of Ukraine; or

(e) leading businesspersons operating in Russia and their immediate family members, or other natural persons, benefitting from them, or businesspersons involved in economic sectors providing a substantial source of revenue to the Government of the Russian Federation, which is responsible for the annexation of Crimea and the destabilisation of Ukraine; or

(f) natural persons:

(i) facilitating infringements of the prohibition against circumvention of the provisions of this Decision, or of Decisions 2014/386/CFSP (1), 2014/512/CFSP (2), or (CFSP) 2022/266 (3), or of Council Regulations (EU) No 269/2014 (4), (EU) No 692/2014 (5), (EU) No 833/2014 (6) or (EU) 2022/263 (7); or

(ii) otherwise significantly frustrating those provisions; or

(g) natural persons benefitting from the compulsory transfer of ownership or control of entities established in Russia, previously owned or controlled by entities established in the Union, where such transfer is made by the Government of the Russian Federation through laws, regulations, other legislative instruments or other action of a Russian public authority, and natural persons who have been appointed to the governing bodies of such entities in Russia without the consent of the Union entities which previously owned or controlled them;

(h) natural persons that own, control, manage or operate vessels that transport crude oil or petroleum products, originating in Russia or exported from Russia, while practicing irregular and high-risk shipping practices as set out in the International Maritime Organisation General Assembly resolution A.1192(33), or that otherwise provide material, technical or financial support to the operations of such vessels; or

(i) natural persons forming part of, supporting, materially or financially, or benefitting from Russia's military and industrial complex, including by being involved in the development, production or supply of military technology and equipment; or

(j) natural persons that have participated in or enabled transfers of ownership, control or economic benefit of the business interests of leading businesspersons who are subject to Union restrictive measures pursuant to the criterion set out in point (e) of this paragraph and listed in the Annex to this Decision, thereby significantly frustrating those measures [...] and natural persons associated with them or with the legal persons, entities or bodies listed under Article 2(1)(i).[34]

The expansion of the circle of potentially targeted individuals and entities is of considerable magnitude. Indeed, the number of entries listed under this sanctions regime reached 2814 by May 2026.[35] The highly diverse professional profiles of designees in sanctions regimes, and their degree of proximity to the wrongdoing addressed has been the object of enquiry in recent research. Some authors distinguish

---

[34] Council Decision (CFSP) 2025a.

[35] Ibid.

between the categories of leaders, administrators, supporters and enablers, affirming that only the first group holds effective decision-making power.[36] Others separate closeness to power from proximity to the wrongdoing at hand.[37] However, such analyses centre on the actual listings found in the annexes to sanctions regimes, rather than on designation criteria properly speaking. In the sanctions regime under scrutiny here, a similar analysis is in order as its complexity surpasses standard sanctions regimes.

The first dimension of the expansion is dictated by the persistence of the condemned actions, namely the continued annexation of Crimea and destabilisation efforts. This entails not only that the listing of perpetrators of the actions that gave rise to the annexation is upheld, but also that those perpetuating it are designated too. In this vein, subparagraph (a) includes persons 'supporting or implementing actions and policies' which undermine the territorial integrity, sovereignty and independence of Ukraine, which goes beyond the retrospective allusion to those 'responsible for' them. In doing so, it extends the currency of the condemned acts to the present day: not having been implicated in bringing about the annexation does not exempt an individual from designation as long as he or she contributes to the persistence of the wrongdoing. This approach removes the temporal limitation of the wrongdoing that characterises the typically retrospective approach of mainstream CFSP sanctions practice. In addition, subparagraph (a) broadens the protection of Ukraine to include its 'security and stability' as well as the action of international organisations, which further enlarges the universe of potential designees. A logical consequence of this expansion consists in penalising those who transact with separatist groups in the Donbas, as stipulated in subparagraph (c).

A second dimension of expansion of the designation criteria consists in the targeting of those who support or benefit from the authorities that orchestrated the annexation and destabilisation efforts. This is observable in subparagraphs (b), (d) and (i), which establish that those involved with, benefiting from or supporting Russian decision-makers, the Government of the Russian Federation or its military establishment—broadly defined to include the defence industry—are susceptible of designation, on account of these authorities' responsibility in the annexation and destabilisation. This group of targets has a more remote link to the actions that gave rise to the annexation and destabilisation efforts than that of the persons under subparagraph (a): beyond the individual involvement of the perpetrators—intellectual or material—of the condemned actions, the entire bureaucracies, entourage, suppliers etc. around them are considered to be implicated, and any relationship to them makes individuals eligible for designation.

A third dimension extends the circle to 'leading businesspersons operating in Russia' or businesspersons who are 'involved in economic sectors providing a substantial source of revenue' to the Russian state budget, which is predicated on the government's responsibility for the annexation of Crimea and the destabilisation of

[36] Wallensteen and Grusell 2012.

[37] Portela et al. 2025.

Ukraine. Under subparagraph (e), we find a further layer of detachment from the original wrongdoing: private individuals can see themselves listed for providing revenue to the Russian state, even if they do not purposefully fund the military operation or expressly encouraged destabilisation efforts. Moreover, their close family members are included too. The conduct of commercial activity and its resulting revenue which is, in part, transferred to state coffers does not need to be associated to the initial wrongdoing. Instead, it suffices that the entity at the receiving end of a significant financial transfer is ultimately responsible for the annexation and destabilisation exercise. The inclusion of these layers, which makes eligible for listing individuals who may bear no responsibility for the acts that gave rise to the sanctions regime, evidences the presence of a logic whose main objective is to deprive the affected state of economic resources, approximating the rationale of traditional economic embargoes rather than the EU's characteristically targeted approach.[38]

The fourth dimension of the expansion is dissociated from the wrongdoing that instilled the imposition of sanctions. By contrast, it is concerned with the desire to improve the implementation of sanctions by fighting circumvention practices. Measures under paragraph (h) address individuals involved with the 'shadow fleet', a group of about 400 vessels assembled by Moscow to transport oil beyond the reach of Western restrictions on oil transfers adopted in December 2022, and generating additional revenue for the war in Ukraine.[39] A significant expansion of targets is stipulated under subparagraph (j) and concerns individuals enabling transfers of ownership, control of leading businesspersons already designated under EU sanctions regimes. Lastly, subparagraph (f) adds a catch-all clause that targets those facilitating circumvention of the present or related sanctions regimes. This represents an unconcealed attempt to limit circumvention of EU bans, a new priority for Brussels which has elicited unprecedented inventiveness within EU institutions.[40]

In addition, paragraph (g) targets those who benefit from expropriated entities following the condemned events. This does not concern exclusively those entities located in the territory annexed or subject to destabilisation, but also those in the state responsible for the commission of aggression. This emphasis is even more manifest in the provision for the freezing of assets contained in Article 2 of the CFSP Decision 2014/145 regime. It includes additional designation criteria targeting expropriated entities, referred to as 'legal persons in Crimea or Sevastopol whose ownership has been transferred contrary to Ukrainian law' (Article 2c), 'entities established in Russia, previously owned or controlled by entities established in the Union, ownership or control of which has been compulsorily transferred by the Government of the Russian Federation' (Article 2j), as well as the entities which have benefited from such a transfer.

If we compare this with the formulation of designation criteria in the initial CFSP act of 2014, we observe a major evolution. In the EU's response to Russia's behaviour in 2014, 'natural persons responsible for actions which undermine or

38 Portela 2023.

39 Wilson 2024.

40 See Chaps. 4 and 5.

threaten the territorial integrity, sovereignty and independence of Ukraine, and of natural persons associated with them' could be blacklisted.[41] This followed a model in which only two levels of responsibility were considered: the core group, i.e. those directly responsible, and their associates. By 2025, we identify at least five:

- Those perpetrating the initial wrongdoings, and those who participate in their perpetuation;
- Those involved in the institutions that orchestrated and executed the condemned actions;
- Those heading firms which produce substantial revenue for Russian state coffers;
- Those helping to circumvent the prohibitions enacted;
- Those profiting from the illegal transfer of firms of EU ownership.

The potentially targeted groups can be understood as three concentric circles', as each of the three first groups feature a different degree of proximity to the initial wrongdoing. The fourth group, by contrast, is linked to a different wrongdoing, i.e. the circumvention of the prohibitions enacted by the EU in response to the original annexation and destabilisation operation. The same is true for the fifth group.

Furthermore, those associated to the circle of potentially targeted individuals, and in the case of businesspersons also immediate family members, are also susceptible of designation, arguably constituting an additional layer. The resulting configuration is one in which even individuals with a tenuous—at best—relationship to the acts giving rise to the sanctions are susceptible of listing: the sibling of the CEO of a successful firm whose taxes amount to a substantial sum may find his or her name on a blacklist because the revenue provided to state coffers can be allocated to the war effort, even if this use if not actively encouraged or desired by the company in question, its leadership or their family members. This construct is based on the idea that circumvention ought to be foreclosed or obstructed to the maximum extent possible. However, it has the effect of enlarging enormously the universe of possible designees, diluting the targeted nature of the sanctions instrument. Moreover, they attribute the same status of designee, with identical material and stigmatising consequences, to individuals who intellectually or materially carried out the annexation and destabilisation exercise as to those who are only tangentially related to, or even disconnected from, such actions. This circumstance does not only invite litigation by designees, but it makes the measures more likely to become the target of criticisms, if not contestation.

[41] Council Decision (CFSP) 2014b.

2.5 Sanctions Regimes Imposed Against Russia Outside the Response to the Aggression of Ukraine (2022)

Outside the reaction to the aggression of Ukraine, the EU has adopted various sanctions regimes directed at Russia. In addition to being in place concurrently, these sanctions regimes feature the peculiarity of having been agreed two years after the 2022 invasion of Ukraine, and reflect the deterioration of relations between Brussels and Moscow (CFSP Decision 2024/2643),[42] as well as the worsening of the Human rights situation in Russia in the post-invasion period (CFSP Decision 2024/1484).[43] The former is geared towards protecting the EU,[44] and that of its partner countries, from Russian interference,[45] while the latter is meant to respond to 'serious Human rights violations or abuses, for the repression of civil society and democratic opposition, and for undermining democracy and the rule of law in Russia'. Notably, the establishment of these two sanctions regimes took place after the EU had adopted three consecutive horizontal sanctions regimes addressing cyber-attacks, the proliferation of chemical weapons and Human rights abuses, all of which featured Russian targets among their listings.[46] Beside Russia, only Iran is at the receiving end of a sanctions regime that deals exclusively with domestic Human rights abuses in parallel to another sanctions regime addressing an international security crisis.[47]

The sanctions regime that addresses Destabilising activities by Russia (CFSP Decision 2024/2643), which responds to Moscow's actions directed against EU members and their allies, contemplates the listing of 'natural or legal persons, entities or bodies that are:

> (a) responsible for, implementing, supporting, or benefitting from actions or policies by the Government of the Russian Federation which undermine or threaten democracy, the rule of law, stability or security in the Union or in one or several of its Member States, in an international organisation, or in a third country, or which undermine or threaten the sovereignty or independence of one or several of its Member States, or of a third country [...]
>
> (b) associated with the natural or legal persons, entities or bodies listed under point (a);
>
> (c) supporting the natural or legal persons, entities or bodies engaged in activities referred to point (a)'.

---

42 Council Decision (CFSP) 2024b.

43 Council Decision (CFSP) 2024a.

44 Recital n. 16 of Council Decision (CFSP) 2024b refers to a broader number of reasons, such as 'to safeguard its values, fundamental interests, security, independence and integrity, to consolidate and support democracy, the rule of law, human rights and the principles of international law, and to prevent conflicts and strengthen international security'.

45 This is despite the fact that the sanctions regime regulated by Council Decision (CFSP) 2024b explicitly refers to the war in Ukraine, featuring the phrase 'in the context of Russia's war of aggression against Ukraine' in its title.

46 Portela 2021.

47 Council Decision (CFSP) 2011b.

This represents a variation of the concentric circles model as the group under (a) refers to those directly responsible, while the outermost group includes associates of both the core group and the facilitators.

The sanctions regime addressing 'the situation in Russia' (CFSP Decision 2024/1484) deals with the repression of the political opposition in Russia and contains designation criteria which resonate with the expansive formula outlined above, referring to 'natural persons who:

> (a) are responsible for serious violations or abuses of Human rights or for the repression of civil society and democratic opposition, or whose activities otherwise seriously undermine democracy or the rule of law in Russia;
>
> (b) provide financial, technical, or material support for, or are otherwise involved in, the acts set out in point (a), including by planning, directing, ordering, assisting, preparing, facilitating or encouraging such acts;
>
> (c) are associated with the natural persons referred to in point (a) or (b)'.

Such formulation entails three different levels of responsibility, again forming 'concentric circles': those directly responsible, those who facilitate, and those who are associated to them. Interestingly, a difference between the two sanctions regimes unrelated to the war in Ukraine is that the regime against destabilisation of the EU and its allies (CFSP Decision 2024/2643) foresees the targeting of those supporting or benefiting from destabilisation actions by Russia. This is a complex construct because one does not need to actively contribute to the actions—benefiting from them is sufficient reason for designation. By contrast, the regime addressing the domestic Human rights situation in Russia (CFSP Decision 2024/1484) does not allude to those who could benefit from the condemned actions. Other than this divergence, the three concentric circles are comparable in their scope, as they encompass the perpetrators (those 'responsible'), supporters and associates.

Overall, this evolution demonstrates a readiness by the Council to target different levels of involvement when designating individuals, consolidating a definitive departure from the narrow approach targeting those directly responsible only. This confirms the overall trend towards a 'de-targetisation' of EU sanctions.[48] However, the comparison between the sanctions regimes directed against individuals outside the context of the Ukraine war (CFSP Decision 2024/2643 and CFSP Decision 2024/1484) shows that these regimes are in tune with EU mainstream practice, while the regime responding to the war in Ukraine (CFSP Decision 2014/145) attained a different quality: designation criteria are unprecedentedly broad and heterogeneous. Uniquely, they encompass the possibility of designation for the circumvention of its own prohibitions or that of germane sanctions regimes. This evidences the EU's commitment to upholding the sovereignty and independence of Ukraine, and the international norms protecting the inviolability of borders, as well as the seriousness of its efforts towards the proper implementation of its bans.

[48] Lepeu 2025.

2.6 The Evolution of Sector-Related Sanctions

The progressive broadening of designation criteria described in the preceding sections has been accompanied by an expansion of sector-related restrictions. These measures fit more faithfully the traditional notion of economic sanctions, as they affect directly trade and financial flows. The expansion of sector-related bans is more difficult to track than that of individual sanctions due to the availability of two separate modalities. One of them consists in banning the import or export of a specific category of goods vis-à-vis third countries. Examples include embargoes on gems, diamonds, gas, oil or cocoa. This form of sanction produces effects which are easy to track by referring to mainstream trade statistics. A second modality, however, consist in the blacklisting of entities. In the latter case, the designation of entities can be so ample as to potentially cover an entire sector if listings encompass an exhaustive list of operators. Moreover, in cases of state companies, a single listing can also have the effect of banning trade in one commodity, especially when the state has the monopoly on trade in a given commodity. The entities listed may be so central to the economy of the country that the ban approximates—or even equates to—a full embargo. Cases in point include the listing of state energy companies, such as the *Société nationale d'opérations pétrolières de la Côte d'Ivoire* or the Central Banks of Libya or Iran. Lastly, certain measures address trade hubs such as harbours, hindering trade across sectors without expressly prohibiting the concerned goods. This modality, which has been criticised for blurring the distinction between targeted and non-targeted sanctions,[49] makes it difficult for outside observers to identify sectoral measures and to assess their coverage.

It is discernible that CFSP sanctions policy experienced a turning point over the decade of the 2010s, most visible in the enactment of sector-related sanctions. Previous experience had seen very few sectoral measures enacted: they merely concerned the European response to the protracted and bloody Yugoslav crises, as well as a ban on gold, gems and precious and semi-precious stones imposed on Myanmar after the repression of the Saffron Revolution in 2007.[50] Then a qualitative leap occurred, even if the overall frequency of sanctions imposition remained stable throughout the decade of the 2010s. Firstly, the EU agreed sanctions on Iran that supplemented UN Security Council bans, including an oil embargo and far-reaching financial restrictions replicating US sanctions. This constituted a novelty in that, for the first time, they adversely affected European enterprises, hitting some sectors badly.[51] Shortly after, this was followed by sanctions against Côte d'Ivoire addressing the political impasse that followed the presidential elections of November 2010. Unprecedented measures such as a ban on the import of cocoa to the EU and a prohibition for European companies to trade through the harbours of Abidjan and San Pedro were enacted.[52] This last measure was particularly severe as these

---

[49] Gordon 2019.

[50] Portela 2010.

[51] Tabrizi and Santini 2012.

[52] Council Decision (CFSP) 2011a.

were the only international ports of the country, providing supplies to landlocked neighbouring countries like Burkina Faso.[53] In Libya, the EU supplemented UNSC measures with additional designations as well as an autonomous ban on equipment for internal repression. Subsequently, it prohibited dealings with Libyan financial entities, the Libyan National Oil Corporation and five of its subsidiaries as well as energy firms, and eventually blacklisted several Libyan harbours.[54] In Syria, the EU imposed its entire sanctions toolbox in just a few months, including a ban on the import of Syrian oil and gas.

This evolution culminated in 2014, when the EU responded to the annexation of Crimea with the almost complete isolation of the peninsula,[55] and to Russian military support for the destabilisation activities of the separatist forces in Eastern Ukraine with a heterogeneous sanctions package, representing the first serious instance of economic restrictions against its powerful Eastern neighbour since the end of the Cold War. Subsequently, economic sanctions have become usual practice. Whereas the EU initially interpreted the concept of sanctions narrowly during the 1990s, it has increasingly enacted sanctions that have affected groups not directly targeted both in the target and sender societies. Examples include the freezing the assets of the Central Bank of Iran and of major Iranian commercial banks adopted in 2010.[56] Following the Russian invasion of Ukraine in early 2022, the EU has established several sanctions regimes against Russia which entail exclusively economic bans.[57] Stand-alone economic sanctions regimes are, again, a novelty introduced in EU autonomous sanctions practice after 2022, given that in prior experiences, sectoral bans were added to sanctions regimes which already entailed individual sanctions like visa bans and asset freezes.

The introduction of the 2022 sanctions against Russia, most of them connected to the invasion of Ukraine, marked a turning point in terms of the economic quality of the measures. It quickly grew into the most important EU autonomous sanctions regime in force. According to data provided by the European Commission, sanctions regimes relating to the Ukraine crisis represent 46% of the volume of CFSP sanctions, topping the ranking with 758 entities and 1960 individuals listed.[58] By way of comparison, the second largest sanctions regime, that imposed on Iran, follows with a distance: it represents 12% of the total volume of CFSP sanctions, with 338 entities and 373 individuals under sanctions.[59] This confirms the unprecedented nature of this sanctions regime in the CFSP context.[60]

---

[53] Vines 2012.

[54] Koenig 2011.

[55] See Chap. 4 in this volume.

[56] Council Decision (CFSP) 2010.

[57] Council Decision (CFSP) 2014c, Council Decision (CFSP) 2022a, Council Decision (CFSP) 2014d.

[58] See EU sanctions tracker, at https://data.europa.eu/apps/eusanctionstracker/, accessed 31 May 2026.

[59] Ibid.

[60] Meissner and Graziani 2023; Helwig et al. 2020.

2.6.1 The CFSP Decision 2014/512 Regime

The CFSP Decision 2014/512 sanctions regime, to be found under the rubric 'Russia' of the EU sanction map,[61] was originally adopted on 31 of July 2014, following the shooting down of Malaysian airlines flight MH17 in Donetsk, an event which brought about a tightening of EU sanctions addressing the destabilisation of Ukraine. At the time of adoption, the regime counted 10 operative paragraphs, which stipulated three sets of restrictions:

- A ban on the provision of financing or investment services or dealing in new bonds or equity or similar financial instruments with a maturity exceeding 90 days issued by state-owned Russian financial institutions;
- A prohibition of both supply and procurement of military equipment, covering also dual use goods for military end-users; and
- Restrictions on the supply of certain sensitive goods and technologies when destined for deep water oil exploration and production, arctic oil exploration and production or shale oil projects.

These measures were perceived at the time as audacious, given the EU's previous reluctance to target Russia with its sanctions[62]; yet their effectiveness was regarded as limited in scholarly assessment.[63]

The sectoral bans contemplated under this regime proliferated after February 2022. In essence, the sanctions regime has expanded the prohibitions along all three areas identified in 2014. The initial 10 paragraphs of July 2014 came to include numerous subparagraphs additional to the main text.[64] Article 1 has 24 subparagraphs and Article 4 features 32, while Article 5 has five, Article 8 has four and Articles 3 and 7 have three each.[65] The text of the CFSP Decision enacted in 2014 originally included a single annex listing designated persons and entities; the current version of 2015 reached twenty-one annexes. From the original adoption of the CFSP Decision in July 2014 until July 2025, this piece of legislation was altered more than 50 times, excluding mere corrigenda from this figure. This shows the intensity of the efforts made by the Council to constantly increase the pressure exerted by the sanctions regimes.

Compared to CFSP Decision 2014/145, which foresees the application of bans against individuals, the CFSP Decision 2014/512 regime features mostly sectoral bans and prohibitions of generic scope. Instead of criteria for designation, the regime specifies derogations. An illustration can be found in Article 1b, which prohibits 'deposits from Russian nationals or natural persons residing in Russia, legal persons, entities or bodies established in Russia or legal persons, entities or bodies established outside the Union and whose proprietary rights are directly or indirectly owned

---

[61] See https://sanctionsmap.eu/#/main, accessed 20 August 2025.

[62] Helwig et al. 2020.

[63] Christie 2016; Connolly 2016.

[64] Articles 2 and 6 did not receive any addition.

[65] Council Decision (CFSP) 2025b.

for more than 50% by Russian nationals or natural persons residing in Russia, if the total value of deposits of that natural or legal person, entity or body per credit institution exceeds EUR 100 000'.[66] This prohibition, generic in nature, is qualified by derogations covering, e.g., the satisfaction of basic needs or the official purposes of diplomatic missions, consular posts or international organisations.[67]

Still, some of the numerous annexes refer to bans that apply only to blacklisted entries, while others refer to derogations. However, it is noteworthy that the prohibitions lack the motivation for the inclusion of entries in the annex. The text of the provision merely indicates that certain entries should be included in the annex. Such is the case, e.g. with Article 1(e), which bans the provision of specialised financial messaging services to entities directly or indirectly owned for more than 50% by an entity listed in Annex VIII, which refers to a list of 23 banks. These lists have the function of specifying the details of those entities subject to the ban, providing legal certainty to European economic operators that have to implement it. This is the case for the most voluminous annex, number IV, which features military end-users, and entries which form part of Russia's military and industrial complex, or which have commercial or other links with or which otherwise support Russia's defence and security sector, and thus contribute to Russia's military and technological enhancement or to the development of Russia's defence and security sector. As of May 2026, it featured 921 entries, some of which are located in jurisdictions other than Russia, such as China, Hong Kong, Kazakhstan, India, Turkey or United Arab Emirates. Annex V lists major credit institutions, institutions with over 50% public ownership or control as of 26 February 2022 and credit institution having a significant role in supporting the activities of Russia and its Government and of the Russian Central Bank and established in Russia, while Annex VI lists entities publicly controlled or with over 50% public ownership and in which Russia, its Government or Central Bank has the right to participate in profits or with which Russia, its Government or Central Bank has other substantial economic relationships. There is also a prohibition to transact with entities 'controlled or with over 50% public ownership or in which Russia, its Government or the Russian Central Bank has the right to participate in profits or with which Russia, its Government or the Russian Central Bank has other substantial economic relationship' or 'whose proprietary rights are directly or indirectly owned for more than 50% by an entity listed in Annex X' or those acting on their behalf (Article 1aa). The relevant annex lists 14 key state companies, including those involved in sectors as consequential as energy—Rosneft, Gazprom-, technology—Rostec—and transport—United Aircraft Corporation, Russian Maritime Register of Shipping.

One of the most controversial measures entails a prohibition of broadcasting, which constitutes a first for the EU,[68] embedded in Article 4(g), whose opening stipulations read:

---

66 Council Decision (CFSP) 2022b.

67 Council Decision (CFSP) 2022b.

68 Poli and Finelli 2023.

> '1. It shall be prohibited for operators to broadcast, or to enable, facilitate or otherwise contribute to broadcast, any content by the legal persons, entities or bodies listed in Annex IX, including through transmission or distribution by any means such as cable, satellite, IP-TV, internet service providers, internet video-sharing platforms or applications, whether new or pre-installed.
>
> 2. Any broadcasting licence or authorisation, transmission and distribution arrangement with the legal persons, entities or bodies listed in Annex IX shall be suspended.'

Annex IX lists 32 broadcasters, including Russia Today in various languages, Russia 24 and Sputnik. However, the provision that serves as a basis for the listing does not contain any details on the criteria which guide the selection of entries, contrary to the approach followed under CFSP Decision 2014/145. This makes it difficult to assess the breath of the prohibition, as they can range from selective lists—including only certain elements—to exhaustive lists which cover the entire universe.

In a clear parallel to the germane regime under CFSP Decision 2014/145, this sanctions regime includes provisions to address its own circumvention. A most obvious illustration concerns the use of vessels to conduct activities covered by the bans. Inclusion in the blacklist is subject to designation criteria. According to Article 4x, this concerns vessels that:

> '(a) transport goods and technology used in the defence and security sector, from or to Russia, for use in Russia or for Russia's warfare in Ukraine;
>
> (b) transport crude oil or petroleum products ... that originate in Russia or are exported from Russia while practicing irregular and high-risk shipping practices as set out in the International Maritime Organisation General Assembly resolution A.1192(33);
>
> (c) are operated in such a way as to contribute or support actions or policies for the exploitation, development or expansion of the energy sector in Russia, including energy infrastructure;
>
> (d) are operated in such a way as to contribute or support actions or policies which undermine or threaten the economic subsistence or food security of Ukraine, such as the transport of stolen Ukrainian grain, or the preservation of cultural heritage of Ukraine, such as the transport of stolen Ukrainian cultural goods;
>
> (e) transport goods originating in or exported from the Union listed in Annexes XI, XX and XXIII to Regulation (EU) No 833/2014, or goods originating in Russia or exported from Russia and imported into the Union listed in Annex XXI to Regulation (EU) No 833/2014 and thereby enabling Russia's actions destabilising the situation in Ukraine;
>
> (f) are operated in such a way as to facilitate or engage in the violation or circumvention or otherwise significantly frustrate the provisions of this Decision or of Decisions 2014/145/CFSP, 2014/386/CFSP or (CFSP) 2022/266, or of Regulations (EU) No 833/2014, (EU) No 269/2014, (EU) No 692/2014 or (EU) 2022/263; or
>
> (g) are owned, chartered or operated by natural or legal persons, entities or bodies listed in the Annex to Decision 2014/145/CFSP and in Annex I to Regulation (EU) No 269/2014, are otherwise used in the name of, on behalf of, in relation with or for the benefit of such persons.'

While the use of vessels is most notorious for the transfer of oil in circumvention of the oil cap, i.e. the restrictions on the price of oil agreed by the EU and the G7, which is being flouted by Russia with the help of a 'shadow fleet' end-of-life tankers, prohibited activities under Article 4 cover a myriad of situations. These notably include supporting other prohibitions embedded in EU sanctions regimes: they reinforce the arms embargo, restrict Russia's exploration activities geared towards expanding its energy sector, address the exploitation of Ukrainian resources, and target other possible breaches of other EU sanctions thanks to the inclusion of a catch-all clause in paragraph (f), again mirroring CFSP Decision 2014/145. Designated vessels are subject to a prohibition to access to ports, anchorage zones and locks in the territory of the Union. Member states are neither allowed to trade in, operate or crew listed vessels, nor may they provide them with flag registration, financial or technical assistance, or engage in ship-to-ship transfers or any other transfer of cargo. Under the relevant annex XVI, 651 vessels are listed as of May 2026.

2.6.2 Sanctions Regimes on Annexed and Occupied Territories: CFSP Decision 2014/386 and CFSP Decision 2022/266

Already at the time of adoption, the sanctions regime CFSP Decision 2014/386 represented a radical departure from CFSP sanctions policy: it constituted the first ever full import embargo instituted by the EU.[69] Prohibitions cover the import into the EU of goods originating in Crimea or Sevastopol unless granted a certificate of origin by the Government of Ukraine, as well as the supply of goods and technology for use in transport, telecommunications, energy and the exploration and production of oil, gas and mineral resources. However, instead of specifying designation criteria, Article 4b stipulates that 'the Union shall take the necessary measures in order to determine the relevant items to be covered by this Article'.[70] The provision of a large number of services to entities in Crimea Sevastopol is also banned: accounting, auditing, bookkeeping or tax consulting services, business and management consulting or public relations services, construction, architectural and engineering services, legal advisory services and IT consultancy services, market research and public opinion polling services, technical testing and analysis services and advertising services, software for the management of enterprises or for industrial design and manufacture as well as tourism services, among others.[71] Derogations apply for judicial expenses, public health emergencies, humanitarian purposes, civil society activities, safety of civil nuclear capabilities etc.[72] In sum, the scope of the restrictions is defined so broadly that they effectively amount to comprehensive prohibitions, making designation criteria irrelevant. Instead, the sanctions regime foresees some derogations to its broad restrictions. The decision's only annex alludes to a derogation.[73]

---

[69] Portela 2010.

[70] Article 4b t point 6.

[71] Article 4c.

[72] Article 4c, points 1(g)–1(j): 4e.

[73] Annex I list third countries whose support to civil society activities is exempted from the sanctions. The same applies to Council Decision (CFSP) 2022a.

When the provinces of Donetsk and Luhansk were recognised by Russia as independent entities, the EU modelled its new sanctions regime on the framework previously applied to Crimea and Sevastopol text, leading to the adoption of Council Decision (CFSP) 2022/266, which closely mirrors the language and structure of CFSP Decision 2014/386. Council Decision (CFSP) 2022/266 includes a standard clause expressly prohibiting circumvention of its stipulations, similar to Council Decision (CFSP) 2014/386.[74] The title was modified in October 2022 to cover other 'non-government controlled areas of Ukraine' like Kherson and Zaporizhzhia, following further escalation of the war.

2.7 Discussion

The evolution of designation criteria evidences a qualitative leap in terms of the expansion of the universe that can be potentially targeted by CFSP measures, corroborating both scholarship claiming that CFSP sanctions policy is losing its targeted character[75] and that the Ukraine war constitutes a turning point.[76] No other autonomous sanctions regime in the EU's *repertoire* features a set of designation criteria of a scope comparable to that of CFSP Decision 2014/145.

However, the significance of the broadening of designation criteria goes beyond the more or less strict application of the notion of targeted sanctions. Rather, this broadening evidence that sanctions are increasingly employed to undermine the economic foundations of Russia, marking a shift away from the original objective of penalising and stigmatising individuals directly responsible for acts of aggression, annexation, destabilization, and other violations of the sovereignty, territorial integrity, and independence of the affected state. This shift was already visible in the statements of leading EU figures, particularly Commission President Ursula von der Leyen. When announcing the fourth package of sanctions in the first year of the war, she claimed that it purported 'to further isolate Russia and drain the resources it uses to finance this...war', alluding to 'pressuring Russian elites close to Putin as well as their families and enablers' and referring to the will to 'stop the group close to Putin and the architects of his war' and 'hit a central sector of Russia's system, deprive it of billions of export revenues and ensure that our citizens are not subsidising Putin's war'.[77] However, the EU discourse was characterised by a certain duality. For his part, then-High Representative for Foreign Affairs and Security Policy Josep Borrell highlighted that, in addition to limiting the economic resources of the target

---

[74] Article 4g in Council Decision (CFSP) 2014c and Article 9b in Council Decision (CFSP) 2022a read: 'It shall be prohibited to participate, knowingly and intentionally, in activities the object or effect of which is to circumvent prohibitions in this Decision, including by participating in such activities without deliberately seeking that object or effect but being aware that the participation may have that object or effect and accepting that possibility'.

[75] Lepeu 2025.

[76] Meissner 2023.

[77] von der Leyen 2022.

country and affecting its vital sectors, sanctions fulfil a symbolic messaging function which underlines the unacceptability of the misdeeds, pointing to the political signal: 'Europe is willing to take significant economic risks to coerce Russia for its invasion and to extend its political margin of manoeuvre vis-à-vis Moscow in the future.'[78]

Sanctions' intent of weakening the Russian economy comes to the fore even more patently in the statements by Baltic decision-makers, who are at the forefront of sanctions advocacy in the Council. Illustratively, in an interview in the spring of 2025, Latvian Minister of Foreign Affairs Ms Baiba Braže, also a former Deputy Secretary-General of the North Atlantic Treaty Organisation, declared: 'Sanctions constitute Europe's main leverage tool and allow it to have a seat at the negotiation table. Latvia will continue to advocate sustained pressure via sanctions in order to encourage Russia to truly engage in peace efforts and to respect agreements.'[79] For their advocates, sanctions ought to be tightened rather than merely kept in place, and their objective has a military dimension—to prevent further aggression—, in addition to a political one, namely, securing participation in negotiations concerning the conflict: 'We ought to exert an even stronger economic pressure on Russia, especially by strengthening sanctions. International and European sanctions limit Russia's ability to wage war and must be further strengthened. The Russian economy is weak and unsustainable. Europe and its partners should do everything to further weaken the Russian war economy, which is in decline. Sanctions are crucial to limit Russia's capacity to recover and commit new acts of aggression against its neighbours'.[80] In a similar vein, EU sanctions envoy David O'Sullivan stresses Russia's economic deterioration whenever the effectiveness of sanctions is questioned. He underlines that the 'economy is struggling and…public finances are in disarray. Interest rates are through the roof; the inflation rate is at least 10% if not more; there is no investment happening in Russia except for the military sector—the sanctions do have an impact on the Russian economy'.[81] He further adduces the following counterfactual argument: 'If we had not imposed sanctions, we estimate that Russia would have had

---

[78] Borrell 2022.

[79] Quoted in Delage 2025, p. 62. Original version in French: 'Les sanctions constituent le principal levier de l'Europe et lui permettent d'avoir une place dans la table des négociations. La Lettonie continuera de plaider en faveur d'une pression soutenue par des sanctions afin d'inciter la Russie à s'engager véritablement dans les efforts de paix et à respecter les accords conclus', author's translation.

[80] Quoted in Delage 2025, p. 62. Original version in French: 'Nous devons exercer une pression économique encore plus forte sur la Russie, notamment en renforçant les sanctions. Les sanctions internationales et Européennes limitent la capacité de la Russie à faire la guerre et doivent être encore renforcées. L'économie russe est faible et insoutenable. L'Europe et ses partenaires doivent tout mettre en œuvre pour affaiblir davantage l'économie de guerre russe, en déclin. Les sanctions sont cruciales pour limiter la capacité de la Russie à se reconstituer et à lancer de nouvelles agressions contre ses voisins', author's translation.

[81] Quoted in Tadeo 2015.

an additional 450 billion euros at its disposal for the war'.[82] This signifies the application of a logic that approximates that of classical, comprehensive embargoes, and has lost sight of the targeted intent that characterised the early days of the CFSP.[83]

2.8 Conclusions

The present chapter has analysed the evolution of the scope and coverage of CFSP sanctions imposed in response to the Russian invasion of Ukraine. To this aim, it singled out two sanctions instruments: one of them providing for the listing of individuals and entities (CFSP Decision 2014/145) and another setting out sectoral restrictions (CFSP Decision 2014/512). Together with the sanctions regimes prohibiting interaction with Crimea and Sevastopol (CFSP Decision 2014/386) and Donetsk and Luhansk alongside other territories illegally annexed,[84] they make up the EU's sanctions response to the aggression, annexation and destabilisation exercises conducted by Russia. The analysis shows that the scope of the measures has not only achieved unseen magnitude at an unprecedented speed. A comparison with other sanctions regimes directed at Russia with different motivations evidences a major discrepancy in terms of scope: sanctions regimes unrelated to the war in Ukraine display continuity with previous CFSP autonomous sanctions practice, while sanctions regimes responding to the war in Ukraine depart radically from this tradition. This dramatic alteration is not merely a change in CFSP practice but also entails the transformation of the EU into a different kind of sender: Brussels is no longer the architect of targeted sanctions but also of measures of quasi-comprehensive nature.

References

Blavoukos S, Bourantonis D (2014) Do Sanctions Strengthen the International Presence of the EU? European Foreign Affairs Review 19: 393–410.

Borrell J (2022) Beyond Sanctions. What future for Russia? WP6/22, Instituto Complutense de Estudios Internacionales, Madrid.

Borzyskowski I, Portela C (2018) Sanctions Cooperation and Regional Organisations. In: Aris S, Snetkov A, Wenger A (eds) Inter-organisational Relations in International Security: Cooperation and Competition. Routledge, Abingdon, pp. 240–261.

Brzoska M (2003) From Dumb to Smart? Recent Reforms of UN Sanctions. Global Governance: A Review of Multilateralism and International Organizations 9: 519–535.

Calleja Crespo D, Rollnert Pellicer B (2025) Las medidas restrictivas de la Unión Europea: Un instrumento en evolución [The European Union's restrictive measures: An evolving tool]. Revista Española de Derecho Europeo 94: 9–29.

[82] Ibid.

[83] Portela 2010; Portela 2023.

[84] Council Decision (CFSP) 2022a.

Christie E H (2016) The Design and Impact of Western Economic Sanctions against Russia. The RUSI Journal 161: 52–64.
Connolly R (2016) The Empire Strikes Back: Economic Statecraft and the Securitisation of Political Economy in Russia. Europe-Asia Studies 68: 750–773.
Council of the European Union (2003) A Secure Europe in a Better World: European Security Strategy. Brussels, 12 December 2003.
Council of the European Union (2004) Basic Principles of on the Use of Restrictive Measures (Sanctions). Council Doc. 10198/1/04 REV 1, Brussels, 7 June 2004.
Council Decision (2010) 2010/413/CFSP of 26 July 2010 concerning restrictive measures against Iran and repealing Common Position (CFSP) 2007/140/CFSP, OJ L 195, 27.7.2010, pp. 39–73, ELI: http://data.europa.eu/eli/dec/2010/413/oj.
Council Decision (2011a) 2011/18/CFSP of 14 January 2011 amending Council Decision 2010/656/CFSP renewing the restrictive measures against Côte d'Ivoire, OJ L 11, 15.1.2011, pp. 36–48, ELI: http://data.europa.eu/eli/dec/2011/18(1)/oj.
Council Decision (2011b) 2011/235/CFSP of 12 April 2011 concerning restrictive measures directed against certain persons and entities in view of the situation in Iran. OJ L 100, 14.4.2011, pp. 51–57, ELI: http://data.europa.eu/eli/dec/2011/235/oj.
Council Decision (2013) 2013/255/CFSP of 31 May 2013 concerning restrictive measures against Syria, OJ L 147, 1 June 2013, ELI: http://data.europa.eu/eli/dec/2013/255/oj.
Council Decision (2014a) 2014/119/CFSP of 5 March 2014 concerning restrictive measures directed against certain persons, entities and bodies in view of the situation in Ukraine. OJ L 66, 6.3.2014, pp. 26–30, ELI: http://data.europa.eu/eli/dec/2014/119(1)/oj.
Council Decision (2014b) 2014/145/CFSP of 17 March 2014 concerning restrictive measures in respect of actions undermining or threatening the territorial integrity, sovereignty and independence of Ukraine. OJ L 78, 17.3.2014, pp. 16–21, ELI: http://data.europa.eu/eli/dec/2014/145(1)/oj.
Council Decision (2014c) 2014/386/CFSP of 23 June 2014 concerning restrictions on goods originating in Crimea or Sevastopol, in response to the illegal annexation of Crimea and Sevastopol. OJ L 183, 24.6.2014, pp. 70–71, ELI: http://data.europa.eu/eli/dec/2014/386/oj.
Council Decision (2014d) 2014/512/CFSP of 31 July 2014 concerning restrictive measures in view of Russia's actions destabilising the situation in Ukraine, OJ L 229, 31.7.2014, pp. 13–17, ELI: http://data.europa.eu/eli/dec/2014/512/oj.
Council Decision (CFSP) (2018) 2018/1544 of 15 October 2018 concerning restrictive measures against the proliferation and use of chemical weapons, OJ L 259, 16.10.2018, pp. 25–30, ELI: http://data.europa.eu/eli/dec/2018/1544/oj.
Council Decision (CFSP) (2019) 2019/797 of 17 May 2019 concerning restrictive measures against cyber-attacks threatening the Union or its Member States, OJ L 129I, 17.5.2019, pp. 13–19, ELI: http://data.europa.eu/eli/dec/2019/797/oj.
Council Decision (CFSP) (2020) 2020/1999 of 7 December 2020 concerning restrictive measures against serious Human rights violations and abuses, OJ L 410I, 7.12.2020, pp. 13–19, ELI: http://data.europa.eu/eli/dec/2020/1999/oj.
Council Decision (CFSP) (2022a) 2022/266 of 23 February 2022 concerning restrictive measures in response to the recognition of the non-government controlled areas of the Donetsk and Luhansk oblasts of Ukraine and the ordering of Russian armed forces into those areas, OJ L 42I, 23.2.2022, pp. 109–113, ELI: http://data.europa.eu/eli/dec/2022/266/oj.
Council Decision (CFSP) (2022b) 2022/884 of 3 June 2022 amending Decision 2014/512/CFSP concerning restrictive measures in view of Russia's actions destabilising the situation in Ukraine, OJ L 153, 3.6.2022, pp. 128–138, ELI: http://data.europa.eu/eli/dec/2022/884/oj.
Council Decision (CFSP) (2024a) 2024/1484 of 27 May 2024 concerning restrictive measures in view of the situation in Russia, OJ L, 2024/1484, 27.5.2024, ELI: http://data.europa.eu/eli/dec/2024/1484/oj.

Council Decision (CFSP) (2024b) 2024/2643 of 8 October 2024 concerning restrictive measures in view of Russia's destabilising activities, OJ L, 2024/2643, 9.10.2024, ELI: http://data.europa.eu/eli/dec/2024/2643/oj.

Council Decision (CFSP) (2025a) 2025/1478 of 18 July 2025 amending Decision 2014/145/CFSP concerning restrictive measures in respect of actions undermining or threatening the territorial integrity, sovereignty and independence of Ukraine, OJ L, 2025/1478, 19.7.2025, ELI: http://data.europa.eu/eli/dec/2025/1478/oj.

Council Decision (CFSP) (2025b) 2025/1495 of 18 July 2025 amending Decision 2014/512/CFSP concerning restrictive measures in view of Russia's actions destabilising the situation in Ukraine, OJ L, 2025/1495, 19.7.2025, ELI: http://data.europa.eu/eli/dec/2025/1495/oj.

Council Regulation (EU) (2014a) No 269/2014 of 17 March 2014 concerning restrictive measures in respect of actions undermining or threatening the territorial integrity, sovereignty and independence of Ukraine. OJ L 78, 17.3.2014, pp. 6–15, ELI: http://data.europa.eu/eli/reg/2014/269/oj.

Council Regulation (EU) (2014b) No 692/2014 of 23 June 2014 concerning restrictions on the import into the Union of goods originating in Crimea or Sevastopol, in response to the illegal annexation of Crimea and Sevastopol, OJ L 183, 24.6.2014, pp. 9–14, ELI: http://data.europa.eu/eli/reg/2014/692/oj.

Council Regulation (EU) (2014c) No 833/2014 of 31 July 2014 concerning restrictive measures in view of Russia's actions destabilising the situation in Ukraine, OJ L 229, 31.7.2014, pp. 1–11, ELI: http://data.europa.eu/eli/reg/2014/833/oj.

Council Regulation (EU) (2022) 2022/263 of 23 February 2022 concerning restrictive measures in response to the recognition of the non-government controlled areas of the Donetsk and Luhansk oblasts of Ukraine and the ordering of Russian armed forces into those areas, OJ L 42I, 23.2.2022, pp. 77–94, ELI: http://data.europa.eu/eli/reg/2022/263/oj.

Delage T (2025) 'Lettonie: La paix n'est pas gratuite, la liberté et l'independance ne vent jamais être tenues pour acquises' [Latvia: Peace is not free of charge; freedom and independence must never be taken for granted]. Diplomatie 133: 58–62.

Dipama S, Dal E P (2015) The Effectiveness of Political Conditionality as an Instrument of Democracy Promotion by the EU: Case studies of Zimbabwe, Ivory Coast and Niger. Perceptions: Journal of International Affairs 20: 109–132.

Ferrero-Waldner B (2006) Speech at European Parliament plenary session discussion on Belarus Elections, European Parliament, Strasbourg, 5 April 2006, http://europa.eu/rapid/pressReleasesAction.do?reference=SPEECH/06/226&format=HTML&aged=0&language=EN&guiLanguage=en, accessed 20 August 2025.

Galtung J (1967) On the Effects of International Economic Sanctions, with examples from the case of Rhodesia. World Politics 19: 378–416.

Gordon J (2019) The Hidden Power of the New Economic Sanctions. Current History 118(804): 3–10.

Helwig N, Jokela J, Portela C (2020) EU-Sanktionspolitik in geopolitischen Zeiten: Europas schärfstes Außeninstrument und seine Herausforderungen [EU sanctions policy in geopolitical times: Europe's sharpest foreign policy tool and its challenges]. Integration 43: 278–294.

Hoffmann F (1967) The Functions of Economic Sanctions: a Comparative Analysis. Journal of Peace Research 4: 140–159.

House of Lords (2017) The Legality of EU Sanctions, European Union Committee, 11th Report of Session 2016–17, 2 February 2017.

Jones L, Portela C (2020) Evaluating the Success of International Sanctions: A new research agenda. Revista CIDOB d'Afers Internacionals 125: 39–60.

Koenig N (2011) The EU and the Libyan Crisis: In Quest of Coherence? International Spectator 46: 11–30.

Lepeu J (2025) Ukraine, the De-targetisation of EU Sanctions, and the Rise of the European Commission as Architect of EU Foreign Policy. International Politics, https://doi.org/10.1057/s41311-024-00649-7.

Meissner K (2023) How to Sanction International Wrongdoing? The design of EU restrictive measures. Rev Int Organ 18: 61–68.
Meissner K, Graziani C (2023) The Transformation and Design of EU Restrictive Measures against Russia. Journal of European Integration 45: 377–394.
Poli S (2017) The Turning of Non-state Entities from Objects to Subjects of EU Restrictive Measures. In: Fahey E, Bardutzky S (eds) Framing the Subjects and Objects of EU Law. Edward Elgar, Cham, pp. 158–181.
Poli S (2018) Effective Judicial Protection and its Limits in the Case Law concerning Individual Restrictive Measures in the European Union. In: Neframi E, Gatti M (eds) Constitutional Issues of EU External Relations Law. Nomos, Luxemburg, pp. 287–306.
Poli S, Finelli F (2023) Context specific and structural changes in EU restrictive measures adopted in reaction to Russia's aggression on Ukraine. Eurojus 3:19–49.
Portela C (2010) European Union Sanctions and Foreign Policy. Routledge, London.
Portela C (2015) The European Union, Human rights and Burma/ Myanmar: Elite perceptions in Southeast Asia. In: Chaban N, Holland M (eds) Europe and Asia: Perceptions from afar. Nomos, Baden-Baden, pp. 25–45.
Portela C (2016) Are EU Sanctions 'Targeted'? Cambridge Review of International Affairs 29: 912–929.
Portela C (2021) Horizontal Sanctions Regimes: Targeted sanctions reconfigured? In: Beaucillon C (ed) Research Handbook on Unilateral and Extraterritorial Sanctions, Edward Elgar, Cheltenham, pp. 441–457.
Portela C (2023) Logiques des sanctions de l'Union européenne contre la Russie au sujet de l'Ukraine [The logics of sanctions of the European Union against Russia over Ukraine]. Études Internationales 54: 287–310.
Portela C, Olsen K (2023) Implementation and Monitoring of the EU Sanctions' Regimes, including Recommendations to Reinforce the EU's Capacities to Implement and Monitor Sanctions. European Parliament.
Portela C, Tilahun N, Peez A (2025) The Effectiveness of the EU Global Human rights Sanctions Regime, European Parliament.
Tabrizi A, Santini R (2012) EU Sanctions against Iran: New wine in old bottles? ISPI analysis.
Tadeo M (2015) A conversation with David O'Sullivan, EU Sanctions Envoy, Groupe d'études géopolitiques, 15 July 2025, https://geopolitique.eu/en/2025/07/15/a-conversation-with-david-osullivan-eu-sanctions-envoy/, accessed 20 August 2025.
Vines A (2012) The Effectiveness of UN and EU Sanctions: Lessons for the twenty-first century. International Affairs 88: 867–877.
von der Leyen U (2022) Statement by President von der Leyen on the fourth package of restrictive measures against Russia, Versailles, 11 March 2022, https://enlargement.ec.europa.eu/news/statement-president-von-der-leyen-fourth-package-restrictive-measures-against-Russia-2022-03-11_en, accessed 20 August 2025.
Wallensteen P, Grusell H (2012) Targeting the Right Targets? The UN Use of Individual Sanctions. Global Governance: A Review of Multilateralism and International Organizations 18: 207–230.
Wilson T (2024) How Russia's shadow fleet gets its ships, Financial Times, 10 October 2024, https://www.ft.com/content/b9dee3f3-c2f8-4aa1-b0d9-d207f815b6e5, accessed 21 August 2025.

Chapter 3
The EU's Reaction to the War in Ukraine Through Restrictive Measures: The Limits of the Council's Discretion as Defined by the Court of Justice of the European Union

Sara Poli

Contents

Abstract This chapter explores the role of the Court of Justice of the European Union (CJEU) in constraining the Council's discretion in the administration of restrictive measures adopted in response to the war in Ukraine. It identifies emerging judicial trends in the case-law concerning both individual and sector-related sanctions. The legal analysis shows that the evidence presented by the Council is subject

S. Poli et al., *The EU's Response to the War in Ukraine and Its Impact on the EU Legal Order*, Global Europe: Legal and Policy Issues of the EU's External Action 7,
https://doi.org/10.1007/978-94-6265-767-0_3

to rigorous judicial scrutiny, and in several instances, listings have been annulled. Yet, the Council enjoys wide discretion in establishing the designation criteria. The General Court (GC) has shown particular attention to ensuring the effectiveness of sanctions, especially in litigation involving prominent business figures and their relatives. Yet, the Court is not deferent to the Council. The *Tokareva* case shows that the GC has imposed an unprecedented limitation on the Council's discretion by ruling that an individual cannot be listed solely on the basis of being associated with another associated person. The analysis of the case-law on sector-related restrictive measures shows that the GC has generally adopted a deferential stance towards the Council, prioritizing the effectiveness of sanctions. This approach is evident in the rejection of annulment actions in *Russia Today France* and *Ordre néerlandais des avocats du barreau de Bruxelles*. The trend is further confirmed in *Jemerak*, where the CJEU permitted Russian nationals to access notarial services for the purpose of divesting property within the Union, thereby introducing a pragmatic exception to the prohibition to provide legal advisory services. An exception to this trend can be found in the *Islentyeva* case, where the GC refused to provide the widest possible interpretation of the prohibitions laid down by restrictive measures, in light of the proportionality principle.

Keywords Court of Justice · Common Foreign and Security Policy · Effective judicial protection · Legal standing · Russian businessmen · Family members · Council's discretion · Sector-related restrictive measures · Broadcasting ban · Principle of proportionality

3.1 Introduction

The objective of this chapter is to show how the Court of Justice (hereafter the 'CJEU' or the 'Court') has limited the discretion of the Council in the administration of restrictive measures enacted in response to Russia's aggression of Ukraine. The author does not intend to exhaustively examine the case-law of the Court, resulting in numerous annulment actions[1] brought by the targets of these measures. The ambition of this chapter is to highlight leading cases showing how the Council is constrained by the Court in the administration of different categories of restrictive measures enacted to end the war in Ukraine. The Court is confronted with the challenge of ensuring that the Council may enact effective restrictive measures that are designed to resist their circumvention, while safeguarding fundamental human rights.

The chapter is composed in the following way. Section 3.2.1 defines the scope of the Court's jurisdiction while Sect. 3.2.2 stresses the Council's freedom to set out

[1] The number of new annulment actions concerning restrictive measures in the first three years of war was 103 in 2022, 63 in 2023 and 63 in 2024. It is the third largest sector after actions introduced in the field of intellectual property rights and the law governing the institutions. Annual Report 2024, Statistics concerning the judicial activity of the General Court, p. 7.

designation criteria and types of restrictions that are necessary to achieve the objectives of restrictive measures of individual restrictive measures (territorial integrity)[2] as well as sector related restrictive measures (destabilisation).[3] Section 3.3 considers what are the limits of the Council's discretion in managing individual restrictive measures in specific cases concerning: the obligation to de-list a member of a state organ who ceases to hold a public office (Sect. 3.3.1), the management of the listing of 'leading businesspersons providing a substantial revenue to the Russian government' (Sect. 3.3.2), of family members or of associated persons (Sect. 3.3.3). In Sect. 3.3.4 a concrete example of the impossibility for the Council to list certain persons is shown. The main interesting cases on sector-related restrictive measures are illustrated in Sects. 3.4 and 3.5, placing special emphasis on cases in which the Court had to balance the need to preserve the effectiveness of restrictive measures with fundamental human rights such as the right to freedom of expression (the judicial decision concerning broadcasting bans) or the right to property (the interpretation of the notion of 'legal advice') or has interpreted the scope of the flight ban imposed on Russia. An assessment of the cases concerning sector-related measures follows in Sect. 3.6, showing on the one hand, how the Court has supported the Council in fighting propaganda for war at the expense of the right to freedom of expression but on the other hand, has helped the Council to counter the circumvention of sanctions without losing sight of general principles such as the principle of proportionality. Concluding remarks seek to capture the way the Court has shaped the Council's discretion in managing EU restrictive measures that intend to maximise the pressure on Russia to cease the aggression to Ukraine and to effectively counter circumvention practices.

---

[2] Council Decision 2014/145/CFSP (territorial integrity) as modified after the start of the aggression to Ukraine with Council Decision (CFSP) 2022/265 of 23 February 2022; Council Regulation (EU) No 269/2014 of 17 March 2014 concerning restrictive measures in respect of actions undermining or threatening the territorial integrity, sovereignty and independence of Ukraine as amended.

[3] Council Decision (CFSP) 2022/264 of 23 February 2022 amending Decision 2014/512/CFSP concerning restrictive measures in view of Russia's actions destabilising the situation in Ukraine; Council Regulation (EU) No 833/2014 of 31 July 2014 concerning restrictive measures in view of Russia's actions destabilising the situation in Ukraine as amended.

3.2 The Practice of Restrictive Measures: The Contribution of the Court of Justice of the European Union

3.2.1 The Jurisdiction of the Court of Justice of the European Union

It is well known that the CJEU has provided an expansive interpretation of its jurisdiction in the field of CFSP, despite the limits posed by the black letter of Article 24(1) TEU and 275(1) TFEU.[4] Exceptions to the lack of jurisdiction are encapsulated in these provisions. In particular, natural and legal persons and non-state entities who are targeted by a CFSP Decision instituting a restrictive measure[5] have the right to challenge the listing decision,[6] under Article 263(4) TFEU. The case law has extended the Court's jurisdiction to preliminary rulings on the validity of Regulation under Article 215 TFEU and to action in damages[7] in light of the right to an effective judicial protection[8] and the rule of law. In addition, the notion of 'legal person' has been broadly interpreted.[9] Scholars have generally considered the interpretation of 'the rule of lawlessness encapsulated in the provisions of Article 24(1) TEU and Article 275(1) TFEU,[10]' as a positive development in line with Article 23 TEU.[11]

After the war in Ukraine started, the judiciary has confirmed this trend.[12] In the ruling in Neves 77 the Court recognised it had jurisdiction to give a preliminary ruling on the *interpretation* of a restrictive measure of general scope (set out by a CFSP

---

[4] The CJEU has performed a gap-filling function which has created tension with the principle of conferral. For a discussion on these issues, see for all scholars who have written on this topic Van Elsuwege 2021, pp. 134–135.

[5] On the definition of this notion see Poli 2019, pp. 19–21.

[6] In order to challenge restrictive measures of general scope, applicants face additional legal challenges with respect to the situation in which restrictive measures of individual nature are challenged. The rules of general application defining the designation criteria are subject to a limited judicial review. T-235/22, *Russian Direct Investment Fund*, 15 May 2024, ECLI:EU:T:2024:31, para 108. Yet, applications for annulment of Regulations, laying down restrictive measures of general application, enacted under Article 215 TFEU, were held admissible insofar as they could be qualified as regulatory act. For an example, see Case T-258/22, *Belaruskali*, 18 September 2024, ECLI:EU:T:2024:633.

[7] CJEU, Case C-134/19 P *Bank Refah Kargaran*, 6 October 2020, ECLI:C:2020:793, para 49. For comments see Poli 2022, pp. 1045–1080.

[8] For criticism regarding the Court's expansive interpretation see Koutrakos 2018, p. 35; for praise of the CJEU's approach to the interpretation of its jurisdiction see Hillion 2023, pp. 260–261.

[9] See Poli 2018, p. 295 and Poli 2022, 1058.

[10] Hillion 2023, p. 261; Wessel 2016.

[11] Hillion 2023.

[12] In a recent ruling the CJEU has recognised that the scope of the Court's jurisdiction stretches to action in damages resulting of various acts and omissions by EU institutions on the implementation of a Joint Action on an EU mission in Kosovo. CJEU, Cases C-29/22 P and C-44/22 P, *KS/KD*, 10 September 2024, ECLI:EU:C:2024:725. See for a positive assessment on the ruling, amongst others, Lonardo 2024.

Decision). This interpretation was necessary for the referring court to decide whether confiscation measures enacted by national authorities were legal. In principle, only restrictive measures of individual nature are subject to judicial review, under a literal interpretation of Article 275 TFUE.[13] The ruling in Neves 77 has reversed the case law that has so far excluded the jurisdiction of the Court on CFSP Decisions setting out restrictive measures of general nature. Admittedly, the circumstances of the case are very specific: in the case at hand, the Council had failed to implement a Regulation, which served as a basis for national sanctions (confiscation) imposed on a natural or legal person.[14] Despite these very specific circumstances, it is important to stress that the ruling in Neves 77 could be considered a precedent that be used in future cases to confirm that the Court's jurisdiction stretches to preliminary ruling on the interpretation of CFSP measures instituting restrictive measures of general nature. Surely, the EU's discussion on EU's accession to the ECHR and opinion 2/13[15] have influenced the decision of the Court to examine the legality of CFSP measures before the Strasbourg Court gains the competence to rule on the legality of the EU's action in the mentioned policy field.[16]

A further illustration of the expansive scope of the CJEU's jurisdiction in the field of CFSP is represented by the ruling in *Ordre néerlandais des avocats du barreau de Bruxelles*.[17] In this case the General Court (GC) has also accepted to examine the legality of restrictive measures of general scope, prohibiting to give legal advice to Russian nationals[18] without previously ascertaining whether it had jurisdiction to do so. The justification provided by the GC was that the action was in any event unfounded.[19]

The reason why the Court proceeded to examine the merits of the action without first determining its admissibility is not readily apparent. A possible explanation is that the GC did not want to leave gaps in judicial protection vis-à-vis CFSP acts that are challenged on failure to respect human rights, pending the finalization of the agreement on the EU's accession to the ECHR.

In the next sections the scope of the Council discretion in enacting restrictive measures and of its obligations will be highlighted, bearing in mind that the Court has never annulled a listing decision on the ground that it disproportionately affects substantive fundamental rights.[20] In contrast, designations of natural persons made

---

[13] Indeed, this provision refers to CFSP, instituting restrictive measures vis-à-vis natural or legal persons and other non-state entities.

[14] The Court reaches this conclusion taking into consideration Articles 19, 24 and 40 TEU and Article 215(1) TFEU, read in the light of Articles 2 and 21 TEU. CJEU, Case C-351/22 *Neves 77 Solutions SRL*, 10 September 2024, ECLI:EU:C:2024:723, para 53.

[15] Opinion 2/13 EU Accession to the ECHR, 18 December 2014, ECLI:EU:C:2014:2454.

[16] See for additional comments Poli and Finelli 2022, pp. 523–568.

[17] CJEU, Case T-797/22, *Ordre néerlandais des avocats du barreau de Bruxelles*, 2 October 2024, ECLI:EU:T:2024:670.

[18] Article 12b(2a) of Regulation No 833/2014, inserted by Regulation 2023/427.

[19] GC, case T-797/22, para 24.

[20] The rights to property or to conduct business are the most frequently invoked by applicants.

in breach of the right to an effective judicial protection (Article 47 CFR) were invalidated by the GC on the ground that the Council has made errors of assessment or has failed to motivate the listing. In Sect. 3.7 the most important trend emerging from the case law of the GC will be highlighted.

3.2.2 *The Scope of the Council's Discretion: The Designation Criteria and the Types of Obligations of Restrictive Measures that Are Not Subject to Judicial Challenge*

The GC had the opportunity to confirm that the Council has a broad discretion in shaping the EU restrictive measures, in line with established case law on this category of CFSP acts.[21] This trend results from litigation concerning both individual[22] and sector-related restrictive measures[23] applied in the context of Russia's aggression. The Council's freedom concerns different aspects of the legal regime of the EU restrictive measures.

The Council is free in defining the types of restrictions that can be enacted in order to tackle new security concerns posed by hybrid threats.[24] The best example of this wide sanctioning powers is provided by the ruling in *Russia Today France*,[25] where the GC acknowledged the competence of the Council to enact for the first time[26] an EU-wide broadcasting ban on selected Russian media outlets (Sputnik and a number of Russia Today's subsidiaries). The purpose of the sanction is to counter the spread of disinformation and the dissemination of propaganda in support of Russia's aggression.

These activities are a form of hybrid threat specifically posed by Russia. The Council does not consider disinformation activities as propaganda for war prohibited under Article 20(1) ICCPR; however, their destabilising effect on the Member States and the neighbours is enough to qualify them as 'a significant and direct threat to the Union's public order and security'.[27]

---

[21] CJEU, Case C-605/13 P, *Anbouba*, 21 April 2015, EU:C:2015:248, para 41.

[22] Council Decision 2014/145/CFSP (territorial integrity).

[23] Council Decision 2014/512 (destabilisation).

[24] See on this issue Alì 2025, p. 345 ff, Casolari 2024, p. 47.

[25] GC, Case T-125/22, *RT France*, ECLI:EU:T:2022:483.

[26] Asset freezes and travel bans vis-a-vis journalists, complicit with authoritarian regimes, were authorised in the practice. See annulment actions introduced by journalists: GC, Cases T-273/13, *Sarafraz v. Council*, ECLI:EU:T:2015:939; T-262/15, *Kiselev v. Council*, ECLI:EU:T:2017:392; T-693/13, *Mikhailchanka v. Council*, ECLI:EU:T:2016:283.

The mentioned restriction was later renewed and extended to other Russian media outlets, such as Voice of Europe, RIA Novosti, Izvestia and Rossiyskaya Gazeta. See https://ec.europa.eu/commission/presscorner/detail/en/ip_24_2682, 17 May 2024 [accessed 20 May 2025].

[27] It should be added that Norway and Switzerland have not aligned for different reasons to the restrictions on media outlets and propagandists enacted by the EU. The former considered that these measures affected the right to freedom of expression; the latter labels this type of sanction

The scope of the prohibition is very wide.[28] The generalisation of the broadcasting prohibition at the EU level[29] has guaranteed a uniform approach to disinformation across the Union and has contributed to promoting the protection of the Union public order to the rank of a general interest of the organisation.

According to the GC in the ruling in *Russia Today France*, the Council cannot be criticised for having considered that 'suitable measures to respond to the serious threat to peace on the borders of the European Union and the violation of international law could include the temporary prohibition of the broadcasting of content of certain media outlets belonging, in particular, to the RT group of channels ('the RT Group'), funded by the Russian State budget, on the ground that they supported that aggression by actions such as those referred to in recital 7 of the contested decision[30]'.

A further dimension of the Council's discretion is that the Council has extensive powers in shaping the designation criterion of individual sanctions and to decide the kind of prohibition that can be enacted in the context of sector-related restrictive measures. For example, in *Vinokurov* the GC rejected the argument that it was disproportionate for the Council to target persons who did not directly or indirectly participate to the illegal activities in Ukraine.[31] The Council is free to define the designation criteria which are the most suitable in a given geopolitical situation. This implies that persons who indirectly support the government's commission of breaches of international law can be sanctioned. Chief amongst these subjects are businesspersons who have featured amongst the addresses of restrictive measures since 2014. In 2017 the CJEU had already had the opportunity to confirm the legality of their inclusion in the backlist.[32]

In the context of its reaction to Russia's aggression of 2022, the GC has validated the designation criterion of Article 2(1) g),[33] enabling the Council to target 'prominent businessmen providing substantial revenue to the government of Russia'.[34]

---

ineffective. In a FAQ of the Secretariat d'État à l'Economie it was specified that in Switzerland it is more effective to counter disinformation through facts rather than through prohibitions. See https://www.seco.admin.ch/seco/fr/home/Aussenwirtschaftspolitik_Wirtschaftliche_Zusammenarbeit/Wirtschaftsbeziehungen/exportkontrollen-und-sanktionen/sanktionen-embargos/sanktionsmassnahmen/faq_russland_ukraine.html. [accessed 20 February 2025].

[28] It is also prohibited 'to facilitate or to make otherwise available' the information content of Sputnik and several Russia Today's subsidiaries in various Member States.

[29] The Baltic States, Poland and Germany had taken similar measures to those of the Council before the latter acted in early March 2022.

[30] GC, case T-125/22, *Russia Today France*, para 52.

[31] GC, case T-302/22, *Vinokurov*, ECLI:EU:T:2024:325, 29 May 2024, para 44.

[32] CJEU, Case C-72/15, *Rosneft*, 28 March 2017, EU:C:2017:236. See Poli 2017.

[33] Article 2 (1) g) Decision (CFSP) 2014/145, as amended by Decision 2022/329 of 25 February 2022 amending Decision 2014/145/CFSP concerning restrictive measures in respect of actions undermining or threatening the territorial integrity, sovereignty and independence of Ukraine, O.J. 2022 L 50/1.

[34] In Joined GC, Cases T-290/22, T-763/22 *Igor Albertovich Kesaev*, 4 September 2024, ECLI:EU:T:2024:575 the designation criteria f) and g) were challenged on grounds, amongst others, that they breached the presumption of innocence and the principle of proportionality. See also other

The rationale for targeting the circle of oligarchs who support Putin's war efforts by contributing to the revenue of the Russian Federation is convincing. Given that it is crucial to decrease the revenues over which Russia counts to continue its war, it seems justified to target these persons, in the light of the proportionality principle. The latter is a general principle whereby the Council must take measures that are appropriate for achieving the legitimate objectives pursued and cannot go beyond what is strictly necessary to achieve those objectives. Certainly, the number of the designated persons under this criterion cannot be compared to those listed under far narrower listing criterion of the EU restrictive measures enacted after the destabilisation of Ukraine in 2014.[35] The fully-fledged aggression of 2022 has justified an expansion of the designation criteria to target leading businesspersons operating in Russia involved in economic sectors providing a substantial source of revenue to the Government of the Russian Federation.

For the GC there is a logical connection between the objective of making pressure on the Russian Federation to cease its illegal behaviour (and the costs of its actions to undermine Ukraine's territorial integrity, sovereignty and independence) and the listing of persons who provide a substantial revenue to the government.[36] The aim of restrictive measure is to reduce the financial support to the continuation of the war.

The GC has also confirmed the Council's power to impose specific obligations on persons who are targeted. For example, in *Fridman, Aven and German Khan*[37] the applicants unsuccessfully contested the legality of the obligation to report the assets and cooperate with the competent authorities.[38] One of the arguments of the applicants in support of their position was that the obligation to disclose their financial position is a form of sanction and not a 'restrictive measure' within the meaning of that provision.[39] Yet the GC confirmed that the Council could impose this new kind of obligation in order to ensure the uniform application of Regulation No 269/2014

actions challenging criteria a) and d) in GC, Case T-237/22, *Alisher Usmanov*, 7 February 2024, ECLI:EU:T:2024:56.

[35] With the outbreak of the war in 2014, the Council had chosen to target 'undertakings or sectors that are reliant on cutting-edge technology or expertise mainly available within the European Union' and this choice was considered legitimate and consistent with the objective of ensuring the effectiveness of the restrictive measures by the GC. See GC, Case T-715/14, *PAO Rosneft Oil Company*, 13 September 2018, ECLI:EU:T:2018:544, para 162. On differences between the 2014 and 2022 legal regimes of restrictive measures to respond to Russia's illegal activities see Meissner and Graziani 2023, p. 381.

[36] See GC, cases T-305/22, *Viktor Filippovich Rashnikov,* para 108, T-193/22 *OT*, 15 November 2023, EU:T:2023:716, para 139. See also T-333/22, *Khan*, 29 November 2023, ECLI:EU:T:2023:758.

[37] GC, Case T-635/22 *Fridman, Aven and Khan*, 11 September 2024, ECLI:EU:T:2024:620.

[38] Article 9(2) and (3) of Regulation No 269/2014, as amended by Article 1, point 4, of Regulation 2022/1273 are the legal bases of obligations to report funds and to cooperate with the competent authorities in that regard, and treat failure to comply with those obligations as a circumvention of fund-freezing measures.

[39] GC, Case T-635/22 *Fridman*, para 44.

and to thwart patterns to circumvent restrictive measures, strategies made possible, in particular, by recourse to complex legal and financial arrangements.[40]

Considering the broad discretion reserved to the Council, the latter is subject as a counterbalance to an intense scrutiny by the judiciary when the persons subject to restrictive measures introduce the annulment of the listing decision before the GC. The applicants often claim that the Council erred in listing them since they do not come within the scope *ratione personae* of the challenged act(s). Renewal of the listing are also challenged. The GC carries out a full review on restrictive measures: a scrutiny of the evidence supporting the listing or re-listing is mostly based on open-source information and more rarely by confidential information.[41]

Looking at the practice, while in most cases annulment actions were rejected, applicants have also been successful, in particular when the Council has not been able to provide sufficiently specific evidence[42]—which is the standard prescribed since the ruling in *Anbouba*[43]—in support of the listing or when such evidence was outdated. In both cases the Council fails to comply with the right to an effective judicial protection (Article 47 of the CFR), which in a Union that is based on the rule of law, must be respected. The Council is under an obligation to gather specific evidence that the targeted persons fulfil the designation criteria or continues to do so after the expiry of the first or subsequent listing decision. Indeed, EU restrictive measures cannot be renewed over time without solid legal justification: listed persons may cease to fall within the scope *ratione personae* of restrictive measures due to changes in their legal[44] or factual situation.[45]

After a defeat in Court, the Council may delete the name of the successful private party from the list or update/change the body of evidence at the basis of the listing in order to maintain the applicant's name on the list. It is also possible to re-shape the designation criterion depending on the evolution of the geopolitical situation. The Council has been very active in introducing changes. An important driver for an expansion of the designation criterion was the problem of the circumvention of sanctions. In June 2023 the controversial criterion Article 2(1)g of Decision 2014/145/CFSP (hereafter 'criterion g')) as amended by Decision 2022/329/CFSP was also expanded. The Council was empowered to target: 'leading businesspersons operating in Russia and their immediate family members, or other natural persons, benefitting from them, or businesspersons, legal persons, entities or bodies involved in economic sectors providing a substantial source of revenue to the Government

---

40 Ibid., para 55.

41 See, for an example amongst others, GC case T-193/22, *OT*.

42 'The activity of the EU Courts is governed by the principle of the unfettered assessment of the evidence, and it is only the reliability of the evidence before the Court which is decisive when it comes to the assessment of its value.' T-193/22, *OT*, para 114.

43 CJEU, case C-605/13 P, *Anbouba*, para 52.

44 A change of status may have occurred. For example, a prominent businessperson may cease to occupy a high-level position in a company that is deemed to be crucial for Russia to continue the war. See Sect. 3.3.1 for a discussion on the conditions for the possible delisting.

45 A family member of a listed person may cease to be associated with the primary target of restrictive measures in case he/she no longer has common interests with the primary target of the sanctions.

of the Russian Federation, which is responsible for the annexation of Crimea and the destabilisation of Ukraine.'[46] The original criterion g) did not include family members and was limited to 'leading businesspersons or legal persons, entities or bodies involved in economic sectors providing a substantial source of revenue to the Government of the Russian Federation.'[47] Therefore the Council has expanded the potential circle of persons who could be subject to restrictive measures. The rationale of this decision is double: on the one hand, the continuation of the illegal activities of the aggressor State has justified the expansion of the number of targeted persons in the hope to increase the pressure on Russia to cease its illegal activities. On the other hand, the Council has strived to make it easier to target family members of the primary designated persons, considering the problem of circumvention of the sanctions. It is also possible that the Council has wished to change the designation criterion to make sanctions more defensible before the judiciary.[48]

Having set out the scope of the Council's discretion, in the next sections we will define the limits emerging from the case-law on its freedom of action.

3.3 The Contribution of the Court of Justice of the European Union to Limit the Discretion of the Council

3.3.1 The Council's Obligation in Case a Member of a State Organ Ceases to Hold a Public Office

The ruling in *Ovsyannikov*[49] deserves attention since it limits the Council's margin of manoeuvre to keep a member of a state organ which has contributed to undermine Ukraine's territorial integrity on the blacklist in case he ceases his public office.[50]

The applicant is a Russian national, the former governor of Sévastol, a Russian-controlled province in Ukraine which was illegally annexed to the Russian Federation, and a former vice-minister of industry and commerce of the Russian Federation. He held office as governor between 2017 and 2019 and as vice-minister until 2020. In both cases, the applicants had ceased to hold office, but the Council confirmed the restrictive measures that were originally enacted against him for the official positions Ovsyannikov had held in the past.

[46] See new Article 2(1) g of Council Decision (CFSP) 2023/1094 of 5 June 2023 amending Decision 2014/145/CFSP concerning restrictive measures in respect of actions undermining or threatening the territorial integrity, sovereignty and independence of Ukraine. O.J. 2023, L 146/20.

[47] Decision (CFSP) 2022/329 amending Decision 2014/145, OJ 2022 L 50, p. 1.

[48] See on this issue Chaps. 1 and 6 of the present book.

[49] GC, Case T-714/20, *Dmitry Vladimirovich Ovsyannikov*, 26 October 2022, ECLI:EU:T:2022:674.

[50] On this issue see Poli 2024, pp. 208–213.

The GC upheld the annulment action on the ground that the factual basis for keeping the applicant on the list referred exclusively to events in the past. The Council could not presume that the concerned person was still responsible for threatening the territorial integrity, the sovereignty and independence of Ukraine after he ceased his mandate. The obligation to re-examine restrictive measures every six months would be deprived of *effet utile* if the Council could avail itself of that presumption. The fact that the applicant no longer held public office showed that he did not actively support the policies threatening Ukraine's territorial integrity. It is up to the Council to prove that, on the contrary, he held links with the ruling class of the Russian Federation. The circumstance that the applicant had not taken the distance from the actions or policies threatening the territorial integrity, the sovereignty and independence of Ukraine cannot justify the decision to maintain the restrictive measures that were originally adopted vis-à-vis Mr Ovsyannikov. As a result of the ruling, the name of Ovsyannikov was deleted from the list.[51]

The lesson to be learnt from this ruling is that the cessation of the status of the member of a state organ is a cause for de-listing. The Council must adapt its sanctions to the evolution of the political context that led to their adoption. More precisely, this institution is obliged by the CFR to individually assess the situations of the listed persons, including those of former members of State organs, and de-list them after they cease their public functions, if this does not jeopardize the objective of the restrictive measures. Indeed, these measures are merely intended to put pressure on the political leadership of a third country to cease illegal conduct. They are not of a punitive nature; this implies, for example, that they cannot be used to make a member of former State organ accountable for international crimes committed during the term of office.

3.3.2 The Case Law on 'Leading Businesspersons Providing a Substantial Revenue to the Russian Government'

The bulk of litigation before the GC concerns the listing of Russian oligarchs and their family members.[52] The Court has engaged in a meticulous case-by case assessment of the evidence provided by the Council to support the legality of restrictive measures instituted vis-a-vis the mentioned targets. This is a way to subject the exercise of the Council's powers in the field of CFSP to the rule of law. The GC has provided clarifications on each of the notions encapsulated in the designation criteria: 'leading businessperson providing a substantial revenue to the government of the Russian Federation'. By so doing the case-law has defined the perimeter of the Council's discretion.

[51] Council implementing Regulation (EU) 2023/253 of 6 February 2023 implementing Regulation (EU) No 269/2014 concerning restrictive measures in respect of actions undermining or threatening the territorial integrity, sovereignty and independence of Ukraine, O.J. 2023, L 35/1.

[52] On this topic see Finelli 2023a.

The highest number of cases revolved around criterion g). First, it is crucial to clarify 'whom' qualifies as a 'leading businessperson'. This notion includes persons who are important 'in the light, amongst other things, of their occupational status,[53] the importance of their economic activities, the extent of their capital holdings or their functions within one or more of the companies in which they pursue those activities.'[54]

The case concerning Mr Khudaverdyan,[55] the former executive director of Yandex, a company active in the sector of information and communication technology, deserves special attention. Even if he had resigned from his position of executive director at the time he was first listed, the GC considered him prominent because of the importance of the activities carried out by Yandex. The applicant's name could be kept in the list since he had maintained an influence on the mentioned company.[56]

In *Mndoiants* the Court has clarified that the Council does not have an unfettered discretion in designating businesspersons. Indeed, neither the applicant's residence in the Russian Federation, nor the fact that he could potentially be appointed minister of culture were relevant factors to qualify a businessperson as prominent.[57] He was involved in a no profit organization and he possessed 30% of the shares of a company with a modest turnover in a specific year.[58] Therefore, this evidence was deemed insufficient to prove that the applicant was a prominent businessperson. The fact that the Minister of economy and banks blacklisted by the Council were customers of the applicant did not matter for the GC. Mr Mndoiants' listing was annulled, and the Council has delisted him.[59]

The GC has also shed light on the second part of criterion g).[60] Should an oligarch be characterised as 'prominent', for example in terms of taxes paid into the budget of the Russian Federation[61] he cannot be listed under criteria g), unless he is active in a sector which is important for the Russian economy.[62] This leads to question what is a 'sector providing a substantial revenue' to Putin's government. The Court has widely

[53] GC, Case T-270/22, *Dmitry Alexandrovich Pumpyanskiy*, 6 September 2023, ECLI:EU:T:2023:490.

[54] GC, T-193/22, *OT*, 15 November 2023, ECLI:EU:T:2023:716, para 143.

[55] GC, T-335/22, *Khudaverdyan*, 6 September 2023, ECLI:EU:T:2023:500.

[56] Ibid., para 111.

[57] GC, Case T-390/22, *Mndoiants*, 20 December 2023, ECLI:EU:T:2023:850.

[58] GC, Case T-390/22, para 103.

[59] Council Decision (CFSP) 2024/847 of 12 March 2024 amending Decision 2014/145/CFSP concerning restrictive measures in respect of actions undermining or threatening the territorial integrity, sovereignty and independence of Ukraine, OJ L, 2024/847, 13.3.2024, ELI: http://data.europa.eu/eli/dec/2024/847/oj.

[60] The Court has stressed that in order to be listed, a leading businessperson must be active in a sector of the economy providing a substantial source of revenue to the Russian Federation. GC, Case T-313/22, *Abramovich*, 20 December 2023, ECLI:EU:T:2023:830, para 98.

[61] The GC has clarified that the taxes paid by the oligarchs are not relevant to determine whether the sector in which he is a prominent businessman provides a substantial source of revenue. T-302/22, *Vinokurov*, para 111.

[62] GC, Case T-283/22, *Moshkovich*, 20 December 2023, ECLI:EU:T:2023:849, para 96.

conceived this notion and has not limited itself to consider the relevance of the sector for the continuation of the war as a determining factor; what matters is the position of the company in which a prominent businessman is active in the context of the Russia's economy and not the global market.[63] Thus, the GC has confirmed the legality of the listing of oligarchs active in the trade in steel pipes[64] in the fields of information and communication technology,[65] agriculture, pharmaceutical[66] metallurgy,[67] and petrochemistry.[68]

The Court has also had the opportunity to dwell on the term 'substantial' revenue, which is not defined in the acts instituting restrictive measures. In *Pumpyanskiy* the GC held that the adjective in question, 'which qualifies the nominal group 'source of revenue', implies that that source of revenue must be significant and therefore not negligible.[69]' Given the applicant enjoyed a high level position in companies active in the oil and gas sectors, the GC presumes that they provide directly or at least indirectly, a substantial source of revenue for the Government of the Russian Federation.[70] A flexible approach is thus adopted: there is no need to provide data by the Council. Only when he resigned from these strategic companies the GC annulled his listing, considering that the Council could not prove that the applicant retained an influence on these firms.[71]

In *Khudaverdyan* the Court took into consideration both the contribution in terms of GDP made by the sector of information and communication technology to Russia's budget as well as the taxes to be paid into it as relevant factors to hold that this sector is a substantial source of revenue.[72] The food retail trade and agricultural sectors are also sources that provide a substantial source of revenue, despite the fact that the tax revenue of the two sectors is small.[73] In another case the GC clarified that the fact that a person is active in an economic sector which contributes to '*entités fédérées locales et non au budget du government russe*[74]' is not relevant to annul the listing.

---

[63] GC, Case T-302/22, para 147.

[64] As clarified in T-270/22, *Dmitry Alexandrovich Pumpyanskiy*, or in T-313/22, para 104. See also T-359/22, *Evgeny Borisovich Zubitskiy*, 6 December 2023, ECLI:EU:T:2023:779.

[65] As confirmed in T-355/22, *Khudaverdyan*.

[66] T-283/22, above n. 62.

[67] GC, Case T-305/22, *Rashnikov*.

[68] GC, Case T-651/22 *Shamalov*, 4 September 2024, ECLI:EU:T:2024:576.

[69] GC, Case T-270/22, *Pumpyanskiy*, para 57.

[70] Ibid.

[71] GC, Case T-740/22, *Dmitry Alexandrovich Pumpyanskiy* 26 June 2024, ECLI:EU:T:2024:418.

[72] GC, Case T-305/22, above n. 67, paras 103 and 106.

[73] The GC reports that the tax revenue is between 3.46% and 0.76%. In order to decide whether the tax revenue is substantial, the GC has also taken into consideration "la taxe sur la valeur ajoutée (TVA), les cotisations de sécurité sociale, les droits d'accise ou les droits d'exportation et d'importation et toute autre recette parvenant directement ou indirectement au budget de l'État." See T-651/22 *Shamalov*, para 154.

[74] GC, Case T-313/22, para 117.

While in most cases the validity of the Council's designation of prominent businesspersons was confirmed, in a few instances the annulment actions were upheld. By way of example two cases may be listed.

In *Shulgin* the Court has recognised that the Council has committed an error of assessment in maintaining in the blacklist a businessperson who no longer held high-level positions in Russian companies active in the field of digital trade.[75]

In *Farkhad Teimurovich Akhmedov*, the applicant was the Vice President of a company active in the field of telecommunication, but he had resigned from his position ten years before the aggression of 2022. He could not be defined as a prominent businessperson considering that he had sold the shares of the companies in which he was active more than 10 years before those measures were adopted. The applicant succeeded in its annulment action against the initial listing; the GC found that the evidence relied upon by the Council was based on situations dating back 10 years before the aggression of 2022 and was also vitiated by mistakes.[76] The renewal of his listing in March 2023 was founded on different grounds: the applicant's 'ongoing business interests in Russia, including in the IT and forestry sectors'. Yet the GC found that the evidence provided for by the Council to maintain the applicant's name on the list was insufficient to prove that he fell within criteria g).[77] The GC acknowledged that taking into consideration of activities pursued by the applicant, which dated back 10 years or more, would have the effect of freezing his situation in a distant, already elapsed past and of depriving the periodic review provided for in the relevant CFSP Decision or Regulation, of all practical effect. It is unsurprising that the rulings in *Akhmedov* and *Shulgin* resulted in the delisting of these persons.[78]

The conclusion that may be drawn from the case law examined in this section is that the Court has considered most of the challenged restrictive measures legal thus making it possible for the Council to achieve the objective of these measures (*in casu* the decrease of the revenue of the Russian Federation) without giving *carte blanche* to this institution in the name of the effectiveness of restrictive measures. Indeed, in

---

[75] GC, Case T-364/22, *Shulgin*, 6 September 2023, ECLI:EU:T:2023:503.

[76] The targeted person was listed by the Council on several grounds: his position of Russian businessman involved in the energy sector and in Russian local politics. In particular, he had founded the company Tansley Trading, which supplied equipment to Russian gas producers, and he had become a minority shareholder in Northgas, an oil and gas company in Siberia. Finally, he was the chairman of another company active in the energy sector. Yet the GC found that he could not be defined as a prominent businessman active in an activity that provides a substantial source of revenue to the Russian Federation. Indeed, the first company was dissolved more than ten years before the aggression; the applicant had sold the shares of Northgas ten years before the aggression to Ukraine started. The applicant's involvement in local politics also dated back to more than 10 years. Finally, it was factually wrong that Mndoiants was the chairman of a company active in the energy sector. See T-363/22, *Akhmedov*, 29 May 2024, ECLI:EU:T:2024:326, paras 73 and 78.

[77] The company of which he was a shareholder was not an important company of the IT sector; neither the company the applicant operated in the forestry sector could be qualified as important.

[78] Council Decision (CFSP) 2023/1767 of 13 September 2023 amending Decision 2014/145/CFSP concerning restrictive measures in respect of actions undermining or threatening the territorial integrity, sovereignty and independence of Ukraine, O.J. 2023, L 226/104.

order to list Russian businessmen, it is necessary to provide evidence that they are capable of contributing to Putin's war machine.

The Council is compelled by the Court to review its decisions in case businessmen step down from their high-level positions within strategic companies or dispose of the shares they possess in these firms.[79] Yet this does not automatically imply that they can be delisted; indeed, there is a risk that the oligarchs circumvent the restrictions. In order to maintain the name on the blacklist, the Council needs to show that the designated person maintains an influence on the company.

3.3.3 The Listing of Family Members and the Interpretation of the Association Criteria with the Primary Target of Restrictive Measures

After February 2022 numerous family members of Russian nationals were listed by the Council since they fell within the following designation criterion: they were natural persons associated with the listed persons[80] and derived an advantage from them.[81] The rationale, which was not explained in the initial listing decisions of 2022, may be derived from the practice of EU restrictive measures: that is, to avoid that the targets of restrictive measures circumvent the sanctions[82] by transferring (for example, through shell companies) to family members part of their assets.[83] At the same time, for EU restrictive measures to be effective, it is necessary that family members who have connections with the primary target may be easily subject to similar measures to avoid the circumvention of sanctions; which is crucial to ensure their effectiveness.[84] The GC had to find a balance between the mentioned CFSP objective and the protection of the fundamental rights of the family member.

In the Iran sanction regime (Weapons of mass destruction) the judiciary was confronted with the problem of circumventing sector-related restrictive measures

---

[79] The applicant must prove that shares were disposed of. For a case in which the evidence was deemed insufficient and the listing decision confirmed see GC, Case T-333/22, *Khan*, para 131. Poli and Finelli 2022, pp. 24–25.

[80] Including persons, who materially or financially support the government of the Russian Federation, leading businesspersons involved in economic sectors providing a substantial source of revenue to, and on persons supporting or benefitting from, the Government of the Russian Federation and on natural persons associated with those persons.

[81] See recital (7) Council Decision (CFSP) 2022/582 of 8 April 2022.

[82] GC, Cases T-296/20, *Amer Foz*, para 174, T-540/19, *Sharif*, 18 May 2022, EU:T:2021:220, para 159, and, by analogy, T-577/12, *NIOC and Others*, 4 September 2015, EU:T:2015:596, para 139.

[83] See, for example, GC, Case T-234/22 *Gulbakhor Ismailova*, 8 May 2024, ECLI:EU:T:2024:287. The applicant was the beneficiary of two trusts that were designed by the oligarch Alisher Usmanov, Ismailova's brother, to circumvent restrictive measures. On the designation of family members see Butler 2023.

[84] CJEU, Cases C-380/09 P, *Melli Bank*, 13 March 2021, ECLI:EU:C:2012:137, para 58 and C-595/15 P, 22 September 2016, *NIOC*, ECLI:EU:C:2016:721, para 89.

while in the case of Syria in many cases the case-law concerned the listing of members of specific families who were presumed to contribute to the illegal activities of the Syrian government.[85] In the *contentiex* concerning Russian restrictive measures post-2022, the applicants have mostly been linked to businessmen or to persons financially or materially supporting the Russian government; only the very first ruling on the listing of a family member concerns Ms Prigozhina, mother of the mercenary who was listed for having benefited from links with the Russian government.[86] The ruling in *Prigozhina*[87] is relevant since it has clarified that the family relation with the targeted person is not enough for the purpose of validating the listing. The GC applied the case-law in *Tay Za*[88] which excluded that family links could justify the listing.

The key test to fulfil the designation criteria is that there must be a link through an economic activity or common interest between the concerned subjects.[89] At the time restrictive measures were enacted *vis-à-vis Prigozhina* she was no longer the co-owner of a company with her son as she had been until 2017. The GC annulled Prigozhina's listing since it was based exclusively on the family relation with her son. The risk of circumvention of restrictive measures, which is at the basis of the need to include family members associated with the primary targets of restrictive measures, is clearly high in this case. Yet, it would be disproportionate to restrict Ms *Prigozhina*'s fundamental rights, considering the remote connection between her and the illegal activities carried out by Russia in Ukraine.

Given that unlike in the Syrian sanction regime, there was no relative presumption that family members could be listed,[90] and considering that family links were not sufficient to justify the listing, the concept of 'association' became of central importance in the case-law.[91] The proof of the 'association', which is primarily expressed by common financial interest, such as transferred assets from the primary target to the family member,[92] was further elaborated upon by the GC.

In *Galina Evgenyevna Pumpyanskaya*[93] the applicant is the wife of a leading businessperson,[94] who fulfil the designation criterion g)[95] since he is involved in

[85] On the establishment of legal presumptions see Hinojosa-Martínez 2023, pp. 118–122.

[86] Prigozhin was listed since he was responsible for deploying mercenaries in Ukraine and had benefited from his links with the Russian defence ministry to obtain public contracts.

[87] GC, Case T-212/22, *Prigozhina* v *Council*, 8 March 2023, ECLI:EU:T:2023:104.

[88] CJEU, Case C-376/10 P, *Tay Za*, 13 March 2012, EU:C:2012:138.

[89] Ibid., paras 93–94.

[90] See for a comparison the Syrian regime in which the Council targeted the Assad and Makhlouf families.

[91] In contrast, the concept of 'advantage' was not questioned by the applicants and consequently the GC did not have the opportunity to explore it.

[92] See, for example, Case T-497/22, *Marina Alexandrova Mordashova* in which Mr. Mordashov transferred assets, amounting to over 1.5 billion EUR, to his partner (after his designation).

[93] GC, Case T-272/22, *Galina Evgenyevna Pumpyanskaya*, 6 September 2023, ECLI:EU:T:2023:491.

[94] Mr Dmitry Alexandrovich Pumpyanskiy.

[95] The companies in which Dmitry Alexandrovich Pumpyanskiy is active support and benefit from cooperation with authorities of Russian Federation and State-owned companies.

companies that support and benefit from the cooperation with authorities of the Russian Federation and State-owned companies. The applicant contested the designation criteria for failing to provide for legal certainty. The GC acknowledges that the Council has not as such defined the concept of 'association' 'and its meaning is contingent on the context and circumstances at issue.[96]' Yet the mentioned criterion did not confer on the Council an arbitrary discretion. The reason for including this criterion, amongst others, is well justified by the Court: when the funds of a person who is a leading businessperson provides a substantial source of revenue to the Russian Federation, there is a non-negligible risk that this businessperson may exert pressure on persons associated with him/her in order to circumvent the effect of the measures to which she/he are subject.[97] The question was whether Galina could be qualified as associated to her husband.

In the case at hand the common interests between the applicant and her husband are represented by an organization that manages the charitable activities of one of the companies whose President is Ms Pumpyanskaya's husband. The lady is involved in that foundation. This is enough to prove that she is associated with her husband. M. Dmitry Alexandrovich Pumpyanskiy, a member of the Pumpyanskiy's family was also considered associated to his father.[98]

The GC has contributed to loosen the link between the family member and the primary target of restrictive measures in the case of *Elena Petrovna Timchenko*.[99] In particular, the GC has made easier for the Council to prove the existence of the association criteria. The applicant is the wife of a billionaire, who was listed on account of his support to Putin; she is the founder of the Timchenko foundation together with her husband. The reasons provided by the Council to justify her listing was that she was associated to her husband by means of the mentioned Foundation; in addition, her participation to public affairs through this entity was beneficial for her husband's social position. The Court rejected MS Timchenko's annulment action. The GC held that a natural or legal person could be considered associated with a person subject to restrictive measures when she/has a link with him/her by means of financial support or by the advantage derived from Russian decision makers.

Yet, this is a narrow interpretation of the concept. The GC selected a broader reading of this notion: an associated person is a family member who has common interests with the person subject to restrictive measures which are not necessarily formalised in a legal structure created for this purpose.[100] Thus, the notion of association is extremely flexible. As a result, a family member of a person whose assets are frozen will quite easily fulfil the condition of being associated to the primary target. The Court found that *Elena Petrovna Timchenko* met the designation criterion. This interpretation of the condition of 'associated person' may seem unsatisfactory since

[96] GC, Case T-272/22, para 63.

[97] Ibid., para 118.

[98] GC, Case T-291/22, *Alexander Dmitrievich Pumpyanskiy,* 6 September 2023, ECLI:EU:T:2023:499.

[99] GC, Case T-361/22, *Elena Petrovna Timchenko,* 6 September 2023, ECLI:EU:T:2023:502.

[100] GC, Case T-361/22, para 76.

it almost creates a presumption that family members have links with the primary target and support them in their attempts to circumvent restrictive measures.

In Mazepin the GC had the opportunity to stress that the commonality of activities or interests between a son and a father had to exist at the time of the adoption of restrictive measures. This condition proved to be tricky for the Council.[101] The applicant has been a driver for the Haas F1 Team until March 2022. His father, a prominent businessman, had appeared in the Council's blacklists since the early days of the war. Nikita was listed in September 2022 on account of his association to his father; the links between the two persons were the family relation and a sponsorship agreement through which Nikita's father had funded the Haas F1 team, thus indirectly supporting his son's career. Challenged before the Court, the mentioned listing decision was considered illegal by the GC: indeed, the renewal of Nikita's listing in September 2022 referred to events of the past, in particular a sponsorship agreement[102] which was terminated before the adoption of contested measures. Therefore, at the time restrictive measures were adopted, the applicant and his father could not be said to be associated by means of economic or capital links or by the existence of common interests.[103]

The applicant could not really benefit from this success in Court; indeed, the Council changed the reasons justifying Nikita's asset freezes and visa ban adding to the statement of reasons that Nikita's Foundation, created after the termination of the sponsorship contract, was funded by Mazepin senior.[104] The second set of restrictive measures, maintaining Nikita's name in the list, was adopted in March 2023. Once again, the GC held that the Council had not proved that the Foundation set up by the applicant was funded by a company belonging to his father. Indeed, the evidence provided by the Council relied on publicly available sources predating the creation of the Foundation.

The case law briefly sketched out in this section shows that it may be difficult for the Council to defend the listing of family members if it is necessary to prove the existence of a common activity or of common interest between the targeted persons at the time restrictive measures were enacted.

The notion of association is also relevant for the designation of family members of targets different from businessmen providing a substantial revenue to the Russian government. The interpretation of the concept of 'association' is broadly similar to

---

[101] GC, Case T-743/22, *Nikita Dmitrievich Mazepin*, 20 March 2024, ECLI:EU:T:2024:180. The case is also known as the first case in which the applicant had succeeded in obtaining interim measures in relation to his application for annulment in respect of the visa ban imposed through the first set of acts maintaining acts of September 2022. See GC, Case T-743/22 R, 20 March 2024, not published, EU:T:2023:102. Nikita Mazepin asked for three additional orders for interim measures. Even if in two cases these applications were initially upheld by the Vice-President of the GC they were subsequently cancelled or annulled by the Vice-President of the Court of Justice. See for references to these orders T-743/22, paras 27–53.

[102] There was a link between the father and the son since the latter, who was a driver for the Haas F1 team, was part of the Team that was funded by one of his father's companies.

[103] T-743/22, above n. 101, para 91.

[104] The second set of acts maintaining the Nikita Mazepin on the list was dated 13 March 2023.

that of 'association' in the context of a family relationship with a businessman. If the advantage derived from the primary target is too remote in time, it is not possible to hold that the family member derives a benefit from the targeted person. This is clear from the ruling in *QF*[105] which was lost by the Council. The primary target of restrictive measures was not a businessperson but the shareholder of an important bank, Mr Fridman; he was listed for providing support to the Russian government. The applicant was placed in the blacklist for being associated to her former husband insofar as she derived an advantage from him: QF had been able to profit from the alimony that she received from her former partner and she had a comfortable life in Paris. The GC was not convinced by the Council's defence. The applicant had divorced in 2005 and she no longer received the alimony at the time restrictive measures were adopted.[106] She might have derived an advantage in the past from her family relation but the grounds for designation[107] were different and as a result the GC annulled the listing.

The difficulties in defending restrictive measures vis-a-vis family members before the court might have driven the Council to change the designation criteria. In June 2023 Article 2(1) g of CFSP decision 2014/145 was amended to include 'immediate family members of businesspersons' benefiting from them. The notion of 'advantage' is replaced by that of 'benefit' and at the same time the 'association' criteria is dropped. The Council's explanation to justify the inclusion of 'immediate family members' is convincing[108] and is in line with the importance that countering the circumvention of restrictive measures has always had in the practice of the Council. According to this institution, leading Russian businesspersons have engaged in a systematic practice of distributing their funds and assets amongst their immediate family members and other persons, often in order to hide their assets, to circumvent the restrictive measures and to maintain control over the resources available to them.

Therefore, should an immediate family member, be it the children, wives and husbands or parents, benefiting from a leading businessperson, he/she should be listed in order to ensure the effectiveness of restrictive measures. The designation criteria are ambiguous as to what kind of benefit must be derived from the primary target and when the benefit must be received with respect to the time restrictive measures were enacted. The case-law has helped to clarify these ambiguities.

It is now necessary to examine whether the changes of the designation criteria of family members introduced in June 2023 has made the listing of these categories of persons more defensible in Court.

Let us start with the example of Nikita Mazepin's application for annulment. He was re-listed in September 2023 for the third time. The justification was that he had benefited from his father sponsorship agreement to support his career of F1 driver, in application of criterion g) as amended. Nikita had derived advantages from his father given that without the sponsorship agreement, Nikita would have not been part of the

[105] T-386/22, *QF*, ECLI:EU:T:2023:670.

[106] Ibid., para 69.

[107] Ibid., paras 66–69.

[108] Preamble n. 5 of Decision (CFSP) 2023/1094, cit.

Haas F1 team. In addition, the Council still relies on the association criteria in arguing that the applicant had common interests with his father through a Foundation. The latter was funded by a company owned by his father and through another company, which was partly owned by his father and whose objective was to support Nikita's career as a motorsport driver.

For the third time, the acts maintaining the applicant's name in the blacklist were considered illegal by the GC. The Court stressed that the applicant had obtained good results as a driver of F2 and F3 before being recruited as F1 driver, thus rejecting the position of the Council that Nikita's recruitment was due to his father's sponsorship agreement. The Council had not shown enough evidence to prove that Nikita derived an advantage from the Foundation funded by a companies controlled by his father. Finally, the GC was not convinced by the argument that the applicant had joint interests with his father through a company which was created to support Nikita's career. Indeed, Nikita's father had transferred the shares of the concerned company before restrictive measures were enacted. Finally, he was not the only racing driver to have been recruited by the company. This ruling clarifies that the benefit must be present at the time restrictive measures were enacted as it was the case when the original designation criteria g) were in force.

In contrast to the ruling in Mazepin, the Council was successful in the *Mordashova* case in which the GC dwelled on the concept of 'benefit' that the family member must derive from the primary target. This notion is such when it is '*quantitativement ou qualitativement non négligeable*'[109]; in the words of the GC the benefit must be widely defined and interpreted 'having regard to the objective of avoiding practices used to circumvent restrictive measures, expressly referred to in recital 5 of CFSP Decision 2023/1094.[110]' As a result, benefits 'may therefore be a financial or non-financial benefit, such as a donation, a transfer of funds or of economic resources, an intervention to further the award of public contracts, an appointment or a promotion.[111]' The GC upheld the Council's argument that the applicant was a family member who derived an advantage from her husband and rejected the action.

In the ruling in *Ezubov*[112] released on the same date as that in *Mordashova*, the GC upheld an annulment action given that the applicant had derived a benefit from the primary target in a remote past with respect to the enactment of restrictive measures. In this case the listed person, Mr Oleg Deripaska, had transferred to his cousin, Mr Ezubov, eight sets of assets, some of which had a value of several million euros. Well, for the GC this was not enough to prove that the applicant benefited from the oligarch concerned and the listing was annulled. Indeed, a substantial transfer of assets escapes the definition of benefit if it is part of a long-standing business relations between a targeted person and his cousin. In other words, the benefit received from the supplier must be relatively recent in time. Thus, a transfer of property, dating back 2014 (as it in the case at hand) does not fall within the definition of 'benefit'.

---

[109] GC, Case T-497/22, *Mordashova*, 11 September 2024, EU:T:2024:604, para 116.

[110] Ibid., para 109.

[111] Ibid.

[112] GC, Case T-741/22, *Pavel Ezubov*, 11 September 2024, ECLI:EU:T:2024:605.

The GC rejected the Council's argument that the transfer of assets, which is an expression of a common interest or a common activity, could be sufficient to conclude that the family member derived a benefit from the primary target. The GC refused to interpret 'the criterion g) as amended in a similar way to the associated person criterion, laid down in Article 2(1) in fine of Decision 2014/145 as amended in so far as it covers persons linked by common interests. Such an interpretation would have the effect of depriving the amended criterion (g) of effectiveness in that it would become meaningless as compared with the associated person criterion where the latter criterion is applied in relation to a listed person on the basis of criterion (g).'[113]

The GC excluded that 'any benefit granted after [February 2014, the annexation of Crimea] necessarily falls within the scope of amended criterion (g), since the circumstances in which it was granted and the passage of time between that grant and the date on which the businessperson's name behind that grant was included on the lists at issue are also factors to be taken into account in assessing whether the inclusion, on those lists, of the name of the recipient of that benefit is well founded. In any event, the benefit received by the person whose name is included on the lists at issue under amended criterion (g), or at least its consequences, must subsist at the time when the restrictive measures against him or her are adopted.[114]'

Finally, the re-listing of both Pumpyanskiy's wife and son on the basis of the amended criterion g) were annulled[115] after the GC annulled the listing of Pumpyanskiy senior since he lost his status of leading businessperson.[116]

In conclusion, the amendment of criterion g) does not make possible to list family members if the benefit they derived from the primary target is too far in time. Therefore, the change of the designation criteria g) has not substantially strengthened the defensibility of the listing of a family member who has connections with the primary subjects. The GC has not made explicit the reason underlying its position. It seems plausible to think that the risk of circumvention of the effects of restrictive measures, which is particularly acute in family relations, is lessened if the benefit received from the primary target of restrictive measure is too distant in time.

The case-law accounted for in this section has shown that the Council faces a limit when listing persons in order to ensure the effectiveness of restrictive measures. It is not possible to subject to sanctions family members of primary targets if they do not have an actual common interest or activity with the primary target or if the benefit they derive from their relatives, regardless of the economic value, concerns a longstanding transaction/business relation.

---

[113] Ibid., para 186.

[114] Ibid., para 189.

[115] GC, Case T-737/22, *Pumpyanskaya*, 26 June 2024, ECLI:EU:T:2024:417.

[116] GC, Case T-740/22, *Pumpyanskiy*.

3.3.4 *The Impossibility of Listing a Person Associated to a Person Associated to a Third Party*

Having defined when family members can be targeted, it necessary to understand when it is possible to rely on the association criterion to list different subjects. This is one of issues at stake in *Tokareva.*[117] In this ruling the GC has put a clear limit on the stretching of the notion of 'associated person', unlike in another case concerning a legal person associated to a bank.[118] In particular, the GC has excluded that the Council could designate persons for their association to family members of a third party. Ms Tokareva was listed on account of her association to a person who was in his turn listed for his association to his father, featuring in the Council's blacklist. Thus, in Tokareva the GC has specified that an associated person to an associated person cannot be listed. It is possible to list a person under the association criterion only if he/she is associated to one of the persons who fall within one of the primary designation criteria of Article 2(1), from a) to h).[119]

The Council's strategy to list a person since she/he is part of a global network of family members of listed persons on account of the risks of circumvention[120] was held illegal. The GC was not sensitive to the effectiveness of restrictive measures on this occasion. '*En effet, une telle interprétation donnerait une portée excessivement large au lien d'association et ne tiendrait pas compte de la lettre de l'article 2, paragraphe 1, in fine, de la décision 2014/145, telle que modifiée, ainsi que de l'exigence d'un lien suffisant entre les personnes concernées et le pays tiers qui est la cible des mesures restrictives adoptées par l'Union, au sens du point 64 de l'arrêt du 13 mars 2012, Tay Za/Conseil [...].*'[121] In this paragraph the GC refers, without mentioning it, to the principle of proportionality to exclude that Tokareva can be listed on account of her connection to an associated person. The GC holds that the literal interpretation of the notion of association is actually an obstacle to list a person in a position similar to that of Ms Tokareva.[122] It could be added that the listing of a person must be functional to the achievement of the objectives of restrictive measure. The targeting of an associated person to another associated person neither presents a sufficient

---

[117] GC, Case T-744/22, *Maya Tokareva*, 11 September 2024, ECLI:EU:T:2024:608.

[118] See T-102/23 *SBK Art*, 30 April 2025, ECLI:EU:T:2025:416. In this case, the applicant, SBK Art, a Russian company, challenged its listing as an associated company to Sberbank, which was in its turn blacklisted as an entity financially supporting the Government of the Russian Federation and as an entity involved in an economic sector providing a substantial source of revenue to it. The applicant was a subsidiary of Sberbank, specifically established for the purpose of holding Sberbank's interests in the Fortenova Group. The link between applicant and Sberbank was that the latter retained the effective control over the applicant, notwithstanding the purported transfer of its shares to a businessman from the United Arab Emirates. The annulment action was rejected and the GC considered the Council's decision to list the applicant justified by the need to counter the circumvention of restrictive measures. See para 218.

[119] GC, Case T-744/22, above n. 117, para 46.

[120] Ibid., para 44.

[121] GC, Case T-744/22, above n. 117, para 50.

[122] Ibid., para 49.

nexus with the EU objective of weakening the capacity of the Russian Federation to continue the war, nor can it be justified by the risk of circumvention. Indeed, the latter justification may be reasonably applied in case there is a family relation between the person concerned and a targeted subject. In the absence of a family link, the potential risk of circumvention is not sufficient to justify the listing.[123] In the postscriptum to this chapter important legal developments concerning the Tokareva case law are accounted for.

3.4 The Case Law of the CJEU on Sector-Related Measures

The legality of sector-related measures was also questioned in a few instances.[124] The first case, Russia Today France,[125] concerns the prohibition to broadcast imposed on selected media outlets.[126] This measure undoubtedly affects the right to freedom of expression and information, protected by Article 11 of the EU Charter of Fundamental Rights and Article 10 ECHR. This is one of the grounds invoked by the applicant to challenge the new type of restriction before the GC.[127] The observance of the right to be heard was also contested by the applicant since the Council had enacted the mentioned measures without notification.

In July 2022, the GC confirmed the legality of these sanctions. The view was taken that the right to be heard was respected; in particular, due to the exceptional situation created by the Russian aggression, the Council could enact the mentioned measures without notifying the applicant. In principle, there was no 'effect surprise' to preserve in imposing a prohibition on broadcasting activities. Therefore, the lack of notification could have been considered a breach of due process rights. Yet, the GC has shown a propensity to derogate from due process rights in time of emergency.

As to the breach of the right to freedom of expression, the GC extensively relied on the case law of the ECHR to confirm that the broadcasting ban was legal. The GC held that there was sufficient evidence showing that the applicant was under the

[123] See *contra* T-102/23 *SBK Art* above n. 118.

[124] GC, Cases T-125/22, *RT France*, T-728/22 *Cogebi*, 17 April 2024, ECLI:EU:T:2024:249, T-235/22, *Russian Direct Investment Fund*, Case C-109/23 *Jemerak*, T 494/22, T-494/22, *NKO AO National Settlement Depository (NSD)*, 11 September 2024, ECLI:EU:T:2024:607, T-797/22, *Ordre néerlandais des avocats du barreau de Bruxelles*.

[125] GC, Case T-125/22 *RT France*, above n. 124.

[126] Council Decision (CFSP) 2022/351 of 1 March 2022 amending Decision 2014/512/CFSP concerning restrictive measures in view of Russia's actions destabilising the situation in Ukraine, O.J. 2022 L 65, p. 5.

[127] T-125/22 *RT France*, above n. 124. The applicant claimed that the impugned CFSP decision, instituting the mentioned restrictive measures, was to be annulled on the following grounds: the lack of competence of the Union to enact such measures since only national authorities may impose sanctions on media outlets; breaches of the rights to be heard, of defence, and to effective judicial protection (Articles 41, 47 and 48 of the EU Charter of Fundamental Rights ('CFR')), freedom of expression (Article 11 CFR and Article 10 ECHR), freedom to conduct business (Article 16) and, finally, the principle of non-discrimination on the grounds of nationality.

permanent direct and indirect control of the Russian Federation. The broadcasting ban was temporary and reversible and did not constitute interference with the essence of the right to freedom of expression. The assessment of the proportionality of the broadcasting ban was contested[128] as well as the effects of the measure which was qualified as an act of censorship to defend EU citizens from propaganda.[129]

A French scholar, Millet, took the view the ruling is against EU values, including pluralism. The impugned restrictive measures are considered an act of censure. In addition, Millet remarks:

> Ce n'est pas un hasard si RT France n'a pas été interdite par l'Arcom, le successeur du CSA. Il s'agit du résultat d une législation française très protectrice des médias en vertu de laquelle il n'est en effet possible de prononcer, sous le contrôle vigilant du Conseil d'État, l'interdiction d'un média contrôlé par un État étranger qu'à des fins répressives et non préventives lorsqu'il est établi que ce média porte atteinte aux intérêts fondamentaux de la Nation.

In the opinion of the present author, the ruling of the GC is convincing: the evidence presented shows that Russian media outlets are a machine for war propaganda. In order to preserve the effectiveness of the restrictive measure in question, the Council had to act at EU level. The concerned sanction certainly restricts the right to freedom of expression and sacrifice the plurality of opinions in a democratic society; however, media outlets, controlled by an aggressor State, abuse of their right to freedom of information if they hide the nature of the serious wrongful activities conducted by Russia in Ukraine. The prohibition is therefore justified in the context of a war. There were no other less restrictive measures that could achieve the objective of safeguarding international security and public order. Therefore, the broadcasting ban complied with the proportionality principle.

The GC's ruling in RT France should be welcomed and is better substantiated than other rulings, such as that in *Kiselev*[130] in which the GC had been more superficial in rejecting the ground that the concerned restrictive measures breached Article 11 of the ECFR. There is little doubt that RT and Sputnik are propaganda machines and that it is more effective to enact restrictive measures to tackle hybrid threats, such as the spreading of false information on the aggression of Russia against Ukraine, at the EU rather than national level. Manipulating information on who bears the responsibility for an armed aggression is unacceptable in a Union which is based on respect of international law.

While it is true that Russian media outlets have abused their right to freedom of expression, the new typology of EU restrictive measures is controversial. The Council has envisaged the possibility to abolish these sanctions when the war ends. Given that the restrictions at stake have an important impact on the rights to freedom of expression and to receive information, it would probably be disproportionate to keep them after the end of the war. Indeed, the restrictions were adopted on the ground that Russia Today and Sputnik carried out disinformation activities which had a destabilising effect on the EU member States and the neighbouring countries.

---

[128] Casolari 2024, p. 52.

[129] Lonardo 2022, p. 51.

[130] GC, Case T-262/15 *Kiselev*, 15 July 2017, ECLI:EU:T:2017:392.

This effect would cease after the end of the war. Failure to lift these measures, once the war is ended, will be more difficult to justify. In this respect, it is noteworthy that the Council has set for itself a broad power of appreciation which was confirmed by the GC; these measures can be maintained until 'the aggression against Ukraine is put to an end, and until the Russian Federation, and its associated media outlets, cease to conduct propaganda actions against the Union and its Member States'.[131] However, as a result of the ruling discussed here, the Council is free to maintain the restrictions to the right of freedom of information 'until the Russian Federation, and its associated media outlets, cease to conduct propaganda actions against the Union and its Member States. As the two criteria are cumulative, if one of them ceased to be satisfied, there would be no further need to maintain the measures at issue.'[132]

The ruling confirms that in times of war the Council may adopt exceptional restrictive measures capable of limiting EU citizens' fundamental rights, such as the right to receive information. It remains to be seen whether the perception of the threat to the Union's public order and security posed by the disinformation campaign of Russian media outlets will change after the end of the war. In this respect, recent events such as the disinformation campaigns which have characterised elections in different countries, such as Georgia, Moldova and Romania, may induce the Council to keep restrictions to Russian media outlets.

3.5 The Court's Assessment of Sector-Related Restrictive Measures: The Effectiveness of Restrictive Measures Versus the Divestment of Russian assets from the Union Market

In a preliminary ruling in *Jemerak*[133] the CJEU has interpreted in a narrow manner the notion of 'legal advice' in the context of Article 1k(2) of Council Decision 2014/512/CFSP as amended, prohibiting the provision of this service to Russian nationals.[134] The reason at the basis of this ban is to avoid that Russian natural or legal persons can seek legal advice to circumvent the EU restrictive measures.[135]

The most important question raised by the referring judge was whether a notary in Germany could authenticate the contract of sale of immovable properties belonging to Russian nationals or whether such an act amounted to the provision of legal advisory services. A further uncertainty was whether the authentication fulfilled the conditions

[131] Recital 11 of Council Decision (CFSP) 2022/351.

[132] GC, Case T-125/22, above n. 124, para 155.

[133] CJEU, Case C-109/23 *Jemerak*, 5 September 2024, ECLI:EU:C:2024:681.

[134] Decision 2022/1909 of 6 October 2022 amending Decision 2014/512/CFSP concerning restrictive measures in view of Russia's actions destabilising the situation in Ukraine, O.J. 2022, L 259 I/122. See Article 5n(1) and (2) of Regulation 2022/1904 of 6 October 2022, O.J. 2022 L 259 I/3. A derogation from this prohibition is made for the exercise of the right to the defence.

[135] This is explained in recital 5 of Decision 2022/1909, cit.

of the derogation to the prohibition to provide legal advisory services provided for in the text of the Regulation. The Commission's guidelines considered 'notary services' as part of 'legal advisory services'. This generated uncertainty since the guidelines were non-legally binding.[136] The Court has reversed the interpretation provided by the Commission.

Notary services to Russian nationals fall outside the scope of the prohibition since they could not contribute to the circumvention of sanctions.[137] The interpretation of the Court does not prevent Russian nationals to carry out commercial activities and to dispose of their immovable properties. A few Member States argued that this conflicted with the objective of restrictive measures. Yet the Council did not support this interpretation and took the view that the purpose of the prohibition in question was to make it more difficult for Russian legal persons operating in the territory of the European Union to continue their commercial activities in that territory.[138]

It is submitted that by ruling that the notary services can be provided to Russian nationals, the CJEU has not weakened the effectiveness of restrictive measures since these persons need to use these services in order to divest their properties from the Union market. This is indirectly confirmed by the fact that few months after the preliminary ruling was raised before the GC, the Council had introduced a temporary derogation from the prohibition to provide legal advice to legal persons, entities or bodies established in Russia in order to expedite the divestment of Russian operators from the Union market.

As a result, Member States were authorised to introduce national legislation making it easier for Russians to sell their assets and to reduce their commercial activities in the EU until 31st March 2024.[139]

---

[136] See ibid., para 30. Another source of uncertainty was whether the authentication fulfilled the conditions of the derogation to the prohibition to provide legal advisory services. Article 5(6) of the Regulation 2022/1904.

[137] CJEU, Case C-109/23, above n. 133, para 55.

[138] Ibid., para 54.

[139] Recital 42 of Council Decision (CFSP) 2023/1217 of 23 June 2023 amending Decision 2014/512/CFSP concerning restrictive measures in view of Russia's actions destabilising the situation in Ukraine, O.J. 2023, L 159I/451.

3.6 The Court's Assessment of Sector-Related Restrictive Measures and the Proportionality Principle

The EU has progressively intensified its anti-circumvention activity seeking to change restrictive measures to better fight the evasion of sanctions.[140] The effectiveness of EU sector-related restrictive measures[141] is probably more important for the achievement of the objective of sector-related restrictive measures that than of individual restrictive measures. Indeed, arguably an effective implementation of the prohibition to export goods and technology suited for use in the war is more crucial to weaken Russia's war machine than depriving the Russian Federation of the revenues of the oligarchs.

While with the rulings in *Russia Today France* and in *Ordre néerlandais des avocats du barreau de Bruxelles* the GC has rejected the annulment actions against sector-related restrictive measures, in another case, *Islentyeva*,[142] the GC has excluded that certain prohibitions of general scope applied to all Russian nationals who are neither involved in the war, nor they contribute to circumvent restrictive measures. In this annulment action a Russian private pilot had sought the annulment of the prohibition to fly imposed on 'non-Russian registered aircrafts which is owned, chartered or otherwise controlled by a Russian natural or legal person.[143]' The Court of Justice had to rule on whether the applicant was directly concerned by the mentioned prohibition which is of general nature and applies to all Russians.[144] The Court gave a negative answer to this question, holding that the notion of 'control' by a Russian natural or legal person of non-Russian registered aircrafts refers to economic or financial control over such an aircraft and not to technical or operational control. It is interesting that the Court has taken advantage of the unqualified notion of 'control' in the act that it was asked to interpret to take a narrow reading of this concept. It selected an interpretation which is favourable to the position of an

[140] So far, the proposal by scholars to create a horizontal sanction regime devoted to the circumvention of sanctions was unheard. Portela and Olsen 2023, p. 53. The present author is not convinced that a separate legal instrument designed to address sanction evasion would really be necessary to contain the phenomenon of circumvention.

[141] G7 members have also considered the circumvention of sanctions a common concern. On early studies on the problem of circumvention of EU restrictive measures see Finelli 2023b, p. 733.

[142] GC, Case T-233/22, *Ekaterina Islentyeva*, 20 December 2023, ECLI:EU:T:2023:828.

[143] The prohibition applies to aircrafts operated by Russian air carriers or to non-Russian-registered aircraft which is owned or chartered, or otherwise controlled by any Russian person or entity, to take off from, land in or overfly the territory of the Union. See Article 1(2) of Council Decision (CFSP) 2022/335 of 28 February 2022 amending Decision 2014/512/CFSP concerning restrictive measures in view of Russia's actions destabilising the situation in Ukraine, O.J. 2022 L 57/4.

[144] Article 3d of Council Regulation (EU) 2022/334 of 28 February 2022 amending Council Regulation (EU) No 833/2014 concerning restrictive measures in view of Russia's actions destabilising the situation in Ukraine, O.J. 2022 L 57/1. The GC excluded that it lacked jurisdiction to examine the legality CFSP Decision enacting restrictive measures enacted though of general application. Ibid., para 30.

individual and is thus in line with the proportionality principle.[145] As a result of this ruling, the Russian pilot may continue using her private pilot licence since she is not affected by the flight ban enacted by the EU. The ruling is important since without disavowing that the objective of restrictive measures is to maximise the pressure on Putin and the Russian government, the CJEU has made clear EU restrictive measures that affect natural or legal persons may not have the widest possible scope.

This ruling shows that the GC has not invariably interpreted restrictive measures so as to maximise their effectiveness; the proportionality principle requires an interpretation of an EU measure that burdens the least individuals.

3.7 The Impact of the War in Ukraine on the Shape of EU Restrictive Measures: An Overall Assessment of the Contribution of the CJEU

Considering the numerous designations[146] made by the Council in the context of the Russian aggression to Ukraine, which is as high as in no other sanction regime, it has been challenging for this institution to gather sufficient evidence to list persons who directly or indirectly contribute to the war in Ukraine. The Court has confirmed that the Council has a broad discretion in laying down the designation criteria of individual restrictive measures and in defining the breath and the quality of the prohibitions. The GC has been particularly sensitive to preserving the effectiveness of sanctions especially in the context of litigation concerning prominent businessmen and family members. Yet, gathering the evidence supporting the re-listing of businessmen and family members has proved to be a more challenging task[147] for the Council than in other sanction regimes. In a non-negligible number of cases the designations were annulled. In the case of *Tokareva* the GC has constrained the Council's discretion in an unprecedented manner given that it has imposed on this institution not to list an associated person to an association person. In the opinion of a scholar, '[…], the General Court has maintained a fairly balanced approach: while the Council may explore legal avenues to improve sanctions effectiveness, combatting circumvention does not allow the indiscriminate listing of individuals under a lower standard of proof.[148]'

[145] Ibid., paras 50–51.

[146] As of 26 March 2025, 1862 persons are included in the consolidated list of travel bans made public by the Commission. https://sanctionsmap.eu/#/main/travel/ban. Accessed 1 July 2025. The number of listed persons and entities whose assets are frozen is 2534 (more precisely, 1899 persons and 635 entities). See https://data.europa.eu/apps/eusanctionstracker/search/WyJyZWdpbWUvVUtSIl0=. Accessed 1 July 2025.

[147] For example, in one case the GC considered that none of the criterion a), f) and g) relied upon by the Council were sufficiently substantiated. Joined cases T-309/22 and T-739/22, *Vladimir Rashevsk*, 10 July 2024, ECLI:EU:T:2024:455.

[148] Challet 2024, p. 9.

Coming to the interpretation of the EU sector-related restrictive measures, the GC has been complacent with the Council in the name of the effectiveness of these measures, as it results from the rejection of the annulment action in Russia Today France and from *Ordre néerlandais des avocats du barreau de Bruxelles*. This trend is confirmed in the ruling in *Jemerak*, in which the CJEU has made possible for Russian nationals to use notary services in order to divest their properties from the Union market. At the same time, the *Islentyeva* case shows that the GC has also interpreted the EU sector-related restrictions in light of the proportionality principle, thus refusing to provide the widest possible scope to restrictive measures. The GC's approach should not be given for granted; the court could have chosen to maximize the effectiveness of restrictive measures rather than to apply the proportionality principle.

3.8 Post scriptum

On 11 February 2026, the General Court delivered an important judgment in Case T-693/25, *Tokareva v Council*. The GC upheld the annulment action, finding that the Council had committed an error of assessment by maintaining the freezing of Ms Tokareva's assets on the ground that she allegedly benefited from her husband, a leading businessperson operating in Russia. The Court concluded that the evidence relied upon by the Council was insufficient to justify her continued listing.

This was not the first time that Ms Tokareva had successfully challenged her inclusion on the sanctions list. Between 2023 and 2025, she had succeded in three separate actions before the GC. In 2024, the Court annulled her listing in Case T-744/22, *Tokareva v Council*. Two further annulment actions were subsequently upheld in March and September 2025 (Cases T-269/24 and T-295/25). Despite these judgments, the Council maintained Ms Tokareva's name on the list, thereby forcing her to bring yet another action for annulment.

The GC observed that the grounds relied upon by the Council to justify the listing decision challenged in the September 2025 proceedings were essentially identical to those that had already been found unlawful in its 2024 judgment. In this context, the Court considered it necessary to examine whether the Council had complied with its obligations under Article 266 TFEU.

Pursuant to the mentioned Treaty provision, the institution whose act has been declared void is required to take the necessary measures to comply with the judgment of the Court. This obligation stems from the binding force and authority of *res judicata* attaching to the annulment judgment. The GC found that the Council had maintained the applicant on the sanctions list on the basis of substantially the same evidence that had already been considered inadequate in two previous annulment proceedings.

The judgment is significant because it confirms that, once a listing decision has been annulled and the judgment has become final, the Council cannot simply disregard the Court's findings and re-adopt substantially the same measures on the basis of evidence that has already been found insufficient. To do so would undermine both the authority of *res judicata* and the obligation of compliance imposed by Article 266 TFEU.

References

Alì A (2025) Le misure restrittive dell'UE in relazione alle minacce ibride della Russia [European Union restrictive measures in response to Russia's hybrid threats]. In: Alì A (ed) Le sanzioni dell'UE nei confronti della Russia tra sicurezza internazionale e diritti umani [EU sanctions against Russia between international security and human rights] Giappichelli/Nomos. pp. 345–370.

Butler G (2023) Of Rulers, Relatives, and Businesspersons: The Imposition of Sanctions on Family members. Legal Issues of Economic Integration 50: 367–390.

Casolari F (2024) EU sanction policy—A legal appraisal in light of the EU's strategic autonomy doctrine. In: Adinolfi G, Lang A, Ragni C (eds) Sanctions by and against International Organization. Intersentia, Cambridge/Antwerp/Chicago, pp. 29–57.

Challet C (2024) How far may the council go to combat sanctions circumvention? Recent CJEU rulings on the restrictive measures against Russia. EU law live, 207, 16 November 2024.

Finelli F (2023a) Who are the Russian oligarchs? Recent Developments in the Case Law of the European Court of Justice. European Papers 8: pp. 1513–1522 https://doi.org/10.15166/2499-8249/727.

Finelli F (2023b) Countering circumvention of restrictive measures: The EU response. Common Market Law Review 60: 733–762.

Hillion C (2023) The EU external action as mandate to uphold the rule of law outside and inside the Union. Columbia Journal of European Law, 29: 260–261.

Hinojosa-Martínez M L (2023) Rule of Law and Effective Judicial Protection versus Raison d'état in EUs Political Sanctions: The Relevance of Individual Conduct. In: Hinojosa-Martínez L M, Pérez-Bernárdez C (eds) Enhancing the Rule of Law in the European Union's External Action. Edward Elgar Publishing, Cheltenham, pp. 108–131.

Koutrakos P (2018) Judicial review in the EU's common foreign and security policy. International and Comparative Law Quarterly 67: 1–35.

Lonardo L (2022) Russia' s War Against Ukraine and the Foreign Policy Reaction of the EU: Context, Diplomacy, and Law. Palgrave Macmillan, Cham.

Lonardo L (2024) How the Court Tries to Deliver Justice in Common Foreign and Security Policy, Where the Need for Judicial Protection Clashes with the Principles of Conferral and Institutional Balance. Joined Cases C-29/22 P and C-44/22 P KS and KD. European Papers 9: 830–844, https://doi.org/10.15166/2499-8249/786.

Poli S (2017) The Common Foreign and Security Policy after Rosneft: Still imperfect but gradually subject to the rule of law. Common Market Law Review 54: 1799–1834.

Poli S (2018) Judicial protection and its limits in the case law concerning individual restrictive measures in the European Union. In: Neframi E, Gatti M (eds) Constitutional issues of EU external relations law. Nomos, Luxembourg, pp. 287–306.

Poli S (2019) Le misure restrittive autonome dell'Unione europea [The EU autonomous restrictive measures]. Editoriale scientifica, Naples.

Poli S (2022) The right to effective judicial protection with respect to acts imposing restrictive measures and its transformative force for the Common Foreign and Security Policy. Common Market Law Review 59: 1045–1080.

Poli S (2024) Judicial challenges to EU restrictive measures by individual state organs, 'emanations of non-EU member states' and third countries: the limits to the council's discretion. In: Lang A, Adinolfi G, Ragni C (eds) Sanctions by and against international organizations. Intersentia, Cambridge/Antwerp/Chicago, pp. 203–224.

Poli S, Finelli F (2022) Le misure restrittive russe davanti alla Corte di Giustizia dell'Unione Europea: le tendenze giurisprudenziali emergenti [The EU restricitve measures against Russia before the European Court of Justice: emerging judicial trends]. Diritto dell'Unione europea 3: 523–568.

Portela C, Olsen K (2023), Implementation and Monitoring of the EU Sanctions' Regimes, Including Recommendations to Reinforce the EU's Capacities to Implement and Monitor Sanctions. European Parliament.

Van Elsuwege P (2021) Judicial review and the Common Foreign and Security Policy: Limits to the gap-filling role of the Court of Justice. Common Market Law Review 58: 1731–1760.

Wessel R (2016) Lex Imperfecta: Law and Integration in European Foreign and Security Policy. European Papers 1: 439–468, https://doi.org/10.15166/2499-8249/52.

Chapter 4
The Implementation and Enforcement of CFSP Sanctions

Clara Portela

Contents

Abstract The implementation and enforcement of CFSP sanctions, a question that has long remained marginalised from European foreign policy debates, acquired a new relevance with the sanctions regimes launched by the EU in response to the Russian annexation of Crimea and destabilisation of Ukraine in 2014. They further intensified with the 2022 invasion of Ukraine, which has seen the deployment of a number of initiatives by the European Commission. These are not only geared at improving a system of implementation and enforcement characterised by decentralisation and stark discrepancies, but also seek to address attempts at evasion and circumvention of CFSP restrictions, opening a new and challenging line of action for EU institutions. Due to the economic nature of many of the imposed measures, and the relevance of these efforts to the Commission's mandate, this institution has benefited from a growing centrality in a policy field traditionally dominated by the Council.

Keywords Implementation · Enforcement · Circumvention · Evasion · Russo-Ukrainian war · CFSP

S. Poli et al., *The EU's Response to the War in Ukraine and Its Impact on the EU Legal Order*, Global Europe: Legal and Policy Issues of the EU's External Action 7,
https://doi.org/10.1007/978-94-6265-767-0_4

4.1 The Transformation of Sanctions Implementation and Enforcement

In contrast to the formulation of sanctions legislation, which is centralised in Brussels institutions, the EU operates a decentralised system of sanctions implementation and enforcement. As a result, the EU enjoys normative competence or *compétence normative* in sanctions policy but lacks operational competence or *compétence opérationnelle*.[1] While the current system remained unaltered and uncontroversial since its creation; it has been subject to a myriad of initiatives and reforms over the past few years. The drive towards revising the system emerged before the Russian invasion of Ukraine: however, the 2022 aggression injected a powerful impulse to those efforts. Accordingly, the present chapter is structured as follows: an initial section opens up by describing the implementation and enforcement system as conceived originally. This is followed by a section which outlines the reforms initiated both before the 2022 invasion and in its aftermath. After that, new efforts at fighting circumvention practices are detailed, before a final section concludes by assessing the reform initiatives.

4.2 Implementation and Enforcement at the Point of Departure

4.2.1 The Initial Design

The implementation and enforcement system is set out in two Council documents: 'Guidelines on implementation and evaluation of restrictive measures in the framework of the CFSP' (henceforth 'Guidelines'), initially adopted in 2003 and updated in 2018, and the 2015 'Best Practices on Effective Implementation of Financial Restrictive Measures'.[2] Both documents deal with the standardisation of wording and common definitions for legal instruments. By contrast, the political aspects of sanctions policy are discussed in the 'Basic Principles for the Use of Restrictive Measures (Sanctions)', a short programmatic document released in 2004.[3]

According to this system, member state authorities are responsible for the implementation of sanctions, ensuring that they are respected by public bureaucracies, economic operators and citizens alike. A key issue are derogations from existing bans, called 'exceptions' and 'exemptions' in EU parlance, depending on whether they are of permanent nature, or decided on a case-by-case basis. EU sanctions legislation stipulates the conditions under which exemptions may be granted.[4] The procedure

---

[1] Martin 2019.

[2] Council of the European Union 2015.

[3] Council of the European Union 2004.

[4] Council of the European Union 2018, p. 12.

for granting exemptions to private operators differs depending on whether the bans originate from the United Nations Security Council (UNSC), or an autonomous[5] EU regime:

(i) When the EU implements sanctions mandated by the UNSC, the authority to grant exemptions rests with the UN Sanctions Committee responsible for the sanctions regime at hand, in accordance with the text of the relevant UNSC resolution.
(ii) For autonomous sanctions regimes, exemptions are granted by national authorities of the member states, which decide on them on a case-by-case basis, ensuring that they are not misused to circumvent the objectives of the ban.[6] Member states notify each other of exemptions granted, informing the Commission as well.

Certain measures are implemented directly by member states, notably visa bans, where a no objection procedure applies: A member state wishing to grant an exemption must notify the Council. The exemption is considered granted unless a member state raises an objection within two working days, in which case the Council, acting by qualified majority, may grant the exemption.[7]

Providing guidance to private operators on how to comply with sanctions is a responsibility of member states exercised via national authorities, which in turn follow guidance issued by the European Commission. Standard bans on armaments, restrictions on admission and asset freezes, traditional CFSP sanctions, present little difficulty in terms of interpretation. Arms embargoes routinely apply to the pre-agreed 'common military list', while visa bans and asset freezes apply to blacklists of individuals and entities featuring identifiers. However, as sanctions practice evolves and Brussels introduces new types of restrictions of increasing sophistication, the need for clarification by affected industries grows. The measures imposed on Russia following the destabilisation of the Donbass in 2014 were a case in point. After the EU enacted its ban on the supply of equipment and services for oil production and exploration in the summer of 2014, numerous inquiries by affected European firms led to the specification of provisions in the EC Regulation. When the legal text presents some ambiguity regarding the scope of the bans, the Commission can issue non-binding guidance on interpretation. Alternatively, the Council may adopt a new version of the legislation specifying their scope.[8]

The enforcement system is similarly decentralised. EU legislation exhorts member states to enact penalties for violations of bans: capitals must ensure that bans are implemented and complied with, and must lay down penalties applicable to breaches

[5] When the UNSC agrees sanctions, the EU passes legislation to implement the bans stipulated in UNSC Resolutions; when the EU decides its own measures, it adopts the same type of legislative acts as when it implements UNSC decisions without acting under its authority, namely a CFSP Decision (formerly: Common Position) and a Regulation.

[6] Council of the European Union 2018, p. 12.

[7] Council Decision (CFSP) 2013, p. 19.

[8] Portela 2020.

of sanctions legislation.[9] Thus, each member state is responsible for designating the authorities in charge of implementation and enforcement and endowing it with appropriate powers, and for passing national laws penalising breaches and determining penalties. The decentralisation that characterises the enforcement system is grounded on the principle of subsidiarity, enshrined in the Treaty on European Union. According to this principle, decisions are best taken at the level closest to the citizens, given that the national legislator is best positioned to consider local conditions. Authorising member states to determine penalties facilitates coherence with the legal traditions of each country and ensures that financial fines are commensurate with local purchasing power.

The Commission is responsible for collecting information on laws and associated penalties in each member state, and for checking their alignment with the provisions of EU sanctions legislation. It oversees whether the implementation and enforcement of individual and sectoral sanctions takes place at the member state level in accordance with EU regulations. In the event of misalignment, the Commission is responsible for approaching the member states at fault and request corrective action. As a last resort, it has the power to launch an infringement procedure against any member state for failing to implement EU legislation. Importantly, given that the CFSP falls outside the responsibility of the Commission, an infringement procedure can only be launched due to the failure to implement the provisions of the EC Regulation, and not of the associated CFSP act.[10] In addition to Commission supervision, the current system foresees a mechanism for information exchange among member states on interpretation, implementation and enforcement issues, keeping the European External Action Service (EEAS) and the Commission in the loop. The 'Guidelines' provide that member states shall inform each other of assets frozen and the amounts concerned, derogations granted, measures taken in implementation of sanctions legislation, violation and enforcement problems and relevant judgments by national courts.[11] The Commission assists member states in monitoring the sanctions' economic effects on the target, which can include overviews of the value of frozen assets from listed individuals and entities or from other finance-sector related measures as well as sanctions' impact on EU trade relations with third countries.

4.2.2 A Recipe for Fragmentation

A glance at the setup of the implementation system suggests that the uniform implementation of EU sanctions is not guaranteed, as individual member states enjoy considerable room for manoeuvre.[12] This encourages significant discrepancies among member states in terms of implementation and enforcement. Despite

[9] Council of the European Union 2018, p. 19.

[10] Gestri 2016.

[11] Council of the European Union 2018, p. 50.

[12] Martin 2019.

the scarcity of publicly available data, extant research on the implementation of EU sanctions points to notable differences.[13] Illustrative of this fragmentation is the number and types of national authorities involved in implementation and enforcements. Member states have designated everywhere from one to 27 competent national authorities[14]; it is calculated that they total about 160 across the EU.[15] This also highlights that they have different definitions of what a national authority competent for sanctions implementation is. Certain capitals define national authorities as authorities that have the right to grant authorisations and binding legal answers, whereas others define them as all authorities that take part in any aspect of the implementation or enforcement of sanctions provisions. Furthermore, national authorities across the EU may differ considerably in terms of size, their ability to detect and prosecute evasion may be at variance, and possible deficiencies in state capacity for sanctions implementation and enforcement remain unaddressed. This heterogeneity of competent authorities, coupled with different legal and administrative traditions, paves the way for vast variation in terms of the centralisation/decentralisation of sanctions implementation at the member state level. In addition, there are no common criteria governing the allocation and coordination of roles to specific agencies within state structures. Whereas some member states regulate the specific responsibilities of individual authorities, others rely on coordination on a case-by-case basis. Since EU restrictive measures mostly have their legal basis in a regulation or implementing regulation, sanctions regimes are directly applicable in the domestic legal orders. Irrespective of the system applied, regulations oblige member states to ensure that every element of an EU sanction regime is allocated to a specific national authority.[16]

Worryingly, several discernible gaps can be identified as potential obstacles to the operation of the system.[17]

4.2.2.1 Mechanisms for Exemptions

A decentralised system for granting exemptions affords third parties opportunities for shopping. While companies incorporated in the EU are obliged to obtain clearance from the national authority in their country, nothing prevents third parties from filing applications in several member states. Since national authorities enjoy discretion in determining whether a specific request falls under an exemption, interpretations may vary from one member state to another. When a national authority rejects an application for an exemption, the requesting entity may approach another member state in the hope of eventually receiving clearance. National authorities face competing incentives. On the one hand, they might interpret prohibitions generously out of humanitarian concern, or to prevent hindering legitimate trade flows. On the other

---

[13] Druláková and Přikryl 2016; Druláková and Zemanová 2020; Portela 2015.

[14] Portela and Olsen 2023.

[15] Olsen and Fasterkjær Kjeldsen 2022.

[16] Ibid.

[17] Portela 2020.

hand, authorising a request rejected elsewhere as doubtful may incur reputational costs.

The only entity foreseen for the settlement of possible controversies is the European Commission. A member state that objects to a derogation granted by another member state may bring the matter to the attention of the Commission, which can approach the national authority allegedly in the wrong and request the withdrawal of the controversial authorisation. Alternatively, the dissatisfied member state can contact the national authorities allegedly at fault directly to voice concern. In both cases, the national authorities having granted the disputed clearance can benefit from the discreet nature of the *démarche*. No publicly accessible data exist on whether member states disagree with authorisations granted by other member states and, if so, with what outcome. While the Commission retains the option of launching an infringement procedure against a state in the hypothetical case that it refuses to enforce sanctions legislation, this scenario has never materialised.

4.2.2.2 Evasion Detection

While equipping the authority competent for implementation and enforcement with the necessary tools is the responsibility of member states, national agencies differ considerably in terms of size, investigative capacity, manpower and expertise at their disposal.[18] Accordingly, their ability to detect and prosecute evasion may be at variance. Neither the 'Guidelines' nor EU legislation stipulate the nature of specific resources member states need to make available to ensure optimal compliance by domestic actors. Thus, potential gaps in state capacity for sanctions implementation and enforcement remain unaddressed. Conspicuously, the Commission has never launched an infringement procedure against a member state on the basis of the deficient application of EU sanctions regulations even in the face of allegations by civil society and the mass media.[19] Since sanctions are a CFSP matter, which ultimately rests in the hands of the Council, the Commission has traditionally been reticent to publicly call out member states for deficient sanctions implementation.[20]

4.2.2.3 Penalties

Administrative penalties for breaches of EU sanctions legislation are substantially higher in some member states than in others. A 2022 cross-European survey found that fines could range from a few thousand euros, as in Romania, to penalties of millions of euros, as in Estonia, to unlimited penalties, as in Croatia.[21] Similarly, vast discrepancies could be found in potential prison sentences. The lowest maximum

[18] Golumbic and Ruff 2013.

[19] European Centre for Constitutional and Human Rights 2018.

[20] Olsen 2022.

[21] Giumelli et al. 2022.

prison sentences are four months in Denmark, which can be increased to four years under particularly aggravating circumstances, and two years in Cyprus. The highest maximum prison sentences are 12 years in Malta and 15 years in Germany, under certain aggravating circumstances. By contrast, Romanian criminal law only prescribes prison sentences for violations of sanctions related to dual-use goods and technologies. For their part, Poland and Spain merely contemplate administrative penalties.[22] Accordingly, the risk assessment for European firms changes substantially depending on the EU jurisdiction where they are incorporated.

The Commission checks national legislation stipulating the penalties for sanctions violations, and if it detects inadequacies, it can approach the member state in question and request their correction. In the event that the member state at fault persistently refuses to rectify identified deficiencies, the Commission could open an infringement procedure. In any case, only blatant deviations, such as disproportionately low fines, would qualify for the Commission's launching of such action. The opening of an infringement procedure is also available to the Commission if the enforcement authorities of a member state manifestly fail to stop evasion of a sanctions regime.

4.2.2.4 Guidance for Private Operators

The issuance of non-binding guidance by the Commission intends to assist economic operators to comply with EU bans. In addition, the Commission may issue opinions at the request of national authorities.[23] This replicates standard practice in other areas of Commission activity. Still, Commission guidance, offered as a Commission Notice following a Q&A format as well as Commission opinions, include the following disclaimer: 'The Commission oversees the application of Union law under the control of the Court of Justice of the European Union. Pursuant to the Treaties, only the Court of Justice of the European Union can provide legally binding interpretations of acts of the institutions of the Union'.[24] According to this disclaimer, adhering to Commission guidance does not fully protect operators from eventual fines, given that, in the event of litigation, the national prosecutor's interpretation of a ban may diverge from the Commission's understanding. Uncertainty is exacerbated as the entity responsible for initiating prosecution, which is located at the national level, is not necessarily the same actor that issues guidance, the Commission. This diverges from the US system, where the Treasury's Office of Foreign Asset Control (OFAC) is empowered to carry out both functions. As a result, private operators may be inclined to overcomply with bans, foregoing operations that the sanctions designers never intended to restrict.[25] In particular, banks are known to overcomply with sanctions legislation as part of their

---

[22] Ibid.

[23] National authorities may also issue guidance. Commission opinions are available under: https://ec.europa.eu/fpi/what-we-do/sanctions_en, accessed 1 September 2025.

[24] European Commission 2017.

[25] Portela 2016.

regular policy of 'de-risking',[26] often guided by specialised software that amplifies the effects of designations.[27] The inability to transact financially with actors in target countries amplifies the breadth of the measures, affecting legitimate trade flows. In addition, economic operators occasionally lament a lack of responsiveness by national authorities. An executive from a major European bank reports that it took him about a year to receive clarification on a question of legal interpretation that he had requested from his national authority, while the US treasury agency, OFAC, replied to the same inquiry in just one week.[28] Both phenomena, purposeful overcompliance by the private sector and protracted processing times by competent national agencies, have been pinpointed as obstructive to the operations of humanitarian actors active in jurisdictions subject to international sanctions.[29]

4.3 The Drive Towards Reform Prior to the 2022 Invasion of Ukraine

Towards the end of the past decade, indications of a new willingness for improved implementation and enforcement of sanctions proliferated. Some suggested the establishment of a centralised agency dealing with implementation and enforcement, following the OFAC model. Then-Minister of France Bruno LeMaire proposed the establishment of an agency comparable to the Us treasury's OFAC, which is endowed with far-reaching powers and staffed with a two hundred-strong workforce,[30] a proposal that resonated with the think-tank community.[31] In March 2016, the UK set up an Office of Financial Sanctions Implementation (OFSI) capable of issuing enforcement actions, one of which fined a bank for dealing with a person blacklisted under the EU's Egypt sanctions regime. The establishment of an EU agency comparable to the Us treasury's OFAC is not readily practicable in the short to medium term given that the OFAC is endowed with competences that are currently in the hands of member states. Since the transfer of such competences would require a qualitative leap in integration, the eventual establishment of a European OFAC can only be understood as part of a long-term vision. Then-Prime Minister of the Netherlands Mark Rutte called for enhanced supervision and coordination in sanctions policy with a view to ensuring a level playing field for European firms, and to strengthening the role of the Commission in monitoring enforcement and providing guidance for private actors, positing: 'A level playing field demands that companies

[26] Giumelli and Onderco 2021; Moret 2015; Elliott 2022.

[27] Jaeger 2021.

[28] French original: 'l'OFAC a répondu en une semaine, tandis que chez nous cela a mis un an' [OFAC replied in one week, while here it took one year], quoted in Martin 2019, p. 20, author's translation.

[29] Debarre 2019.

[30] France24 2018.

[31] Geranmayeh and Lafont 2019.

know that any breach of sanctions will trigger enforcement action throughout the EU. The European Commission can serve as a linking pin for the national enforcement authorities, prompting them to take effective action and calling them to account if they fail to do so. The Commission can also inform companies across the EU about what they can and cannot do'.[32] The Foreign Ministers of Czechia, Denmark and the Netherlands laid out their vision for EU foreign policy, arguing as follows: 'Sanctions need swifter implementation, better guidance and stricter compliance. This is above all a national responsibility. But we also must strengthen European institutions to ensure maximum coordination and full compliance with the sanctions regime'.[33]

These ideas resonated with the first von der Leyen Commission, inaugurated in 2019. In her mission letter to Commissioner Valdis Dombrovskis, Executive Vice President for an Economy that Works for People, new President of the European Commission Ursula von der Leyen provided an explicit mandate to enhance implementation: 'Given that any legislation is only as good as its implementation, I want you to focus on the application and enforcement of EU law within your field. You should provide support and continuous guidance to Member States on implementation, and be ready to take swift action if EU law is breached'.[34] The simultaneous transfer of the Commission's sanctions unit from Foreign Policy Instruments to the Directorate General for Financial Stability, Financial Services and Capital Markets Union (DG FISMA) as part of the ensuing reshuffling of Commission portfolios[35] made clear that the monitoring of sanctions implementation was part of that endeavour. Placing the sanctions unit in the directorate-general responsible for financial stability, financial services, and capital markets union was seen as an indication of the Commission's willingness to align sanctions implementation closer with its technical oversight of the EU's financial sector.[36] President von der Leyen explicitly mandated Commissioner Dombrovskis 'to ensure that the sanctions imposed by the EU are properly enforced, notably throughout its financial system'.[37]

Following the transfer of the sanctions unit from EEAS, where it had been based as a section of the Foreign Policy Instruments, DG FISMA became the Commission's main responsible directorate-general for sanctions issues. The foregrounding of the Commission by those political actors advocating enhanced implementation and enforcement relies on its role as the 'guardian of the Treaties', whereby the Commission holds the main responsibility relating to the monitoring of the correct implementation of EU Council decisions and regulations, including on restrictive measures. Other Commission directorate-generals assist with the monitoring of sanctions implementation, including DG TRADE, which monitors trade flows between the EU and the economy under sanctions, as well as third countries used as proxies

[32] Rutte 2019.

[33] Kofod et al. 2019.

[34] Mission letter to Valdis Dombrovskis, Executive Vice-President-designate for An Economy that Works for People, Brussels, 10 September 2019.

[35] European Commission 2019.

[36] Portela and Olsen 2023.

[37] Ibid.

for sanctions circumvention and DG TAXUD, which oversees the customs union and the joint customs borders.

In January 2021, the Commission presented a Communication featuring a wide range of reform initiatives to strengthen the EU's implementation of sanctions. The communication, confusingly titled 'The European economic and financial system', presented a covered blueprint of what the Commission set out to accomplish in the field of sanctions implementation and enforcement in the following years, undoubtedly aided by the persistence of the Ukraine crisis.[38] The communication was preceded, and partly inspired, by a confidential non-paper prepared by Czechia, Denmark and the Netherlands, among others, calling for a strengthening of the EU's overall sanctions implementation and enforcement system as well as an overall review of the effectiveness and relevance of existing EU sanctions regimes.

Another intriguing development took place only a few months later. For a long time, researchers had been unable to produce cross-EU comparisons of sanctions implementation policies because they faced difficulties in the data collection, not least motivated by the existence of multiple legal systems in the EU. Due to these data gathering constraints, research in the field had only produced comparisons between two countries, generic discussions or overviews which remained inevitably incomplete.[39] In December 2022, a group called 'Genocide Network' associated with EUROJUST published a comparative study exposing the stark discrepancies between penalties faced by sanctions violators across different EU members.[40] As the first publicly available cross-country comparison, it paved the way for efforts towards approximation.[41]

4.4 The Drive Towards Reform Following the 2022 Invasion of Ukraine

Notwithstanding the existence of plans for reform announced by the Commission in its 2021 communication, a powerful impulse to upgrade implementation and enforcement emanated from Russia's military invasion of Ukraine in February 2022 and the extensive sanctions response that it elicited. Since the Council's adoption of the first sanctions packages against Russia and Belarus in early 2022, both EU institutions and member states strengthened their determination to tighten sanctions implementation across the EU.

A first outcome was increased activity by the Commission in its traditional roles of monitoring implementation and issuing guidance, including the introduction of

[38] European Commission Communication: The European economic and financial system: fostering openness, strength and resilience, COM(2021) 32 final, see especially page 15 ff.

[39] Giumelli 2020; Drulákova and Přikryl 2016; Drulákova and Zemanová 2020; Meissner and Portela 2022.

[40] EUROJUST 2022.

[41] See Chap. 7 in this volume.

some innovations. A Dutch-sponsored non-paper on the strengthening of the EU's sanctions capacity and its countering of sanctions circumvention[42] called for a platform for common analysis on individual cases of circumvention to be established at the EU-institutional level. Several capitals supported a more proactive monitoring role by the Commission, both in terms of enhancing a systemic overview of implementation structures, processes, and results at member state level as well as attempts to actively guide capitals and private actors to counter possible sanctions violations and circumvention. Traditionally, the main tool employed by the EU to assist economic operators in their efforts to comply is the issuing of guidance. This practice has seen a major expansion since February 2022, commensurate to the fast pace at which the sanctions waves were adopted, which produced certain wordings that required further specification. The practice of issuing guidance in Q&A format had been cultivated in previous years in order to address possible obstacles to humanitarian action[43]; however, the volume of guidance produced after February 2022 is unprecedented. While the issuing of guidance has been applauded in jurisdictions like Canada where this practice is less developed, European operators have occasionally expressed dissatisfaction with their non-binding nature: indeed, guidance notices continue to be invariably accompanied by the disclaimer stating that only the Court of Justice of the European Union can issue binding interpretations of EU law. Moreover, this was confirmed by the EU judicature.[44] Other initiatives to support EU businesses and economic operators in their implementation efforts include the allocation of funding to support the development of information technology tools to improve the dissemination of information on sanctions. The Commission set up a contact point for non-EU authorities and operators, endowed with a dedicated mailbox. The contact point is meant to encourage non-EU authorities and operators to reach out directly to the Commission when they face difficulties in interpreting EU sanctions legislation. There is also an anti-disinformation dimension to this initiative, as it designed to dispel narratives about bans putatively affecting food supplies,[45] and to help ensure that the flow of agri-food products and fertilisers to their countries continues unimpeded.

The fragmented and diverse approaches to sanctions implementation at national level require relevant data to be shared and compiled by the Commission. Indeed, the Commission has boosted its role in developing guidance for sanctions implementation. DG FISMA and other DGs respond more comprehensively to requests by national authorities and European firms on how to interpret certain provisions in the various sanctions regimes, and the Commission's provision of guidance and FAQs increased significantly.[46] Nevertheless, stakeholders resented the insufficient guidance received during the first year of the expanded Russia sanctions of 2022.

---

[42] For the full text, see the following link: https://open.overheid.nl/documenten/ronl-9af192a9dbdd615b48854e341be0c3e5b88c2594/pdf, accessed 1 September 2025.

[43] Manfredi and Jugl 2024.

[44] See Chap. 3 in this volume.

[45] Palestini and Portela 2025.

[46] Portela and Olsen 2023.

The Commission significantly increased its work on compiling data to better monitor sanctions implementation across the EU thanks to the newly-established 'Sanctions Information Exchange Repository', a database designed to enable prompt reporting and exchange of information between the Commission and member states. Similarly, the Commission endeavoured to enhance its understanding of member state implementation via the circulation of questionnaires and visits to national authorities.

In addition to the monitoring of sanctions effects at the level of economic operators, the Commission also traces cumulative trade data relating to sanctioned goods and services, including dual-use items. The trade data, compiled and assessed by DG TRADE and DG TAXUD, is used for monitoring abnormalities in export or import flows with third countries in order to detect possible instances of sanctions circumvention. As for the dual-use measures incorporated in the Russia sanctions regime, DG TRADE expanded existing dual-use reporting systems to include sanctions-relevant data. The formal reporting about member states' authorisations and denials relating to dual-use provisions are often preceded by informal exchanges between relevant national authorities and consultations with exporters. The Commission's internal coordination on the monitoring of sanctions implementation and enforcement was strengthened. Since February 2023, DG FISMA and several directorate-general with responsibilities for trade, taxation, energy or transport (DG TRADE, DG TAXUD, DG ENER and DG MOVE), alongside other stakeholders like the Secretary-General's Office, the EU's Anti-Fraud Agency OLAF and the Joint Research Centre, formalised their coordination practices in a new Inter-Service Group.[47] This group has replaced various informal coordination formats, often led by the Secretary-General's Office, which had developed during 2022 between different directorate-generals and services.

A whistle-blower tool, which had been announced as part of the January 2021 package of initiatives, became operational in March 2022. It provides two avenues for individuals and entities to supply information about possible breaches of EU sanctions: either via a direct message to DG FISMA or via an online form that ensures the anonymity of the informant. Allegations are then assessed with a view to determining whether the Commission or a national authority should investigate the raised concern. While stakeholders confirm that the whistle-blower tool has been used on multiple occasions, confidentiality requirements prevent an evaluation of the tool's overall performance.[48] Non-governmental stakeholders point out that the tool provides for better protection than the previous system, where suspicions about sanctions violations had to be raised informally with either EU institutions or national authorities. This was particularly challenging for potential non-EU whistle-blowers, who were not previously reassured that the information conveyed would be treated confidentially in the EU system.

The Commission also took bold steps to mitigate the EU's decentralised system's potential for fragmentation outside its traditional field of competence. While the Commission's renewed activity in this regard pre-dates the Russian invasion of

[47] Portela and Olsen 2023.

[48] Ibid.

Ukraine launched in February 2022, the wave of sanctions it unleashed added new impetus to these efforts. A most evident outcome was the criminalisation of sanctions violations.[49] The Commission first proposed to identify the violation of EU sanctions as an area of crime that meets the criteria specified in Article 83.1 TFEU, popularly known as 'Eurocrimes', a classification that enabled the Commission to propose legislation to approximate the definition of criminal offences as well as penalties in the member states.[50]

4.5 The Fight Against Circumvention

Sanctions circumvention refers to third-party states or groups which engage in activities that help economic operators to obviate prohibitions stipulated under sanctions legislation. Evasion and circumvention are closely related concepts describing methods to avoid the effects of prohibitions. However, evasion refers to the deliberate act of avoiding sanctions by bypassing the rule, i.e. via breaching prohibitions, while circumvention alludes to activities which are in appearance legally permissible but designed to skirt bans, such as via the export to third countries which later re-export materials to the forbidden destination.[51] While evasion can be tackled via regular domestic enforcement, circumvention has an international dimension that makes it more difficult to address.[52] The problem of sanctions circumvention is not new to the EU: instances were documented with regards to the sanctions regimes imposed on Iran,[53] DPRK[54] or Libya.[55] Still, the EU's political focus on the avoidance of circumvention was, until recently, modest. With the imposition of far-reaching sanctions against Moscow following the invasion of Ukraine, concerns about the risk of circumvention became acute. Such concerns intensified once dual-goods restrictions were in place, as it became clear that, instead of switching to alternative suppliers, Russian authorities were obtaining Western technology via circumvention channels.[56] Indeed, trade between the EU and countries like Armenia, Belarus, Kazakhstan, Kyrgyzstan and Turkey grew conspicuously following the imposition of sanctions.[57]

The European Commission stepped up its efforts to curtail opportunities for circumvention, which resulted in the adoption of a battery of new measures. A most

[49] European Parliament and the Council of the European Union 2024.

[50] European Commission 2022. See also Chap. 7 in this volume.

[51] Preble 2025.

[52] In fact, the EU had even been accused by US stakeholders of aiding the circumvention of the extraterritorial effects of US sanctions against Iran through the creation of the Instrument in Support of Trade Exchanges, INSTEX. See Johnson 2019.

[53] Early 2015.

[54] Habib 2016; Esteban and Portela 2022.

[55] Portela and Romanet 2022.

[56] Sibona 2024.

[57] Wiśniewska 2025.

visible step is the creation of a Special envoy for the Implementation of EU Sanctions. Despite the fact that its title is now commonly abbreviated to 'EU Sanctions Envoy', its mandate focuses specifically on improving implementation. The position is organisationally tied to the Office of the Director-General of DG FISMA and has, since January 2023, been held by Mr David O'Sullivan, a former Secretary-General of the European Commission as well as a former Director General for external trade. The Envoy's international engagement on sanctions circumvention intends to attract support for its bans beyond those partners which already align with them,[58] or at a minimum, to dissuade third parties from facilitating circumvention. Despite the generic job title, the trigger and focus of this position is the sanctions efforts against Russia.[59]

Most innovations have taken legal form and are discernible in the text of the sanctions instruments. EU exporters of sensitive goods and technology are now required to contractually prohibit re-exportation to Russia or 'for use in Russia'.[60] In addition, the most significant innovation has been the introduction of provisions prohibiting circumvention. Such clauses are present in all relevant EU sanctions regimes: the sanctions regime targeting individuals and entities for their actions against the territorial integrity, sovereignty and independence of Ukraine, CFSP Decision 2014/145, the regime imposing sectoral sanctions against Russia for its destabilisation of Ukraine, CFSP Decision 2014/512,[61] and the sanctions regimes imposing restrictions on interaction with annexed and occupied territories concerning Crimea and Sevastopol, CFSP Decision 2014/386, and Donetsk and Luhansk, CFSP Decision 2022/266. In addition to expressly prohibiting circumvention, penalties are foreseen for those attempting it.

Of all four sanctions regimes responding to the war in Ukraine, the sanctions regime CFSP Decision 2014/145 is designed for the listing of individuals and entities. Tellingly, out of the ten designation criteria contemplated in its Article 1, two are intended to avoid circumvention. The main anti-circumvention provision is to be found under subparagraph (f), which allows for the designation of those facilitating breaches of the prohibition against circumvention of the provisions of CFSP Decision 2014/145, of any of the three remaining sanctions regimes, or for 'otherwise significantly frustrating' those provisions. This key anti-circumvention prohibition was introduced with the adoption of the eighth sanctions package in October 2022.[62] Following a revision of the clause in June 2023, Article 1(f) and Article 2(h) read as follows:

> natural or legal persons, entities or bodies facilitating infringements of the prohibition against circumvention of the provisions of this Decision, of Council Regulations (EU) No 269/2014

[58] Cardwell and Moret 2023.

[59] Timofeev 2023.

[60] Article 5.b.1.

[61] Council Decision (CFSP) 2014c.

[62] Council Decision (CFSP) 2022b.

> (*1), (EU) No 692/2014 (2), (EU) No 833/2014 (*3) or (EU) 2022/263 (*4), or of Council Decision 2014/386/CFSP (5), 2014/512/CFSP (*6) or (CFSP) 2022/266 (*7).[63]

Similarly, the germane regime CFSP Decision 2014/512 features an equivalent clause geared towards preventing the circumvention of bans on the supply of goods and technology. Here, the rationale for the measure is specified in the preamble, which introduces the option to:

> restrict the sale, supply, transfer or export of sensitive dual-use goods and technology, or goods and technology that might contribute to the enhancement of Russia's military, technological or industrial capacities or to the development of Russia's defence and security sector, in a way that strengthens its ability to wage war, and whose export to Russia is prohibited under Decision 2014/512/CFSP and Regulation (EU) No 833/2014 to third countries whose jurisdiction is demonstrated to be at a continuing and particularly high risk of being used for circumvention.[64]

In view of the sensitivity of adopting measures affecting third country-entities, the preamble announced a few precautions to be considered when making decisions on listings, which it describes as a last-resort measure. The Council aims do decide on listings after having been briefed on the outreach actions taken, considering a thorough technical analysis by the Commission on the circumvention issues in question and evidence demonstrating that the alternative measures taken have been ineffective, and after having sought the views of the government of that third country.[65]

Both the listing of entities engaging in circumvention as that of third countries is contemplated. Article 5a prohibits the sell, supply and transfer of goods and technology to designated third country entities.[66] The same article specifies that this provision concerns only 'sensitive dual-use goods and technology, or goods and technology that might contribute to the enhancement of Russia's military, technological or industrial capacities or to the development of Russia's defence and security sector, in a way that strengthens its ability to wage war, and whose export to Russia is prohibited under this Decision', and that third countries will only be listed after having been 'identified by the Council as having systematically and persistently failed to prevent the sale, supply, transfer or export to Russia of goods and technology, as listed in that Annex, exported from the Union despite the Union's prior outreach and assistance to the country in question'.[67] The relevant annex, number XIV, remains empty to this day. The fact that, for the two years that elapsed after the adoption of this provision, no designation had been made offers various interpretations. One of them is that the Council prefers to hold to account the firm responsible for the circumvention exercise, something that it has done by listing plenty of third-country enterprises elsewhere. By contrast, the Council is wary of antagonising other states via designation, in order to prevent the ensuing diplomatic fallout. A second reading

---

[63] Council Decision (CFSP) 2014a, Articles 1(f) and 2(h).

[64] Council Decision (CFSP) 2023, at recital 13.

[65] Ibid., recitals 15–17.

[66] Article 5.a.1.

[67] Article 5.a.3.

is that third countries have been willing to adopt the regulatory framework necessary to avoid circumvention, but individual firms still breach relevant legislation. As explained by the Special envoy on sanctions implementation, while companies based in China and Hong Kong are responsible for 80% of the transhipment of Western components used by Russia to make drones, missiles and shells of higher precision, much of this circumvention 'is not officially run by the Chinese government'.[68] Lastly, the procedure detailed in the preamble, and the last resort character that the Council ascribed to designations, can result in lengthy processes led by the Special envoy for sanctions implementation, whose outcome may still be unknown. Current efforts have reportedly encouraged countries like Armenia or Kazakhstan to introduced mechanisms to prevent the re-export of sensitive products.[69]

Several additional anti-circumvention prohibitions were progressively added. Article 2, which provides for the freezing of assets and includes an even longer catalogue of designation criteria—three more than Article 1 providing for prohibitions of entry-, foresees the listing of entities 'that have participated in or enabled transfers of ownership, control or economic benefit of the business interests of leading businesspersons who are subject to Union restrictive measures'.[70] Notably, a number of provisions were introduced to tackle the sale of oil originating from Russia. Subparagraph (h) takes issue with the 'shadow fleet', targeting individuals who operate vessels transporting crude oil or petroleum products from Russia and practicing 'irregular and high-risk shipping practices' foreseen in resolution A.1192(33) of the International Maritime Organisation General Assembly, or who support their operations.[71] While the CFSP Decision 2014/145 regime provides for the listing of those individuals who operate the 'shadow fleet', CFSP Decision 2014/512 foresees the designation of vessels.[72] These are subject to a prohibition to access ports, anchorage zones and locks in the territory of the Union. EU member states are prevented from to trading in, operating or crewing listed vessels, providing them with flag registration, financial or technical assistance, or engaging in ship-to-ship transfers or any other transfer of cargo. However, the listing of vessels does not end with the shadow fleet. Their operation in favour of actions breaching other sanctions constitute additional reasons for designation. This includes supporting the expansion of the energy sector in Russia, and obviously the transport of stolen items from Ukraine—be it grain or cultural heritage—as well as the flouting of the arms embargo. This is complemented by catch-all clauses designed to support the remaining sanctions regimes, closing possible loopholes: one foresees the use of vessels to facilitate the violation or circumvention or 'otherwise significantly frustrate' prohibitions embedded in the same sanctions regime or in the 2014/145/CFSP, 2014/386/CFSP or CFSP 2022/266 sanctions regimes and accompanying regulations[73]; or are 'owned, chartered or

---

68 O'Sullivan quoted in Tadeo 2025.

69 Kaca 2025, Kyrgyzstan became the first listed country in April 2026.

70 Article 2m.

71 Council Decision (CFSP) 2025a.

72 Article 4 x.

73 Article 4 x 2.(f).

operated by individuals or entities designated under the regime CFSP 2014/145' or used on their behalf.[74] Under this clause, more than 600 vessels have been listed.[75]

Lastly, the sanctions regimes CFSP Decision 2014/386 and CFSP Decision 2022/266, concerning Crimea Sevastopol and Donetsk and Luhansk, deliberately designed as parallel texts instituting quasi-embargos on the territories they cover, equally include an anti-circumvention clause: 'It shall be prohibited to participate, knowingly and intentionally, in activities the object or effect of which is to circumvent prohibitions in this Decision, including by participating in such activities without deliberately seeking that object or effect but being aware that the participation may have that object or effect and accepting that possibility'.[76] Contrary to the preceding regimes, these clauses do not foresee designations for breaches, which already feature elsewhere: on account of the quasi-comprehensive character of their provisions, listings annexed to these two regimes are mostly linked to carve-outs.[77]

4.6 Discussion

Overall, the anti-circumvention provisions introduce a number of key innovations that help the EU tackle circumvention. Firstly, they prohibit circumvention. Simple as this measure may seem, it had been absent from previous CFSP sanctions practice; as a result, operators were free to engage in circumvention as it was not technically in breach of sanctions legislation. Secondly, it establishes a penalty for engaging in circumvention practices—nothing less than the same penalty contemplated for the same wrongdoing that gives rise to the sanctions, i.e. inclusion in the blacklist, which implies being subject to an asset freeze, a prohibition on financial transfers, and as an individual, a prohibition on entry. Thirdly, the circumvention provisions have been organised in a circular fashion: they refer to each other and support each other mutually. Circumvention of one of the four sanctions regimes responding to the war in Ukraine may entail designation under the same sanctions regime or alternatively, perhaps additionally, another one (CFSP Decision 2014/145 or CFSP Decision 2014/512). Moreover, the wording of the anti-circumvention clauses feature such an ample scope that any unanticipated loopholes can be easily filled. This is largely accomplished via two methods. Firstly, engaging in behaviour that contributes to prolong the condemned wrongdoing is equated to the condemned wrongdoing for the purposes of the designation. In other words, one is equally likely to be listed for engaging in the condemned wrongdoing—in our case, the war in Ukraine—than for engaging in actions that contribute to the continuation of the wrongdoing, such as the operation of a vessel of the shadow fleet or the acquisition of the expropriated subsidiary of an EU company. The second method is to include various

[74] Article 4 x 2.(g).

[75] Council Decision (CFSP) 2025b.

[76] Article 4 g in Council Decision (CFSP) 2014b, Article 9 b in Council Decision (CFSP) 2022a.

[77] See Chap. 2 in this volume.

layers of proximity to the wrongdoing, which contemplates the listings of individuals 'supporting', 'benefiting from', or 'associated with' those directly engaging in any of the condemned actions. Thanks to this approach, Brussels has moved from leaving circumvention almost unaddressed to equipping itself to curtail it. What is probably most remarkable about the development of anti-circumvention clauses is that Brussels has skilfully avoided replicating Washington's use of secondary sanctions. While the anti-circumvention clauses embedded in CFSP Decision 2014/145 and CFSP Decision 2014/512 display clear extraterritorial effects, they merely restrain EU suppliers from providing technology and technical assistance.[78]

In addition, these legal arrangements to counter circumvention and the post of Special envoy for the implementation of sanctions, a sui-generis position in the EU foreign policy landscape, reinforce each other. When the position was first created, details on his mandate were very scarce, to the extent that the public did not know what to expect of him. A large part of his task consists in persuasion. EU officials reported that the initial reaction of third countries approached about their participation in circumvention was to adduce that they were not bound by EU sanctions, but the risk of reputational damage helped bringing them on board of anti-circumvention efforts.[79] However, the prospect of being blacklisted for failing to adopt the necessary regulatory framework to avoid circumvention contributes to support these efforts. In any case, as recognised by the Special envoy himself, the objective of these efforts it to reduce the extent of these practices, but its full eradication is unrealistic: 'there will be circumvention. We will never eliminate it fully. What we have to do is to make circumvention harder, less predictable, less reliable and more expensive'.[80]

4.7 Conclusions

Our brief overview over initiatives undertaken to improve the EU's system of implementation yields several insights. Firstly, the main input for the long-neglected focus on implementation did not emerge with the 2022 invasion of Ukraine. Rather, the aftermath of the 2014 annexation of Crimea and the ensuing destabilisation of Eastern Ukraine set the stage for enhanced reform efforts.[81] The even greater shock represented by the 2022 invasion, which led to unprecedented sanctions,[82] facilitated the implementation of the Commission's ambitious agenda. Moreover, the urgency injected to the process of improving implementation, led by some determined member states, displayed another noticeable effect: that of promoting a leap in integration that would have been difficult to effect absent a major geopolitical crisis like an interstate war in Europe. The Commission enhanced its powers in

[78] Sibona 2024.

[79] Anonymous EU official quoted in Korkea-aho and Lonardo 2025, p. 17.

[80] O'Sullivan quoted in Tadeo 2025.

[81] Portela et al. 2021.

[82] Meissner and Graziani 2023; Miadzvetskaya and Challet 2022.

the process, acquiring a new centrality.[83] Perhaps the most obvious illustration is the transfer of sanctions violations to the realm of Article 83.1 TFEU, a veritable integration leap and an incursion into criminal law as it allows the Commission to establish the definition of the crime and set minimum penalties.

Yet, current efforts, speedy and far-reaching as they were, remain insufficient. The implementation and enforcement machinery continues to lack a standardised system for assessment of sanctions impacts and for the integration of lessons learned. Economic impacts are monitored: the 2014 EU sanctions regime on Russia compelled the Commission to start monitoring economic effects both on the Russian economy and on that of the member states, an exercise it conducts jointly with national authorities. By contrast, developments concerning the political impact are followed in the absence of an evaluative framework assessing their effectiveness. The Council's practice of reviewing sanctions regimes periodically when the legal act approaches its expiry date has been lauded because it invites member states and institutions to regularly take stock of the political evolution of the target, preventing inertia in sanctions regimes. The evaluation of sanctions regimes performance in bringing about the desired political outcomes in the target country is traditionally conducted in the framework of the geographical Council Working Party responsible for the target country in question. Their work is supported by the EEAS; however, there is no specific mandate for the EEAS sanctions unit or geographical sections to monitor progress driven by the sanctions regime. The EU lacks an agreed evaluative framework that could be applied to the assessment of sanctions performance.[84] Neither is there a mechanism foreseen for the provision of institutional memory on previous sanctions regimes in the EEAS machinery.[85]

Despite the renewed commitment of EU institutions and member states to take implementation seriously, it remains unclear if Brussels will extend the approach taken to the Russo-Ukrainian war to other sanctions regimes, with a view to tackling the challenge of sanctions circumvention more globally. Circumvention is not unique to the Russia sanctions regime; however, most of the latest innovations in exclusively concern the sanctions regimes established in response to the Russian aggression of Ukraine. It has been proposed that clauses relating to sanctions circumvention should become a standard feature in all EU sanctions regimes.[86] Alternatively, in order to address the circumvention issue in a more horizontal fashion, Brussels could also ponder to establish a dedicated sanctions regime, along the lines of current thematic EU sanctions regimes on terrorism, chemical weapons, cyber-attacks and human rights abuses.[87]

---

83 Håkansson 2023; Korkea-aho and Lonardo 2025.

84 Druláková et al. 2010.

85 Portela and Olsen 2023.

86 Portela and Olsen 2023.

87 Portela 2021.

References

Cardwell P, Moret E (2023) The EU, Sanctions and Regional Leadership. European Security 32: 1–21.
Council of the European Union (2004) Basic principles on the use of restrictive measures (sanctions), Brussels, 7 June 2004.
Council of the European Union (2015) EU Best Practices for the effective implementation of restrictive measures (10254/15).
Council of the European Union (2018) Guidelines on implementation and evaluation of restrictive measures (sanctions) in the framework of the EU Common Foreign and Security Policy, doc. 5664/18.
Council Decision (2013) 2013/255/CFSP of 31 May 2013 concerning restrictive measures against Syria, OJ L 147, 1 June 2013. pp. 14–45, ELI: http://data.europa.eu/eli/dec/2013/255/oj.
Council Decision (2014a) 2014/145/CFSP of 17 March 2014 concerning restrictive measures in respect of actions undermining or threatening the territorial integrity, sovereignty and independence of Ukraine, OJ L 78, 17.3.2014, pp. 16–21, ELI: http://data.europa.eu/eli/dec/2014/145(1)/oj.
Council Decision (2014b) 2014/386/CFSP of 23 June 2014 concerning restrictions on goods originating in Crimea or Sevastopol, in response to the illegal annexation of Crimea and Sevastopol, OJ L 183, 24.6.2014, pp. 70–71, ELI: http://data.europa.eu/eli/dec/2014/386/oj.
Council Decision (2014c) 2014/512/CFSP of 31 July 2014 concerning restrictive measures in view of Russia's actions destabilising the situation in Ukraine, OJ L 229, 31.7.2014, pp. 13–17, ELI: http://data.europa.eu/eli/dec/2014/512/oj.
Council Decision (CFSP) (2022a) 2022/266 of 23 February 2022 concerning restrictive measures in response to the recognition of the non-government controlled areas of the Donetsk and Luhansk oblasts of Ukraine and the ordering of Russian armed forces into those areas, OJ L 42I, 23.2.2022, pp. 109–113, ELI: http://data.europa.eu/eli/dec/2022/266/oj.
Council Decision (CFSP) (2022b) 2022/1907 of 6 October 2022 amending Decision 2014/145/CFSP concerning restrictive measures in respect of actions undermining or threatening the territorial integrity, sovereignty and independence of Ukraine, OJ L 259I, 6.10.2022, pp. 98–117, ELI: http://data.europa.eu/eli/dec/2022/1907/oj.
Council Decision (CFSP) (2023) 2023/1217 of 23 June 2023 amending Decision 2014/512/CFSP concerning restrictive measures in view of Russia's actions destabilising the situation in Ukraine, OJ L 159I, 23.6.2023, pp. 451–525, ELI: http://data.europa.eu/eli/dec/2023/1217/oj.
Council Decision (CFSP) (2025a) 2025/1478 of 18 July 2025 amending Decision 2014/145/CFSP concerning restrictive measures in respect of actions undermining or threatening the territorial integrity, sovereignty and independence of Ukraine, OJ L, 2025/1478, 19.7.2025, ELI: http://data.europa.eu/eli/dec/2025/1478/oj.
Council Decision (CFSP) (2025b) 2025/1495 of 18 July 2025 amending Decision 2014/512/CFSP concerning restrictive measures in view of Russia's actions destabilising the situation in Ukraine, OJ L, 2025/1495, 19.7.2025, ELI: http://data.europa.eu/eli/dec/2025/1495/oj.
Debarre A (2019) Safeguarding Humanitarian Action in Sanctions Regimes. International Peace Institute, New York.
Druláková R, Přikryl P (2016) The Implementation of Sanctions Imposed by the European Union. Central European Journal of International and Security Studies 10: 134–160.
Druláková R, Rolenc J M, Travnickova Z, Zemanová S (2010) Assessing the Effectiveness of EU Sanctions Policy. Central European Journal of International and Security Studies 4: 101–121.
Druláková R, Zemanová S (2020) Why the Implementation of Multilateral Sanctions does (not) Work: Lessons learnt from the Czech Republic. European Security 29:524–544.
Early B (2015) Busted Sanctions: Explaining why economic sanctions fail. Stanford University Press, Stanford.

Elliott KA (2022) U.S. Approaches to Multilateral Sanctions: Co-operation and coercion intertwined. In: Charron A, Portela C (eds) Multilateral Sanctions Revisited. Lessons learned from Margaret Doxey. McGill-Queen's University Press, Montreal, pp. 34–50.
European Centre for Constitutional and Human Rights (2018) Joint letter: 14 Syrian and international human rights organisations support ECCHR's complaint against Italy, 28 June 2018.
European Commission (2017) Commission guidance note on the implementation of certain provisions of Regulation (EU) No 833/2014, Commission Notice, C(2017) 5738 final, Brussels, 25 August 2017.
European Commission (2019) Allocation of portfolios and supporting services note, Brussels, 7 November 2019.
European Commission (2022) Communication to the European Parliament and the Council: Towards a Directive on criminal penalties for the violation of Union restrictive measures, COM/2022/249 final, 2022.
Esteban M, Portela C (2022) EU Sanctions against North Korea: Making a stringent UN sanctions regime even tougher, In: Casarini N et al (eds) Routledge Handbook of EU-Korea Relations, Routledge, Abingdon, pp. 382–395.
EUROJUST (2022) Prosecution of Sanctions (Restrictive Measures) Violations in National Jurisdictions: A Comparative Analysis, The Hague.
European Parliament and Council of the European Union (2024) Directive (EU) 2024/1226 of the European Parliament and of the Council of 24 April 2024 on the definition of criminal offences and penalties for the violation of Union restrictive measures and amending Directive (EU) 2018/1673, OJ L, 2024/1226, 29.4.2024, ELI: http://data.europa.eu/eli/dir/2024/1226/o.
France24 (2018) France urges Europe to push back against "unacceptable" US sanctions on Iran, 11 May 2018.
Geranmayeh E, Lafont M (2019) Meeting the Challenge of Secondary Sanctions. In: Leonard M, Shapiro J (eds) Strategic Sovereignty: How Europe can regain the capacity to act. ECFR, London, pp. 61–84.
Gestri M (2016) Sanctions Imposed by the European Union: Legal and institutional aspects. In: Ronzitti N (ed) Coercive Diplomacy, Sanctions and International Law. Brill Nijhoff, Leiden, pp. 70–102.
Giumelli F (2020) Implementation of Sanctions: European Union. In: Asada M (ed) Economic Sanctions in International Law and Practice. Routledge, Abingdon, pp. 116–135.
Giumelli F, Onderco M (2021) States, Firms, and Security: How private actors implement sanctions, lessons learned from the Netherlands. European Journal of International Security 6: 190–209.
Giumelli F et al (2022) United in Diversity? A Study on the Implementation of Sanctions in the European Union. Politics and Governance 10: 36–46.
Golumbic C, Ruff R (2013) Who Do I Call for an EU Sanctions Exception? Why the EU economic sanctions regime should centralize licensing. Georgetown Journal of International Law 44:1007–1053.
Habib B (2016) The enforcement problem in Resolution 2094 and the United Nations Security Council sanctions regime: Sanctioning North Korea. Australian Journal of International Affairs 70: 50–68.
Håkansson C (2023) The Ukraine War and the Emergence of the European Commission as a Geopolitical Actor. Journal of European Integration 46: 25–45.
Jaeger M D (2021) Circumventing Sovereignty: Extraterritorial sanctions leveraging the technologies of the financial system. Swiss Political Science Review 27: 180–192.
Johnson K (2019) EU offers up a meagre workaround to U.S. Iran sanctions. Foreign Policy, 31 January 2019.
Kaca E (2025) Countering the Circumvention of EU Sanctions against Russia by Foreign Companies. Polish Institute of International Affairs, Bulletin No. 71, Warsaw.

Kofod J, Blok S, Petricek T (2019) How to revamp EU foreign policy. Politico, 9 December 2019.

Korkea-aho E, Lonardo L (2025) How Russia's War against Ukraine Changed EU Sanctions Decision-making. Journal of European Integration.

Manfredi S, Jugl M (2024) Tackling Unintended Consequences of EU Sanctions: NGOs' Advocacy for Humanitarian Exceptions. Journal of Common Market Studies 62: 1519–1537.

Martin E (2019) La politique de sanctions de l'Union Européenne. Ambition multilatérale contre logique de puissance [The sanctions policy of the European Union. Multilateral ambition versus power logic]. Etudes de l'Ifri, Paris.

Meissner K, Graziani C (2023) The Transformation and Design of EU Restrictive Measures against Russia. Journal of European Integration 45: 377–394.

Meissner K, Portela C (2022) Beyond Foreign Policy? EU Sanctions at the Intersection of Development, Trade and CFSP. Politics and Governance 10(1): 1–4.

Miadzvetskaya Y, Challet C (2022) Are EU Restrictive Measures really Targeted, Temporary and Preventive? Europe and the World: A Law Review 6: 1–19.

Moret E (2015) Humanitarian Impacts of Economic Sanctions on Iran and Syria. European Security 24(1): 120–140.

Olsen K B (2022) The Geoeconomic Diplomacy of European Sanctions: Networked Practices and Sanctions Implementation. Brill, Leiden.

Olsen K B, Fasterkjær Kjeldsen S (2022) Strict and uniform: Improving EU Sanctions Enforcement. DGAP Policy Brief 29.

Palestini S, Portela C (2025) The Global South and the Contestation of Unilateral Sanctions against Russia. Cooperation and Conflict.

Portela C (2021) Horizontal Sanctions Regimes: Targeted sanctions reconfigured? In: Beaucillon C (ed) Research Handbook on Unilateral and Extraterritorial Sanctions. Edward Elgar, Cheltenham, pp. 441–457.

Portela C (2015) Member states' Resistance to EU Foreign Policy Sanctions. European Foreign Affairs Review 20(3): 39–61.

Portela C (2016) Are EU Sanctions 'Targeted'? Cambridge Review of International Affairs 29: 912–929.

Portela C (2020) Implementation and Enforcement. In: Helwig N et al (eds) Sharpening EU Sanctions Policy. FIIA Report 63, Study commissioned by the Office of the Prime Minister of Finland, Finnish Institute for International Affairs, Helsinki, pp. 105–115.

Portela C, Olsen K B (2023) Implementation and Monitoring of the EU Sanctions' Regimes, including Recommendations to Reinforce the EU's Capacities to Implement and Monitor Sanctions. European Parliament, Brussels.

Portela C, Pospieszna P, Skrzypczyńska J, Walentek D (2021) Consensus against all Odds: Explaining the persistence of EU sanctions on Russia. Journal of European Integration 43: 683–699.

Portela C, Romanet J L (2022) Mediation and Sanctions in Libya: Synergy or obstruction? Global Governance: A Review of Multilateralism and International Organizations 28: 228–250.

Preble K (2025) Evasion and Circumvention. In: Portela C, Charron A, Sossai M (eds) Encyclopedia of International Sanctions. Edward Elgar, Cheltenham, pp. 180–183.

Rutte M (2019) The EU: From the power of principles towards principles and power. Churchill Lecture, Europa Institute of the University of Zurich, 13 February 2019.

Sibona M (2024) Tackling Circumvention of EU Sanctions. Jacques Delors Institute, Paris.

Tadeo M (2025) A conversation with David O'Sullivan, EU sanctions Envoy, Groupe d'études géopolitiques, 15 July 2025, https://geopolitique.eu/en/2025/07/15/a-conversation-with-david-osullivan-eu-sanctions-envoy/, accessed 20 August 2025.

Timofeev I (2023) What to expect from the EU Special envoy on sanctions? Valdai Expert Opinions, 3 February. https://valdaiclub.com/a/highlights/what-to-expect-from-the-eu-special-envoy/ (accessed 19 July 2026).

Wiśniewska I (2025) A game of cat and mouse. How Russia is Circumventing Sanctions. OSW Centre for Eastern Studies Report, April. https://www.osw.waw.pl/sites/default/files/OSW%20REPORT%20-%20A%20game%20of%20cat%20and%20mouse%20%E2%80%93%20how%20Russia%20is%20circumventing%20sanctions-www.pdf (accessed 19 July 2026).

Chapter 5
The War in Ukraine and Its Influence on the Council's Decision-Making in the Context of the Common Foreign and Security Policy

Luca Paladini and Sara Poli

Contents

Abstract This chapter examines the impact of the war in Ukraine on decision-making within the EU's Common Foreign and Security Policy (CFSP), with particular focus on the adoption of restrictive measures against Russia and key developments in the Common Security and Defence Policy. The current practice in the field of sanctions reveals that Member States avoid invoking the constructive abstention mechanism under Article 31 TEU, in order to safeguard the unity and effectiveness of the EU's sanctions regime. Dissenting positions within the Council were expressed through 'simple abstention' pursuant to Article 238(4) TFEU or through the inclusion of ad hoc derogations in sector-related restrictive measures. Next, the chapter

This chapter is the result of the two authors' joint thinking. That being said, Sects. 5.1 and 5.3 and Sects. 5.3.1 to 5.3.3 have been written by Luca Paladini, while Sara Poli wrote Sects. 5.2, 5.2.1 and 5.4.

S. Poli et al., *The EU's Response to the War in Ukraine and Its Impact on the EU Legal Order*, Global Europe: Legal and Policy Issues of the EU's External Action 7,
https://doi.org/10.1007/978-94-6265-767-0_5

examines arguments that may lead the EU Court of Justice to uphold the annulment action brought by the European Parliament against the Council challenging the use of unanimity in the adoption of implementing measures in the context of EU restrictive measures. Turning to the Common Security and Defence Policy the chapter explores the use of constructive abstention in connection with the launch of the EUMAM Ukraine mission and the operational deployment of the European Peace Facility (EPF), particularly in relation to the provision of lethal military equipment. These instances highlight the different positions of certain Member States vis-à-vis EU initiatives in support of Kiev. The second case that is examined in this chapter concerns a pending action brought by Hungary to seek the annulment of its exclusion from EPF-related decision-making. The future ruling will clarify whether a country relying on constructive abstention has still the possibility to participate in the adoption of subsequent implementing decisions. The chapter concludes with reflections on the broader implications of the war in Ukraine for the CFSP decision-making process.

Keywords War in Ukraine · CFSP · Decision-making process · Article 31 TEU · Article 40 TEU · Restrictive measures · Article 215 TFEU · CSDP · EUMAM Ukraine · European Peace Facility

5.1 The CFSP Decision-Making Process After the Outbreak of the War in Ukraine: Introductory Remarks

The outbreak of the war between Russia and Ukraine compelled the European Union to take a number of measures in the framework of the Common Foreign and Security Policy (CFSP) whose implications for the Council's decision-making process in this area are particularly interesting.

It is necessary to recall the procedure regulating Council deliberations under the CFSP and the Common Security and Defence Policy (CSDP),[1] as delineated in Article 31 TEU. As a general rule, the Council acts by unanimity, and this threshold is deemed satisfied in cases where a Member State constructively abstains.[2] This flexibility mechanism enables the Council to adopt decisions by 'quasi-unanimity', thereby exempting the dissenting Member State from the obligation to implement the decision, while simultaneously requiring it not to obstruct the Union's actions that are based on that decision. However, if constructive abstentions account for at least one-third of the Member States and one-third of the EU population, the decision will not be adopted.

[1] ESDP is an integral part of the CFSP—see Article 24(1) and Article 42(1) TEU.

[2] Article 31(1) TEU.

By way of derogation, certain categories of decisions may be adopted by qualified majority,[3] except those with military or defence implications.[4] These qualified-majority decisions include: (i) decisions defining a EU action or position pursuant to a decision of the European Council concerning the Union's strategic interests and objectives[5]; (ii) decisions proposed by the High Representative of the Union for Foreign Affairs and Security Policy (High Representative), either following a specific request from the European Council or on their own initiative; (iii) decisions implementing a previously defined EU action or position; and (iv) decisions relating to the appointment of special representatives.[6] Two additional legal provisions deserve attention: the so-called 'passerelle clause', which allows the European Council, acting unanimously, to authorise the Council to decide by qualified majority in other cases[7]; and Article 41(3) TEU, which defines procedures for access to appropriations within the EU budget for urgent initiatives. In all instances, the adoption of a decision by qualified majority may be blocked by a Member State invoking 'vital and stated reasons of national policy.' This is the so-called 'emergency brake'. Should this mechanism be activated, the High Representative and the Member State concerned must endeavour to reach an acceptable compromise. Failing that, the Council, acting by qualified majority, may request that the matter be referred to the European Council for a unanimous resolution.

Finally, procedural matters are decided by simple majority.[8]

In practice, the Council has traditionally adopted decisions by consensus.[9] Only in instances where vetoes are raised—i.e., in the absence of unanimous agreement[10]—does the question of initiating a formal vote under Article 31 TEU arise. To date, the practical application of this provision has remained limited.[11] Constructive abstention was used for the first time in 2008, when Cyprus abstained from the decision to launch

---

3 Article 31(2) TEU.

4 Article 31(4) TEU. See the exceptions referred to in Article 45(2) TEU (on the European Defence Agency) and Article 46(2–5) TEU (on the Permanent Structured Cooperation).

5 Article 22(1) TEU.

6 Article 33 TEU.

7 Article 31(3) TEU.

8 Article 31(5) TEU.

9 See Klabbers 2022, p. 157 ff.

10 Such instances remain a constant possibility and are subject to criticism, especially when they result from a "blocking for blocking's sake" strategy, which certain Member States occasionally use. That strategy essentially reflects a withdrawal from constructive consensus-building and consists in the imposition—or threat—of a veto on CFSP decisions, with no substantive justification or prior deliberation. See European Parliamentary Research Service 2023, p. 18 ff.

11 The Council's Rules of Procedure (RoP) appear to corroborate this interpretation. When the Foreign Affairs Council is convened to discuss matters with a view to a formal decision—particularly within the scope of the CFSP—items pertaining to such legal acts are marked with an asterisk. Pursuant to Article 3(2) RoP, an asterisk is indicative of the right to request a vote. Crucially, the asterisk does not mean that a CFSP proposal will necessarily be put to a vote; rather, it indicates that the vote may take place. This graphical indicator seems to reflect an established institutional practice, insofar as it does not preclude the adoption of a CFSP proposal by consensus, even when marked with an asterisk.

the EULEX Kosovo mission.[12] Cases involving qualified majority voting remain exceedingly rare,[13] despite repeated calls for its broader use since the Commission's 2018 Communication on the subject.[14] There is no known instance of the emergency brake having been triggered; the same goes for the 'passerelle clause.' Furthermore, no official record exists concerning the use of voting to reach a simple majority on procedural matters.

Nevertheless, the war in Ukraine has introduced remarkable changes in CFSP decision-making procedures under Article 31 TEU. First, constructive abstention has been used in relation to several decisions supporting Ukraine, highlighting the impossibility of achieving consensus and making it necessary to vote and to trigger the flexibility mechanism of Article 31(1) TEU. Second, the decision-making procedure leading to the adoption of restrictive measures—which is characterised by its own specificities[15]—has led the Council to grant temporary derogations from energy import bans on Russia to certain Member States experiencing supply constraints.

Two Council decisions adopted in response to the war in Ukraine were challenged before the EU Court of Justice (ECJ) on grounds related to breaches of Article 31(1) TEU. These two cases will give the ECJ the opportunity to provide important clarifications on the decision-making applicable both in the context of restrictive measures and in that of the CFSP. The European Parliament instituted proceedings to annul a Council decision on restrictive measures targeting Russia's destabilising activities. The Parliament contended that the requirement of unanimity to amend the list of sanctioned entities was in breach of Article 31(2), third indent, TEU, which provides that Council decisions must be made by qualified majority voting. In addition, Hungary brought an action for annulment against a decision of the European Peace Facility Committee adopted on 24 May 2024.[16] Hungary contested its exclusion from voting on the implementing measure of a decision from which it had constructively abstained.

---

[12] Council, doc. CM 448/08, Brussels, 4 February 2008.

[13] See Szép and Wessel 2023, p. 6.

[14] European Commission 2018. For a commentary, see Poli 2019, p. 391 ff. Among other EU documents advocating the use of qualified majority voting (QMV), see European Parliamentary Research Service 2022 and 2023. Several Member States have also expressed their support for QMV. See, for instance, *Joint Statement of the Foreign Ministries on the Launch of the Group of Friends on Qualified Majority Voting in EU Common Foreign and Security Policy*, 4 May 2023 (Belgium, Finland, France, Germany, Italy, Luxembourg, the Netherlands, Slovenia, and Spain—later joined by Romania and Denmark). See also the declaration *It's time for more majority decision-making in EU foreign policy* of 12 June 2023 in which the foreign ministers of Germany, Belgium, Luxembourg, the Netherlands, Romania, Slovenia, and Spain declared their support for the use of voting methods and flexibility mechanisms provided for under Article 31 TEU, with the aim of enabling the EU to act more effectively and promptly in "an increasingly uncertain global arena", while also ensuring the proper functioning of its institutions in view of the Union's seventh enlargement.

[15] *Infra*, Sect. 5.2.

[16] Council Decision (CFSP) 2024/1471 of 21 May 2024 of 21 May 2024 on the allocation of the amounts of the financial contribution paid to the European Peace Facility pursuant to Decision (CFSP) 2024/1470 (OJ L 2024/1471).

In light of the above, this chapter will continue by examining recent developments in the application of Article 31 TEU. Section 5.2 will draw attention to the challenges of building the necessary consensus to adopt or renew restrictive measures in response to the conflict in Ukraine, and the use of temporary or calibrated derogations granted to specific Member States will also be discussed in this context. Section 5.2.1 will provide a commentary on the arguments invoked by the European Parliament in support of its annulment action against a CFSP Decision.[17] This is an important judicial development which contributes to strengthening the Parliament's role as a litigant in the context of the CFSP. This pending action constitutes a genuine opportunity to expand the use of qualified majority voting.

Next, the chapter will explore the impact of the war on the CSDP, with a special focus on constructive abstentions concerning the EUMAM Ukraine mission and the use of the European Peace Facility (EPF). It will argue that invoking the flexibility mechanism under Article 31(1) TEU has two possible effects. On the one hand, compensatory mechanisms may counterbalance the non-implementation of CFSP and CSDP decisions by Member States that have invoked constructive abstention; on the other hand, there may be a 'domino effect' attached to reliance on the flexibility mechanism: the loss of voting rights on implementing measures, an effect that is contested by Hungary in a pending case.[18]

Finally, the chapter will offer some concluding remarks on the war in Ukraine and its impact on the CFSP decision-making process, as well as on the persistent tension between preserving the unity of EU action and accommodating flexibility for Member States.

5.2 Restrictive Measures in Response to the War in Ukraine: The Challenge of Building Consensus

Following Russia's aggression against Ukraine in February 2022, the EU significantly intensified its restrictive measures against Moscow, which had already been sanctioned since 2014 for the unlawful annexation of Crimea. To date, the EU has

---

[17] Council Decision (CFSP) 2024/2643 of 8 October 2024 concerning restrictive measures in view of Russia's destabilising activities ST/8742/2024/INIT, OJ L 2024/2643.

[18] T-457/24, Hungary v Council and European Peace Facility Committee, action brought on 3 August 2024, in OJ C 2024/6266.

adopted eighteen sanctions packages,[19] with a nineteenth reportedly under consideration.[20] Belarus[21] and Iran[22] have also been subjected to EU restrictive measures for their support to Russia.

As is well known, sanctions targeting third countries, non-state actors, or individuals are enacted through a CFSP decision pursuant to Article 29 TEU, which must be adopted unanimously, upon proposal by the High Representative. Such a decision may directly impose restrictive measures, such as visa bans, which are to be implemented by Member States, economic measures, or other forms of bans.[23] CFSP decisions may be adopted to implement UN Security Council resolutions, or autonomously by the EU in response to internationally wrongful acts. Where a CFSP decision so requires, the Council, based on a joint proposal by the High Representative and the Commission and acting by qualified majority, will adopt a regulation under Article 215 TFEU, providing for the interruption or reduction of economic and financial relations with third countries, or other economic measures against individuals. Examples include restrictions on imports and exports of goods or services and asset freezes.

Consensus among Member States has at times proven difficult to achieve, particularly due to the strategic use of veto powers. A prominent example occurred in 2020, when the Council sought to expand the list of individuals sanctioned in Belarus in response to the government's repression of street protests against a rigged presidential election. The Republic of Cyprus exercised its veto, citing the Council's failure to consider a parallel proposal to sanction Turkey over its unauthorised drilling within Cyprus's territorial sea and in contested waters of the eastern Mediterranean. During negotiations with the other Member States in the Council, Nicosia did not consider the option of simple abstention or any other flexibility mechanism. Instead, Cyprus made the withdrawal of its veto subject to an EU common position against Turkey. The European Council adopted a position on Turkey on 1 October 2020[24]; Cyprus lifted its veto the following day; as a result the Council unanimously adopted the

---

[19] The framework for restrictive measures relies mainly on Decision 2014/512/CFSP of 31 July 2014 concerning restrictive measures in view of Russia's actions destabilising the situation in Ukraine, in OJ 229/2014, which, as of today, has undergone 51 amendments. It also relies on Decision (CFSP) 2024/2643 of 8 October 2024 concerning restrictive measures in view of Russia's destabilising activities, in OJ L 2024/2643.

[20] See Politico.eu 2025. On the impact of the war on the EU sanctions decision-making, with specific regard to the proposal phase, see Korkea-aho and Lonardo 2025. On the emergent role of the Commission as the leading institution in the domain of EU sanctions packages, see Miadzvetskaya 2025. See also Chap. 2 of this book for further comments.

[21] Council Decision 2012/642/CFSP of 15 October 2012 concerning restrictive measures in view of the situation in Belarus and the involvement of Belarus in the Russian aggression against Ukraine, in OJ L 285/2012.

[22] Council Decision (CFSP) 2023/1532 of 20 July 2023 concerning restrictive measures in view of Iran's military support to Russia's war of aggression against Ukraine and to armed groups and entities in the Middle East and the Red Sea region, in OJ L 186/2023.

[23] See Chap. 1.

[24] Conclusions, Brussels, 1–2 October 2020, points 16 ff.

decision to tighten sanctions on Belarus.[25] Shortly thereafter, the Council issued a CFSP decision updating the sanctions regime established in 2019 against Turkey.[26] It is worth noting that Cyprus could have opted for simple abstention to express its dissent. Its deliberate refusal to do so arguably constituted a breach of the duty of solidarity under Article 24(3) TEU[27] and, more broadly, of the principle of sincere cooperation enshrined in Article 4(3) TEU, as noted by scholars.[28] The use of the veto as a "bargaining chip for other negotiations"[29] in the context of sanctions against Minsk is a way to obstruct EU action.

Similar patterns have emerged in Hungary's conduct since 2022, with repeated instances of opposition to relevant decisions related to the war in Ukraine, including threats to veto restrictive measures in response to Russia's aggression. In January 2025, Prime Minister Orbán announced Hungary's intention to block the renewal of sanctions against Russia, set to expire on 31 January 2025,[30] arguing that they were detrimental to the European economy.[31] Hungary linked its veto to the cessation of Russian gas transit through Ukraine at the end of 2024, demanding its restoration as essential for Central European energy supply. Following intense negotiations and a commitment by the Commission to involve Hungary and Slovakia in discussions with Kiev to ensure energy continuity,[32] Orbán withdrew the veto,[33] allowing the sanctions to be extended for a further six months.[34] Slovakia also posed obstacles, particularly following the formation of the government led by Robert Fico. Most recently, after a month-long impasse,[35] Bratislava withdrew its veto on the eighteenth sanctions package against Russia, enabling its formal adoption on 18 July 2025.[36]

Thus, the requirement of consensus within the Council has at times necessitated prolonged negotiations to secure successive rounds of sanctions in response to the conflict. Despite the reluctance of certain Member States, the EU has nonetheless

---

[25] Council Implementing Decision (CFSP) 2020/1388 of 2 October 2020 implementing Decision 2012/642/CFSP concerning restrictive measures against Belarus, in OJ 319/2020.

[26] Council Decision (CFSP) 2020/1657 of 6 November 2020 amending Decision (CFSP) 2019/1894 concerning restrictive measures in view of Turkey's unauthorised drilling activities in the Eastern Mediterranean, in OJ L 372/2020.

[27] Along the same lines, see Poli and Pau 2020, p. 1511 ff.

[28] See Bottner and Wessel 2013, p. 1058.

[29] European Parliamentary Research Service 2023, p. 21.

[30] Council Decision (CFSP) 2024/2026 of 22 July 2024 amending Decision 2014/512/CFSP concerning restrictive measures in view of Russia's actions destabilising the situation in Ukraine, in OJ L, 2024/2026.

[31] See Euractiv.com 2025.

[32] See Europeannewsroom.com 2025, and Abouthungary.hu 2025.

[33] See Dailynewshungary.com 2025.

[34] Council Decision (CFSP) 2025/175 of 27 January 2025 amending Decision 2014/512/CFSP concerning restrictive measures in view of Russia's actions destabilising the situation in Ukraine, in OJ L, 2025/175.

[35] See Eunews.it 2025a.

[36] See Eunews.it 2025b.

succeeded in enacting an unprecedented sanctions regime in response to the Russo-Ukrainian war.

Building consensus has also been challenging for other reasons.

Special difficulties arose in connection with the approval of energy-related sanctions in June 2022, such as those prohibiting the import, purchase, or transfer into Member States of crude oil and certain petroleum products from Russia.[37] Several Member States, due to their geographical position, are significantly dependent on Russian pipeline gas, with no viable short-term alternatives. Consequently, the prohibition was not applied to those States until a further Council decision was adopted.[38] The technique used to accommodate the needs of a group of Member States without abandoning the adoption of the relevant restrictions is noteworthy. Derogation clauses were devised to overcome the vetoes of Russian-oil-dependent countries. The need to ensure unity in the EU's response to Russian aggression led the Council to carve out derogations in one of the most sensitive import prohibitions. This reflects an unprecedented willingness to compromise. The Council also approved 'calibrated derogations' for Bulgaria, Croatia, and Czechia. Bulgaria was permitted to import crude oil and petroleum products for a limited period; Croatia was granted a derogation to purchase vacuum gas oil from Russia under specific conditions; and Czechia obtained a ten-month suspension to enact the prohibition and secure alternative supplies. Landlocked States also received authorisation to import prohibited oil in exceptional circumstances.[39] In December 2022[40] these derogations were expanded in certain cases,[41] adjusted to prevent circumvention,[42] or tempered "in a spirit of solidarity with Ukraine".[43]

Thus, a certain degree of variable geometry applies to oil import restrictions. In our view, the reliance on derogations constitutes a pragmatic technique enabling the EU to reach agreement on 'sensitive' restrictive measures within the Council, while accommodating the specific needs of certain Member States. In this case, the uniform application of restrictive measures is sacrificed for the greater good—namely, the

[37] Council Decision (CFSP) 2022/884 of 3 June 2022 amending Decision 2014/512/CFSP concerning restrictive measures in view of Russia's actions destabilising the situation in Ukraine, in OJ L 153/2022.

[38] Ibidem, recital 8: "Those Member States should take all necessary measures to obtain alternative supplies as soon as possible".

[39] Ibidem, recital 12.

[40] Council Decision (CFSP) 2022/2478 of 16 December 2022 amending Decision 2014/512/CFSP concerning restrictive measures in view of Russia's actions destabilising the situation in Ukraine, in OJ L 322/2022.

[41] Bulgaria was allowed to export refined oil to third countries "in order to mitigate environmental and safety risks since such products cannot be stored safely in Bulgaria" (ibidem, recital 15).

[42] Bulgaria was also prohibited from selling petroleum products obtained from Russian crude oil imported to buyers located in other Member States or in third countries (ibidem).

[43] In that spirit, "it is appropriate to nevertheless allow Hungary, Slovakia and Bulgaria to export to Ukraine certain refined petroleum products obtained from Russian crude oil imported on the basis of the derogations in question, including, when necessary, by transiting through other Member States" (ibidem).

adoption of a common position on the conflict and a coordinated financial contribution to its resolution. It should be stressed that derogations are sometimes temporary and do not enable the countries concerned to avoid the application of restrictive measures indefinitely. As a result, derogations represent a form of flexibility in the CFSP decision-making process to reach temporary compromise solutions; yet, they cannot entirely replace the need to build consensus on the adoption or renewal of restrictive measures.

In this regard, one may wonder whether it would be possible and legitimate to have the Council approve restrictive measures by qualified majority voting—a development suggested by the Commission in 2018 and on subsequent occasions. As is well known, that could be achieved by activating the 'passerelle clause' under Article 31(3) TEU, thereby enabling the European Council to unanimously authorise the Council to adopt CFSP decisions by qualified majority, including those on restrictive measures. Should this development be implemented, outvoted Member States would be bound to respect the CFSP decision—unlike in cases of constructive abstention, which is therefore not a viable option for the adoption of CFSP decisions instituting restrictive measures.[44] However, if a dissenting Member State refused to comply with its obligations, the Commission would lack enforcement powers, and the ECJ would not have jurisdiction. By contrast, the Commission is empowered to act with respect to regulations enacted under Article 215 TFEU, and the ECJ has, in principle, jurisdiction to receive infringement actions against regulations. To date, the Commission has never exercised its enforcement powers in this context, given the inextricable link between TFEU regulations and the underlying CFSP decisions. This practice may be subject to changes.

Unity in the EU's sanctions policy is essential to ensuring the effectiveness of restrictive measures—not only for the substantive reasons outlined above, but also with regard to the credibility and long-term sustainability of those measures.[45] The positions of the Member States are therefore deeply interdependent in the implementation of sanctions, a dynamic that is unique to the CFSP framework. In this context, it is doubtful whether qualified majority voting is suitable for adopting the initial CFSP decisions that provide for restrictive measures.[46] The aforesaid interdependence applies both to individual restrictive measures adopted by the Council under a CFSP decision—such as visa bans—and to regulations enacted under Article 215 TFEU, which are necessary for sanctions of an economic nature. It is worth recalling that unity and unanimous implementation are imperative not only when the EU acts autonomously, but even more so when restrictive measures are coordinated with third countries. This is particularly true in relation to the so-called like-minded partners, which impose identical sanctions on the same targets, thereby amplifying their

44 Bartoloni 2023, pp. 1121–1130.

45 See also Beaucillon 2018, p. 396.

46 See Poli 2019.

impact and effectiveness.[47] The same applies to third countries that are candidates for EU accession, as well as to members of the European Free Trade Association and the European Economic Area, whom the EU regularly invites to align with its restrictive measures, with the aim of maximising their overall effect.[48]

Although numerous legal scholars have advocated for the use of constructive abstention as an alternative to qualified majority voting in the adoption of restrictive measures, its practical viability remains questionable.[49] In our view, the imperative of uniform implementation makes constructive abstention unsuitable in this context. Unsurprisingly, there are no recorded instances of constructive abstention in CFSP decisions imposing or amending sanctions against third States, State organs, or private parties. Uniformity would be compromised in case of differentiated application across Member States.[50] Consider, for example, a visa ban prohibiting a sanctioned individual from entering or transiting through the territory of EU Member States. If even one Member State were to constructively abstain from the CFSP decision establishing or modifying such a measure, the ban would not be uniformly applied, thereby enabling the individual to access part of the EU territory. As a result, the deterrent effect of the EU sanction at stake would be undermined. Similar concerns apply to other restrictive measures—such as asset freezes, arms embargoes, or trade restrictions on specific goods—whose impact likewise depends on uniform implementation.

In practice, Member States occasionally resort to simple abstention under Article 238(4) TFEU to express dissent in this specific area of the CFSP. In our opinion, this happens in order to avoid jeopardising the unanimous application of restrictive measures. It is the case, for instance, of Hungary's simple abstention on restrictive measures targeting individuals affiliated with Hamas and Islamic Jihad.[51] Reliance on constructive abstention by Hungary when discussing restrictive measures may be interpreted as an indication that this country feels bound by the duty of solidarity enshrined in Article 24(3) TEU.[52] This interpretation, however, does not hold true for CFSP decision-making after the outbreak of the war in Ukraine. The challenge of building consensus in response to this war lies in managing potential vetoes raised by

---

[47] See Reuters.com 2024 about Council Decision (CFSP) 2024/2783 of 29 October 2024 amending Decision 2013/184/CFSP concerning restrictive measures in view of the situation in Myanmar/Burma, in OJ L 2024/2783.

[48] See EEAS 2024. E.g., see the sanctions against Turkey for unauthorised drilling in the Eastern Mediterranean, with which Albania, Armenia, Bosnia and Herzegovina, Iceland, North Macedonia, Montenegro, and Serbia aligned. See also *Statement by the High Representative on behalf of the EU on the alignment of certain third countries with Council Decision (CFSP) 2025/484 concerning restrictive measures in view of Türkiye's unauthorised drilling activities in the Eastern Mediterranean*, 21 March 2025.

[49] See Pomorska and Wessel 2021.

[50] See Portela and Olsen 2023.

[51] Council Decision (CFSP) 2024/1837 of 28 June 2024 amending Decision (CFSP) 2024/385 establishing restrictive measures against those who support, facilitate or enable violent actions by Hamas and the Palestinian Islamic Jihad, in OJ L 2024/1837. In that regard, see Eunews.it 2024.

[52] See Bartoloni 2023, p. 1128.

one or more Member States—whether for legitimate concerns, such as energy supply, or for strategic purposes. In the latter case, the political motivations underlying the instrumental use of the veto—Hungary being a prominent example—reveal a deliberate attempt to undermine European unity on the position to be taken on Russia's aggression against Ukraine. As a result, appeals to loyal cooperation fall on the deaf ears of the Member State concerned.

Ultimately, given that invoking constructive abstention in the context of the approval of restrictive measures is not possible, simple abstention and temporary derogations assume a more prominent role, alongside the political negotiations conducted in Brussels, which frequently prove decisive in resolving seemingly intractable disagreements.

That said, while the above considerations apply specifically to restrictive measures, the application of Article 31(2), third indent, TEU cannot be excluded in other areas. A transition to a faster decision-making procedure within the CFSP is both feasible and desirable. Such a development could be pursued in other domains of the CFSP—for instance, to adopt common positions in UN bodies in response to human rights violations, as suggested by the Commission in its Communication of 2018[53]—or within the specific framework of the CSDP.

5.2.1 Restrictive Measures in Response to Russian Aggression Against Ukraine: A Test Case for the First-Ever Use of Article 31(2), Third Indent, TEU

While unanimity is bound to remain the prevailing voting rule for the adoption of EU restrictive measures, the action for annulment brought by the Parliament in October 2024 may represent a golden opportunity towards a wider use of qualified majority voting in the CFSP.[54]

The action concerns a Council Implementing Decision of an initial CFSP decision, which in the applicant's view should have been adopted on the basis of Article 31(2), third indent, TEU. More specifically, the Parliament requests the annulment of CFSP Decision 2024/2643[55] on restrictive measures in response to Russia's destabilising activities. The adoption of this act proved contentious, with Slovakia and Hungary introducing political and negotiating obstacles within the Council, thereby delaying

[53] European Commission 2018, p. 11. The Commission suggested to rely on Article 31(3) TEU to introduce qualified majority voting in the Council for the adoption of EU positions on human rights in international fora.

[54] C-883/24, *Parliament v Council*, action brought on 19 December 2024, in OJ C 2025/899.

[55] Council Decision (CFSP) 2024/2643 of 8 October 2024 concerning restrictive measures in view of Russia's destabilising activities ST/8742/2024/INIT, OJ L, 2024/2643, 9.10.2024, ELI: http://data.europa.eu/eli/dec/2024/2643/oj.

and influencing its adoption.[56] We contend that the Parliament's legal challenge reflects, on the one hand, a broader frustration with the strategic use of veto powers in the realm of restrictive measures and, on the other hand, the wish to test to the full potential the opportunities to vote by qualified majority provided for by the Lisbon Treaty.

It is useful to examine the legal pleas and main arguments advanced by the Parliament, while offering some preliminary reflections on them.

The applicant alleges that Article 31(2), third indent, TEU is breached insofar as Article 4(1) of the contested CFSP Decision stipulates that the Council, acting by unanimity, shall decide to establish and amend the list of sanctioned natural and legal persons, entities, and bodies. Yet, the primary provision of Article 31(2) TEU explicitly provides that certain decisions shall be adopted by qualified majority when implementing a prior unanimous decision that defines an EU action or position. By requiring unanimity for the implementation of the prior Decision, the Council arguably contravened the express wording of Article 31(2) TEU.

In our view, the Parliament's claim is well-founded.

Given that the initial Decision adopting a common position on Russia's destabilising activities was adopted unanimously, subsequent implementing decisions may be qualified as acts to be adopted by qualified majority voting, under Article 31(2), third indent, TEU. Thus, it is essential to clarify the meaning of 'implementing measure' within the meaning of the third indent of Article 31(2) TEU, as the scope of this term determines which decisions following an initial CFSP decision—namely, Council implementing decisions—may be adopted by qualified majority. A possible interpretation of the aforesaid provision is that once the decision to sanction specific legal persons, entities, and bodies has been taken and an initial list established, the inclusion of new entries in this initial act does not alter the political content of the original decision, which therefore may be adopted by qualified majority voting.

A possible supporting argument is that the CFSP decision that includes specific names of individuals and other non-state entities in the blacklist of sanctioned legal persons, entities, and bodies is an 'implementing act', because the Council applies objective criteria—the designation criteria[57]—and simply selects the subjects who meet them. There could be a parallel between an 'implementing act' and the notion of "subsequent acts applying or otherwise putting in motion the basic Council Decision", which the Council has distinguished from "legal acts amending substantially the basic Council Decision",[58] in the context of EU peace missions. In our view, the inclusion of new entries in the blacklist is an example of a subsequent act that 'puts in motion' the initial decision and can therefore be voted by qualified majority. This clearly differs from a legal act that 'substantially amends' the initial decision"—for instance by extending the types of sanctions of the original sanction regime, or

[56] See The Moscow Times 2024.

[57] See Chaps. 2, 3 in the present book.

[58] Statement made by a representative of the Council Legal Service during the vote on the CFSP decision concerning EUMAM Ukraine, in respect of which Hungary constructively abstained.

by adding new designation criteria—and would require unanimous approval by the Council.

The case-law concerning Article 291(2) TFEU (as well as the provisions of the EU treaties that preceded it) also seems to support the Parliament's position. In general, the ECJ has repeatedly affirmed that "the concept of 'implementation' comprises both the drawing-up of implementing rules and the application of rules to specific cases by means of acts of individual application".[59] Moreover, in the field of restrictive measures the Court provided more detailed guidance in its judgment of 2016 on sanctions imposed on the National Iranian Oil Company (NIOC).[60]

The case concerned the appeal against the judgment by which the General Court had dismissed the application for annulment brought by NIOC against two acts imposing restrictive economic and financial measures on Iran, namely (i) Decision 2012/635/CFSP[61] amending Decision 2010/413/CFSP,[62] and (ii) Council Implementing Regulation 945/2012[63] implementing Regulation 267/2012.[64] For the purposes of this analysis, it should be recalled that the Grand Chamber observed that Council Implementing Regulation 945/2012 constituted "a specific application of the general listing criterion relating to the provision of support to the Government of Iran and was intended to ensure, within the framework of the FEU Treaty, that the imposition on NIOC of the restrictive measures dictated by the situation in Iran was implemented uniformly throughout the European Union".[65] The ECJ thus classified the inclusion of a new entity in an existing list of sanctioned individuals and entities as an act of an executive nature, insofar as the listing was based on predetermined general criteria and, therefore, devoid of discretionary elements.

In our view, not all CFSP decisions implementing a CFSP act must be adopted unanimously. Indeed, the inclusion of a new entry, based on predetermined criteria, in the list of individuals and entities constitutes a purely implementing act. Such listings are implemented by the Council through decisions adopted pursuant to the underlying CFSP decision.[66] It follows that if CFSP decisions add new names to pre-established

[59] C-521/15, *Spain v Council*, Opinion of Advocate General, 1 June 2017, ECLI:EU:C:2017:420.

[60] C-440/14 P, 1 March 2016, *National Iranian Oil Company v Council*, 1 March 2016, ECLI:EU:C:2016:128.

[61] Council Decision 2012/635/CFSP of 15 October 2012 amending Decision 2010/413/CFSP concerning restrictive measures against Iran, in OJ L 282/2012.

[62] Council Decision of 26 July 2010 concerning restrictive measures against Iran and repealing Common Position 2007/140/CFSP, in OJ L 195/2010.

[63] Council Implementing Regulation (EU) No 945/2012 of 15 October 2012 implementing Regulation (EU) No 267/2012 concerning restrictive measures against Iran, in OJ L 282/2012.

[64] Council Regulation (EU) No 267/2012 of 23 March 2012 concerning restrictive measures against Iran and repealing Regulation (EU) No 961/2010, in OJ L 88/2012.

[65] C-440/14 P, above n. 60, paras 37 ff. (in particular, para 40).

[66] See Article 291(2) TFEU, which stipulates that, in duly justified specific cases and within the framework of the CFSP, the Council shall exercise implementing powers conferred by legally binding acts of the EU—which include initial CFSP decisions. On this topic, see C-521/15, *Spain v Council*, 20 December 2017, ECLI:EU:C:2017:982, para 47. For a commentary on the case, see Chamon 2018.

lists of sanctioned entities, they may be adopted by qualified majority voting under Article 31(2), third indent, TEU, rather than by unanimity, as they do not constitute legal acts that—to borrow the words of the Council Legal Service—"substantially" amend the "basic decision".[67]

The Council may claim that the power of implementing CFSP decisions belongs to it, since there is a clear basis for that power in the treaties, namely in Article 291(2) TFEU, Article 24(1), second indent, TEU and Article 26(2) TEU. The implementing powers of the Council in the context of the CFSP are different from those enshrined in non-CFSP areas,[68] which are much more limited and reserved to specific circumstances and conditions.[69] Therefore, even if the decision to include specific names of individuals in the blacklist can be regarded as an "implementing act[70]" rather than a political act, the implementing powers in the context of the CFSP belong to the Council, and the Court has broadly construed the Council's prerogative to reserve these powers for itself.[71] Or, by relying on another interpretation, the Council could claim that the inclusion of a subject in the blacklist amounts to a political decision, thus requiring the unanimity vote. The Court might take a narrow interpretation of the Council's CFSP implementing powers in order to protect the "effect utile" of Article 31(2), third indent, TEU and the possibility of adopting an "implementing act" by qualified majority—and in doing so, it would be upholding the Parliament's argument. As a matter of fact, such an interpretation would be in line with the CJEU's case-law, which has progressively knocked down the specificities of the CFSP. Moreover, the Council may argue that not all inclusions in the list of sanctioned individuals carry equal weight, as the political profile of certain figures may warrant unanimous consent prior to their inclusion. A case in point is the proposed listing of Patriarch Kirill of Moscow under the EU's sixth sanctions package of May 2022. As is well known, his name was removed from the final list following Hungary's opposition,

---

[67] In this regard, it is worth recalling the "Non-Binding Criteria for the application of Articles 290 and 291 of the Treaty on the Functioning of the European Union"—18 June 2019, in OJ C 223/2019. In particular, Rule D stipulates that "additional rules implementing or giving effect to the rules already established in the basic act by specifying in further detail the content of that act, without affecting the substance of the legislative framework, should be laid down in implementing acts. This would be the case where a *sufficiently precise legal framework* has been laid down by the legislator, for example where the main conditions and criteria are laid down by the legislator" (emphasis added). In the case at hand, the 'sufficiently precise legal framework' may well be constituted by the predetermined general criteria governing the listing of sanctioned individuals and entities.

[68] Article 291(2) TFEU.

[69] For a discussion of this issue see Chamon 2023, pp. 1696–1697.

[70] This is so because, by amending the list of names in the annexes of the basic act, the Council applies objective designation criteria to a specific situation without amending the text of the basic act itself. Authority for this interpretation may be found in *National Iranian Oil Company*, above n. 60, para 36, where the Court stated: 'It should be added that, according to the case-law of the Court, the concept of 'implementation' comprises both the drawing-up of implementing rules and the application of rules to specific cases by means of acts of individual application (judgment in *Commission v Council*, 16/88, EU:C:1989:397, para 11).'

[71] See above n. 60.

which resulted in a veto.[72] In this respect, the Court could side with the Council and consider that the decision to include an individual's name in the list is a political decision and, therefore, cannot be the subject of an implementing act that is put to a vote. As a consequence, the Court could find that Ar. 31(2), third indent, TEU is not applicable.

The second plea advanced by the Parliament concerns the alleged violation of Article 40 TEU. According to the applicant, the requirement for the Council to act unanimously within the CFSP framework influences the subsequent procedure under Article 215 TFEU, thereby altering the conditions for adopting the implementing Regulation. The Parliament contends that this undermines the procedural parallelism between the TEU and the TFEU, both of which are generally based on qualified majority voting. Consequently, the shift from qualified majority to unanimity in the contested CFSP Decision is said to distort the institutional balance envisaged by the Treaties for the adoption of restrictive measures.

On this point, we respectfully disagree with the Parliament.

The alleged procedural parallelism is deprived of a solid foundation. On the one hand, regardless of the voting rule used to adopt a Council implementing decision, any subsequent Regulation is adopted by qualified majority under Article 215(1) TFEU, a provision that sets out autonomous procedural rules which are independent from Article 31 TEU. On the other hand, the CJEU has never recognised a procedural parallelism between the CFSP and the TFEU. Rather, the Court has referred to the substantive link between the objectives pursued under the TEU in the CFSP and the actions falling within the scope of the TFEU, thereby enabling the enactment of restrictive measures of an economic and financial nature.[73] As noted by the CJEU, the wording of Article 215 TFEU plays a crucial role in interpreting primary law. In the *Neves 77* case, the use of the modal verb 'shall' in para 1 of Article 215 TFEU—"shall adopt", as opposed to "may adopt" in para 2—led the Court to conclude that the Council is under a binding obligation to implement a CFSP decision within the TFEU framework.[74] Similarly, it may be argued that since Article 215(1) TFEU explicitly provides for adoption by qualified majority of the "necessary measures," the voting threshold is unequivocal and should not be altered merely because the Council's implementing decision or the measure that gives effect to a CFSP decision (usually a Regulation) was adopted unanimously. These considerations may lead the CJEU to conclude that the alleged breach of Article 40 TEU is unfounded.

Nonetheless, two aspects of this pending case deserve closer attention.

First, the High Representative was granted leave to intervene in support of the form of order sought by the Parliament, on the grounds that it had an interest in the outcome of the case.[75] The contested decision was adopted on the basis of a

[72] See Politico.eu 2022.

[73] C-130/10, *Parliament v Council*, 19 July 2012, EU:C:2012:472, para 59, and subsequent consistent case law.

[74] C-351/22, *Neves 77 Solutions*, 10 September 2024, ECLI:EU:C:2024:723, para 46.

[75] C-883/24, *Parliament v Council*, Order of the President of the Court, 8 April 2025, ECLI:EU:C:2025:277.

proposal by the High Representative, who exercised her right of initiative under Article 30(1) TEU. Notably, the High Representative's original proposal did not include the requirement contested by the Parliament—namely, that the envisaged decision be adopted by unanimity.[76] Once the Council introduced this requirement, the High Representative challenged the amendment, arguing that it infringed Article 31(2) TEU by disregarding the prescribed use of qualified majority voting. The participation in the proceedings is therefore likely to have a decisive impact on the interpretation of her institutional powers.[77]

Second, this case sheds light on the inconsistent practice surrounding restrictive measures, particularly with respect to the voting procedure applicable to implementing acts. Unlike the contested decision that the Parliament is seeking to have annulled, not all CFSP decisions specify the voting rule required for subsequent amendments. In some cases, the Council is expressly required to adopt and amend restrictive measures by unanimity.[78] In others, the relevant decisions merely refer to the Council adopting and amending sanctions,[79] without further specifications, and this may be taken to mean that qualified majority voting can be used to enact the

---

[76] Proposal from the High Representative of the Union for Foreign Affairs and Security Policy to the Council of 02/05/2025 for a Council Decision amending Decision (CFSP) 2024/2643 concerning restrictive measures in view of Russia's destabilising activities, ST 8423 2025 INIT, 7 May 2025.

[77] Ibidem, paras 10 ff.

[78] Council Decision (CFSP) 2024/385 of 19 January 2024 establishing restrictive measures against those who support, facilitate or enable violent actions by Hamas and the Palestinian Islamic Jihad, in OJ L 2024/385; Council Decision (CFSP) 2024/254 of 12 January 2024 concerning restrictive measures in view of the situation in Guatemala, in OJ L 2024/254; Council Decision (CFSP) 2023/2135 of 9 October 2023 concerning restrictive measures in view of activities undermining the stability and political transition of Sudan, in OJ L 2023/2135; Council Decision (CFSP) 2023/1574 of 28 July 2023 amending Decision (CFSP) 2022/2319 concerning restrictive measures in view of the situation in Haiti, in OJ L 192/2023; Council Decision (CFSP) 2023/1532 of 20 July 2023 concerning restrictive measures in view of Iran's military support to Russia's war of aggression against Ukraine, in OJ L 186/2023; Council Decision (CFSP) 2021/1277 of 30 July 2021 concerning restrictive measures in view of the situation in Lebanon, in OJ L 277/2021; Council Decision (CFSP) 2019/797 of 17 May 2019 concerning restrictive measures against cyber-attacks threatening the Union or its Member States, in OJ L 129/2019; and Council Decision (CFSP) 2016/849 of 27 May 2016 concerning restrictive measures against the Democratic People's Republic of Korea and repealing Decision 2013/183/CFSP, in OJ L 141/2016.

[79] Council Decision (CFSP) 2017/1775 of 28 September 2017 concerning restrictive measures in view of the situation in Mali, in OJ L 251/2017; Council Decision (CFSP) 2015/1333 of 31 July 2015 concerning restrictive measures in view of the situation in Libya, and repealing Decision 2011/137/CFSP, in OJ L 206/2015; Council Decision (CFSP) 2015/740 of 7 May 2015 concerning restrictive measures in view of the situation in South Sudan and repealing Decision 2014/449/CFSP, in OJ L 117/2015; Council Decision 2014/450/CFSP of 10 July 2014 concerning restrictive measures in view of the situation in Sudan and repealing Decision 2011/423/CFSP, in OJ L 203/2014; Council Decision 2013/255/CFSP of 31 May 2013 concerning restrictive measures against Syria, in OJ L 147/2013; Council Decision 2012/642/CFSP of 15 October 2012 concerning restrictive measures against Belarus, in OJ L 285/2012; Council Decision 2011/101/CFSP of 15 February 2011 concerning restrictive measures against Zimbabwe, in OJ L 42/2011; Council Decision 2010/788/CFSP of 20 December 2010 concerning restrictive measures against the Democratic Republic of the Congo and repealing Common Position 2008/369/CFSP, in OJ L 336/2010; Council Decision 2010/656/CFSP of 29 October 2010 renewing the restrictive measures against Côte d'Ivoire, in OJ L

implementing act. A separate mention must be made of Decision 2014/512/CFSP on restrictive measures against Russia. Until June 2024, this decision contained no provision regarding the voting rule for amending the annexes listing sanctioned individuals. However, Decision (CFSP) 2024/1744 introduced Article 8c, which states: "The Council, acting by unanimity on the basis of Articles 29 and 30 of the Treaty on European Union, shall amend Annexes".[80] Should the CJEU consider the Parliament's application admissible and uphold the Parliament's action, thus confirming that qualified majority voting could be used in adopting Council Implementing Decisions, a substantial portion of existing practice on restrictive measures would require reconsideration.[81]

In any event, these reflections remain preliminary, given the pending nature of the case. We will need to wait for the conclusions of Advocate General Ćapeta and the Court's final decision.

5.3 The Impact of the War in Ukraine on the Adoption of CSDP Decisions

The EU has responded to the outbreak of the war in Ukraine by supporting Ukraine in the context of the CSDP.

On one hand, in October 2022, the EU launched the EUMAM Ukraine mission, aimed at training Ukrainian armed forces in the territory of selected Member States. The mission's objective is to enhance Ukraine's capacity to defend its territorial integrity and to protect civilians in the context of ongoing hostilities.[82] On the other hand, the Union provided financial assistance to bolster Ukraine's defence capabilities through the EPF,[83] by supplying lethal and non-lethal military equipment. The decision to deliver the former category of military material was controversial. At the institutional level, the EU adopted the Strategic Compass in March 2022, shortly after the outbreak of the war, thereby reaffirming its strategic orientation in the field of security and defence.[84]

The provision of lethal equipment to third States via the EPF has prompted an increase in the use of constructive abstention under Article 31(1) TEU, particularly by

285/2010; and Council Decision 2010/231/CFSP of 26 April 2010 concerning restrictive measures against Somalia and repealing Common Position 2009/138/CFSP, in OJ L 105/2010.

80 Article 1(25) of the Council Decision (CFSP) 2024/1744 of 24 June 2024 amending Decision 2014/512/CFSP concerning restrictive measures in view of Russia's actions destabilising the situation in Ukraine, in OJ L 2024/1744.

81 In this regard, one may wonder why the Parliament did not also challenge Decision (CFSP) 2024/1744.

82 Council Decision (CFSP) 2022/1968 of 17 October 2022 on a European Union Military Assistance Mission in support of Ukraine (EUMAM Ukraine), in OJ L 270/2022.

83 Council Decision (CFSP) 2021/509 of 22 March 2021 establishing a European Peace Facility, and repealing Decision (CFSP) 2015/528, in OJ L 102/2021.

84 On the Strategic Compass and recent developments in the ESDP, see Chap. 10 in this book.

neutral Member States (Austria, Ireland and Malta).[85] Hungary joined this group but its conduct warrants specific attention: it constructively abstained from Council decisions concerning support to Ukraine, more precisely those involving 'lethal supplies' and the establishment of the EUMAM Ukraine mission. This behaviour illustrates Budapest's selective use of the flexibility mechanism provided under Article 31(1) TEU, an approach shaped by the pro-Russian orientation of the Orbán government.[86]

The following sections will examine this practice in greater detail, with a special focus on the legal implications of constructive abstention in the context of CSDP decision-making.

5.3.1 *The Legal Consequences of Constructive Abstention and the Principle of Mutual Solidarity*

In October 2022 Hungary constructively abstained from Council Decision (CFSP) 2022/1968, which established the EUMAM Ukraine mission. In its accompanying statement—offering no substantive justification for its refusal to support the decision—Budapest specified that "Hungary's constructive abstention is on the understanding that Hungary will participate in any future deliberations of the Council concerning proposals for the amendment of the Council Decision on EUMAM Ukraine. Hungary reserves the right to exercise its voting rights at its full discretion when the Council votes on such proposals".[87] Budapest's intention to preserve its ability to influence subsequent measures adopted in implementation of the initial CFSP decision is clear. Yet, it does not seem legally justified. Indeed, reliance on constructive abstention triggers a 'domino effect': a Member State that has constructively abstained from an initial CFSP decision cannot participate in the adoption of implementing measures whose existence is inextricably linked to that underlying instrument.

From a theoretical perspective, this effect is grounded in the concept of logical-legal interdependence between legal acts—a notion rooted in the classical legal tradition. This appears to be the meaning of the statement made by the Council Legal Service during the meeting in which Hungary declared its constructive abstention. As clarified by a representative of the Council Legal Service, "the legal consequence of the formal declaration of constructive abstention, pursuant to the second subparagraph of Article 31(1) TEU concerning the Council Decision on EUMAM Ukraine,

[85] See Council Decision (CFSP) 2023/927 of 5 May 2023 on an assistance measure under the European Peace Facility to support the Ukrainian Armed Forces through the provision of ammunition, ST/7344/2023/INIT OJ L 123/2023.

[86] For an analysis of such conduct prior to the outbreak of the war, see Pomorska and Wessel 2021, p. 356. Slovakia appears to be adopting a comparable stance, having ceased the provision of military assistance to Ukraine and currently contemplating its withdrawal from both the EUMAM UA and EPF initiatives. Moreover, it has reportedly threatened to veto forthcoming sanctions against Russia (see Genini 2025, p. 25).

[87] Council, doc. 13777/22, Brussels, 27 October 2022, point 5.

is that, in accordance with the Treaty, Hungary will not be obliged to apply that Council Decision, while, in a spirit of mutual solidarity, it will have to refrain from any action likely to conflict with, or impede, Union action based on that Decision; the other Member States will have to respect Hungary's position. The Legal Service clarified that this means that the constructive abstention will necessarily cover all subsequent acts applying or otherwise putting in motion the basic Council Decision, such as the approval of the mission plan or appointment of the mission commander. On the other hand, Hungary will have the possibility to use its voting rights differently for legal acts amending substantially the basic Council Decision, such as its renewal or the decision to move the mission in Ukraine".[88]

We do not fully endorse the interpretation offered by the Council Legal Service, which appears to construe in an unduly narrow manner the scope of subsequent acts deriving from the basic decision—acts to which constructive abstention should apply, thereby excluding the dissenting Member State from the vote. While we agree that such acts include, for example, the approval of the mission plan or the appointment of the commander, it remains unclear why the renewal of the mission or the decision to conduct training of Ukrainian forces on their own territory should be classified as "legal acts substantially amending the basic Council Decision", and thus fall outside the scope of the 'domino effect'. In our view, a "substantial" amendment to the basic decision—one that, according to the Council Legal Service, would require the participation of the dissenting Member State in the vote—should concern changes of the decision that significantly alter the original mandate of the mission, such as the inclusion of operational tasks in a wartime context or, more significantly, direct defensive activities on Ukrainian soil (e.g., the protection of civilian infrastructure such as hospitals). That said, in our view, considering the aforementioned logical-legal interdependence between legal acts, one could argue that the so-called 'domino effect' ought to be interpreted in a more expansive manner, reflecting the fact that the Member State invoking constructive abstention has, from the outset, dissociated itself from the substance of the underlying CFSP decision. Accordingly, it should no longer be entitled to participate in decisions that shape or implement the action initially adopted by the Union.

Coming back to the position of the Council Legal Service, this is unequivocal: the invocation of constructive abstention entails the impossibility of voting on, at the very least, "all subsequent acts applying or otherwise putting in motion the basic Council Decision". As we shall see, the 'domino effect' triggered Hungary's reaction not in relation to EUMAM Ukraine itself, but rather with respect to the use of the EPF for the provision of lethal equipment to Kiev.[89] Nevertheless, Hungary's constructive abstention from EUMAM Ukraine appears to have marked a turning point in its position on supporting Ukraine, including in relation to the EPF. Indeed, prior to the establishment of EUMAM Ukraine in on 17 October 2022,[90] there is no

[88] Ibidem, Ad "A" item 9.

[89] *Infra*, Sect. 5.3.4.

[90] In this regard, see Genini 2025, p. 25. See also Council Decision (CFSP) 2022/338 of 28 February 2022 on an assistance measure under the European Peace Facility for the supply to the Ukrainian

record of Hungary invoking constructive abstention in connection with the provision of lethal weapons to the Ukrainian armed forces. However, just one month later, Budapest began to systematically use constructive abstention for all decisions on this matter. In its statement at the meeting of 14–15 November 2022,[91] the Hungarian government maintained that its abstention with regard to the delivery of lethal force corresponded "to its constructive abstention from Council Decision (CFSP) 2022/1968 on a European Union Military Assistance Mission in support of Ukraine".[92]

A precedent for the use of constructive abstention had already been set during the adoption of the CFSP decision establishing the EPF, namely Council Decision (CFSP) 2021/509 of 22 March 2021 (hereinafter, the EPF Decision).[93] Sweden, Austria, Ireland, and Malta issued statements in which, while expressing support for the CFSP decision under adoption, they nonetheless voiced concern over the potential use of the EPF to deliver lethal equipment in sensitive contexts. Notably, Sweden employed a formulation that was not entirely unequivocal, stating that its "right to constructively abstain is not in any way contingent on the character of its security and defence policy. Any such decision will be based on national considerations, including a context-based and case by case risk assessment of the proposed assistance measure".[94] These Member States thereby signalled their intention to invoke constructive abstention in future decisions concerning individual deliveries.[95]

Following the entry into force of the EPF and the emergence of concrete needs to supply lethal equipment to certain third States—including Ukraine—Austria, Ireland, and Malta formally invoked constructive abstention.[96] Their declarations adopted a largely standardised format, structured around three core elements.[97] First, each State expressed its intention to abstain from the Council decision "in accordance

Armed Forces of military equipment, and platforms, designed to deliver lethal force, in OJ L 60/2022; Council Decision (CFSP) 2022/636 of 13 April 2022 amending Decision (CFSP) 2022/338 on an assistance measure under the European Peace Facility for the supply to the Ukrainian Armed Forces of military equipment, and platforms, designed to deliver lethal force, in OJ L 117/2022; and Council Decision (CFSP) 2022/1971 of 17 October 2022 amending Decision (CFSP) 2022/338 on an assistance measure under the European Peace Facility for the supply to the Ukrainian Armed Forces of military equipment, and platforms, designed to deliver lethal force, in OJ L 270/2022.

[91] Council, doc. 14945/22, Brussels, 9 January 2023.

[92] Ibidem.

[93] Council Decision (CFSP) 2021/509.

[94] Council, doc. 7397/21, Brussels, 19 April 2021, especially the statements on item "A".

[95] See European Parliamentary Research Service 2022, p. 62 ff.

[96] E.g., see Council, doc. 8900/1/24, Brussels, 30 May 2024 regarding constructive abstentions declared by Austria, Ireland and Malta on Council Decision (CFSP) 2024/1713 of 13 June 2024 on an assistance measure under the European Peace Facility to support the Armed Forces of the Republic of Moldova with military equipment designed to deliver lethal force, in OJ L 2024/1713.

[97] As of 30 August 2025, there have been a total of nineteen cases. The first dates back to Council Decision (CFSP) 2022/338 of 28 February 2022 on an assistance measure under the European Peace Facility for the supply to the Ukrainian Armed Forces of military equipment, and platforms, designed to deliver lethal force, in OJ L 60/2022, while the latest concerns Council Decision (CFSP) 2025/809 of 23 April 2025 on an assistance measure under the European Peace Facility to support the Armed Forces of the Republic of Moldova with military equipment designed to deliver lethal

with the second subparagraph of Article 31(1) of the TEU". Second, they affirmed their commitment to refrain from any action that might conflict with or hinder the implementation of EU action based on that decision, in a spirit of mutual solidarity. Third, they signalled their willingness to financially support assistance measures benefiting the third State through a voluntary elective contribution, provided such measures did not entail the provision of lethal equipment. By contrast, Sweden has not, to date, issued any formal declaration of constructive abstention, despite having expressed reservations during the adoption of the EPF's founding act. Its earlier statements indicated a cautious approach, but no formal invocation of the flexibility mechanism has followed.

In the case of Hungary, its constructive abstentions have specifically concerned lethal assistance measures adopted after the establishment of EUMAM Ukraine. In particular, Hungary has voted in favour of similar measures directed toward other third States. To date, there is no record of constructive abstention by the Hungarian government with respect to lethal supplies approved for various third countries.[98] Hungary's declarations largely mirror those issued by neutral Member States, yet differ in their final clause, whereby Budapest reserves the right to identify, pending on a decision that will be made later, an existing or possible future assistance measure or propose a new one, to which it will provide a corresponding contribution pursuant to Article 5(3)[99]". This formulation reflects Hungary's intention to retain discretion over its financial participation in EPF-supported measures, while maintaining its political distance from providing lethal weapons to Ukraine. Furthermore, Hungary invoked constructive abstention in relation to sostituisci con 'weapons' the decision establishing the Ukraine Assistance Fund[100]—a dedicated allocation within the EPF financed through windfall profits generated from frozen Russian assets, following the imposition of restrictive measures against Moscow.[101] This abstention underscores Hungary's broader reluctance to endorse measures perceived as directly supporting Ukraine's military efforts, even when such initiatives are framed within the Union's financial and strategic instruments.

force, in OJ L, 2025/809. Half of these supplies were destined for Ukraine, while the remaining supplies were sent to the armed forces of Benin, Moldova, Nigeria and Somalia.

[98] E.g., in the case of Decision (CFSP) 2024/1713 on an assistance measure to support the Armed Forces of Moldova.

[99] E.g., *supra* fn. 91.

[100] Council Decision (CFSP) 2024/890 of 18 March 2024 amending Decision (CFSP) 2021/509 establishing a European Peace Facility, in OJ L 2024/890. See dailynewshungary.com 2024 and budapesttimes.hu 2024.

[101] See Chap. 6. Council Decision (CFSP) 2024/1470 of 21 May 2024 amending Decision 2014/512/CFSP concerning restrictive measures in view of Russia's actions destabilising the situation in Ukraine, in OJ L 2024/1470, and Council Decision (CFSP) 2024/1471 of 21 May 2024 on the allocation of the amounts of the financial contribution paid to the European Peace Facility pursuant to Decision (CFSP) 2024/1470, in OJ L 2024/1471, and also Council Regulation (EU) 2024/1469 of 21 May 2024 amending Regulation (EU) No 833/2014 concerning restrictive measures in view of Russia's actions destabilising the situation in Ukraine, in OJ L 2024/1469.

5.3.2 Are Compensatory Measures Mandatory for Member States Invoking Constructive Abstention in the CSDP?

This limited yet significant practice illustrates the underlying rationale of constructive abstention: transforming a veto into a non-obstructive stance, thereby enabling the EU to act on the international stage. The dissenting Member State is not required to implement the CFSP decision but must refrain from obstructing its execution. As a consequence, the operational burden must be redistributed among the Member States that supported the decision. To date, the effects of such redistribution have remained minimal, largely due to the limited number of constructive abstentions declared. Nonetheless, a novel and controversial issue has emerged in the context of the EPF.

In fact, neutral Member States that have used constructive abstention and refrained from financing the delivery of lethal weapons have at the same time declared their intention to fund non-lethal assistance of an equivalent value. Within the EPF framework, therefore, the exempting effect of constructive abstention has been offset by a compensatory financial contribution. As previously noted, Hungary has adopted a less proactive stance, merely reserving the right to identify a compensatory measure, but without ever actually identifying it. The lack of reactions to Hungary's ambiguous position by Member States that voted in favour of the delivery of lethal weapons appears to suggest that compensatory measures are voluntary. Yet, the matter remains unsettled. It is not unconceivable that the duty of loyal cooperation imposes an obligation to identify compensatory measures on the abstaining Member State. To find a clear answer, let us first look at the text of the EPF Decision[102] and, then, at the Member States' statements on its proposal.

Article 5(3) of the EPF Decision seems to point towards an obligation for the Member State that has formally invoked constructive abstention, since it provides that "that Member State *shall* make an additional contribution" (emphasis added) to assistance measures, other than those concerning the supply of military equipment, or platforms, designed to deliver lethal force.[103] However, this interpretation seems undermined by Article 27 of the same decision. Under this provision, the abstaining Member State "*may* identify" (emphasis added) the alternative assistance measures "to which it will make an additional contribution" (para 1), but if it fails to do so within six months, "the High Representative or other Member States *shall* identify the measures to which such additional contributions will be made" (para 2, emphasis added). After this, the High Representative "shall present proposals as necessary to the Council for adoption" (para 3). When taken together, Article 5(3) and Article 27(1–2) suggest that compensatory measures must ultimately be ensured—either voluntarily by the abstaining Member State or, in the event of inaction by the latter, by the High Representative or other Member States.

---

[102] Council Decision (CFSP) 2021/509.

[103] Along the same line, see Article 26, para 7, EPF.

Turning now to the statements annexed to the proposal for the EPF Decision, certain neutral Member States explicitly stressed the voluntary nature of the compensatory contributions. This position is clearly articulated in the Austrian statement, which reads: "As regards the Council Decision establishing a European Peace Facility, Austria underlines that this Council Decision does in no way affect the consequences of constructive abstentions as set out in Article 31(1) TEU".[104] Ireland expressed a similar view. Furthermore, as previously mentioned, the voluntary nature of compensatory measures was explicitly emphasised by Austria, Ireland, and Malta when they constructively abstained from decisions on lethal supplies. Finally, the EPF implementation guidelines adopted a few months after its establishment also employ discretionary language regarding compensatory measures.[105] In addition to reiterating that the abstaining Member State "*may*" indicate alternative assistance measures to which it intends to contribute, the guidelines state that if the Member State concerned does not identify or request other assistance measures (AMs) within six months, "the High Representative or other Member States *should* identify the AMs to which such additional contributions will be made" (emphasis added).[106] The use of "should" instead of "shall" weakens the obligation imposed by Article 27 of the EPF Decision, which requires the High Representative and other Member States to take action where the abstaining Member State fails to do so, thereby making the compensatory mechanism even less certain. Thus, the guidelines seem to provide an interpretation of the EPF Decision that, by departing from the clear wording of its text, turns a mandatory obligation more into a recommendation.

Be it as it may, we agree with the view that the nature of the compensatory measures is voluntary. Indeed, despite the ambiguity of the legal framework and the clarity of the emerging practice, we do not believe it is legally tenable for a secondary law instrument—such as the EPF Decision—to attach new legal effects to a flexibility mechanism whose contours are defined by primary law. Article 31(1) TEU gives constructive abstention an exempting effect, which is coupled with a negative obligation: namely, to refrain from obstructing the Union's action. But if constructive abstention needs to entail additional positive obligations—more specifically, the duty to provide compensatory measures—this should be established by primary law, either expressly or by reference to secondary law (as for the 'passerelle clause' under Article 31(3) TEU, for example). Yet, this is not currently the case.

On this point, it is worth noting the position taken by France in its statement annexed to the proposal for the EPF Decision. According to France, providing compensatory contributions does not affect the interpretation of Article 31(1) TEU, or the Member States' obligation to actively and unreservedly support the CFSP in a spirit of loyalty and mutual solidarity, as provided for in Article 24(3) TEU. As a result, a formal declaration of constructive abstention does not affect the duty of the abstaining Member State to contribute to the financing of alternative support

---

[104] Council, doc. ST 6618 2021, Brussels, 18 March 2021.

[105] Council, doc. 10134/21, Guidelines on the preparatory and decision-making process for assistance measures under the European Peace Facility, Brussels, 24 June 2021, point 28.

[106] Ibidem.

measures, on the basis of a derogation concerning the financial aspects of the CFSP enshrined in Article 41 TEU. In France's view, when the Council established the aforesaid obligation, it "decided, on the basis of the second subparagraph of Article 41(2) TEU, to create, by way of exception, a derogation mechanism allowing those Member States, under certain conditions, not to contribute financially to measures relating to the delivery of equipment specifically designed to deliver lethal force, while preserving the principle of financial solidarity for the Facility as a whole".[107]

We do not find this interpretation persuasive, for two reasons. First, Article 41 TEU states that Member States invoking constructive abstention are not required to contribute to the financing of expenditure with military or defence implications. This excludes the existence of any form of obligation and makes no reference to other burdens. Moreover, the exemption applies to all military-related expenses, including those concerning non-lethal supplies, which have thus far been subject to the compensatory mechanism. Second, Article 41(2) TEU refers to secondary law, allowing the Council, acting unanimously, to establish an alternative cost-sharing arrangement to the default GNI-based method. In our view, while this reference certainly authorises the Council to adopt additional criteria for distributing military costs among participating Member States,[108] it does not empower it to regulate other aspects of CFSP governance, such as decision-making procedures or related flexibility mechanisms.

Regardless of whether compensatory contributions are mandatory or discretionary, the importance of the practice whereby Member States that invoke constructive abstention provide them should not be underestimated, given that the practice is increasingly widespread. An indirect confirmation of this can be found in the latest amendment to the EPF. Decision (CFSP) 2024/3185 changed the text of Article 5(3) of the EPF to clarify that the additional contribution will be in an amount equivalent to "the reference amount of the assistance measure from which the Member State has abstained". Quite meaningfully, one of the recitals introducing the amendment emphasises that, "(d)rawing on the experience gathered, the financial planning of the EPF should be improved, and the effects of the constructive abstentions should be adjusted accordingly".[109] This is indeed reflected in the new text of Article 5(3), which suggests that the practice of compensatory measures is now well established, since it lays down a rule on the amount of the said contributions.

The issue of compensatory measures does not arise in the context of peace missions. In these cases, the initial CFSP decisions remain silent on the possibility of invoking constructive abstention. As a consequence, the exempting effect of constructive abstention has meant that Cyprus did not contribute to EULEX Kosovo and Hungary abstained from participating in EUMAM Ukraine. This, in turn, has placed

---

[107] EU Council, doc. ST 6618 2021, Brussels, 18 March 2021, p. 6 ff. Article 41(2) TEU states that "Operating expenditure to which the implementation of this chapter gives rise shall also be charged to the Union budget, except for such expenditure arising from operations having military or defence implications and cases where the Council acting unanimously decides otherwise".

[108] See Schmidt-Radefeldt 2013, p. 1192, and Ramopoulos 2019, p. 270.

[109] Council Decision (CFSP) 2024/3185 of 16 December 2024 amending Decision (CFSP) 2021/509 establishing a European Peace Facility, in OJ L 2024/3185, recital 8.

a greater burden on the other Member States in terms of financial, military, human, and logistical resources. In the case of EUMAM Ukraine, a compensatory contribution—or, as Budapest typically phrases it, "the reservation to identify one"—is not mentioned in Hungary's formal declaration of constructive abstention. However, since Norway participated in EUMAM as a third State, Hungary's absence from this mission was partially offset by Norway's contribution to the delivery of training to the Ukrainian armed forces in Poland and Germany.[110]

In principle, compensatory measures to alleviate the burden on other Member States are theoretically feasible in the context of different, non-contentious peace missions. Had such a practice been established, both Cyprus and Hungary would have been able to respectively offset their non-contributions to the EULEX Kosovo civilian mission and the EUMAM Ukraine military assistance mission. Alternatively, in the specific case of military operations—even non-operational ones—a viable solution might consist in undertaking non-military activities. For instance, in the case of EUMAM Ukraine, Hungary could have contributed to the training of medical personnel, a task ultimately carried out by Bulgaria. These examples show that identifying compensatory measures in the context of peace missions is indeed possible, albeit more complex than in the case of the EPF. Indeed, it is necessary to identify compensatory measures on a case-by-case basis and adjust them to the nature and characteristics of the contested peace mission as well as to the military and civilian capacity of the abstaining Member State.

A number of conclusions may be drawn from the analysis of compensatory measures. Firstly, this practice, previously unknown, emerged after Russia's 2022 invasion of Ukraine and the subsequent urgent need to provide support to Kyiv, including through the supply of lethal military equipment. While Cyprus's constructive abstention from the EULEX Kosovo mission in 2008 did not raise significant issues, the decision to supply lethal equipment to Ukraine has, in contrast, given rise to constitutional concerns for neutral Member States and political objections from Hungary. It may therefore be posited that the outbreak of the war in Ukraine has led to the development of a novel and intriguing practice within the CFSP decision-making process. Secondly, we can conclude that a dissenting Member State, that constructively abstains from a CFSP decision, is not required to provide a compensatory contribution. This is because it remains subject to the negative obligation to refrain from obstructing or impeding the decision's implementation. It may be argued that Hungary has complied with this obligation.

Nonetheless, it may be concluded that compensatory measures represent concrete steps taken by dissenting Member States to support the Union's action. As a result, they are the clearest expression of the duty to actively and unreservedly support the CFSP in a spirit of loyalty and mutual solidarity.[111] This is exemplified by the constructive abstentions declared by neutral Member States in relation to the EPF and

[110] Political and Security Committee Decision (CFSP) 2023/495 of 28 February 2023 on the acceptance of a third State's contribution to the European Union Military Assistance Mission in support of Ukraine (EUMAM Ukraine), in OJ L 69/2023.

[111] See Article 24(3) TEU.

the voluntary compensatory contributions they have offered. In our view, the offer of the said contributions, while constituting a voluntary commitment under Article 31(1) TEU and the EPF, can be regarded as a conduct consistent with the duty of solidarity underpinning the CFSP. It could even be considered a derivative obligation stemming from the general duty enshrined in Article 24(3) TEU.

5.3.3 *The 'Domino Effect' of Constructive Abstention and the Action Brought by Hungary Before the ECJ*

The 'domino effect' of Hungary's constructive abstention became apparent not only in relation to the EUMAM Ukraine mission, but also in connection with the establishment of the Ukraine Assistance Fund.

Following its abstention, Budapest threatened to veto decisions concerning the fund's disbursement. This obstructionist stance provoked strong reactions from several Member States and the former High Representative for CFSP, who described Hungary's conduct as "unacceptable" and "unbearable".[112] Once again, as was the case with EUMAM Ukraine, the Council Legal Service reiterated that constructive abstention from the initial CFSP decision precludes participation in the adoption of subsequent acts, in particular those concerning the allocation of the dedicated fund.

In contrast to the EUMAM Ukraine episode, Budapest responded by filing an action before the General Court on 30 August 2024. The application seeks the annulment of the EPF Committee's decision of 21 June 2024 concerning the allocation of funds to assistance measures for the supply of military support to the Ukrainian Armed Forces, pursuant to Council Decision (CFSP) 2024/1471 of 21 May 2024.[113] Hungary also seeks the partial annulment of the minutes of the EPF Committee's meeting of 25 June 2024, which recorded the adoption of that decision.[114]

Hungary contends that the contested decision infringes Article 31(1) TEU and Council Decision (CFSP) 2021/509,[115] particularly with respect to the vote held within the EPF Committee. According to Hungary, the Committee violated these provisions by excluding it from the vote on the grounds that it was not a contributing Member State, thus disregarding its vote. Hungary takes the view that its exclusion constitutes a breach of the principle of equality among Member States and undermines the democratic functioning of the Union. The legal issue raised by Hungary precisely concerns the 'domino effect': the vote of the Hungarian representative was

[112] Foreign Affairs Council: Press remarks by High Representative Josep Borrell at the press conference, Brussels, 22 July 2024.

[113] Council Decision (CFSP) 2024/1471 of 21 May 2024 on the allocation of the amounts of the financial contribution paid to the European Peace Facility pursuant to Decision (CFSP) 2024/1470, in OJ L 2024/1471.

[114] T-457/24, Hungary v Council and European Peace Facility Committee, action brought on 3 August 2024, in OJ C 2024/6266.

[115] Council Decision (CFSP) 2021/509.

not counted because it had constructively abstained from the basic Council decision. Recalling the clarifications provided by the Council Legal Service, participating to the adoption of any subsequent act implementing the basic decision-namely, the decision of the EPF Committee—was thus precluded.

In our view, Hungary's objections are not well founded. The exclusion from voting is a legal consequence of invoking constructive abstention.

First of all, we do not believe that the principle of equality between Member States has been infringed. This principle, which underpins membership in international organisations, guarantees equal status within the institutional framework.[116] Hungary enjoys the same rights as all other Member States under EU law and may invoke the flexibility mechanisms provided therein. In this case, Budapest opted to declare a constructive abstention. This Member State could have voted in favour of the Council decision, thereby assuming both the implementation obligations and the right to vote on subsequent implementing measures. Instead, Hungary freely chose to invoke constructive abstention, thereby acquiring the right not to implement the underlying decision—unlike those Member States that voted in favour and are bound by its application.

The alleged violation of the principle of democratic functioning is also unpersuasive. In the Treaty framework, democracy is invoked in relation to the EU's engagement with its citizens, as enshrined in Articles 9 to 12 TEU under Title II. In particular, Article 10(2), second indent, TEU states that: "Member States are represented in the European Council by their Heads of State or Government and in the Council by their governments, themselves democratically accountable either to their national Parliaments, or to their citizens". However, this provision must be interpreted in light of Article 10 TEU as a whole and, more broadly, within the context of Title II. A systematic reading of these provisions leads to the conclusion that the EU's democratic legitimacy is rooted in the representation of its citizens, expressed in two forms: directly, through the European Parliament, and indirectly, through the European Council and the Council, whose legitimacy derives from a "chain of legitimation" based on national elections.[117] It is difficult to see how such representation has been violated in the present case, merely because Hungary's vote was not counted in the adoption of a measure implementing a Council decision. Even if one were to accept that the exclusion of Budapest's vote deprives Hungarian citizens of the indirect representation envisaged by Article 10(2), second indent, TEU, it could be equally maintained that the Hungarian government freely chose to invoke constructive abstention under Article 31(1) TEU, thereby accepting both the benefits and the inherent consequence of abstaining on a certain decision, which is not to participate in the vote on subsequent acts which originate from the underlying decision.

As with the pending case discussed in Sect. 5.2.1, it will be for the General Court to ascertain the correct interpretation of this matter.

---

[116] For an extensive discussion, see Efraim 2000.

[117] See Lock 2019, p. 109 ff. and Porras Ramìrez 2013, p. 424.

5.4 Conclusions: The Impact of the War in Ukraine on the CFSP Decision-Making Process

As shown in this chapter, the outbreak of the war in Ukraine has triggered significant changes to the CFSP decision-making process.

The difficulties in achieving consensus among Member States regarding both restrictive measures against Russia's aggression and support for Ukraine have led the Council to rely on Article 31 TEU—a provision that was traditionally underused. This shift has resulted in a more systematic recourse to voting procedures and, in several instances, to the use of constructive abstention. Where this mechanism has proved inapplicable, alternative ones, such as simple abstention or other forms of flexibility, have been employed. The General Court will clarify whether the 'domino effect' of constructive abstention will take place or not. A rejection of the action would diminish the disrupting potential of certain Member States within the decision-making process in the context of defence.

While the unanimity requirement for the adoption of Council decisions has increased the sense of ownership of CFSP Decisions, the practice of voting by qualified majority is almost non-existent.[118] A potential turning point may be the ruling of the GC in the pending case *Parliament v Council*,[119] should the application be considered admissible. Following the intervention of the High Representative/Vice-President of the Commission in the judicial proceedings[120] in favour of a broader use of qualified majority voting within the CFSP, new legal developments may be expected in the near future. This is also confirmed by statements made by the President of the Commission in the 2025 State of the Union Address before the Parliament on 10 September 2025.[121] In this context, the ruling of the Court in the pending case *Parliament v Council* is eagerly awaited.

Finally, it should also be noted that that the level of flexibility within the CFSP decision-making framework has increased. The search for equilibrium—or compromise, as it might be termed—is not confined to the decision-making process under Article 31 TEU. New 'procedural mechanisms' have been introduced to mitigate the effects of dissent, particularly in relation to Hungary's stance on assistance to Ukraine or to its path to EU's membership. These include Hungary's withdrawal from Council sessions (for instance, on Ukraine's accession *dossier*[122]) and its refusal to endorse

[118] This voting procedure was used only in a limited number of instances. See Szép and Wessel 2023, p. 6.

[119] C-883/24, *Parliament v Council*, action brought on 19 December 2024, in OJ C 2025/899.

[120] C-883/24, *Parliament v Council*, Order of the President of the Court, 8 April 2025, ECLI:EU:C:2025:277.

[121] See Chap. 11 (conclusions) in this book.

[122] See Lang 2023. It is worth noting that, in order to support Ukraine's path towards, among other goals, EU membership, the Union has allocated substantial financial resources through the Ukraine Facility, which entered into force on 1 March 2024. Under Pillar III, dedicated to Union accession assistance and related support measures, the Facility provides for up to €50 billion, including €4.76 billion specifically earmarked for technical assistance and measures aimed at facilitating Ukraine's alignment with EU legislation and regulatory standards. Overall, total payments to Ukraine under

the conclusions of European Council meetings (for example, the renewal of support for Ukraine following the Zelensky–Trump meeting of 28 February 2025[123]). These ad hoc expedients—unexplored before February 2022—may be recorded as part of the practice of compromises on consensus building, demonstrating the significant impact that the war in Ukraine has had on the EU legal order.

References

Abouthungary.hu (2025) Bóka: Hungary has won guarantees from EU over energy security. 29 January. https://abouthungary.hu

Bartoloni ME (2023) Simple Abstention and Constructive Abstention in the Context of International Economic Sanctions: Two Too Similar Sides of the Same Coin? European Papers 7:1121–1130.

Beaucillon C (2018) Opening up the horizon: the ECJ's new take on country sanctions. Common Market Law Review 55:387–415.

Bottner R, Wessel RA (2013) Article 31 [Procedures for the Adoption of CFSP Decisions]. In: Blanke H-J, Mangiameli S (eds) The Treaty on European Union (TEU). A Commentary. Springer, Heidelberg, pp. 1051–1080.

Budapesttimes.hu (2024) EU Peace Facility top-up adopted with Hungarian Constructive abstention, minister says. 18 March. https://budapesttimes.hu

Chamon M (2018) Fining Member States under the SGP, or how enforcement is different from implementation under Article 291 TFEU: Spain v. Council. Common Market Law Review 55:1495–1519.

Chamon M (2023) Only Fans of the Council's implementing powers in Luxembourg: Fenix International. Common Market Law Review 60:1683–1704. https://doi.org/10.54648/cola2023120

Dailynewshungary.com (2024) No veto: EU Peace Facility top-up adopted with Hungarian constructive abstention. 18 March. https://dailynewshungary.com

Dailynewshungary.com (2025) EU sanctions against Russia: that's why Hungary has withdrawn its veto. 27 January. https://dailynewshungary.com

EEAS (2024) Increasing the effectiveness of sanctions. 9 January. https://eeas.europa.eu

Efraim A D (2000) Sovereign (In)Equality in International Organizations, in Legal Aspects of International Organization (Vol. 34). The Hague-Boston-London.

Eunews.it (2024) Sanctions on violent Israeli settlers, EU finds political agreement. 18 March. https://eunews.it

Eunews.it (2025a) Ukraine: Slovakia continues to block sanctions against Russia. 16 July. https://eunews.it

Eunews.it (2025b) Slovakia backs down; EU adopts 18th sanctions package against Russia. 18 July. https://eunews.it

Euractiv.com (2025) Hungary upholds veto against Russia sanctions roll-over as talks continue. 13 March. https://euractiv.com

European Commission (2018) Communication from the Commission 'A stronger global actor: a more efficient decision-making for EU Common Foreign and Security Policy'. COM(2018) 647 final.

---

the Facility in 2024 will amount to €16.2 billion, with disbursements in 2025 expected to reach €12.5 billion. See European Council, conclusions, EUCO 50/24, Brussels, 19 December 2024, point 4.

[123] Conclusions, Brussels, 6 March 2025, and conclusions on Ukraine, firmly supported by 26 Heads of State or Government (EUCO 10/25).

European Parliamentary Research Service (2022) The implementation of Article 31 of the Treaty on European Union and the use of Qualified Majority Voting—Towards a more effective Common Foreign and Security Policy? Brussels.

European Parliamentary Research Service (2023) Qualified majority voting in common foreign and security policy—A cost of non-Europe report. Brussels.

Europeannewsroom.com (2025) EU assures energy stability as Slovakia slams Ukraine's gas transit cut. 10 January. https://europeannewsroom.com.

Financial Times (2024) EU seeks to insulate itself from Viktor Orbán's vetoes. 25 June. https://ft.com

Genini D (2025) How the war in Ukraine has transformed the EU's Common Foreign and Security Policy. Yearbook of European Law 44:1–35. https://doi.org/10.1093/yel/yeaf003

Klabbers J (2022) An Introduction to International Organizations Law, 4th edn. Cambridge University Press, Cambridge.

Korkea-aho E, Lonardo L (2025) How Russia's war against Ukraine changed EU sanctions decision-making. Journal of European Integration 47:745–766.

Lang A (2023) Una "sedia vuota" al Consiglio europeo del 14–15 dicembre 2023 [An 'Empty Chair' at the European Council of 14–15 December 2023]. Eurojus, 18 December

Lock T (2019) Article 10 TEU. In: Kellerbauer M, Klamert M, Tomkin J (eds) The EU Treaties and the Charter of Fundamental Rights. A Commentary. Oxford University Press, Oxford, pp. 108–124.

Miadzvetskaya Y (2025) EU sanctions decision-making in times of war: Procedural changes and rise of the Commission. Maastricht Journal of European and Comparative Law 32:269–288. https://doi.org/10.1177/1023263X251345672

Poli S (2019) Recenti sviluppi in materia di PESC: verso l'attenuazione della sua specificità? [Recent Developments in the CFSP: Towards a Weakening of Its Legal Specificity?]. In: AA.VV. (eds) Temi e questioni di diritto dell'Unione europea—Scritti in onore di Claudia Morviducci [Themes and Issues in European Union Law—Essays in Honour of Claudia Morviducci]. Cacucci Editore, Bari, pp. 387–405.

Poli S, Finelli F (2023) Context specific and structural changes in EU restrictive measures adopted in reaction to Russia's aggression to Ukraine. Eurojus 3:19–49.

Poli S, Pau A (2020) La reazione dell'Unione europea di fronte alla crisi del Mediterraneo orientale: tra misure restrittive e la proposizione di "un'agenda politica positiva" alla Turchia [The European Union's Response to the Eastern Mediterranean Crisis: Between Restrictive Measures and the Proposal of a 'Positive Political Agenda' for Turkey]. European Papers 5:1511–1530.

Politico.eu (2022) Hungary throws new spanner into EU sanctions talks. 1 June. https://politico.eu

Politico.eu (2024) EU approves up to €1.4B military aid to Ukraine from Russian frozen assets. 24 June. https://politico.eu.

Politico.eu (2025) Von der Leyen sees 19th sanctions package against Russia in early September. 17 August. https://politico.eu

Pomorska K, Wessel RA (2021) Editorial: Qualified Majority Voting in CFSP: A Solution to the Wrong Problem? European Foreign Affairs Review 26:351–358.

Porras Ramírez JM (2013) Article 10 [Representative Democracy]. In: Blanke H-J, Mangiameli S (eds) The Treaty on European Union (TEU). A Commentary. Springer, Heidelberg, pp. 417–447.

Portela C, Olsen KB (2023) Implementation and monitoring of the EU sanctions' regimes, including recommendations to reinforce the EU's capacities to implement and monitor sanctions. European Parliament, Brussels.

Ramopoulos T (2019) Article 41 TEU. In: Kellerbauer M, Klamert M, Tomkin J (eds) The EU Treaties and the Charter of Fundamental Rights. A Commentary. Oxford University Press, Oxford, pp. 269–272.

Reuters.com (2024) UK, EU and Canada impose new sanctions targeting Myanmar military. 29 October. https://reuters.com

Rossi LS (2025) A Legal Scalpel Instead of an Axe. How a Reinterpretation of Article 7 TEU Could Neutralise Hungary's CFSP Veto Strategy. Verfassungsblog, 9 July. https://verfassungsblog.de/a-legal-scalpel-instead-of-an-axe/

Schmidt-Radefeldt R (2013) Article 41 [Financing the CFSP]. In: Blanke H-J, Mangiameli S (eds) The Treaty on European Union (TEU). A Commentary. Springer, Heidelberg, pp. 1187–1199.

Szép V, Wessel RA (2023) Assessing Current CFSP Structures and Processes and Formulating Recommendations. ENGAGE Working Paper Series, No. 23, April.

Themoscowtimes.com—Agence France-Presse (2024) EU Moves to Sanction Russia Over Hybrid Attacks. 2 October. https://themoscowtimes.com

Chapter 6
The EU's Response to Russia's Aggression Through Restrictive Measures: Limits Imposed by International Law and Opportunities for Its Development

Sara Poli

Contents

This chapter is based on and further develops the following publications: Poli 2025, pp. 97–113 and Poli and Finelli 2023, pp. 19–49. The author wishes to thank Maruša Veber for her comments and Dr Isaac David Freckleton for his editorial assistance. The usual disclaimer applies.

S. Poli et al., *The EU's Response to the War in Ukraine and Its Impact on the EU Legal Order*, Global Europe: Legal and Policy Issues of the EU's External Action 7,
https://doi.org/10.1007/978-94-6265-767-0_6

Abstract This chapter examines to what extent the EU has respected and developed international law in its response to Russia's aggression of Ukraine through restrictive measures. First, the legal nature of these acts is explored; second, it is stressed that they serve multiple purposes. The analysis of the different objectives pursued by the EU in adopting restrictive measures in response to the 2022 conflict shows that the latter are consistent with international law, albeit with some critical observations concerning restrictive measures aimed at preventing the commission of international crimes. The EU's response to the 2022 proclamation of independence of non-government-controlled areas of Ukraine through restrictive measures represents a development of international law since by enacting sanctions the EU has gone beyond the obligation not to recognise the legality of that political initiative, as required by Article 41(2) of the Articles on State Responsibility for Internationally Wrongful Acts (ARSIWA). The designation criteria underlying individual restrictive measures are analysed and assessed, leading to the conclusion that, save for minor exceptions, these criteria are consistent with international law. The chapter further focuses on the legal framework designed to counter the circumvention of sector-related measures and argues that so far there have been no instances of extraterritorial application of EU law, despite the global reach of EU sanctions. The latter may impact third country operators without violating the rules of prescriptive jurisdiction. The EU has probably reached the maximum 'territorial extension' of its restrictive measures. The chapter also examines the legality of the mechanism that was established to transfer the extraordinary revenues generated by the immobilised assets of the Russian Central Bank to Ukraine and argues that it is an innovative lawful measure, in reaction to breaches of *jus cogens* rules of international law. By enacting this mechanism, which was also implemented by other G7 members, the EU may have contributed to the development of international law. Finally, the chapter addresses the package of measures adopted in December 2025, which represents a watershed moment for the EU in light of the form and the substance of the Council Regulation (EU) 2025/2600, which is qualified as an emergency measure. This new act is hybrid in nature, as it constitutes a lawful countermeasure adopted to support Ukraine while also serving as an instrument to safeguard the Union's economic stability.

Keywords International law · Circumvention · Confiscation · Countermeasures · Designation criteria · Extraordinary revenues · Extraterritoriality · Assets of the Russian Central Bank · Emergency measures · Retorsions

6.1 Introduction

The aims of this chapter are twofold: the first is to examine whether the EU has respected international law when adopting restrictive measures[1] in its reaction to Russia's aggression against Ukraine; the second is to assess whether in enacting some of these sanctions the organization has contributed to consolidating principles of international law[2] and 'to the strict observance and the development of international law'.[3] Rather than attempting a comprehensive evaluation of all the issues raised, this chapter concentrates on the most legally contentious aspects of the debate, assessed against the evolving law and practice of EU external relations over four years of war in Ukraine. Both the serious nature of the breaches of international law committed by Russia in 2022 and the wide range of restrictive and emergency measures enacted by the EU in response to the conflict in Ukraine,[4] render this context particularly suitable for addressing some of the thorniest legal issues of international law. For example, what kind of response measures may the international community adopt in response to breaches of *erga omnes* obligations and other kinds of violations of international law when the wrongdoer State holds a veto right within the UN Security Council? The EU has provided various forms of support to Ukraine. In some cases, new legal instruments, such as the channelling of the extraordinary cash balances generated by frozen Russian sovereign state assets, were deployed to assist the victim of the aggression, thus contributing to the development of international law. At the same time, the intensification of anti-circumvention efforts designed to protect the effectiveness of restrictive measures has pushed the EU into contested legal territory under international law, raising concerns about its compliance with the duty to ensure strict observance of international law.

This chapter presents the discussion on the EU's response to the war in Ukraine across seven sections. The qualification of EU restrictive measures under international law is examined in Sect. 6.2, which argues that most of the measures

---

[1] The word 'sanctions' is used interchangeably with 'restrictive measures.'

[2] As required by 21(2)b TEU.

[3] Article 3(5) TEU.

[4] These measures include prohibitions to access ports and locks, flight bans as well as traditional economic prohibitions such as import and export bans or prohibitions to provide (financial) services or to invest. A new type of sanctions is the broadcasting ban on a number of Russian media outlets. The prohibition of transactions related to the management of reserves and assets of the Central Bank of Russia is one worth drawing attention to. These assets were temporarily frozen by Council Decision (CFSP) 2022/335 amending Decision 2014/512/CFSP and Council Regulation (EU) 2022/334.

enacted in the context of the war in Ukraine are acts of retorsion rather than collective countermeasures. Specific examples of retorsions are provided in Sect. 6.2.1. Section 6.3 illustrates how restrictive measures were also adopted as an expression of the duty not to recognise unlawful situations resulting from serious breaches of an obligation arising under a peremptory norm of international law while Sect. 6.4 shows that in some cases restrictive measures were misused as a reaction to the commission of international crimes committed by individuals. Next, Sect. 6.5 dwells on the connection between the designation criteria of individual restrictive measures[5] and the purpose of these acts, which is to cease the aggression, showing that such a link does not always exist.

Section 6.6 explores the extraterritorial effects of the EU restrictive measures. The position of the EU institutions denying that sanctions are adopted beyond the jurisdiction of the Union is illustrated and commented upon in Sect. 6.6.1. The following subsection addresses the anti-circumvention activity of the Union and discusses the extent to which the EU may protect the effectiveness of the restrictive measures without enacting secondary sanctions. Indeed, the need to counter the circumvention of sanctions has forced the EU to expand the territorial reach of export bans on specific goods or technology which are used, directly or indirectly, by Russia to continue the war efforts. Other measures concern access to ports. Section 6.6.3 examines the way EU operators are required to ensure the effectiveness of EU restrictive measures by imposing on non-EU subsidiaries an obligation not to re-export sensitive goods or technology to Russia and comments on the global reach of these measures.

Section 6.7 scrutinises the EU's efforts to ensure Ukraine's reconstruction and in particular, the legality of the *sui generis* mechanism created to use the revenues generated by the frozen assets and reserves of the Central Bank of Russia ('CBR') to support Ukraine's reconstruction, without affecting Russia's sovereign state assets, which are protected by international law. After briefly summarising how the EU developed the idea of using the revenues in Sects. 6.7.1 and 6.7.2, other legal options to support Ukraine's reconstruction are examined in Sect. 6.7.3 while the next one describes the way the windfall tax works. Finally, a positive assessment of the compatibility of the latter instrument with international law is made in Sect. 6.7.5. Subsequent sections address the Ukraine Loan Cooperation Mechanism (in Sect. 6.7.6) and the manner in which the EU's contribution to the observance of international law safeguards the integrity of the assets (in Sect. 6.7.7). Finally, the package of measures adopted at the end of December 2025 is commented on in Sect. 6.7.8, providing an overall positive assessment of their compatibility with obligations stemming from international law. Concluding thoughts sum up the main findings of the chapter in Sect. 6.8.

[5] Council Decision 2014/145/CFSP; Council Regulation (EU) 269/2014.

6.2 The Qualification of EU Restrictive Measures Under International Law

There is no doubt that the aggression[6] carried out by Russia constitutes a violation of a peremptory norm of international law, whose observance is owed to all members of the international community, including the EU Member States which may act through the EU in the area of the CFSP. The Council has explicitly acknowledged the breach of an *erga omnes* obligation by Russia in the text of a CFSP Decision.[7] The violation of such obligations constitutes the condition that, in principle, may justify the adoption of third-party countermeasures or collective countermeasures (or counter measures in the general interest),[8] under Article 54[9] of the ARSIWA.[10] Yet, the legality of these measures remains controversial, even 24 years after the adoption of the draft articles mentioned above. The cautious approach adopted in the qualification of restrictive measures as collective countermeasures is understandable, given that this may lead to abuses that threaten the peaceful coexistence of States. At the same time, one may wonder in what circumstances should these measures be taken if not when a State, holding a veto right in the UN Security Council, commits an act of aggression. Is there not a common legal interest in the performance of the obligation to cease an aggression? The EU is not an injured Party, but is rather a *sui generis* regional organization that is suited to take collective countermeasures in reaction to the aforementioned *erga omnes* breach of international law due to its proximity to the victim of the aggression. Proximity as well as the very many economic interests shared by EU Member States and Russia makes the EU's attempts to cease the aggression particularly important.

The EU has not qualified its restrictive measures as countermeasures,[11] but it is rare for subjects of international law to do so; it should also be stressed that France is

[6] The European Council qualifies Russia's special operation as an unprovoked and unjustified military aggression against Ukraine. See European Council conclusions on Russia's unprovoked and unjustified military aggression against Ukraine EUCO 18/22, 24 February 2022.

[7] See recital 3 of CFSP Decision (CFSP) 2023/191. Yet there are some variations in the language used by the Council. In some cases, the text of CFSP Decisions imposing individual restrictive measures is ambiguous since it states that Russia has committed 'a manifest violation of the Charter of the United Nations.' In other contexts, the Council is more explicit. 'Russia's war of aggression against Ukraine grossly violates international law and is causing massive loss of life and injury to civilians. Russian's attack of 24th February is a blatant violation of the territorial integrity, sovereignty and independence of Ukraine. Recital 3, Council decision (CFSP) 2022/335.

[8] Jackson and Paddeu 2024, p. 40, footnote 43.

[9] 'This chapter does not prejudice the right of any State, entitled under Article 48, para 1, to invoke the responsibility of another State, to take lawful measures against that State to ensure cessation of the breach and reparation in the interest of the injured State or of the beneficiaries of the obligation breached.'

[10] ILC, Articles on State Responsibility of States for Internationally Wrongful Act (ARSIWA) 2001.

[11] The Council states that: 'The introduction and implementation of restrictive measures must always be in accordance with international law.' Council, 'Guidelines on Implementation and Evaluation of Restrictive Measures (Sanctions) in the Framework of the EU Common Foreign and Security Policy' (Annex to Doc n. 5664/18, 4 May 2018) para 9, [accessed on 19 September 2025]. In other

one of the EU members that considers them as impermissible. While scholars have recognised that international law has developed after the ARSIWA were agreed in 2001 and that such measures may now be regarded as permissible,[12] it is not possible to argue that there has been an evolution in state practice on collective countermeasures in the context of the war in Ukraine. Only G7 countries enacted sanctions and therefore, even assuming that some of these acts qualify as countermeasures, the practice of imposing unilateral coercive measures remains dominated by the Western component of the international community. As to Russia's reaction, this country has banned European officials, scientists and activists in response to the EU restrictive measures[13] and has considered sanctions as unlawful considering that they are not imposed by the UN Security Council.[14]

It is noteworthy that, in a much-criticised ruling, the General Court has had the opportunity to exclude the possibility that the EU's restrictive measures enacted in reaction to breaches of human rights, in a situation of deterioration of democracy and the rule of law, could be qualified as unlawful countermeasures.[15] Although the restrictive measures adopted vis-à-vis Venezuela, and the breaches committed by that State, are distinct from those at stake in the context of the war in Ukraine, the stance taken by the General Court is of particular relevance. The latter did not state what the legal nature of the concerned acts was, though. Since the challenged measures were considered legal, it could be argued that by implication the GC recognised that the measures at issue were acts of retorsion.

Leaving aside collective countermeasures, there are other legal bases in the ARSIWA that justify the adoption of the EU prohibitions enacted in reaction to Russia's aggression. Unilateral restrictive measures may be considered as 'lawful means' enacted by a group of States within the international community that cooperate to bring to an end a serious breach of international law, under Article 41 (1) of

---

parts of the guidelines, specific Treaty obligations, stemming from the WTO are illustrated. Ibid., para 11.

[12] For references see Jackson and Paddeu 2024, pp. 241–242.

[13] https://www.themoscowtimes.com/2025/03/13/russia-expands-eu-entry-ban-in-retaliation-to-war-anniversary-sanctons-a88351 [accessed on 19 September 2025].

[14] https://www.mid.ru/en/press_service/minister_speeches/1905317/ [accessed on 19 September 2025].

[15] In the ruling in GC, T-65/18 RENV, *Bolivarian Republic of Venezuela v Council* the GC took the view that restrictions imposed by the Council in 2017 in view of the situation in Venezuela and consisting in prohibiting the export of goods and technology that could be used for internal repression purposes in this country did not qualify as unlawful countermeasures. Ibid., paras 90-92. The reasoning leading to this conclusion may be criticised for a number of reasons which will not be deepened here. See for a discussion, see Kassoti 2024, pp. 247–259. Suffice to say that the GC, after rejecting Venezuela's claim that the EU restrictive measures were illegal countermeasures, did not state what was the nature of the sanctions at stake. Yet, the GC described restrictive measures as an expression of the EU independent sanctioning power in accordance with the objectives and values of the Union as set out in Article 3(5) TEU and Article 21 TEU, namely (amongst other things) the objective of promoting, in the wider world, democracy, the rule of law, the universality and indivisibility of human rights and fundamental freedoms, respect for human dignity, and respect for the principles of the United Nations Charter and international law.

the ARSIWA.[16] The EU, which is not a State, as the Court of Justice itself recognises,[17] has legal personality[18] and is authorised by its Member States, which are represented within the Council, to enact restrictive measures. The possibility for the EU to react to *erga omnes obligations* was also recognised by the General Court in the ruling in *Russia Today France.*[19] As mentioned, proximity to Russia is a factor that places the EU in a particularly favourable situation to authorise lawful measures designed to make the cost of continuing the war in Ukraine remarkably high for Russia. Economic coercion is a legal form of action to inhibit an aggression, and it is a substitute for direct military engagement to support the victim of the aggression. Even if restrictive measures cause damage to their addressees, this does not render them unlawful.

The fundamental question is whether the EU restrictive measures can be regarded as lawful under international law. In an internal document of the working party on public international law of 2022, it is stated that 'most of the initial sanctions imposed by the EU and its Member States may be seen as acts of retorsions.'[20] In the act referred to, neither is it specified which of the adopted restrictive measures qualify as acts of retorsions, nor is the possibility of adopting collective countermeasures excluded.

The EU's restrictive measures *vis-à-vis* a third country, be it Russia or other members of the international community that support Russia's war efforts,[21] can be considered as lawful counter measures when they breach a Treaty obligation, enshrined in a bilateral or multilateral Treaty, of which both the EU and the affected third country are parties. Indeed, the security exceptions clauses of international agreements justify the adoption of restrictive measures that may conflict with the provisions of EU agreements. For example, prohibitions concerning the export of arms or dual-use technology or the provision of services may respectively breach the GATT[22] or the GATS or even the terms of the Partnership and Cooperation agreement ('PCA') with Russia[23] or other bilateral agreements that the EU may have concluded with the target country. Bilateral Investment Treaties ('BITs') may also be relied upon by Russia to challenge Member States' enactment of restrictive measures. It is regretful that 23 out of 27 Member States have agreements of this kind in force with Russia.[24] Leaving BITs aside and focusing only on the two WTO agreements

---

[16] See also conclusion 19 (1) of the ILC, Draft conclusions on the identification and legal consequences of peremptory norms of general international law (jus cogens) peremptory norms 2022.

[17] CJEU, Opinion n. 2/2013, para 156.

[18] Article 47 TEU.

[19] GC, Case T-125/22, *Russia Today France v Council*, para 86.

[20] WK 15858/2022 INT p. 27 on file with the author.

[21] Such as Belarus, Iran, China and DRNK.

[22] In particular, Articles I and XI.

[23] Partnership and Cooperation Agreement between the EU, its Member States and the Russian Federation, https://eur-lex.europa.eu/eli/agree_internation/1997/800/oj/eng, [accessed on 19 September 2025].

[24] Darvas, Demertzis et al. 2023, p. 4.

mentioned above, the EU may avail itself of security exceptions such as Article XXI(b) iii GATT 1994[25] and Article XIVbis GATS.[26] It is noteworthy that a Panel report in a dispute between Ukraine and Russia has confirmed that restrictions of trade in goods can be taken in times of war or other emergencies in international relations, subject to the scrutiny of the Dispute settlement body of the WTO which may decide whether the State invoking the exception fulfils the condition of Article XXI(b)iii.[27] On the basis of this ruling, the EU and its Member States may also decide how to best protect their security interests in a situation which falls within the notion of 'emergency in international relations,' defined by the Panel, as including 'heightened tension or crisis, or general instability engulfing and surrounding a state.[28]' Without any doubts the war in Ukraine fulfils these conditions.

As to the PCA with Russia, the Court of Justice had already confirmed that, under Article 99 of this agreement, it is possible for the EU to impose trade restrictive measures vis-à-vis Russia for the purpose of protecting the security of the EU.[29] In contrast, the GC could not rule on the compatibility of EU restrictive measures with GATS in the *Vnesheconombank* case[30] given that the complainants had not adduced any evidence that the contested act breached that agreement. Yet, the GC recalled that only in exceptional circumstances is it possible to review the legality of EU measures in light of the WTO agreements and that, in any case, the GATS included security exceptions in Article XIV *bis* on which the Council could rely to justify the contested measures.[31]

Should there be restrictive measures that breach WTO law, it is unlikely that the Court of Justice will interpret the EU acts as being in conflict with the obligations stemming from that body of law, considering the case law on denial of direct effect of the WTO agreements.[32] It should also be mentioned that Russia has not complained before the Dispute Settlement Body about the EU prohibitions.

A final issue deserves further attention. So far, we have assumed that the EU is not an 'injured State' within the meaning of Article 48 of the ARSIWA. May the EU transition from a non-affected party by the war in Ukraine to a Party that has been at least indirectly touched by it, considering the extended duration of the

---

[25] Nothing in this Agreement shall be construed [...] b) to prevent any contracting party from taking any action which it considers necessary for the protection of its essential security interests. [...] (iii) taken in time of war or other emergency in international relations.'

[26] 'Nothing in this Agreement shall be construed: [...] to prevent any Member from taking any action which it considers necessary for the protection of its essential security interests (i) relating to the supply of services ... for the purpose of provisioning a military establishment; (ii) relating to fissionable or fusionable materials; (iii) taken in pursuance of obligations under the UN Charter for maintenance of international peace and security.'

[27] Russia-measures concerning traffic in transit, WT/DS512/7, 29 April 2019, esp 7.100.

[28] Ibid., p. 7.76.

[29] CJEU, C-72/15 *Rosneft*, paras 113–116.

[30] GC, Case T-737/14, *Bank for Development and Foreign Economic Affairs (Vnesheconombank) v Council of the European Union.*

[31] Ibid., paras 155–157.

[32] Gallo 2025, chap. 7, Sect. 6.3.

war and the breach of its territorial integrity by Russian drones? This problem is particularly important: indeed, should it be possible to acknowledge the change of its legal position, the EU would then be an 'injured Party' within the meaning of Article 42 of ARSIWA; this would make it possible for the EU to take countermeasures[33] to protect its interests.

6.2.1 Retorsions

There are many EU restrictive measures that are clearly acts of retorsion. This is the case of the suspension of agreement with Russia such as the bilateral visa facilitation agreement as of 9 September 2022. The EU is not obliged to continue issuing visas[34] under the same conditions that were applicable before the war. Taking other fields of EU competence into consideration, the Union is not compelled to provide services to Russian nationals or companies or to other non-state entities of that State, such as banks; nor is there an obligation to authorise the broadcasting activities of Russian media outlets. Although there are certain EU services that are used worldwide, this does not mean that the EU is obliged to provide them to Russian nationals. The EU has banned the Russian government, operators of the target third country and financial institutions established in this country from having access to services provided in the internal market.[35] These measures may have disruptive effects and may interfere with the right to conduct business or to operate on the financial markets, particularly in the case of Russian banks. However, this does not render them unlawful. They constitute acts of retorsion, adopted in order to exert pressure on the aggressor State to bring its unlawful conduct to an end. Once Russia ceases its aggression, the conditions for lifting the sanctions would be met.

One of the first initiatives taken by the EU after Russia started its aggression was to impose on the Society for Worldwide Interbank Financial Telecommunication (SWIFT) the obligation to cease providing services to a number of Russian operators. Cutting off several banks from access to SWIFT messaging services is a clear example of the denial of access to services. The mentioned company is Belgian and has a prominent role in global financial services: it serves 11,500 institutions in different countries worldwide. As of July 2025, 45 Russian and 4 Belarusian banks were cut off from those services[36]; as a result, it has become more difficult and expensive for them to carry out international transactions. It is submitted that even if the EU

---

[33] Jackson and Paddeu 2024, p. 245. On this issue see Sect. 6.7.8.

[34] Gestri 2022, p. 70.

[35] A sample of this type of prohibition includes services related to military goods, dual use goods, energy sector technology, services, accounting, auditing, bookkeeping or tax consulting services, business and management consulting or public relations services, architectural and engineering services, legal advisory services and IT consultancy services, market research and public opinion polling services, technical testing and analysis services or advertising services.

[36] Council Regulation (EU) 2025/1470.

has 'weaponised SWIFT,'[37] taking advantage of its global leadership by prohibiting the provision of services to operators in Russia, this does not make the restrictive measures unlawful. The prohibition in question is an act of retorsion: the EU does not breach any rule of international law when it decides to exclude selected Russian banks from the services provided by SWIFT. Its prohibition makes it more difficult or more expensive for the mentioned entities to carry out their activities, but they can continue to carry out financial transactions without SWIFT.[38] Yet, there are also authors who consider some of these measures as a 'weaponisation of the internal market' or an example of the exercise of jurisdiction which unduly stretches the territorial or the nationality principles to make jurisdiction 'ubiquitous'.[39] Therefore, they cast doubts on the legality of restrictive measures which have a global reach.

The EU is also free to deny Russian vessels permission to access EU ports or to prohibit any aircraft registered in Russia, and non-Russian aircraft that are owned, chartered, or controlled by Russian individuals or entities, from flying into, across, or taking off from EU territory.[40] It is noteworthy that Russia has filed a statement before the Convention on International Civil Aviation Organization (ICAO) Council against Canada, all EU Member States, the USA, and the UK in October 2023.[41] The complaining country took the view that the prohibitions related to the flight ban and other airspace-related restrictions[42] breach obligations in the framework of ICAO: the EU measures are unlawful since they are discriminatory in relation to the Russian Federation and its airlines. More precisely, Russia contests the legality of the ban on the use of airspace for aircraft of Russian airlines, the ban on the supply of aircraft and spare parts to them, the prohibition on the maintenance and provision of insurance services for aircraft, the detention of aircraft abroad, and the restriction of access to meteorological information for air navigation.[43] Furthermore, the concerned State argues that limiting the supply of spare parts jeopardizes flight safety.

Some of these restrictions, particularly the flight ban, are similar to a measure enacted in 1998 against former Socialist Federal Republic of Yugoslavia.[57] The difference is that the EU is not acting to fulfil the requirements of the United Nations Security Council resolution as it happened in the late 1990s. It has chosen unilateral coercive measures. As noted by Hoffmeister, 'the ILC qualified the 1998 Yugoslav flight ban as a third-party countermeasure in reaction to a breach of obligations *erga omnes*, but left it open whether non-directly affected States have a right to adopt

[37] Ruys and Rodríguez Silvestre 2024, p. 469. On the weaponisation of finance and the role of European central banks and financial sanctions against Russia, see Quaglia and Verdun 2023.

[38] We shall see, the CBR has created an alternative financial messaging system: the System for Transfer of Financial Messages (SPFS).

[39] Ruys and Rodríguez Silvestre 2024, p. 480.

[40] Since February 2022, the EU has closed its seaports and airports, as well as airspace, to Russia.

[41] https://report.az/en/region/russia-files-statement-with-icaoI-council-about-violation-of-air-tra ffic-rules-by-western-countries/, [accessed on 18 August 2025].

[42] Ibid.

[43] Ibid.

such measures.'[44] It may be wondered whether by closing its airspace and seaports through unilateral restrictive measures in reaction to Russia's aggression, the EU is applying collective countermeasures. Hoffmeister argued that similar measures might have conflicted with bilateral commitments of some Member States towards Russia (in the case of access to ports) or with the ICAO obligations.[45] The mentioned scholar considers that by prohibiting access to airports and seaports as a reaction to Russia's illegal use of force against Ukraine, the EU could further contribute to the development of customary international law concerning the use of collective countermeasures.[46] In the opinion of the author, it is not sure that the EU breached the Convention on Civil Aviation of 1944 in enacting the mentioned airspace-related restrictions. The statements made by Russia to the ICAO Council in October 2023, and further elaborated in a working paper of 2025 on the occasion of the 42nd ICAO Assembly in September 2025, are quite vague and do not refer to the source of obligation of non-discrimination. Russia also mentions other breaches of obligations, but the arguments raised are not convincing. The complainant holds that the human right to freedom of movement, included in the Universal Declaration of Human Rights, is breached by the coercive restrictive measures.[47] Yet, the mentioned right is not an absolute one and is subject to derogations prescribed by law for various reasons, including public order and national security. A further argument is that the principle of equality of States as well as the duty not to interfere in domestic affairs are violated by unilateral coercive measures. Finally, the point is made that the bans on aircraft maintenance and insurance services cause safety concerns. In sum, although Russia is significantly affected by the flight ban and other airspace-related restrictions—given that it is the world's largest country by territory—in the absence of specific obligations requiring EU Member States to grant access to their airspace, and in light of the impact of the war in Ukraine on EU security as well as documented incursions into Member States' airspace, the EU's unilateral measures are lawful and, in particular, cannot be regarded as disproportionate.

Having identified a number of retorsions, it is necessary to examine the nature of the prohibition of transactions related to the management of reserves as well as of assets of the CBR[48] enacted on 28 February 2022. It is not the first time that the EU has adopted similar measures: important precedents are represented by the

---

[44] Hoffmeister 2023, p. 690.

[45] Hoffmeister 2023, p. 691.

[46] Ibid. For a discussion of this issue see Veber 2026.

[47] ICAO Assembly, Incompatibility of unilateral coercive measures with the provisions of the convention on international civil aviation, their impact on international civil aviation and the consequences of their application, A42-WP/2561 EX/188, 28/7/25, Revision No. 1, 12/9/25, p. 2, [accessed on 20 September 2025].

[48] 'Transactions related to the management of reserves as well as of assets of the Central Bank of Russia, including transactions with any legal person, entity or body acting on behalf of, or at the direction of, the Central Bank of Russia, are prohibited.' Article 3e), Council Regulation (EU) 2022/334.

cases of Iran[49] and Syria.[50] The frozen assets of the CBR initially consisted of debt securities in the form of bonds, which subsequently matured and were converted into cash. The EU prohibition is temporary and subject to review, as is any other EU restrictive measure. Scholars are divided as to whether executive measures of this kind implicate immunity and inviolability rules in relation to the assets of CBR.[51] There are no straightforward answers to this question; a leading scholar of international law, Moseienko, regards these sanctions as 'lawful (third party) countermeasures.[52]' In the author's opinion, precluding the use of sovereign assets by Russia is justified by the breaches committed by this country.[53] The EU prohibition under examination serves the purpose of assisting Ukraine in ending the aggression, which constitutes a breach of international obligations owed by Russia to the whole international community. The question of whether the immobilised assets of the Russian Central Bank could be used to support Ukraine's reconstruction, or in the context of peace negotiations, or to repay EU loans is examined in Sects. 6.7.2 and 6.7.7.

In Sects. 6.3 and 6.4, we shall see that, on the one hand, the EU has relied on different forms of restrictive measures with respect to those described in this section and, on the other hand, the Union has resorted to sanctions for purposes different from exerting pressure on Russia to withdraw from Ukraine's territory.

6.3 The Enactment of Restrictive Measures Go Beyond the Obligation not to Recognise the Independence of the Non-Government-Controlled Areas of Ukraine

In the practice of the EU's response to the war in Ukraine there are also restrictive measures which were adopted in reaction to the Russian recognition of the independence of the non-government-controlled areas of the Donetsk and Luhansk oblasts of Ukraine in February 2022. The EU adopted a number of prohibitions related to the import into the Union of goods originating in those areas or to the sale or supply of goods and technology to people of those areas in various sectors.[54] The legal basis was the CFSP Decision enacted in 2014 through which the EU had not recognised

---

[49] See Article 23 of Council Regulation (EU) No 267/2012, as amended by Council Regulation (EU) 2025/1975.

[50] On 28 May 2025, the Council has removed the Syrian Central Bank from the list of entities subject to sanctions. The latter were originally enacted in 2012. The decision was taken as a consequence of the fall of the Assad's regime in 2024.

[51] Moseienko 2023, p. 1015.

[52] Moseienko 2023, p. 1008.

[53] On the legal basis for the freezing of the sovereign assets of the RCB see Sect. 6.7.2.

[54] See also in the statement of the High Representative of the Union on this issue: on 22 February 2022, Michel defined the recognition of independence of the non-government-controlled areas of the Donetsk and Luhansk oblasts of Ukraine as a severe breach of international law and international agreements.

the illegal annexation of Crimea and Sevastopol.[55] The mentioned Council's position go beyond the obligation not to recognise as lawful situations resulting from the violation of a serious breach of an obligation arising from a peremptory norm of international law.[56] Scholars have observed that unlawful situations of the kind at issue may, over time, be cured or validated through a gradual process, including acquiescence.[57] The EU's response to the 2022 proclamation of independence, however, was not confined to the non-recognition of the legality of that political initiative; rather, the Union sought to impose economic and political costs in response to the unlawful situation created in the non-government-controlled areas of Ukraine. Since the EU has adopted restrictive measures, this practice may represent an initial step towards expanding the scope of the obligations arising under Article 41(2) of the ARSIWA. On this reading, members of the international community would be understood as being under a positive obligation to adopt sanctions. However, any progress towards the formation of a new rule of customary international law to that effect would require more extensive and consistent State practice.

The EU has also enacted sanctions when Russia did not directly use force but was aiding in organising illegal referenda, aimed at the annexation of the occupied territories (including Ukraine's Donetsk, Kherson, Luhansk, and Zaporizhzhia regions), which were organised in September 2022. While Russia's initiatives are not per se forcible acquisitions of territory, which is certainly an example of a violation of *jus cogens*, Russia has carried out a serious violation of the territorial integrity of Ukraine, in breach of Article 2(4) of the UN Charter. The UN General Assembly invited all States, international organizations and UN agencies not to recognize any alteration of status purportedly based on those referenda.[58] Beyond complying with this call for non-recognition, the EU adopted sanctions, thereby contributing to the practice of imposing coercive measures even in situations where the responsible State has not necessarily breached a peremptory norm of international law. In the next section we shall see that in some cases the EU has also imposed restrictive measures in a situation in which individuals carry out serious breaches of human rights.

---

[55] Council Decision (CFSP) 2025/1204.

[56] Article 41(2) ARSIWA states: 'No State shall recognize as lawful a situation created by a serious breach [by a State of an obligation arising under a peremptory norm of general international law] ...'.

[57] Dawidowicz 2010.

[58] UN General Assembly Resolution ES-11/4 of 12 October 2022 was adopted by 143 votes in favour, 5 against and 35 abstentions. A comparable resolution had previously been adopted in response to the illegal referendum held in Crimea (Resolution A/RES/68/262 of 27 March 2014). However, the level of support for the 2014 resolution was significantly lower: it was adopted by 100 votes in favour, 11 against and 58 abstentions. In this issue see Asada 2024, pp. 17–18.

6.4 Restrictive Measures as Instruments to Hold Perpetrators of Serious Violations of Human Rights Accountable

The EU has not only made use of restrictive measures in reaction to Russia's breaches of *erga omnes* obligations and other kinds of obligations of international law, but has also adopted sanctions against perpetrators of serious violations of human rights.

Shortly after the massacres in Bucha and Mariupol, the Council adopted measures against military personnel (including Colonel Azatbek Asanbekovich Omurbekov, a.k.a. 'the Butcher of Bucha')[59] who had carried out the killing of civilians. The justification was that: 'The Union supports all measures to ensure accountability for human rights violations and violations of international humanitarian law in Ukraine by the Armed Forces of the Russian Federation.[60]' The legality of these sanctions in international law may be contested, since their objective does not seem to be the prevention of the violations in question, in line with the nature of restrictive measures but rather the punishment of the authors of the breaches. It is submitted that the sanctions under examination have a symbolic character; they are designed to stigmatise the commission of serious violations of human rights in a situation in which the failure to impose restrictive measures would imply that the EU is not regarding the violations committed by the wrongdoers as sufficiently serious. The atrocities committed in Bucha are qualified as war crimes or crimes against humanity by the Council.[61] Yet, the assertion of criminal responsibility for the listed officers, in the absence of a trial or independent verification systems, is problematic.[62] In principle, restrictive measures are of a *preventive* (rather than repressive) nature and are supposed to be temporary: the EU autonomous sanctions under exam are subject to review after 12 months. Accordingly, in principle, restrictive measures are not suitable instruments to hold perpetrators of crimes accountable. In other cases, the Council has been more cautious and has listed individuals for the commission of serious breaches of human rights rather than for international crimes[63]; in other cases, it has linked illegal activities, such as the deportation of children, to the violation of the territorial integrity and independence of Ukraine.[64]

While restrictive measures present clear limits in ensuring accountability for crimes, they could nonetheless serve the purpose of deterring individuals from committing those crimes; as such, they complement other initiatives taken by the EU. The Union has significantly engaged and cooperated with Ukraine in order to

---

[59] Council Decision (CFSP) 2022/883.

[60] Recital n. 3, Council Decision (CFSP) 2022/883.

[61] Recital n. 4, Ibid.

[62] Sexton 2022.

[63] For instance, in March 2023, the lists of the EU Global Human Rights Sanctions Regime (EU GHRSR) were updated to include police officials and commanders of unit active in occupied territories in Ukraine; they were held responsible for serious human rights violations, including systematic sexual and gender-based violence. See Council Decision (CFSP) 2023/501 of 7 March 2023.

[64] See Council Implementing Regulation (EU) 2023/429.

bring the authors of international crimes to justice. The EU has also cooperated with the International Criminal Court (ICC) to avoid impunity of crimes and human rights abuses committed in Ukraine. Since Russia's aggression, the European Commission has repeatedly stated that justice will be served for Ukraine and its people. Accordingly, it has reiterated its support for the investigations of the ICC Prosecutor and has provided over EUR 10 million to finance the activities of the Office of the Prosecutor related to Ukraine.[65] In addition, the Commission, the Council, and the Member States have been engaged in an unprecedented coordination to investigate the international crimes committed in Ukraine.

In March 2022, Lithuania, Poland, and Ukraine signed a Joint Investigation Team (JIT) agreement to enable the exchange of information and to facilitate investigations of war crimes, crimes against humanity, and other core crimes.[66] The main aim of the JIT is to support the gathering of evidence and its swift and secure exchange among partners. In this context, Eurojust has supported the set-up of the JIT in order to coordinate national investigations.[67] In April 2022, Eurojust and the ICC signed an agreement enabling the Office of the Prosecutor of the ICC to become a participant in the JIT.[68] This is the first time that the Office of the Prosecutor of the ICC has ever participated in a JIT. Estonia, Latvia, and Slovakia also joined the JIT,[69] followed by Romania.[70] In March 2023, seven national authorities involved in the JIT signed a Memorandum of Understanding (MoU) with the United States Department of Justice to facilitate closer coordination in their respective investigations in connection with the war in Ukraine.[71]

Given the urgent need to coordinate investigative efforts, EU institutions have also worked together to amend and reinforce Eurojust's mandate to collect and preserve evidence of war crimes.[72] The new mandate allows Eurojust to (i) store and preserve evidence related to war crimes, including digital evidence, such as satellite images,

[65] See Opening remarks by Commissioner Reynders at the Justice Ministers Conference on Support to the International Criminal Court and its Investigations into the Situation in Ukraine, press release https://ec.europa.eu/commission/presscorner/detail/eN/speech_23_1786. See also https://ec.europa.eu/commission/presscorner/detail/en/IP_22_3543 [accessed on 10 October 2025].

[66] The JIT is the result of a coordination meeting, which was held on 2 March at the initiative of the Prosecutor General of Lithuania, the Polish Minister of Justice and Prosecutor General and the Ukrainian Prosecutor General.

[67] Press released 18 March 2022, https://www.eurojust.europa.eu/news/eurojust-supports-joint-investigation-team-alleged-core-international-crimes-ukraine [accessed on 10 October 2025].

[68] See Statement by ICC Prosecutor, Karim A.A. Khan QC, https://www.icc-cpi.int/news/statement-icc-prosecutor-karim-aa-khan-qc-office-prosecutor-joins-national-authorities-joint [accessed on 10 October 2025].

[69] See https://www.eurojust.europa.eu/news/estonia-latvia-and-slovakia-become-members-joint-investigation-team-alleged-core-international [accessed on 10 October 2025].

[70] https://www.eurojust.europa.eu/news/romania-becomes-seventh-member-joint-investigation-team-alleged-core-international-crimes [accessed on 10 October 2025].

[71] https://www.justice.gov/opa/pr/us-attorney-general-and-ukrainian-prosecutor-general-met-strengthen-joint-efforts-hold [accessed on 10 October 2025].

[72] Article 1, Regulation (EU) 2022/838 of the European Parliament and of the Council of 30 May 2022 amending Regulation (EU) 2018/1727 as regards the preservation, analysis and storage at

photographs, videos, audio recordings, DNA profiles and fingerprints, and to process and analyse this evidence, in close cooperation with Europol, and (ii) share it with the relevant national and international authorities, including the International Criminal Court and other countries. Eurojust is also empowered to set up a dedicated database to centrally preserve, store, and analyse evidence of core international crimes, i.e. the Core International Crimes Database (CICED).[73] Eurojust and Europol are sharing the information with the relevant national and international judicial authorities, including the ICC. Finally, an International Centre for the Prosecution of the Crime of Aggression Against Ukraine (ICPA) was set up in July 2023 'to enhance investigations into the crime of aggression by securing key evidence and facilitating the process of case building at an early stage.'[74]

Finally, it worth of mentioning that in 2025 the EU also endorsed the establishment of the ad hoc Special Tribunal for the Crime of Aggression against Ukraine through an agreement signed by Ukraine and the Council of Europe.[75] As a result, Ukrainian authorities will be able to refer ongoing domestic investigations and prosecutions related to the crime of aggression to the Prosecutor of the Special Tribunal.[76]

6.5 The Broadening of the Designation Criteria of Individual Restrictive Measures: Are There Any Limits?

The Council has never, prior to the Russian aggression against Ukraine, frozen assets or issued visa bans on a comparable scale. The designation criteria of individual restrictive measures have been considerably expanded since the initial versions of EU acts that imposed the first individual restrictive measures in 2014. It may be wondered whether the categories of addressees of EU sanctions as defined by the Council are in line with international law. More precisely, two questions may be raised: are the groups of private parties who may potentially end up on the blacklists functional to the achievement of the objective of restrictive measures? Or is there a disconnection between the targeting of these persons and the cessation of the aggression? How has the Council applied the sanctions in practice?

Eurojust of evidence relating to genocide, crimes against humanity, war crimes and related criminal offences, OJ L 148, 31.05.2022, p. 1.

[73] https://www.eurojust.europa.eu/publication/core-international-crimes-evidence-database-ciced [accessed on 10 October 2025].

[74] https://www.eurojust.europa.eu/news/international-centre-prosecution-crime-aggression-made-official-united-justice-conference [accessed on 10 October 2025].

[75] https://www.coe.int/en/web/portal/-/president-zelenskyy-and-council-of-europe-secretary-general-berset-to-sign-agreement-on-special-tribunal-for-aggression-against-ukraine [accessed on 02 January 2026].

[76] https://www.eeas.europa.eu/delegations/ukraine/international-coalition-agrees-establishment-special-tribunal-crime-aggression-against-ukraine_en?s = 232&utm_source = chatgpt.com [accessed on 2 January 2026].

It is necessary to start from the category of 'leading businesspersons active in a sector providing a substantial source of revenue.[77]' The reason why they are targeted is in line with the objective of restrictive measures, which is to put an end to Russia's aggression. Indeed, by curbing the sources of revenue of the aggressor State, maintaining the war machine becomes increasingly difficult. It should be immediately clarified that the listing of prominent businessmen was resorted to in the context of other regimes of restrictive measures and is devoid of any punitive purpose.[78]

In June 2023 Council (CFSP) Decision 2023/1094[79] changed the listing criterion of Article 2(1) g) of Decision 2014/145 as amended which was extended to include three categories of persons in addition to the leading businesspersons: their immediate family members and other natural persons, benefiting from businessmen, businesspersons, legal persons, entities or bodies involved in economic sectors providing a substantial source of revenue to the Government.

It may be wondered whether the expansion of the designation criteria introduced by Decision (CFSP) 2023/1094 is justified by the need to ensure that the objective of restrictive measures is achieved. Listing family members does not increase the pressure on the Russian government to cease the aggression; therefore, it may appear incompatible with the nature of restrictive measures. Yet, the Council's explanation set out in the preamble to the mentioned CFSP Decision convincingly justifies the listing of these persons[80]: leading Russian businesspersons have engaged in a systematic practice of distributing their funds and assets amongst their immediate family members and other persons, often in order to hide their assets, to circumvent the restrictive measures and to maintain control over the resources available to them. The importance of countering circumvention has also been highlighted in the case law.[81] Therefore, listing family members makes the EU sanctions more effective and is compatible with the principle of proportionality since not all family members are eligible for listing: only those who derive a benefit from the primary target.

Coming to businessmen who are not prominent but provide a substantial source of revenue to the government of Russia, their inclusion in the designation criterion is necessary considering that they fund the war machine. In contrast, it may be more difficult for the Council to prove that 'persons other than the immediate family members' who benefit from businesspersons should be targeted. Indeed, these subjects neither present a sufficiently strong connection with the authors of the breaches of international law, nor do they have any influence on the ability of businessmen to fund the war. They do not even indirectly contribute to the continuation of the aggression. The only plausible justification to include these persons in

---

[77] For an illustration of the different designation criteria see Chap. 2 in this book.

[78] GC, Case T-193/22, *OT*, par. 144.

[79] See Council Decision (CFSP) 2023/1094.

[80] Recital n. 5, Ibid.

[81] For individual restrictive measure see GC, Case T-102/23, *SBK Art OOO*, paras 165, 167, 218, CJEU, Cases C-703/23 P, *Elena Petrovna Timchenko*, par. 32, C-72/11, *Afrasiabi and Others*, par 46. In the context of sectoral restrictive measures see AG's Medina Opinion of 26 June 2025 in Cases C-313/24 (*Opera Laboratori Fiorentini*), C-380/09 P, *Melli Bank*, par. 58 and C-595/15 P, *NIOC*, par. 89. On the circumvention of individual restrictive measures see Finelli 2025.

the designation criteria is that they could be used by businesspersons to circumvent the asset freezes/visa bans. Yet, while there is a real risk of circumvention when it comes to family members of the designated persons, that risk is merely potential in the case of persons other than family members (i.e. friends) of the primary targets being listed. The inclusion of this category of subjects on the sanctions list should be conditional upon the Council establishing, on the basis of sufficient evidence, that the circumvention of restrictive measures has increased.

It is noteworthy that the preamble of (CFSP) Decision 2023/1094 widens the circle of persons who could potentially be placed on the blacklist.[82] It is unusual to identify potential targets of restrictive measures in the preamble whose provisions are in principle not legally binding.[83] In the light of the case law of the GC, it could be argued that the Council has provided an interpretation of the provisions of the act which is contrary to the wording of Article 1. The preamble states that the designation criteria should cover 'leading businesspersons operating *in any economic sector*' of Russia[84] thus adding a further category of persons to those of Article 2(1) g. This time the justification provided by the Council is not entirely convincing: persons are listed since they have been allowed to exploit natural or public resources by the government and as such, they have a relation of interdependence with the Russian government.[85] While there is little doubt that a relationship of mutual benefit and support exists between the Government of the Russian Federation and leading businesspersons operating across economic sectors in the country, where the sector concerned does not generate substantial revenue for the Russian state budget, it becomes difficult to link the designation of such individuals to the attainment of the primary objectives of restrictive measures. Yet, the targeting of a businessperson continues to be consistent with the purpose of EU sanctions where that individual is active in sectors of strategic relevance, such as the energy sector. A further element of interest in the practice is that the Council appears to rely on a combination of listing criteria when designating individuals and generally refrains from invoking the criterion under consideration as the sole basis for a listing.

A second category of persons referred to in the Preamble is represented by 'other businesspersons who are involved in economic sectors providing a substantial source

[82] Council Decision (CFSP) 2023/1094, recital n. 5.

[83] As the Court has stressed, 'The preamble to an EU act has no binding legal force and cannot be relied on as a ground either for derogating from the actual provisions of the act in question or for interpreting those provisions in a manner that is clearly contrary to their wording, it may explain their content, since the recitals in that preamble constitute important elements for the purposes of interpretation that may clarify the intentions of the author of that act (CJEU, Case C-422/19 and C-423/19 *Hessischer Rundfunk*, EU:C:2021:63, par. 64 and the case-law cited).' GC, Case T-741/22, *Ezuvov v Council*, par. 183.

[84] The reasons justifying the inclusion of business persons is the following: '[...] the Council considers that the designation criteria should be extended to allow for the listing as appropriate of *other businesspersons* (emphasis added) who are involved in economic sectors providing a substantial source of revenue to the Government of the Russian Federation, in order to increase pressure on the Government of the Russian Federation to bring an end to its war of aggression against Ukraine.' See Recital 4, Council Decision (CFSP) 2023/1094.

[85] Ibid.

of revenue to the Government of the Russian Federation.[86]' In this case the justification offered by the Council is convincing: these persons contribute to financially supporting the continuation of the war; therefore, freezing their assets serves the purpose of increasing the pressure on the Government of the Russian Federation to bring to an end the aggression against Ukraine.

Having identified the main objective of most restrictive measures in Sect. 6.2.1, that is to say the cessation of the hostilities in Ukraine, it is crucial to ensure that sanctions are effective. The effectiveness of sector-related measures is even more important than that of individual restrictive measures since Russia's war machine is more affected by sector-related measures than individual ones.[87]

In order to avoid the circumvention of its sanctions, the EU has targeted private parties who frustrate both individual and sector-related sanctions.[88] In addition, the Council has expanded the scope of the prohibitions to trade and the provision of services in Crimea and Sevastopol so as to avoid that these territories become a vehicle of circumvention.[89] It is necessary to examine what the outer limits of the mentioned extended anti-circumvention activities are. This will be discussed in the next section.

---

[86] Ibid.

[87] Arguably, violations of sector-specific restrictive measures have a more severe impact on the European Union's sanctions regime than breaches of individual asset freezes imposed on oligarchs. Certain sectoral measures—particularly those targeting the import of oil, arms, and dual-use goods and technologies—are specifically designed to increase the economic, technological, and military costs for Russia of continuing the war.

The effectiveness of these measures is, however, significantly undermined by widespread circumvention practices. Numerous documented cases show violations of EU prohibitions carried out by third countries or by economic operators established outside the Union. Through these channels, Russia may continue to acquire weapons, strategic goods, or sensitive technologies that enhance its military, industrial, or technological capabilities. This may occur, *inter alia*, through subsidiaries of EU companies operating in third countries, or as a result of deliberate policies by third states aimed at exporting prohibited items to Russia or circumventing bans on services essential for oil exports.

A notable example is the so-called 'shadow fleet' which enables Russia to bypass restrictions on maritime services linked to oil transportation. Likewise, the involvement of third countries in facilitating the circumvention of export controls on drones, weapons, and other warfare-related technologies plays a critical role in sustaining Russia's war effort and contributes to serious violations of international humanitarian law.

[88] Section 6.6.1.

[89] Council Decision (CFSP) 2025/397.

6.6 The Extraterritorial Effects of EU Restrictive Measures: False Extraterritoriality and the Factors Triggering Prescriptive Jurisdiction

6.6.1 The Position of the EU Council: Restrictive Measures Are Not Extraterritorial in Nature

The extraterritorial application of sanctions has often been a matter of contention in the practice of unilateral coercive measures; in particular, US sanctions were contested for imposing the so-called 'secondary sanctions', an expression that can be taken as a synonym for extraterritorial sanctions.[90] The latter were defined by scholars as 'sanctions that are imposed on foreign economic operators whose activities have no nexus whatsoever with the sanctioning state.'[91] These measures do not apply against a State that has committed a breach of international law, but rather vis-à-vis third countries (including operators subject to their jurisdiction) that engage with the mentioned State (or entities under its jurisdiction), even if the sanctioning State does not have a cause of action against these subjects. The designation by the US of EU companies that had contractual relations[92] with entities included in the special designated list (SDL) of the Iran sanction regime after 2018 is a notorious example of the extraterritorial application of these measures.

The Union has criticized the US for applying sanctions beyond its jurisdiction[93] and has taken protective measures for its operators,[94] including a trade instrument aimed at adopting countermeasures in cases of economic coercion.[95]

The EU institutions have always stated that restrictive measures do not apply extraterritorially in breach of the principle of prescriptive jurisdiction, and this is reiterated in the Commission's FAQs.[96] The Council defines the standard clause on jurisdiction in the following terms. Restrictive measures apply: (a) within the territory of the Union, including its airspace; (b) on board of any aircraft or any vessel under the jurisdiction of a Member State; (c) to any person inside or outside the territory of the Union who is a national of a Member State; (d) to any legal person, entity or body, inside or outside the territory of the Union, which is incorporated or constituted under the law of a Member State; (e) to any legal person, entity or body in respect of any business done in whole or in part within the Union.[97]'

---

90 Ruys and Ryngaert 2020, p. 8.

91 Ryngaert et al. 2024, p. 3.

92 CJEU, C-124/20, *Bank Melli Iran v Telekom Deutschland GmbH*.

93 Beaucillon 2021, p. 121.

94 The EU has also enacted blocking statutes to protect EU companies from the US secondary sanctions against those who traded with Cuba and Iran. Ibid., pp. 122–123.

95 This is the anti-coercion instrument regulated by Council Regulation (EU) 2023/2675.

96 See FAQs p. 296 (29 October 2025) [accessed on 10 November 2025].

97 Council Guidelines on implementation and evaluation of restrictive measures (sanctions) in the framework of the EU Common Foreign and Security Policy, document 5664/18, 2018, p. 42.

Scholars have never contested the EU restrictive measures for their extraterritorial application until the EU's response to the war in Ukraine in 2022: EU individual restrictive measures (the 'territorial integrity' sanction regime) and sector-related restrictive measures (the 'Russia destabilisation' sanction regime), enacted to exert pressure on Russia to cease the aggression, include prohibitions affecting the right to conduct business of operators in third countries (different from Russia) as a result of an unprecedented anti-circumvention action of the EU. For this reason, the EU has been criticised for potentially imposing secondary sanctions.[98] It is necessary to understand whether this criticism is justified or not.

The challenges faced by the EU in countering the circumvention of EU restrictive measures are remarkable and will be illustrated in Sect. 6.6.2.

Before turning to this issue, two observations can be made. The first is that primary sanctions target the country responsible for an illegal behaviour; yet, even if, for this reason, they have extraterritorial effects in the sense that they may influence the behaviour of the target country,[99] it does not follow that they are extraterritorial by nature.[100] Indeed, the EU exercises its jurisdiction on the basis of a territorial or nationality nexus, or by reference to the place of incorporation of the companies subject to its extensive export and import bans on specific goods, technologies, and services. In addition, the EU often takes political and diplomatic initiatives to broaden the reach of its primary sanctions by encouraging like-minded partners—such as EU candidate countries, Norway, and Switzerland—to align with its sanctions policy.[101] This constitutes an instance of false extraterritoriality, since the third countries concerned are not coerced into aligning with the EU's foreign policy choices; rather, they do so voluntarily and remain free to decline the EU's invitation.[102] Therefore, the Union cannot be said to have imposed its choices in foreign affairs on other States, thus interfering with their sovereignty. In the next section, we will scrutinise more in detail the issue of the jurisdictional nexus of EU restrictive measures, by providing examples of circumvention practices.

6.6.2 *The EU Anti-circumvention Practices and the Limits in Protecting the Effectiveness of Restrictive Measures*

The EU has engaged in an unprecedented fight against the circumvention of its restrictive measures. The effectiveness of these measures is essential for undermining

[98] 'It is difficult to escape the impression that the European Union is increasingly moving in the direction of adopting the very extraterritorial and secondary sanctions it once denounced.' Ruys and Rodríguez Silvestre 2024, p. 497; Terlinden 2024, p. 11.

[99] Kerbrat 2021, p. 166.

[100] Silingardi 2024, p. 1138.

[101] Sossai 2020, p. 67.

[102] Neither Georgia nor Serbia have aligned with EU restrictive measures enacted in reaction to Russia's aggression.

Russia's military, industrial and economic capacity to continue the war. There are numerous examples of anti-circumvention clauses in the 2014 sanction Regulations, as amended. This is certainly not new per se: for example, sanction regimes, including those of UN origin, concerning the non-proliferation of weapons of mass destruction in DRNK[103] or the situation of Libya,[104] impose on Member States the obligation to take steps to avoid vessels circumventing import or export prohibitions.

Yet the intensity of the efforts undertaken by the EU in countering circumvention of EU sanctions related to Russia's aggression is unprecedented. Most of the new criteria inserted in the legal framework of restrictive measures between June 2023 and October 2025 were aimed at closing the loopholes of the sanctions. An innovative aspect of individual restrictive measures is that the obligation to avoid the circumvention of EU prohibitions is broadly defined, as illustrated by the black letter of Article 12 of Regulation 269/2014 as amended.[105] There is also a specific designation criterion in this act that includes a catch-all clause on circumvention,[106] whereby it is possible to list natural or legal persons, entities or bodies facilitating infringement of the prohibition against circumvention of Regulations setting out restrictive measures or significantly frustrating those measures. The wording of this prohibition is extremely wide: the GC not yet confirmed its legality.[107] The author takes the view that Parties instituting unilateral coercive measures have a wide power to protect their effectiveness, especially when sanctions are adopted in reaction to a breach of a peremptory norm of international law. The opportunities to circumvent restrictive measures are numerous and the efficacy of these measures can be put at stake not only by natural or legal persons located in the EU, but also by operators/entities of third countries, which are not subject to EU law. It is well known that EU neighbouring States such as Turkey and Armenia or Azerbaijan have not imposed sanctions against Russia, while China, Iran and North Korea are actively supporting Russia's continuation of the aggression. The EU neighbour countries help Russia to circumvent prohibitions to export technology and sensitive goods, thus making the EU prohibitions ineffective. The attempts to sidestep the EU sanctions concern the

---

[103] See Article 37 of Council Regulation (EU) 2017/1509: 'Member States shall seize, inspect and impound any vessel in their ports, and may seize, inspect and impound any vessel subject to their jurisdiction in their territorial waters where there are reasonable grounds to believe that the vessel has been involved in activities, or the transport of items, prohibited by the relevant UN Security Council Resolutions.'

[104] See Article 21 of Council Regulation (EU) 2016/44 of 18 January 2016 concerning restrictive measures in view of the situation in Libya and repealing Regulation (EU) No 204/2011OJ L 12, 19.1.2016, p. 1: 'Member States shall inspect the cargo of vessels and aircraft bound to or from Libya, if they have information that the cargo of contains prohibited items. Upon discovery, Member States shall seize and dispose prohibited items.'

[105] See Article 12 of Council Regulation 269/2014 as amended: 'It shall be prohibited to participate, knowingly and intentionally, in activities the object or effect of which is to circumvent the provisions of this Regulation, including by concealing the identity of parties, misrepresenting the nature of goods or services, or using intermediaries to avoid compliance.'

[106] See Article 3(1)d of Council Regulation 269/2014, as amended.

[107] For a case where the the legality of the designation criteria in relation to the issue of curcmvention was confirmed see GC Case T-1113/23 *Aleksandra Melnichenko v Council*.

full range of prohibited activities. For example, entities outside Russia favour the circumvention of the prohibition to provide access to SWIFT by using the System for Transfer of Financial Messages, developed by the CBR as an alternative to the EU based company that manages the system of payments. While the EU cannot impose its foreign policy choices upon third countries, it should be stressed that the behaviour of the latter amounts to assisting Russia in the continuation of its unlawful activities. Vessels flying a flag of countries different from those of EU Member States, or Russia, may be used to circumvent the prohibition to import (dual-used) goods/technology or oil or gas from the aggressor country into the Union.[108] Subsidiaries of EU parent companies located in third countries may seek to escape the EU prohibitions to export unmanned aerial vehicles or missiles to Russia.

It is particularly important not to defeat the very same purpose of Regulation 833/2014, which is to weaken Russia's military, industrial and economic capacity to continue the war. The sector-related sanction regime concerning Russia's destabilization seeks to prevent that import/export bans or the prohibition to provide services are circumvented by third countries.

International law sets limits to the Union in the adoption of its sanctions. The jurisdictional provision of Regulation 833/2014 is incorporated in Article 13. Where restrictive measures purport to regulate the conduct of private parties falling under the jurisdiction of another State beyond the EU's accepted jurisdictional bases, they may be contested as encroachments upon that State's sovereignty. It is as if the EU imposed secondary sanctions, that is to say coercive measures 'that apply to the relations between a third country (and its entities) and the targeted State.'[109] Therefore, the EU must exercise prescriptive jurisdiction solely where a territorial or nationality nexus can be established, or where the entity operating outside the EU is controlled by an EU parent company.

As noted above, Regulation 833/2014 includes several provisions aimed at ensuring the effectiveness of its prohibitions. Those provisions appear to be consistent with international law, insofar as they apply to EU operators or are based on a sufficient territorial nexus with the Union. Moreover, they appear to comply with the principle of proportionality, given that the prohibitions are subject to exemptions and derogations.

A number of examples can be made.

In order to safeguard the effectiveness of the export prohibitions on dual-use goods and technology to Russia, it is forbidden to sell, supply, transfer, or export—directly or indirectly—such items to private parties in Russia and *for their use* in Russia (emphasis added). As a result of the latter element of this provision, EU operators are required to refrain from selling dual-use goods to third countries where there is a risk that such goods or technology may be re-sold for use in Russia. The transit of these goods (whether or not they originate in the Union) via the territory of Russia

[108] There are also other anti-circumvention clauses concerning restrictions on road transport and the flight ban.

[109] Silingardi 2024, p. 1138.

is also banned,[110] since there are risks that the prohibited items are intercepted by the target country.[111] Another transit ban applies in respect of goods and technology which might contribute to Russia's military and technological enhancement or to the development of its defence and security sector, as listed in Annex VII, exported from the Union.[112] The powers of national competent authorities ('NCAs') include the revocation of export authorisations[113] granted by way of derogation where there is a substantiated risk of circumvention of EU sanctions. In this context, NCAs are under the obligation to take all necessary measures to ensure the effective implementation of the Regulation when they manage the authorisations.[114]

Next, the EU prohibits the export of certain goods and technologies to countries such as Iran and Belarus insofar as such items may support Russia's war efforts when re-exported from those countries.[115]

Turning to Article 5ae of Regulation 833/2014 as amended in October 2025, this provision lays down a ban on EU operators from engaging in transactions with specific ports, locks as well as airports in Russia and with ports and locks in third countries other than Russia that are used for the circumvention of various export bans.[116] As the Commission has clarified, a third country national is not covered by the mentioned ban; this is a confirmation that the transaction ban rests on solid legal ground.[117]

As a measure of last resort aimed at preventing the circumvention of restrictive measures, particular significance attaches to Article 12f (1) of Regulation 833/2014, which provides that:

> It shall be prohibited to sell, supply, transfer or export, directly or indirectly, goods and technology as listed in Annex XXXIII, whether or not originating in the Union, to any natural or legal person, entity or body in the third country identified in that Annex.' The latter shall only include third countries that have been identified by the Council [unanimously] as having systematically and persistently failed to prevent the sale, supply, transfer or export to Russia of goods and technology exported from the Union, despite the Union's prior outreach and assistance to the country in question.[118]

---

110 See Article 2(1)(a) of Council Regulation 833/2014, as amended.

111 It is not the first time that the EU bans the transit through the target country. For example, the EU prohibited the transit of any petrochemical products originating in Iran or exported from Iran, even if they pass through third countries. See Article 13 of Council Regulation (EU) No 267/2012.

112 See Article 2a(1)(a) of Council Regulation 833/2014, as amended. See also Article 3c(1a) concerning a similar prohibition for goods and technology suited for use in aviation or the space industry.

113 See Article 2(7) and 2a(7) of Council Regulation 833/2014 as amended.

114 See Article 2(8) and 2a(8) of Council Regulation 833/2014, as amended.

115 For example, goods and technology suited for use in aviation or the space industry cannot transit through Belarus; it is also prohibited to export goods and technology which might contribute to Iran's capability to manufacture Unmanned Aerial Vehicles (UAVs) or missiles as listed in specific Annexes.

116 Council Regulation (EU) 2025/2033.

117 Commission's FAQs, Question 9 p. 455 of 19 December 2025 [accessed on 30 December 2025].

118 Article 12f (3) of Council Regulation 833/2014 as amended.

At present, the list set out in Annex XXXIII is empty. Should the Union decide to populate it, such action would not be unlawful. Pursuant to Article 16 of the ARSIWA, States are prohibited from aiding or assisting another State in the commission of an internationally wrongful act; accordingly, the EU Member States may decide to restrict exports of the goods or technologies concerned as an act of retorsion vis-à-vis third countries that breach this obligation. Even where such restrictions were to conflict with WTO law, the EU measures could nonetheless be justified under the relevant provisions of the GATT, as discussed in Sect. 6.2.

Another example of an anti-circumvention measure is set out in Article 3d, which establishes the flight ban. In this context, the national competent authority of the Member State of departure, destination, or overflight may refuse authorisation where it has reasonable grounds to suspect the circumvention of the prohibition, on the basis of factors such as the routing and origin of the flight or information relating to the operator concerned. This measure is grounded in a territorial connection with the Union and is therefore lawful.

In order to counter circumvention practices relating to the prohibitions on oil imports, the EU has, as of 24 July 2023, prohibited access to ports and locks within the territory of the Union for *any* vessel (emphasis added) that has engaged in ship-to-ship transfers at any point during its voyage to a Member State's ports or locks, where the competent authority has reasonable grounds to suspect that the vessel is in breach of the prohibitions laid down in Regulation 833/2014, as amended.[119] A similar provision applies to 'any vessel which the competent authority has reasonable cause to suspect of illegally interfering with, switching off or otherwise disabling its shipborne automatic identification system at any point of the voyage to a Member State's ports or locks, in breach of SOLAS Regulation V/19, point 2.4, when transporting crude oil or petroleum products subject to the prohibitions set out in Article 3 m(1) and (2) and Article 3n(1) and (4).[120]'

In March 2025 the designation criteria of individual restrictive measures were expanded to include 'natural persons that own, control, manage or operate vessels that transport crude oil or petroleum products, originating in Russia or exported from Russia, while practicing irregular and high-risk shipping practices as set out in the International Maritime Organisation General Assembly resolution A.1192(33), or that otherwise provide material, technical or financial support to the operations of such vessels.[121]' This provision seeks to address the issue of the so-called 'shadow fleet' and, as such, merits closer examination. It has rightly been noted that the international endorsement or institutional embedding of a unilateral measure with extraterritorial effects within an intergovernmental organisation such as the IMO is of particular importance, since it 'tend(s) to confer legitimacy, pre-empt international protest, and thus softens the rough edges of unilateralism.'[122] Along the same lines,

[119] Article 3eb(1).

[120] Article 3ec(1).

[121] Recital 6 of Council Decision (CFSP) 2025/388.

[122] Ruys, Ryngaert 2020, p. 108.

Krisch stresses that jurisdictional claims are more widely accepted if measures are linked to international standards.[123]

A further EU initiative, in connection to the shadow fleet, is noteworthy: the Union is seeking to develop international law, in particular in the context of the United Nation Convention on the Law of the Sea (UNCLOS) of 1982, in order to tackle the problems caused by the shadow fleet which not only threaten the effectiveness of restrictive measures but also pose challenges to the protection of submarine cables and pipelines.[124]

Coming back to anti-circumvention measures of Regulation 833/2014, the prohibition on access to ports and locks also affects the transport of goods generating revenue for Russia and applies to vessels irrespective of the flag, except for the Union-flagged vessels[125]; as a result, ships registered in third countries may be listed if they aim at circumventing the EU sanctions. It is noteworthy that as of October 2025, about 1090 vessels are subject to restrictive measures and most of them were inserted into the list in 2025.[126]

The EU has also introduced ancillary sanctions in connection with the prohibitions on access to ports and locks. In particular, EU operators are prohibited from providing, directly or indirectly, technical assistance, brokering services, or financing or financial assistance related to the trading, brokering, or transport—including through ship-to-ship transfers—of crude oil or petroleum products listed in Annex XXV, where such products originate in Russia or have been exported from Russia.[127] This measure has a direct impact on operators in third countries. The reason for the EU to refuse to sell the mentioned services is to counter the circumvention of its primary sanctions: indeed, operators in third countries may use the mentioned services to sidestep the EU prohibition on import of oil and petroleum products from Russia, whose purpose is to decrease the revenues generated by the export of this product.

It is necessary to assess whether the EU may lawfully take measures that make it more difficult for private parties subject to the jurisdiction of another State to engage in the transport of oil, for the purpose of combating the circumvention of its primary sanctions. This raises the question whether such anti-circumvention clauses are compatible with the limits of prescriptive jurisdiction. It is submitted that the prohibition on providing brokering services, or other services necessary for the maritime transport of oil, to operators in third countries is lawful, since the EU is under no obligation to make its services available to operators of third States, even where it is a major provider of such services, as explained in Sect. 6.2. The EU's ban is designed to exert pressure on private parties, who support Russia's circumvention

[123] Krisch 2022, p. 501.

[124] Declaration of the European Union and its Member States on making full use of the international law of the sea framework relating to threats from the 'shadow fleet' and to the protection of critical undersea infrastructure, 16,719/25, par. 10, 15 December 2025, https://data.consilium.europa.eu/doc/document/ST-16829-2025-INIT/en/pdf [accessed on 3 January 2026].

[125] Recital 13 of Council Regulation (EU) 2024/1745.

[126] About 170 vessels were listed in 2024; the rest of the vessels were listed in 2025.

[127] Article 3n.

of sanctions, to cease their activities; therefore, it is lawful since it directly applies to EU service providers.

One of the unintended collateral consequences of the EU's refusal to make its services available to operators of third countries is the potential emergence of safety and environmental risks linked to the transport of oil from Russia, in particular where vessels are unable to secure alternative service providers or seek to circumvent safety requirements in order to evade EU restrictions, including port State control. Such risks[128] associated with the operation of the so-called 'dark fleet' or 'shadow fleet' have been recognised not only by the EU but also by the General Assembly of the International Maritime Organization in its resolution of 6 December 2023.[129] But it is also by virtue of these risks and of other security threats,[130] that the EU may forbid access to ports and locks.

Another example of the global effects associated with EU restrictive measures merits attention. In June 2024, the EU prohibited Union entities operating outside Russia from directly connecting to the SPFS of the CBR, or to equivalent specialised financial messaging services established by this bank.[131] In October 2025, this ban was extended to the connection 'of any systems of the Central Bank of Russia or to systems provided by any other legal person, entity or body incorporated or constituted under the law of Russia that include a financial messaging functionality, including the Fast Payment System (SBP) and Mir.'[132] In addition, since 2024 the Council has provided for a prohibition on engaging in any transactions with a legal person, entity or body established outside Russia as listed in a specific annex, which lists banks that use the SPFS or other equivalent systems. These entities were targeted since by using the SPFS, they '(i) increase Russia's financial resilience and (ii) support the circumvention of the prohibitions in this Decision and Decision 2014/145/CFSP, and in Regulations (EU) No 833/2014 and (EU) No 269/2014.'[133] In June 2024, the list was empty; in 2025 three banks registered in Belarus, Kazakhstan and China were added[134] and the list has grown to seven in October 2025.[135] It may be questioned whether the transaction ban is lawful, given that it affects entities operating within the jurisdiction of third countries. Admittedly, such measures may appear to have extraterritorial effects; however, they are in fact addressed to Union entities operating

[128] The 'shadow fleet' may operate without insurance and with disregard for safety and environmental standards.

[129] Resolution A.1192(33) adopted on 6 December 2023 [accessed on 10 October 2025].

[130] See the Declaration of the European Union and its Member States on making full use of the international law of the sea framework relating to threats from the 'shadow fleet' and to the protection of critical undersea infrastructure, 16719/25, par. 10, 15 December 2025 [accessed on 10 October 2025].

[131] Article 5ac(1) of Council Regulation (EU) 2024/1745.

[132] Article 5ac(1) as amended by Council Regulation (EU) 2025/2033. The prohibition under exam applies as from 25 January 2026. For examples of US sanctions see Abely 2025, p. 48 and ff.

[133] Article 1ad of Council Decision (CFSP) 2024/1744.

[134] See annex XLIV of Council Regulation (EU) 2025/395.

[135] See annex XLIV of Council Regulation (EU) 2025/2033.

outside Russia and therefore remain connected to the EU through a territorial nexus or by virtue of the EU registration of the entities concerned.

The Council states that the aim of the transaction ban is to contain the development of the SPFS and to reduce Russia's capacity to wage war as well as to prevent the frustration of the measures established in Regulation (EU) No 833/2014.[136] This example suggests that the argument based on the notion of 'frustration' is relied upon extensively, in order to justify the adoption of EU restrictive measures. It is noteworthy, and to some extent paradoxical, that the EU imposes a transaction ban on Union entities operating in third countries that use the SPFS, while at the same time allowing Union entities to engage in transactions with Russian entities that make use of that payment system.[137] It is likely that the EU has refrained from extending the prohibition in order to comply with the principle of proportionality and/or to allow the continuation of certain transactions that cannot be suspended in the EU interest.

To sum up, it is undeniable that EU restrictive measures have a global reach extending to operators in third countries. However, this is due to the fact that those operators are connected to the EU through a territorial nexus or by virtue of their links with EU-registered companies. It may therefore be concluded that the EU has not exceeded the limits of its prescriptive jurisdiction. By contrast, the United States may designate in the SDN list individuals and entities lacking any direct territorial or personal nexus with the country.[138] Such designations are not necessarily grounded in a specific cause of action, but rather in the determination that the conduct of the listed entities runs counter to U.S. foreign policy objectives.[139] From an international law perspective, this approach raises concerns, as it may encroach upon the freedom of third States to conduct their own foreign policy, a core element of State sovereignty, and may therefore be viewed as an interference in their internal affairs. Yet an alternative justification for the transaction ban deserves attention, in case the transaction ban is considered a secondary sanction. Drawing on the work of Silingardi,[140] we can say that the measure adopted by the EU can be seen as an instrument to operationalise the obligation of all States to cooperate, through lawful means, to bring to an end any serious breach of peremptory norms of international law, as provided for in Article 41(1) of the ARSIWA and Article 19(1) of the 2022 Draft Conclusions on the Identification and Legal Consequences of Peremptory Norms of General International Law.[141] In this sense, the EU transaction ban may be understood as a measure giving concrete effect to the duty of cooperation referred to above—which the International Law Commission characterised in ARSIWA as a

---

[136] Recital n. 16 of Council Regulation (EU) 2024/1745.

[137] Ibid.

[138] In addition, The US apply penalties to non-US companies rather than access restrictions. Abely 2023, p. 42.

[139] Gordon 2024, p. 93.

[140] Silingardi 2024, p. 231.

[141] See also the advisory opinion of the International Court of Justice, *Legal Consequences of the Construction of a Wall in the Occupied Palestinian Territory (Advisory Opinion) [2004] ICJ Rep* 136, paras 159–160.

progressive development of international law[142]—in a situation in which there are States such as Belarus, Kazakhstan and China that do not comply with the obligation stemming from Article 41(1) ARSIWA.

6.6.3 *The Case of the So-Called 'No Re-export to Russia Clause'*

A set of obligations which may be suspected of being extraterritorial in nature concerns the so-called 'no re-export to Russia clause' in contractual obligations, between an EU parent company and its non-EU subsidiaries, concerning the export of specific technology (used for warfare), provided for in Article 12g of Regulation 833/2014. Before examining this clause in greater detail, it should be emphasised, once again, that the EU trade prohibitions—which are essential to ensuring the effectiveness of its sanctions—are grounded in a territorial nexus or in the place of incorporation of the entities concerned. In particular, export bans on certain items that are instrumental to the continuation of the aggression are addressed to companies incorporated in the EU and to subsidiaries of Russian companies established within the Union. By contrast, as stated by the Commission in its FAQs, Russian subsidiaries of EU parent companies do not fall within the scope of Regulation 833/2014,[143] but remain subject to Russian law.

At the same time, EU law imposes on EU parent companies to avoid circumventing the EU restrictive measures through their subsidiaries in Russia. This implies that EU companies cannot delegate to their subsidiaries in Russia decisions that undermine the effectiveness of restrictive measures.

In June 2024 the Council has imposed extensive due diligence obligations in the text of restrictive measures. It is worth reproducing the text in full:

> It is appropriate to require that Union operators undertake their best efforts to ensure that legal persons, entities and bodies established outside the Union that they own or control do not participate in activities that undermine the restrictive measures provided for in Regulation (EU) No 833/2014. Such activities are those resulting in an effect that those restrictive measures seek to prevent, for example, that a recipient in Russia obtains goods, technology, financing or services of a type that is subject to prohibitions under Regulation (EU) No 833/2014.[144]

'Best efforts obligations' were defined as 'comprising all actions that are suitable and necessary to achieve the result of preventing the undermining of the restrictive measures in Regulation (EU) No 833/2014.' The scope of those obligations was further clarified through examples illustrating the conditions[145] under which they

[142] Silingardi 2024, p. 232.

[143] See FAQs (answer to question 14 of Regulation 833(2014), 29 October 2025 [accessed on 10 November 2025].

[144] Recital n. 29 of Council Regulation (EU) 2024/1745.

[145] Those actions can include, for example, 'the implementation of appropriate policies, controls and procedures to mitigate and manage risk effectively, considering factors such as the third country

may be considered fulfilled. It is submitted that those conditions, which may arguably lead to a degree of overcompliance, are not unreasonable. As to the compatibility of best-efforts obligations with the rules governing prescriptive jurisdiction, this does not appear to be especially contentious, given the existence of a territorial nexus between the EU and the entities upon which the obligation is imposed. Non-EU subsidiaries are required to comply with EU restrictive measures only in the context of their contractual relationships with an EU-based company.[146]

Coming to the 'no re-export to Russia clause,' as expressed by Article 12g) of Regulation 883/2014, this was introduced in EU restrictive measures since December 2023.[147] Under this provision, Union operators who sell, supply, transfer or export sensitive goods to third countries[148] must, as a general rule, include a clause in their contracts prohibiting the re-export of those goods to Russia or for use in Russia. This obligation applies from 20 March 2024.[149] The objective of Article 12g) is clear: in order to prevent EU export bans from being circumvented through trade diversion to Russia via third countries, the Council has required EU operators to include the relevant contractual clause. As a result, the purchaser of the goods concerned—even if located in a third country—is obliged not to re-export them to Russia, including where the purchaser is established in a State that has chosen not to impose sanctions on Russia. It is submitted that such clauses have a sufficient territorial nexus with the EU to justify the exercise of its prescriptive jurisdiction.

But how far can the EU go in preventing the effectiveness of its restrictive measures from being undermined? This question warrants particular attention. The Commission was tasked with assessing the impact of the use of the 'no re-export to Russia clause' on deterring circumvention.[150] Depending on the circumvention patterns identified through this monitoring process, this institution may decide to require Union operators to ensure that their subsidiaries in third countries also use the 'no

---

of establishment, the business sector and the type of activity of the legal person, entity or body that is owned or controlled by the Union operator. At the same time, best efforts should be understood as comprising only actions that are feasible for the Union operator in view of its nature, its size and the relevant factual circumstances, in particular the degree of effective control over the legal person, entity or body established outside the Union. Such circumstances include the situation where the Union operator, due to reasons that it did not cause itself, such as the legislation of a third country, is not able to exercise control over a legal person, entity or body that it owns.' Recital n. 30, ibid.

[146] For a more nuanced position, see Van Damme and Matthaiou 2025, p. 208.

[147] Council Regulation (EU) 2023/2878.

[148] Partner countries such as Norway, Switzerland, Iceland, Liechtenstein, Australia, New Zealand, South Korea and non-EU G7 members are excluded. See annex VIII of Council Regulation (EU) 833/2014 as amended. Sensitive goods and technology include certain common high priority items or specific firearms and ammunition.

[149] In the latest version 'When selling, supplying, transferring or exporting to a third country, with the exception of partner countries listed in Annex VIII to this Regulation, goods or technology as listed in Annexes XI, XX and XXXV to this Regulation, common high priority items as listed in Annex XL to this Regulation, or firearms and ammunition as listed in Annex I to Regulation (EU) No 258/2012, exporters shall, as of 20 March 2024, contractually prohibit re-exportation to Russia and re-exportation for use in Russia.'

[150] Recital n. 32 of Council Regulation (EU) 2024/1745.

Russia clause.' It is submitted that requiring a subsidiary to include this clause in its contractual relations with a non-EU company cannot be justified on the basis of the principle of territoriality, which constitutes one of the recognised grounds for the exercise of prescriptive jurisdiction. Nor does the 'effects doctrine' appear capable of supporting the EU's assertion of prescriptive jurisdiction in this context. Under that doctrine, a State may regulate the conduct of foreign nationals only where such conduct produces a 'direct, substantial, and reasonably foreseeable effect within the State invoking the doctrine'.[151] Bogdanova argues that US sanctions cannot be said to meet the conditions mentioned above since they aim to reinforce the effectiveness of their restrictions/prohibitions by expanding their application extraterritorially.[152] In a similar fashion, the EU aims at preventing the circumvention of restrictive measures rather than to inhibit a conduct that has direct, substantial and reasonable effects on the Union.

In the next sections, this chapter examines another legal problem: this is the use of the assets of CBR to support Ukraine's reconstruction. This issue is of particular significance for the European Union, as the bulk of the mentioned frozen assets are held within the territory of its Member States.

6.7 The EU's Contribution to Ukraine's Reconstruction: The Use of the Extraordinary Revenues Generated by the Immobilised Assets and Reserves of the Central Bank of Russia

6.7.1 The EU's Contribution to Ensure the Reparation of the War Damages Caused by Russia: Preliminary Remarks

The UN General Assembly has recognised that Russia must bear the legal consequences of all its internationally wrongful acts, including the obligation to make reparation for the injury and any damage,[153] caused by such acts.[154] Regional international organisations play an important role in the implementation of this Resolution.

---

[151] Bogdanova 2022, p. 96. The latest basis of the 'effects doctrine' in the EU is Case C-413/14 P *Intel v. Commission*, par 49. The latter states: 'The qualified effects test allows the application of EU competition law to be justified under public international law when it is foreseeable that the conduct in question will have an immediate and substantial effect in the European Union.'

[152] Bogdanova 2022, p. 97.

[153] According to estimations of the World Bank, Ukraine needs 486 billion euros to reconstruct the country. See https://www.worldbank.org/en/news/press-release/2024/02/15/updated-ukraine-recovery-and-reconstruction-needs-assessment-released [accessed on 10 October 2025].

[154] Resolution A/RES/ES-11/5 of 15 November 2022 [accessed on 10 October 2025].

For example, a Register of Damage caused by the aggression of the Russian Federation against Ukraine was established on 12 May 2023 by the Council of Europe,[155] with financial support from the EU. This represents the first step towards the establishment of a compensation mechanism for the victims of the aggression of the Russian Federation against Ukraine.[156] At the same time, given the EU's geographical proximity to Ukraine and this State's status as a candidate country, the EU bears a special responsibility to support its reconstruction, in cooperation with the G7 members. To this end, the EU has assisted the victim of the aggression by providing macro-financial assistance under Article 212 TFEU and military support through the European Peace Facility (EPF).[157] In February 2024, the decision to establish the Ukraine Facility was adopted, marking a groundbreaking step.[158] This new legal instrument addresses Ukraine's financing needs, promotes private investment, and supports the country's recovery, reconstruction, and modernisation. In particular, the EU undertakes to provide exceptional macro-financial assistance to Ukraine in the form of a loan (the 'MFA Loan') and non-repayable financial support intended to assist the country in servicing loans granted in its support,[159] backed by the Multiannual Financial Framework (MFF).[160] Hungary opposed this decision, but the measure was nonetheless adopted. It is worth stressing that the EU institutions regard this new instrument as an exceptional measure, in light of its direct implications for the Union's security.[161] In this context, Recital 49 of the Regulation establishing the Ukraine Facility expressly acknowledges the possibility of using potential revenues generated under the relevant legal acts concerning the use of extraordinary revenues held by private entities—namely central securities depositories—stemming directly from immobilised assets of the CBR. This, in turn, prompts an examination of one of the most controversial initiatives undertaken by the EU, as well as by several G7 countries: the use of revenues generated by the sovereign assets of the CBR to support Ukraine's reconstruction.[162] Seventy per cent of these assets—approximately €210 billion—are held within the jurisdictions of EU Member States, such as Belgium, France, Germany, and Luxembourg. Additional funds are located in the United Kingdom, Switzerland, Japan, and Canada, while a relatively small amount is held in the United States.[163] As of February 2024, the total value of Russian sovereign assets immobilised by the EU and other G7 countries was estimated at

[155] See Council of Europe Committee of Ministers resolution, CM/Res (2023)3, establishing the Enlarged Partial Agreement on the Register.

[156] European Commission, COM (2024) 224, p. 3.

[157] See Chap. 10 in this book.

[158] Council Regulation (EU) 2024/792.

[159] Recital n. 9, Ibid.

[160] The total budget of the Ukraine Facility is 50 billion euros of which 33 billion in loans and 5.27 billion in grants (to be paid using the EU budget) between 2024 and 2027.

[161] Joint declaration of the European Parliament, the Council and the Commission relating to the exceptional nature of the Ukraine Facility, C/2024/1969, 29 February 2024.

[162] See n. 4.

[163] Five billion out of 300 US dollars, https://www.wilsoncenter.org/article/making-russia-pay-enforcement-russian-obligation-repair-war-damages-ukraine [accessed on 10 December 2024].

€260 billion.[164] Over the course of the war, a significant share of the debt securities reached maturity and generated cash. The following section, and the subsections that follow, examine how the extraordinary revenues derived from the immobilised assets of the CBR have been used.[165]

6.7.2 The EU's Interest in Using the Frozen Assets of the Central Bank of Russia and the Debate on the Legality of Their Confiscation

Since May 2022, the European Council has expressed an interest in using the frozen assets and reserves of the CBR to support Ukraine's reconstruction, while remaining within the limits of EU and international law. In October 2022, the Commission was invited to explore possible options for the use of those frozen assets. One proposal envisaged the creation of a structure to manage the frozen public funds, invest them, and direct the resulting proceeds towards Ukraine. This approach was premised on the idea that, once EU sanctions were lifted, the assets and reserves of the CBR would revert to its control. Such a step could be linked to a peace agreement providing for compensation to Ukraine for the damage suffered, with the CBR's assets being set off against war reparations.[166]

The Commission's proposal was consistent with international law, as the frozen assets, which cannot be seized, were to be returned to the Russian Federation once the EU restrictive measures freezing the assets and reserves of the CBR were lifted. At the same time, the Commission left open the possibility of confiscating those assets should Russia refuse to provide compensation for the damage caused by the war. This institution adopted a highly cautious approach in defining the circumstances under which such confiscation might occur. Legal constraints were imposed by state immunities; any decision to make use of state funds required particularly careful consideration in light of the significant legal implications involved in re-purposing a state property. In addition, the confiscation of CBR assets located within EU Member States also entailed significant risks of retaliation.[167]

The central question was whether the assets of a State organ such as the CBR, belonging to a member of the international community that has breached Article 2(4) of the UN Charter by waging a war of aggression, could be transferred to Ukraine

---

[164] Caprile and Peters 2025, p. 2.

[165] They amount to 300 billion US dollars.

[166] https://ec.europa.eu/commission/presscorner/detail/es/ip_22_7311 [accessed on 10 October 2023].

[167] The aggressor country could respond to the confiscation of the CBR's assets and reserves by expropriating EU citizens' properties in its own territory and could have sued Member States for expropriation on the basis of the BITs. Yet, in the author's opinion, there is more than one doubt as to whether the confiscation of the assets of RCB could fall within the scope of the protection afforded by BITs.

on the basis of legislation repurposing those assets. The legality of such a measure is contested. Some scholars argue that customary international law affords central bank assets absolute protection from execution.[168] Others stress that such an immunity enforcement is no longer considered absolute in European Courts but they argue that the principle that property of central banks or other monetary authorities should be immune from enforcement measures is generally accepted by these courts.[169]

In order to settle this matter, it is necessary to distinguish between freezing and seizing sovereign assets. The freezing of the assets can be seen as a breach of the immunity from enforcement of the Central banks, which is taken as a countermeasure in order to make pressure on Russia to cease the aggression. This is a prior sufficiently serious violation of international law[170] which justifies the adoption of countermeasures which are temporary and reversible.[171] The EU initially froze the assets with a view to inducing Russia's compliance with its obligation of cessation under international law. Even if Russia were to bring its internationally wrongful act to an end, the EU could arguably maintain the asset freeze against the RCB insofar as the measure qualifies as a lawful countermeasure. In that case, the freeze could remain in place not only to secure cessation (Article 30 ARSIWA) but also to ensure compliance with the obligation of full reparation (Article 31 ARSIWA), reflecting the normative continuum between cessation and reparation in the law of State responsibility.

Seizing the assets of the CBR differs fundamentally from freezing them, as seizure entails a permanent transfer of ownership associated with confiscation. Such a permanent deprivation of property is generally considered incompatible with the temporary and reversible nature of lawful countermeasures under international law.

The practice does not give final answers to the legality of confiscation measures. In the US the 'Rebuilding Economic Prosperity and Opportunity for Ukrainians Act' (the 'REPO for Ukrainians Act'[172]) authorises the President to confiscate and vest in the U.S. government any sovereign assets of Russia or Belarus that are under U.S. jurisdiction. This Statute makes it possible to allocate Russian sovereign assets[173] (except for what is covered by diplomatic immunities) to a 'Ukraine Support Fund,' which may then be used for 'providing assistance to Ukraine for the damage

[168] Kotanidis 2024, pp. 49–52; Wuert 2019, pp. 281–284. See also Sect. 6.2.1.

[169] Reinisch 2006, pp. 155, 165.

[170] Van der Horst 2023, p. 1031.

[171] An interesting alternative explanation to justify the freezing of the assets is offered by Cinelli. This author argues that the adoption of these measures could be seen as a 'further consequence' that Article 41(3) attaches to breaches of *jus cogens*. This provision states: 'This article is without prejudice to the other consequences referred to in this part and to such further consequences that a breach to which this chapter applies may entail under international law.' Cinelli 2024, p. 857 ff.

[172] See for the text: https://www.foreign.senate.gov/imo/media/doc/06-14-23_repo_act.pdf [accessed on 3 January 2026].

[173] 'The President may seize, confiscate, transfer, or vest any Russian aggressor state sovereign assets, in whole or in part, and including any interest or interests in such assets, subject to the jurisdiction of the United States.' Sect. 104(b)(1).

resulting from' the 2022 invasion.[174] In Canada, the *Special Economic Measures (Russia) Regulations*[175] makes it possible to pursue the seizure and forfeiture of assets belonging to designated persons. The Governor in Council may order the seizure of such property, and the Minister may apply to a superior court for an order of forfeiture, pursuant to which the assets may be permanently vested in the Crown. The proceeds resulting from the forfeiture may be used to support the reconstruction of Ukraine and to provide compensation to victims of the Russian Federation's illegal and unjustifiable invasion.[176]

Leaving aside the two jurisdictions mentioned above, there is no clear indication that EU Member States would favour the confiscation of sovereign State assets. The same appears to apply to the United Kingdom.[177]

Turning to legal scholarship, the possibility of seizing central bank assets has been opposed by authors such as Brunk, on the ground that such measures would violate the immunity from execution enjoyed by central banks under international law.[178] She argues that 'Using countermeasures to seize money for reparations, rather than as a measure to induce the payment of reparations, is in fundamental tension with the basic structure of countermeasures.'[179] Wuerts takes the view that international customary law requires immunity from execution of central bank or monetary authorities assets not used for a commercial activity.[180]

By contrast, the Parliamentary Assembly of the Council of Europe[181] has expressed support for the confiscation of the assets and reserves of the Central Bank of the Russian Federation, a position that has also been endorsed by a number of legal scholars. A group of scholars have suggested to seize and forfeiture Russian state assets and set up a compensation fund through a multilateral Treaty. They consider the concerns raised by the suspension of Russia's sovereign assets as misplaced, and take the view that the seizure and forfeiture in this context is a remedy in extremis and in wartime.[182]

---

[174] Poli 2025, pp. 104–105.

[175] SOR/2014-58, as amended in 2025, Canada Gazette, Part II, Volume 159 (2025), Number 24.

[176] See Chap. 5, Sects. 5.3–5.6. Forfeitures orders were granted twice. See https://gazette.gc.ca/rp-pr/p2/2023/2023-06-21/html/sor-dors120-eng.html [accessed on 3 January 2026].

[177] Butchard 2024, p. 76.

[178] Brunk 2023. See also on this issue Nakatani 2024.

[179] Brunk 2023, p. 1654.

[180] Wuerth 2019, p. 280.

[181] This organ had envisaged the confiscation of the Russian Federation's assets to pay for damage caused by the war in Ukraine in Resolution 2516 (2023) 'Ensuring a just peace in Ukraine and lasting security in Europe.' In a later resolution the Parliamentary Assembly had been open to other solutions such as the confiscation of private assets following a criminal conviction for sanctions violations, the introduction of windfall taxes on the interest or profits derived from frozen Russian state assets or these use of these assets as collateral for loans to Ukraine. Resolution *Ukraine's reconstruction*, 2539 (2024), par. 12.9.

[182] Grant 2022, p. 9.

According to Kamminga,[183] the confiscation of CBR reserves is permissible under international law, in case an agreement on a peace settlement between Russia and Ukraine is not reached:[184] the waging of a war of aggression by a permanent member of the UN Security Council, combined with the immobilisation of its reserves in the territory of third States, allows such confiscation to be characterised as a lawful measure within the meaning of Article 54 of the Articles on State Responsibility (ARSIWA).[185] The author finds this justification convincing to justify the freezing of funds as a last resort tool in case a peace settlement, including the payment of war damages, is not reached. In the author's opinion, the immobilisation of Russian sovereign assets could be seen as a lawful countermeasure which the EU Member States take collectively through the Union. On this view, the legal basis for EU action could be found in Articles 48(1)(b) and 48(2)(b) of the ARSIWA. These provisions allow non-injured States to invoke the responsibility of a State that has breached an obligation owed to the international community as a whole—most notably the prohibition of aggression—and to seek performance of the obligation of reparation in the interest of the injured State. Article 48(2) ARSIWA could therefore provide the legal basis for the EU to confiscate Russian assets in the interest of Ukraine, with a view to ensuring cessation of the breach and compliance with the obligation to repair the damage caused by the war. The logical implication of this approach is that Russian state assets, including the reserves of the CBR, may be repurposed through an act of the executive. This reasoning, in turn, opens the door to the permissibility of collective countermeasures, a development which would represent a progressive development of international law. According to Kamminga, 'state practice appears to be moving to a situation in which the entitlement to take countermeasures no longer distinguishes between directly and indirectly injured states.[186]'

It should be acknowledged that so far EU Member States have shown caution. Turning to the positions adopted by the EU institutions, differences emerge. While the European Parliament has taken the view that Russia's sovereign assets should be confiscated in order to support Ukraine's self-defence and reconstruction,[187] the President of the European Central Bank has, by contrast, adopted a different position, ruling out the confiscation of the assets of the CBR. As she puts it, 'seizing some $260 billion in Russian assets currently frozen in Europe would undermine the *international rule of law* (emphasis added),[188] with unforeseeable consequences. Moving from freezing the assets to confiscating the assets, disposing of them, is something that needs to be looked at very carefully.' President Lagarde added that

---

[183] Kamminga 2023, p. 15.

[184] For other scholars the confiscation of the mentioned assets could be qualified as a counter measure taken to react to Russia's violation of Article 2(4) of the UN Charter. Goldmann 2022.

[185] 'This chapter does not prejudice the right of any state, entitled under Article 48, para 1, to invoke the responsibility of another state, to take lawful measures against that State to ensure cessation of the breach and reparation in the interest of the injured state or of the beneficiaries of the obligation breached.'

[186] Kamminga 2023, p. 7.

[187] European Parliament 2025, par. 24.

[188] Poli 2025.

such an initiative would 'break the international legal order that one seeks to protect, and that one would want Russia and all countries around the world to respect.'[189]

Given the legal uncertainty surrounding the seizing of sovereign assets as a countermeasure,[190] a possible solution for the EU could be to facilitate their transfer to an international reparations mechanism.[191]

Finally, attention should be given to an alternative legal characterisation of the immobilisation of State assets, according to which the measure would not require independent justification under international law, since it is addressed to EU financial institutions and does not, strictly speaking, constitute a freezing of funds.[192] The proposed explanation is not fully convincing since it does not take into account the actual effects of the immobilisation of sovereign assets.

Having set out the debate on the use of sovereign assets, other avenues for supporting Ukraine's reconstruction will be considered in the next section.

6.7.3 Further Options for Supporting Ukraine's Reconstruction

A second option to support Ukraine's reconstruction consists in the confiscation of private assets frozen by G7 members. This measure could enable the EU to mobilise approximately €28 billion.[193] Estonia had adopted legislation of this kind, enabling the use of the assets as prepayment compensation of war damages, in 2024.[194] Although these funds would be insufficient to cover the overall costs of Ukraine's reconstruction, it must be emphasised that the confiscation of such assets raises serious concerns with regard to the fundamental right to property. According to Rosas, 'confiscating Russian property on the sole basis that it has been frozen should probably be excluded,'[195] as confiscation cannot qualify as a lawful countermeasure where it interferes with obligations relating to the protection of human rights. He nevertheless observes that 'the right to property is far from an absolute right,' and argues that it could be contended that persons supporting an act of aggression should not benefit from the exclusion of countermeasures provided for in Article 50(1)(b) of the ILC Articles.[196] At the same time, Rosas maintains that, under EU law, no legal

---

[189] https://www.politico.eu/article/ecbs-lagarde-digs-in-as-us-pushes-europe-on-using-russian-assets-for-ukraine-aid/, [accessed on 10 December 2024].

[190] In the risks associated to the expansion of counter measures see Wuert 2024.

[191] On Veber 2025, pp. 41–43.

[192] Hoffmeister and Köppen 2026.

[193] European Commission, Sanctions against individuals, companies and organisations, available on online [accessed on 10 December 2025].

[194] https://www.riigikogu.ee/wpcms/wp-content/uploads/2024/05/Rahvusvahelise-sanktsiooni-seaduse-muutmine-P-46.pdf [accessed on 10 December 2025].

[195] Rosas 2023, pp. 337, 347.

[196] Rosas 2023, p. 345.

basis currently exists for general confiscation measures. In his view, '[…] in light of the constraints imposed by public international law and EU law, outright and general confiscation of frozen property is neither possible nor, in any event, desirable.'[197]

A third legal avenue for supporting Ukraine's reconstruction lies in the confiscation of assets belonging to persons who breach EU restrictive measures. As emphasised by the Council in its Guidelines on Best Practices on Restrictive Measures, 'if national legislation on penalties applicable in cases of sanctions breaches so provides, preventive freezing, seizure and confiscation may be applied as penalties for infringing restrictive measures.'[198] In such circumstances, confiscated assets could be allocated for the benefit of Ukraine.

Pursuant to Directives (EU) 2024/1226[199] and (EU) 2024/1260,[200] the assets of persons who violate restrictive measures may be confiscated by national authorities. Consequently, the proceeds of such confiscation may be used to support Ukraine. Directive (EU) 2024/1226 lays down minimum rules concerning criminal offences and penalties for violations of Union restrictive measures. One of its key objectives is to facilitate the confiscation of assets and economic resources subject to sanctions where a link to criminal activity can be established. Accordingly, persons subject to the jurisdiction of the EU who engage in conduct amounting to a breach of restrictive measures, may face asset confiscation.

Directive (EU) 2024/1260 on asset recovery and confiscation, which entered into force on the same date as Directive (EU) 2024/1226, governs the management and use of confiscated property, including assets confiscated in connection with violations of restrictive measures.[201] Notably, Article 19 of this Directive allows Member States to use instrumentalities, proceeds, or property confiscated in relation to the offences referred to in Directive (EU) 2024/1226 'to contribute to mechanisms to support third countries affected by situations in response to which Union restrictive measures have been adopted, in particular in cases of war of aggression.'[202] The Commission is empowered to provide guidance on the arrangements governing such contributions. A significant limitation is expressly articulated: the Union must comply with international law when contributing to these support mechanisms.[203] This provision clearly aims to encourage Member States to allocate confiscated assets in support of Ukraine only insofar as such use remains compatible with international law.

It is submitted that the allocation of confiscated assets for the benefit of Ukraine, under these conditions, is consistent with international law. While the confiscation

---

197 Ibid.

198 Council—Update of the EU Best Practices for the effective implementation of restrictive measures, Council document n. 11,623/24, 3 July 2024, par. 29, [accessed on 10 October 2025].

199 Directive (EU) 2024/1226. See Chap. 7.

200 Direct 2024/1260. See Chap. 7.

201 See Article 2(1)p of Directive 2024/1226. Member States will have to comply with the terms of this Directive by 20 May 2025.

202 Article 19 of Directive 2024/1226.

203 The provision opens with the following expression: 'Without prejudice to international law.'

of assets of natural and legal persons solely through restrictive measures is impermissible, given their non-criminal nature, seizure of assets belonging to individuals who have breached restrictive measures is lawful, as such conduct has been criminalised under Directive (EU) 2024/1226. The mechanism established by the latter Directive is likely to make only a modest contribution to Ukraine's reconstruction; nonetheless, the availability to transfer the confiscated assets constitutes a significant expression of the EU's political and legal support for a State that is the victim of an act of aggression.

6.7.4 The Financial Contribution on the Cash Balances of Assets and Reserves Accruing from the Immobilised Assets: A New Instrument to Support Ukraine's Recovery and Reconstruction

In light of the uncertainty surrounding the confiscation of the CBR's assets and reserves, as well as the illegality of seizing private funds belonging to Russian nationals, the Union has devised *a sui generis* mechanism to support Ukraine's reconstruction, namely the use of the revenues generated by the immobilised assets of the CBR, leaving the principal assets untouched. This approach was advanced by the Commission and welcomed by the G7 members.[204] This mechanism constitutes a compromise solution, rendered necessary by the need to provide support to Ukraine without breaching international law and without undermining 'the trust in the euro as a global currency and cause greater losses for the EU than the potential benefits for Ukraine.'[205]

The Union established the legal framework for the use of the revenues generated by the CBR's assets and reserves in February 2024, when the Council imposed a number of obligations on Central Securities Depositories (CSDs) holding CBR assets and reserves with a total value exceeding EUR 1 million. Those obligations served the purpose of making the extraordinary revenues accruing from the cash flows of the frozen assets available to Ukraine.

In early 2024 the Council clarified that the 'balance sheet management transactions linked to assets and reserves of the CBR, or linked to assets and reserves of any legal person, entity or body acting on behalf of, or at the direction of, the CBR, such as the Russian National Wealth Fund, [were] not within the scope of the

[204] G7 Leaders' Statement 24 February 2024, https://www.g7italy.it/wp-content/uploads/G7-Leaders-Statement.pdf. In December 2023 G7 members had advanced the idea of directing the extraordinary revenues held by private entities stemming directly from Russia's immobilised sovereign assets to support Ukraine. G7 Leaders' Statement, 6 December 2023, https://www.consilium.europa.eu/media/68615/g7-leaders-statement-2023-12-6.pdf [accessed on 10.10.2025].

[205] https://www.reuters.com/legal/transactional/legal-challenges-confiscating-russian-central-bank-assets-support-ukraine-2024-08-01/ [accessed on 10 October 2025].

prohibition of transactions which applies since 28 February 2022'.[206] In addition, certain CSDs[207] were required to account for the relevant cash balances separately; a similar obligation applied to the revenues accruing from, or generated by, those cash balances as from 15 February 2024.[208] Finally, the net profits derived from the revenues accumulated by the CSDs could not be disposed of—whether through the distribution of dividends or in any other form for the benefit of shareholders or third parties—until the Council decided on the possible establishment of a financial contribution to the Union budget to be levied on those net profits in order to support Ukraine's recovery and reconstruction.[209] These preliminary steps were necessary to distinguish the revenues generated by the reinvestment of the extraordinary cash balances accumulating due to the immobilisation of the frozen funds of the CBR.

Interestingly, the preamble of the Regulation on the Ukraine Facility refers to the possibility to use the potential revenues generated by the use of extraordinary revenues held by private CSDs stemming directly from immobilised CBR assets.[210]

In May 2024, the Council established a 'financial contribution' to be applied to revenues accruing from, or generated by, the cash balances of assets and reserves held by CSDs, where the total value exceeds EUR 1 million, with effect from 15 February 2024.[211]

As mentioned, most of these reserves and assets (some $207 billion) are held by CSD Euroclear, which is based in Brussels and has derived extraordinary profits from the reinvestment of the cashflow. The financial contribution was levied by the EU at a rate of 99,7% of the net profits determined in respect of revenues accruing from or generated by the cash balances accumulating exclusively due to the restrictive measures.[212] By adopting Council Decision (CFSP) 2024/1470, the Council decided that 90% of the funds raised through the financial contribution would be allocated to the European Peace Facility (EPF),[213] through which the Union provides military support to Ukraine, while the remaining 10% would be directed to Union programmes financed from the Union budget.[214] Hungary abstained from the adoption of this measure and has subsequently challenged it before the General Court, illustrating its systematic opposition to the adoption of common positions in the field of the CFSP. The legal question arising is whether, by abstaining, Hungary forfeited its right to participate in decisions concerning the allocation of those funds. This issue is expected to be clarified by the Court.[215]

---

[206] Recital n. 14 of Council Decision (CFSP) 2024/577.

[207] Only those CSDs holding reserves and assets with a total value of more than 1 million euro.

[208] Article 1, Council Decision (CFSP) 2024/577.

[209] Ibid.

[210] Preamble n. 49 of Council Regulation 2024/792.

[211] Council Decision (CFSP) 2024/1470.

[212] Article 1(2), ibid.

[213] Council Decision (CFSP) 2021/509.

[214] Article 1(2) of Council Decision (CFSP) 2024/1470.

[215] GC, Case T-457/24, *Hungary v Council and European Peace Facility Committee*, action brought on 3 August 2024, in OJ C 2024/6266. See Chap. 5.

In July 2024, the first transfer of EUR 1.5 billion[216] was made available by Euroclear and channelled to Ukraine through the European Peace Facility and the Ukraine Facility[217] to support the country's military capabilities and reconstruction efforts. It is noteworthy that Russia considered this transfer to be illegal, while Switzerland announced that it could not generate any extraordinary income in connection with the CBR's funds, thereby illustrating that not all Western countries are willing to make use of the revenues generated by immobilised assets.

A few comments are now warranted on the allocation of the financial contribution. Initially, the contribution was earmarked to support the European Peace Facility (EPF). This choice reflects the Council's decision to prioritise Ukraine's right to self-defence over the country's recovery and reconstruction.[218] Such a political choice may be justified, given that priority must be accorded to the preservation of Ukraine's very existence over post-conflict reconstruction, as emphasised by the Union's High Representative Josep Borrell in April 2024.[219] Ukraine's capacity for self-defence depends on the provision of weapons not only by the United States, but also by EU Member States through the EPF; as the disbursement of the funds was blocked by Hungary for over a year,[220] there was a need to provide a constant flow of money which was also conveniently used to reimburse Member States's delivery of weapons to Ukraine.

On 24th October 2024 the allocation of the financial contribution was reversed with respect to the previous one: 5% was allocated to the EPF and 95% to Union programmes financed from the Union budget.[221] The Ukraine Facility was one such programme and was designed, amongst other things, to favour reconstruction and modernisation of Ukraine. Yet, on the same day a new instrument, the Ukraine Loan Cooperation Mechanism ('ULCM' or 'The Mechanism')[222] was set up to provide 'Ukraine with non-repayable financial support with a view to assisting the country to repay both the loans provided by the EU (up to 35 billion euros) and other loans provided by third countries.

This instrument, which is managed by the Commission, is complementary to the Ukraine Facility and is additional to other programs of macro financial assistance

---

[216] https://neighbourhood-enlargement.ec.europa.eu/news/first-transfer-eu15-billion-proceeds-immobilised-russian-assets-made-available-support-ukraine-today-2024-07-26_en. l.

[217] Council Regulation (EU) 2024/792.

[218] The new instrument has a double objective: to support Ukraine and its recovery and reconstruction as well as its self-defence against the Russian aggression.

[219] The HR stated: 'We initially envisaged to use revenues [generated by CSDs] to support Ukraine's recovery and reconstruction." He then concluded that "before thinking on reconstruction, we need to think about avoiding destruction.' https://www.eeas.europa.eu/eeas/russia-ukraine-speech-high-representative-vice-president-josep-borrell-ep-plenary-moscows-frozen_en [accessed 3 June 2024].

[220] https://www.euronews.com/my-europe/2024/10/14/what-is-the-european-peace-facility-and-why-hungary-is-blocking-the-disbursements-to-ukrai?utm_source=chatgpt.com [accessed 10 June 2025].

[221] Article 1 of Council implementing Decision (CFSP) 2024/2760. The new allocation started as from the second half of 2025.

[222] Council Regulation (EU) 2024/2773.

enacted to the benefit of Ukraine in 2022 and 2023.[223] The advantage of the Mechanism, which is based on Article 212 TFEU and therefore did not require unanimous approval in the Council, was that the disbursement of funds was managed by the Commission, thereby circumventing Hungary's systematic opposition to supporting Ukraine through the EPF.

The first novelty of this mechanism is that it enabled the Union to make use of the extraordinary revenues generated by the frozen assets of the CBR to service the loans granted to Ukraine. To that end, the Commission would finance the loan by borrowing the necessary funds on the capital markets or from financial institutions.[224] A second innovation was that lenders other than the EU were also entitled to channel their loans through the mechanism. Finally, Recital 14 of the ULCM Regulation allows Member States in which Russian sovereign assets are immobilised to make voluntary contributions to the Mechanism, consisting of the extraordinary revenues accruing from the reinvestment of the cash balances generated by the frozen assets.

A final note is warranted. It should be recalled that, pursuant to Article 19 of Directive (EU) 2024/1260, Member States may use instrumentalities, proceeds, or property confiscated in relation to the offences referred to in Directive (EU) 2024/1226 'to contribute to mechanisms supporting third countries affected by situations in response to which Union restrictive measures have been adopted, in particular in cases of war of aggression.'[225] The ULCM clearly fulfils this condition. It is noteworthy that Member States were not obliged to use confiscated assets for the benefit of Ukraine; rather, the provision in question merely opened a legal avenue enabling them to do so. It remains to be seen if the confiscated funds will be used as envisaged by the Directive.

In conclusion, the ULCM marked an important step in enabling the use of the extraordinary revenues generated by the immobilised assets of the CBR for the benefit of Ukraine and paved the way for the mechanism to serve as a vehicle for coordinating the efforts of G7 members to support Ukraine in compliance with international law, as illustrated in the following section.

6.7.5 An Assessment of the EU's Financial Contribution: A Lawful but Limited Instrument to Support Ukraine

It is now necessary to examine the legality, under international law, of the financial contribution designed by the EU. Paragraph 17 of Council Decision (CFSP) 2024/

---

[223] The EU has provided 7.2 billion euros in 2022 and 19 billion euros 2023 in macro financial assistance to Ukraine. See https://commission.europa.eu/strategy-and-policy/eu-budget/eu-borrower-investor-relations/mfa-programmes-including-ukraine_en [accessed on 10 October 2025].

[224] Under Article 14 of Council Regulation 2024/2773, 'In order to finance the MFA Loan, the Commission shall be empowered, on behalf of the Union, to borrow the necessary funds on the capital markets or from financial institutions in accordance with Article 224 of the Financial Regulation.'

[225] See Sect. 6.7.3.

1470 states that 'the unexpected and extraordinary revenues do not have to be made available to the CBR under the applicable rules, even after the transaction ban has been lifted. As such, they do not constitute sovereign state assets. Consequently, the rules protecting sovereign assets do not apply to these revenues.' Through this statement, the Council implies that the EU has neither breached the rules governing the protection of sovereign assets, nor violated Article 345 TFEU.[226] This conclusion is based on the premise that no transfer of property from the CBR to Euroclear or other CSDs has taken place: the revenues generated by the frozen CBR assets are deemed not to belong to the Russian Federation, but rather to the depositories themselves, which, under EU law, are required to reinvest the cash flows generated by the immobilised assets.[227] Fabbrini has questioned the legality of the financial contribution under international and EU law,[228] suggesting that the tax may represent the first step taken by the EU towards the expropriation of foreign sovereign assets and may conflict with Article 345 TFEU, which governs the system of property ownership.

It is submitted that the financial contribution constitutes a lawful legal instrument, as the principal assets of the CBR remain unaffected by this contribution; no breach of state immunities from execution is associated with this exceptional instrument. While it is true that the revenues generated through the reinvestment of cash balances arising from the immobilised assets would not exist in the absence of those frozen assets, this fact alone does not amount to the confiscation of sovereign property. The transfer of a substantial share of the net profits to the EU by means of a financial contribution does not constitute a measure of confiscation of sovereign state assets. In particular, the EU is not seizing interests accrued on capital belonging to the owner of the funds.[229] Rather, the concerned CSD retains the profits generated by the reinvestment operations, as they are the legal holders of the assets concerned. Accordingly, the use of revenues generated by the frozen assets does not amount to a forced transfer of property. The EU therefore does not act in breach of international law, but rather adopts lawful measures designed to support the victim of an armed aggression in countering the attack and ensuring recovery and reconstruction.[230] It should further be noted that the financial contribution does not violate the international rule of law insofar as that principle governs horizontal relations between States.[231] The concept of the 'international rule of law' encompasses, *inter alia*, the following elements: legal order and stability, equality before the law, the protection of human

---

[226] 'The Treaties shall in no way prejudice the rules in Member States governing the system of property ownership.'

[227] https://www.euroclear.com/newsandinsights/en/press/2023/2023-mr-15-euroclear-delivers-robust-performance-q3-2023.html [accessed on 6 October 2024].

[228] Fabbrini 2024, p. 374. For a discussion on the legality of the use of extraordinary revenues see Kotanidis 2024, pp. 41–42.

[229] Fabbrini 2024, p. 374.

[230] The purpose of the financial contribution is 'to support Ukraine and its recovery and reconstruction, as well as its self-defence against the Russian aggression'. See Recital n. 23 of Council Decision (CFSP) 2024/1470.

[231] On this issue see De Sadeleer and Damjanovic 2024, p. 484.

rights, and the settlement of disputes by an independent judicial body.[232] In the present context, the financial contribution at issue may be seen as safeguarding a 'fair, stable and predictable legal framework,'[233] which constitutes a core component of the international rule of law and lies at the heart of the concerns expressed by the President of the European Central Bank.[234]

That said, the revenues generated by the immobilised assets are likely to be insufficient to compensate Ukraine fully for the damage suffered as a result of the protracted aggression. For this reason, it has been crucial for the Commission to raise the necessary funds on the capital markets, within the framework of the ULCM, in order to provide effective support to Ukraine, as illustrated in the next section.

6.7.6 The EU and G7 Countries' Contributions to Ukraine's Reconstruction: A Coordinated Effort Under the Ukraine Loan Cooperation Mechanism

On the day following the entry into force of the ULCM, the finance ministers of the G7 agreed to launch the Extraordinary Revenue Acceleration Initiative (ERA),[235] which provides for the establishment of a €45 billion loan in support of Ukraine by the end of 2024. The most significant legal development associated with this instrument concerned the mechanism for the repayment of the loans.

> Principal and interest will be repaid by *extraordinary revenues stemming from the immobilisation of Russian sovereign assets (RSA)* (emphasis added) held in European Union (EU) jurisdictions, and possibly in other G7 countries, in line with our respective legal systems and international law, and by any other voluntary contributions.[236]

As a consequence of this G7 initiative, both EU and non-EU G7 lenders would rely on the extraordinary revenues generated by the CBR to finance Ukraine's immediate budgetary needs and long-term reconstruction efforts. The quotation cited above appears to suggest that the repayment of the loans would be secured through the CBR's immobilised assets held within the EU.[237] For these countries, it was

[232] McCorquodale 2016, p. 292.

[233] For a definition of the various aspects of the international rule of law see UN General Assembly Resolution 67/1 'Declaration of the High-level Meeting of the General Assembly on the Rule of Law at the National and International Levels' (30 November 2012) UN Doc A/RES/67/1, in particular par. 6.8 [accessed on 6 October 2024].

[234] See Sect. 6.3.

[235] The G7 members committed to making USD 50 billion available to fund Ukraine's military, budget and reconstruction needs by the end of 2024, https://www.g7italy.it/wp-content/uploads/Joint-Declaration-1.pdf [accessed on 6 October 2024].

[236] https://www.consilium.europa.eu/media/vexjsedk/g7-finance-ministers-statement-on-extraordinary-revenue-acceleration-era-loan-initiative.pdf [accessed on 6 November 2024].

[237] For a confirmation of this interpretation see the Commission press release stating: 'These funds [i.e. the frozen assets of the CBR] will be disbursed to Ukraine to repay the principal and interest on

also possible to make direct use of the extraordinary revenues arising from the immobilisation of Russian sovereign assets within their respective jurisdictions.[238]

On the basis of the ERA initiative, on December 2024 the USA disbursed US$20 billion using the windfall proceeds earned from Russia's own immobilised assets.[239] A comparable initiative, likewise relying on the proceeds generated by immobilised Russian sovereign assets, was undertaken by Canada, which committed to disburse US$3.7 billion and emphasised that it was the first country to advocate the use of the Central Bank of Russia's assets in support of Ukraine.[240] Japan disbursed a loan amounting at US$3.3 billion in April 2025[241]; as to the UK, this country was expected to commit up to £4.5 billion by the end of 2025.[242]

In January 2025, the EU disbursed €3 billion under an exceptional macro-financial assistance programme to be repaid with the proceeds from immobilised Russian state assets in the EU.[243] As a result of the EU loans, Ukraine will receive €18 billion by the end of 2025. While Ukraine's financial needs for 2025 were secured through the ERA Loan initiative, the question of how to provide sustained assistance to Ukraine in the subsequent years remained open. This prompted Ukraine to request a new loan, as discussed in Sect. 6.7.8.

6.7.7 The EU's Contribution to Respect for International Law and the Choice Not to Contribute to the Development of a New Customary Rule of International Law

In previous sections we have seen that the proceeds generated from immobilised Russian sovereign assets held within the EU have been lawfully used to support Ukraine's right of self-defence and to contribute to its reconstruction. The assets themselves were left untouched. This implies that, at present, the Union has refrained from contributing to the emergence of a new rule of customary international law under which the sovereign assets of an aggressor State—particularly one holding a veto power within the United Nations Security Council—could be used to repair the damage suffered by the victim of an armed aggression. Given that the majority of

---

eligible bilateral and multilateral loans to Ukraine from the EU, G7, and possible other partners.' https://ec.europa.eu/commission/presscorner/detail/cs/ip_25_223 [accessed on 6 October 2025].

[238] Article 10 (1) of Council Regulation 2024/2773.

[239] https://home.treasury.gov/news/press-releases/jy2744 [accessed on 18 December 2024].

[240] https://www.canada.ca/en/department-finance/news/2024/10/statement-by-the-deputy-prime-minister-and-minister-of-finance-on-the-extraordinary-revenue-acceleration-loan-mechanism-and-russian-sovereign-assets.html [accessed on 6 October 2025].

[241] https://ceias.eu/the-kyiv-tokyo-axis-japans-normative-response-to-russian-aggression/ [accessed on 6 October 2025].

[242] https://www.gov.uk/government/news/45-billion-military-boost-to-ukraine-front-line-to-support-uk-growth-and-jobs [accessed on 6 October 2025].

[243] https://ec.europa.eu/commission/presscorner/detail/en/ip_25_223 [accessed on 6 October 2025].

those assets were held within the jurisdiction of EU Member States, the Union could have taken the lead in promoting their use. In practice, however, the concentration of CBR assets within EU jurisdictions—particularly in Belgium—has constrained the Union from pursuing the most radical option, which could be contested in light of the protection afforded to sovereign state assets under the law of immunities. The confiscation of the CBR's assets and reserves would expose both the EU and its Member States to heightened legal and financial risks. Such a measure could jeopardise the stability of the euro. For these reasons, the EU ultimately opted for a pragmatic approach. It is noteworthy that one possible alternative option would be to transfer Russian state assets to an international mechanism after the end of the war. Well-established scholars of international law[244] regard this option as lawful. At present, however, the EU has shown reluctance to adopt such a solution, and until the end of 2025 the debate on the full use of the CBR's assets has largely remained taboo.

6.7.8 The December 2025 Package of Assistance Measures for Ukraine: Conditional Asset Immobilisation and the Transformation of a CFSP Act into an Emergency Measure

At the end of 2025, while various efforts were being made to engage Russia and Ukraine in peace talks, the EU Member States adopted significant decisions concerning the use of Russia's frozen sovereign assets, following Ukraine's request for a new loan to finance its budgetary needs for the period 2026–2027. Ukraine's application for financial assistance raised four issues for the EU. The first concerned the need to continue supporting Ukraine's macro-financial stability through a new loan, complementary to those already in force. The second related to the necessity of overcoming a renewed refusal by Hungary to engage with Ukraine's request for financial support.[245] The third involved the need to maintain Russia's sovereign assets in a frozen state for as long as necessary to support the injured State in obtaining reparation for the damage caused by the responsible State. The fourth consisted in ensuring managing those assets while respecting international law.

The meeting of the G7 financial ministers of October 2025 deserves special attention to address the mentioned issues. Indeed, the ministers recognised the possibility to make use of 'the full value of the RSAs immobilised in G7 jurisdictions to end the

[244] Akande et al. 2024, p. 10.

[245] All Member States except Hungary supported the adoption of a document of the President of the European Council entitled 'The latest development on Ukraine' including a commitment to financially assist Ukraine in 2026–2027, including for its military and defence efforts (para 8), 23 October 2025, https://www.consilium.europa.eu/media/zs3a30wp/20251023-text-ukraine-en.pdf [accessed on 6 December 2025].

war and ensure a just and lasting peace in Ukraine'.[246] At that juncture, had the EU made the political choice to use the frozen assets as indicated, it would have encouraged other members of the G7 to do likewise, given that approximately 70% of the assets were located within the Union and that most of them were held by Euroclear. At its meeting of 23 October, the European Council decided to ensure that Ukraine's financial needs would be covered for the following two years; however, no determination was made regarding the use of the frozen assets, owing to Belgium's firm opposition to their use as collateral for a loan to Ukraine. Instead, the Commission was tasked with proposing solutions to address Ukraine's financial needs in time for the subsequent European Council meeting of 18–19 December 2025. Before the Commission disclosed its proposals, in late November the Prime Minister of Belgium wrote to Ms von der Leyen to reject the idea of a possible reparation loan to Ukraine.[247] Such a loan would have required CSDs to transfer to the Commission the cash balances generated by the immobilised assets, which the Commission would then have used to extend a loan to Ukraine. He argued that the assets of the CBR could not be repurposed during an ongoing war, as discussions on war reparations were usually held only in the context of post-war arrangements. Mr De Wever also contested the use of the assets for multiple purposes, such as financing Ukraine's reconstruction, supporting its war effort, or covering its budgetary needs. In addition, he maintained that such use would undermine the prospects of a peace settlement, since the EU would no longer be able to deploy the assets as a bargaining chip in peace negotiations with Russia. A further concern raised by Mr De Wever was that a reparation loan would expose Belgium to legal action by Russia for expropriation under a bilateral investment treaty (BIT) that remained in force between the two countries and Luxembourg.[248] Regrettably, the concerned Member State—like several others—had not denounced the treaty following the outbreak of the war in 2022. It should nevertheless be noted that it is unclear whether the agreement could in fact be relied upon by the CBR. Significant legal uncertainties persist as to whether the Bank, even if regarded as a legal person, would fall within the treaty's *ratione personae* scope.[249] The breadth of the protection afforded to investors under the treaty is likewise uncertain. Finally, even if these legal hurdles were overcome, the enforcement of an award granting damages in favour of the claimant would remain

[246] Statement of G7 financial ministers, https://g7.canada.ca/en/news-and-media/news/g7-finance-ministers-statement/, 2 October 2025 [accessed on 6 December 2025].

[247] https://multimedia.lecho.be/echo-assets/pdf/251127_FinancingforUkraine.pdf [accessed on 6 December 2025].

[248] Agreement between the Belgium–Luxembourg Economic Union and the Union of Soviet Socialist Republics on the Reciprocal Promotion and Protection of Investments (signed 9 February 1989, entered into force 27 May 1991).

[249] This issue is not solved by the ruling of ICJ, *Certain Iranian Assets (Islamic Republic of Iran v. United States of America)*, Judgment, 30 March 2023, General List No. 164.

highly problematic, in light of the protective shield afforded to Member States by the 18th package of restrictive measures.[250]

Turning to the requests put forward by the Belgian Prime Minister, he called for the provision of guarantees by willing Member States to enable Euroclear to maintain the liquidity of the assets for their full amount. The share of the guarantees corresponding to Member States choosing not to participate would have to be borne by the remaining, willing States. The Prime Minister further made it clear that, if necessary, not all Member States were prepared to enter into arrangements for the benefit of Belgium.

In this context, in early December the Commission responded to the European Council's request to put forward alternative solutions to support Ukraine's financial resilience. Two options[251] were proposed. The first option involved borrowing on the capital markets on the basis of the EU budget 'headroom,' following the model already used for the Ukraine Facility. The drawback of this option was that EU taxpayers would ultimately bear the costs if Ukraine failed to repay the loan.

The second option consisted in a reparations loan of EUR 210 billion, available until 2030, to be adopted through an amendment to Regulation (EU) 2024/792 establishing the Ukraine Facility. This loan would be financed by the cash balances held at financial institutions within the Union, such as Euroclear, which had accumulated because of the transaction ban concerning the assets and reserves of the CBR.[252] The Commission proposed borrowing only the cash balances from CSDs, rather than the full value of the underlying assets. Nevertheless, Euroclear would remain liable to repay the loan to the CBR in the event that Ukraine failed to honour its obligation to repay it.

Crucially, the Commission's proposal did not call into question the special protection enjoyed by Russia's sovereign assets under the law of international immunity.[253] To channel the cash balances of CBDs, a debt instrument was to be created through an agreement between the Commission and Ukraine to 'fund a limited-recourse Ukraine Reparations Loan.'[254] Under the proposed scheme, Ukraine was to repay the loan once it received 'cash or non-monetary assets as war reparations, indemnities or any

[250] It is prohibited to recognise and enforce in the EU Member States any injunction, order, relief or judgment issued by non-EU courts or arbitral tribunals in investor-State dispute settlement proceedings relating to EU sanctions, where such decisions could result in the satisfaction of a claim to the benefit of sanctioned persons or entities in connection with measures imposed under EU sanctions regulations. See new Article 11 (2)(a) and (b) of Regulation (UE) n. 833/2014, as amended by Regulation (EU) 2025/1494.

[251] 'Commission unveils two solutions to support Ukraine's financing needs in 2026–2027,' https://ec.europa.eu/commission/presscorner/detail/en/ip_25_2903, 3 October 2025 [accessed on 6 October 2025].

[252] European Commission, COM (2025) 3502, p. 2.

[253] This is confirmed by recital 26 that stated: 'These specific measures are without prejudice to the claim of the Central Bank of Russia. That asset is not impacted by the measures provided under this Regulation.'

[254] European Commission, COM (2025) 3502, p. 4.

financial settlement from Russia, other than territory.'[255] At that point, the EU would be able to repay its borrowing from financial institutions and the latter could return the sovereign assets to the CBR, in full respect of international law.

The disadvantage of the Reparations Loan was that Euroclear remained liable *vis-à-vis* the CBR. Addressing Belgium's concerns, the Commission's proposal protected CSDs from the risk highlighted by Mr De Wever. The first tier of the protection system relied on Member States providing irrevocable, unconditional, and on-demand guarantees to the Union to support such borrowing, in line with their respective shares of the Union's total Gross National Income.[256] It is noteworthy that the guarantees provided to the Union by Member States would cease to be callable once it was possible to rely on the Union budget to guarantee the loan. The Commission had also envisaged that Member States suffering damage as a result of the enforcement, in a third country, of investor-State arbitral awards, connected with measures imposing restrictions on the CBR could rely, in a spirit of solidarity, on other Member States that had concluded guarantee agreements with the Member State concerned covering the risk of such damages.[257]

The second element of the protection system established by the Commission relied on a liquidity mechanism; finally, the third component consisted of Union borrowing to support repayments and of Union debt securities. The Commission stressed that 'there was no scenario under which relevant financial institutions would not be repaid in order to ensure that they were able to honour all contractual commitments related to the assets and reserves of the CBR.'[258]

An interesting aspect of the proposed legal instrument was that the loan pursued multiple objectives, namely: (1) ensuring Ukraine's budgetary resilience; (2) the reparation of war-related damage; and (3) strengthening Ukraine's defence industrial capacity by enabling the country to use the assistance measures 'to launch large-scale procurements of defence products from the Ukrainian Defence Technological and Industrial Base and the European Defence Technological and Industrial Base through procurements under the SAFE Instrument.'[259] While objective (1) is typical of macro-financial stability instruments, objectives (2) and (3) are atypical. Nevertheless, the use of the proposed loan to ensure that Ukraine receives compensation for war damages (objective (2)) is consistent with international law, given that the EU is adopting lawful measures—namely, the transfer of cash balances that do not constitute Russia's sovereign assets—to ensure that Russia fulfils its obligation to pay for war-related damage. Objective (3) warrants particular attention, as it is instrumental in protecting the Union's security: for the first time, a loan to Ukraine

---

[255] European Commission, COM (2025) 3502, p. 3.

[256] Third countries could also contribute to the Reparations Loan by providing irrevocable, unconditional and on-demand guarantees over and above the guarantees provided by Member States.

[257] An agreement between the Commission and each Member State would be concluded to provide the guarantees.

[258] European Commission, COM (2025) 3502, p. 3.

[259] Recital 28, ibid.

was used to indirectly strengthen Member States' defence capacity and investment, as defined in the context of the SAFE Regulation.[260] Accordingly, the loan is not merely designed to support macro-financial stability in Ukraine, underpinned by the usual conditionality requirements,[261] but also constitutes an investment in the Union's security.

As regards the compatibility of the proposed loan with international law obligations, the Commission was keen to stress that the scheme constituted a reversible mechanism, reversibility being a crucial condition for lawful countermeasures. In the Commission's words, '[…] once the conditions for lifting the sanctions as expressed by the European Council and the G7 are met—namely Russia ceases its war of aggression against Ukraine and compensates it for the damage caused by this war—Ukraine will repay the Union, the Union will repay its borrowing from financial institutions, and those financial institutions will repay the CBR.'[262] The triggering factor leading to the return of the sovereign assets to Russia would be this country compliance with its obligations under international law. In the author's view, the Commission's proposal could have assuaged Belgium's concerns.[263] Indeed, it is noteworthy that the proposed Regulation made clear that the Union would use the cash proceeds to fund the Reparations Loan to Ukraine *only* if it could rely on the headroom of the MFF as a guarantee.

The third proposed Regulation,[264] included in the package of measures, disclosed by the Commission in December 2025 concerned an amendment to the MFF. Irrespective of the option chosen by the Member States to support Ukraine, the MFF had to be amended in order to extend to the new form of assistance the budgetary guarantee already applicable to other macro-financial assistance instruments for Ukraine. An amendment to Regulation (EU) 2020/2053 was therefore necessary to enable the mobilisation of the amounts required to honour the Union's repayment obligations under borrowing-and-lending operations, in the event that the beneficiary State failed to make the due payment on time. The proposed change consisted in authorising such mobilisation over and above the MFF ceilings,[265] up to the limit of the Union's own resources (the 'headroom'). The difficulty raised by this measure, based on Article 312 TFEU, was that it required the consent of all Member States, including Hungary.

The fourth legal instrument proposed by the Commission was particularly innovative: a proposed Regulation based on Article 122(1) TFEU, providing for the temporary prohibition on transferring the frozen assets to the CBR and authorising the lifting of that prohibition subject to a number of lawful conditions. The proposed

---

[260] Council Regulation (EU) 2025/1106.

[261] For example, as any macro-financial assistance measure, preconditions were attached to the loan, related to Ukraine's commitment to respect EU values.

[262] European Commission, COM (2025) 3502, p. 4.

[263] There were voices that considered overinflated the litigation risks incurred by Belgium. See https://www.politico.eu/article/legal-opinions-contradict-belgiums-claims-over-russian-assets-euroclear/ [accessed on 6 January 2026].

[264] European Commission, COM (2025) 3500 final.

[265] European Commission, COM (2025) 3500 final, p. 2.

act took the form of an emergency measure in response to the serious economic difficulties caused by Russia's actions in the context of the war in Ukraine. The title of the proposed Regulation referred to 'emergency measures' in the plural. This was because the act addressed, on the one hand, a situation of economic emergency within the Union resulting from four years of war in Ukraine and the potential deterioration of that situation and, on the other hand, the need to continue providing financial assistance to Ukraine.[266] In reality, the contextual interpretation of Article 122(1), which is located in Chapter 1 'Economic policy' of Title VIII 'Economic and monetary Policy' TFEU, justifies the adoption of appropriate measures in relation to first rather than the second emergency. Yet, the two emergencies are interconnected.

Two substantive aspects of the proposal deserve attention and help justify the adoption of the proposed Regulation on the basis of Article 122(1) TFEU. First, the measure under examination considers that the Union's economic stability is undermined not only by Russia's aggression against Ukraine, but also by hybrid actions attributable to Russia targeting the territory of the Union, its Member States, or its undertakings. Second, the Commission stated that 'action at Union level to preserve the stability of the economy of the Union ensures solidarity between the Member States and for all the Member States',[267] thereby seeking to demonstrate that recourse to Article 122(1) TFEU was legally justified. It may be argued that the proposed legislation created a form of insurance against two distinct risks. The first concerned the possible failure to renew the restrictive measures freezing the CBR's assets due to a Member State's persistent opposition to maintaining sanctions. The temporary immobilisation of those assets was a precondition for ensuring that the Union could make use of them in the event that Russia failed to comply with its obligation to compensate for war-related damage. The second risk was that Russia might refuse to pay war reparations to Ukraine, thereby preventing Ukraine from repaying the loan. At its meeting of 18–19 December 2025, the European Council was required to decide which of the legal options advanced by the Commission to support Ukraine could be selected. As stated in the conclusions of the President of the European Council—endorsed by 25 Member States—the Council and the European Parliament would continue to work on the technical and legal aspects of the instruments establishing a Reparations Loan based on the cash balances associated with Russia's immobilised assets.[268] Accordingly, the Reparations Loan was not set aside but merely postponed. This decision was influenced by the announcement that the European Central Bank would not provide monetary support to Member States in the event that they extended loans to Ukraine, as such support would be contrary to Article 123 TFEU. The compromise reached was that the European Council opted to provide Ukraine with a loan of EUR 90 billion for the years 2026–2027, based on EU borrowing on the capital markets and backed by the EU budget headroom,[269] in a manner similar to the Ukraine Facility.

---

[266] European Commission, COM (2025) 3501 final, point 5.

[267] Ibid., p. 3.

[268] Conclusions of the President of the European Council of 18 December 2025, EUCO 26/25, p. 4.

[269] European Council Conclusions of 18 December 2025, EUCO 24/25, p. 1.

While some commentators have regarded Belgium's concerns concerning possible retaliatory measures by Russia in the event that the cash balances were used to support Ukraine as excessive,[270] it is nevertheless understandable that borrowing by the Union on the capital markets was preferable for most Member States. However, not all were in agreement. Following intense discussions, the Czech Republic, Slovakia, and Hungary were unwilling to agree to guarantee a loan to Ukraine. As a result, and as a measure of last resort, it was decided to authorise the loan under Article 212 TFEU by way of enhanced cooperation, while all Member States would give their consent to the amendment of the MFF Regulation. As a consequence of the political compromise reached on 20 December 2025, 24 Member States requested the Commission to submit a proposal to trigger enhanced cooperation for the establishment of a Reparations Loan for Ukraine.[271] On 23 December, the Commission tabled the proposal: it is the first time ever that the procedure of Article 20 TEU is activated to provide a loan to a third country in the context of macro-financial assistance. The three Member States that remained outside the enhanced cooperation will not be impacted by the decision to support Ukraine, in line with Article 332 TFEU.[272]

Ukraine is expected to repay the loan once reparations are received from Russia; should the aggressor State refuse to do so, the Union would, for the first time, reserve the right to make use of immobilised assets to repay the loan, in full compliance with EU and international law.[273]

In conclusion, the decisions adopted by the EU institutions in December 2025 concerning Ukraine represent a watershed moment for the Union. Two exceptional instruments were adopted or are in the process of being finalised. The first is the forthcoming Regulation on macro-financial assistance to Ukraine, which, for the first time, was decided on the basis of enhanced cooperation in the context of one of the Union's external policies. The second is Regulation 2025/2600[274] immobilising the assets of the CBR. The decision to adopt the latter act on the basis of Article 122 TFEU was supported by 25 Heads of State or Government meeting within the European Council, which took note of the Commission's exceptional, temporary, and duly justified emergency measures immobilising the CBR's assets 'on a more sustained basis.[275] The compromise solution was set out in the Conclusions of the President of the European Council, as Hungary and Slovakia chose not to endorse it. The new emergency measure keeps the CBR's assets and reserves immobilised for as long as a number of conditions remain unfulfilled. Article 6 is the most significant provision of the act under examination, as it defines the circumstances that would

[270] Nesterchuk and others (2025) Legal Analysis: Reparations Loan Ukraine, https://libmod.de/legal-analysis-reparations-loan-ukraine/ [accessed on 20 December 2025].

[271] European Commission, COM (2025) 806 final.

[272] As a result of the enhanced cooperation, 'Any mobilisation of resources of the Union's budget as a guarantee for this loan will not have an impact on the financial obligations of these three countries.' Ibid.

[273] Conclusions of the President of the European Council of 18 December 2025, EUCO 26/25, p. 4.

[274] Council Regulation (EU) 2025/2600.

[275] Conclusions of the President of the European Council of 18 December 2025, EUCO 26/25, p. 3.

bring the application of the temporary measures—namely, the prohibition on transferring sovereign assets to the CBR and the related ancillary prohibitions[276]—to an end. These mentioned measures

> shall be maintained as long as the making available of the significant resources to Russia to continue its actions in the context of its war of aggression against Ukraine poses, or threatens to pose, serious economic difficulties within the Union and the Member States and the risk of causing further serious deterioration of the economic situation in the Union and the Member States persists. To this effect, the measures set out in this Regulation shall cease to apply when the following conditions are met:
>
> (a) Russia ceases its war of aggression against Ukraine;
>
> (b) Russia provides reparations to Ukraine to the extent necessary to allow for reconstruction without adverse economic or financial consequences for the Union; and
>
> (c) Russia's actions in the context of its war of aggression against Ukraine have objectively ceased to pose a serious risk of severe difficulties to the economy of the Union and its Member States.

With the adoption of the Regulation in question, the EU has crossed the Rubicon by transforming the temporary freeze of the CBR's assets held within the Union[277] into a freezing order which, while not permanent,[278] is prolonged over time. The Regulation may be regarded as an instrument of last resort, rendered necessary by an exceptional context in which the EU was required to support Ukraine despite the objections of Hungary and other Member States, while remaining in compliance with international law. The novelty of the Regulation lies in the fact that it was enacted by stretching to its limits the Union's competence to adopt (internal) economic emergency measures. The modification of the conditions under which the CBR's assets remain frozen was adopted on the basis of Article 122(1) TFEU, which provides for Union action to address situations of economic emergency, rather than Article 215 TFEU. The legality of the new Regulation could be questioned under international law, in light of the prolonged duration of the prohibitions, as well as under EU law, given that the primary purpose of this measure pursues a CFSP objective. Nevertheless, the author is of the view that, should an action for annulment be brought by one or more of the outvoted Member States before the General Court, the contested measure could be regarded as lawful.

The most obvious criticism that could be levelled against the legality of this countermeasure is that, by immobilising sovereign assets, it arguably undermines

---

[276] These are the prohibitions on satisfying any claims brought by the Russian Federation and prohibition on recognition and enforcement of decisions within the Union of any judicial, arbitral, or administrative decisions obtained by those actors in connection with the restrictive measures (Article 4 of Council Regulation (EU) 2025/2600).

[277] More precisely, the EU 'prohibits, on a temporary basis, any direct or indirect transfer of assets and reserves of the Central Bank of Russia, or of any legal person, entity or body acting on behalf of, or at the direction of, the Central Bank of Russia, such as the Russian National Wealth Fund (the 'Central Bank of Russia or related entities'), in order to ensure that the assets and reserves of the Central Bank of Russia or related entities are not transferred to or for the benefit of Central Bank of Russia or related entities and ultimately Russia.' Recital n. 12 of Council Regulation (EU) 2025/2600.

[278] *Contra* see Leichsenring and Popp 2025.

the requirement that such measures be temporary. In the author's view the Union continues to act in accordance with international law by prolonging the freezing of Russia's assets. Those funds could still be unfrozen should the aggression and the threat to the Union's economy and security cease, and reparation for the damage caused to Ukraine be provided. Therefore, the freezing order is reversible and is subject to periodic review.[279] The term 'temporary' is used repeatedly throughout the Regulation. There is no intention to confiscate the assets, unless Russia fails to offset, as far as possible, the consequences of its violation of peremptory norms of international law. Ukraine must be re-built after 4 years of an unprovoked and unjustified aggression.

A second source of tension with international law obligations lies in the fact that the Union appears to have adjusted the original rationale underlying the freezing of the CBR's assets in 2022. The justification for the conditional freezing order is no longer confined to inducing Russia to cease its aggression, but also extends to exerting pressure on Russia to provide reparation for war-related damage and to cease posing a security threat to the Union. It is noteworthy that the final condition that must be met for the lifting of the prohibition to return the funds—namely, that 'Russia's actions in the context of its war of aggression against Ukraine have objectively ceased to pose a serious risk of severe difficulties to the economy of the Union and its Member States'[280]—is novel and arguably the most problematic. Indeed, the EU is not only acting to the benefit of Ukraine but also to protect its own security.

Nevertheless, the inclusion of this condition may be defended on the ground that the Union may be regarded as a directly affected subject of international law as a result of the war. The rationale underpinning the new emergency measure is that Russia's aggression against Ukraine has both direct and indirect repercussions on the Union's economy. While this assertion may be open to debate in abstract terms, the recitals of the Regulation point to the significant social and economic costs borne by the Member States as a consequence of nearly four years of war. There can be little doubt that the prolonged conflict has adversely affected the Union's economy and that Russia's violation of Ukraine's territorial integrity continues to pose risks to the economic stability of the Member States. It is therefore submitted that, even if the conditions for lifting the mentioned prohibition have evolved, insofar as they remain compatible with international law, they may still render the emergency measure lawful. In this context, the release of the sovereign assets is envisaged only once Russia ceases to pose a threat to the Union. The measure may thus be characterised as hybrid in nature, as it was not adopted solely for the purpose of assisting Ukraine.

Turning to the legality of the new measure within the EU legal order, a number of criticisms were levelled by scholars in the early reactions to the package of measures announced by the Commission. In particular, it has been argued that the new Regulation encroaches upon Article 40(2) TEU,[281] the non-affectation clause safeguarding the prerogatives of the EU institutions in the field of the CFSP. From this perspective,

---

[279] Article 5 of Council Regulation (EU) 2025/2600.

[280] Article 6(1)c of Council Regulation (EU) 2025/2600.

[281] On this issue see Van Elsuwege 2025.

the Regulation could be regarded as a CFSP measure in disguise. In 2022, the CBR's assets were frozen by means of a CFSP Decision and a Regulation, adopted respectively on the basis of Articles 29 TEU and 215 TFEU, in order to support Ukraine. Those measures were subsequently amended in 2024, while their legal bases were maintained. The reason why the restrictive measures could not simply be preserved was that Hungary might have voted against their renewal, thereby obliging Belgium and the other Member States holding the CBR's assets and reserves to return them to Russia. Against this background, it has been suggested that the Commission sought to sidestep Hungary's opposition by relying on the emergency legal basis provided for in the TFEU, namely Article 122, to justify the prohibition on transferring the CBR's assets and reserves. There is little doubt that the Regulation was adopted in order to prevent the unfreezing of the immobilised assets, a prospect threatened by Hungary's opposition. The advantage of relying on Article 122 TFEU lies in the fact that the emergency measure is adopted by qualified majority voting in the Council, thereby preventing Hungary and other Member States that might oppose the renewal of the asset freeze from achieving their ojectives.[282] However, reliance on Article 122(1) TFEU as a legal basis appeared to be the only viable solution once Hungary had persistently exercised its veto power. It is submitted that the transformation of a CFSP measure into a non-CFSP emergency measure constitutes a compromise that is legally sound. The new measure is justified by the existence of an economic emergency arising from *four* years of war in Ukraine, as well as by the direct economic damage inflicted by Russia on the Union.[283] This situation could be further aggravated if Russia were able to make use of the CBR's assets.

6.8 Concluding Remarks

This chapter has demonstrated that the EU's use of restrictive measures serves multiple purposes: (1) ensuring the cessation of Russia's aggression and enhancing Ukraine's financial resilience, which is instrumental to the exercise of its right to self-defence; (2) imposing additional economic and political costs in relation to the proclamation of independence by self-proclaimed separatist entities, thus contributing to expand the scope of the obligations stemming from Article 41(2) ARSIWA[284]; (3) making pressure on States that fails to discharge their obligation of cooperation to bring to an end a violation of a peremptory norm of international law to do so; (4) contributing to the prevention of international crimes; (5) directly supporting the reconstruction of Ukraine, after a violation of *jus cogens* rules. The analysis has

[282] A scholar suggested that the EU should make sure to be able to prolong the freeze of the assets, until Russia has ceased hostilities and paid reparations to Ukraine, thereby removing uncertainties regarding its possible lifting every 6 months. Veber 2025, p. 63.

[283] 'Russia has been negatively impacting the Union economy and business through the seizure, confiscation or forced sale of economic assets within Russia belonging to Union investors.' Recital n. 28 of Council Regulation (EU) 2025/2600.

[284] The EU went beyond the non-recognition obligation stemming from Article 41 (2) ARSIWA.

shown that, while the use of sanctions for the prevention of international crimes remains contested and the nexus between individual designation criteria and the stated objectives is at times tenuous,[285] the Union has generally acted in accordance with international law in adopting restrictive measures in response to multiple serious violations committed by Russia.

Several restrictive measures take the form of retorsions. The risks for the Union of violating international law are primarily connected with the expansion of its anti-circumvention framework, which has been progressively tightened since 2023, as well as with the potential confiscation of Russian sovereign assets. With regard to the former risk, this chapter concludes that anti-circumvention obligations—despite their impact on third-country subsidiaries of EU parent companies or on vessels flagged in third countries—do not amount to an extraterritorial exercise of prescriptive jurisdiction, since EU restrictive measures are based on sufficient jurisdictional links, such as territory or the place of incorporation of the relevant companies or operators.

It is noteworthy, first, that the Union increasingly links the application of restrictive measures to compliance with international standards, as illustrated by the prohibitions targeting the so-called 'shadow fleet,' which are tied to respect for IMO standards. Second, the expanding global reach of EU sanctions and the Union's robust engagement in countering circumvention may be explained by the direct challenge posed by Russia to the Union's territorial integrity, including repeated violations of the airspace of several Member States since 2023.[286] Third, even where sanctions may appear extraterritorial—as in the case of the prohibition on transactions with certain non-Russian entities connected to the SPFS—they remain compatible with international law insofar as the primary obligations are imposed on EU-based legal entities.

That said, it should be noted that if the Union were to impose direct obligations governing contractual relations between non-EU subsidiaries and third-country operators, it would effectively move towards the application of secondary sanctions.

In principle, the EU could also restrict trade in sensitive goods with *third countries* suspected of facilitating re-exports to Russia. To date, however, the Union has refrained from adopting such measures and has instead relied on the Sanctions Envoy to engage with countries that favour the circumvention of sanctions. Should the EU decide to enact trade restrictions, such measures could be taken under Article 16 of

[285] For example, in some cases the designation criteria are unsuited for reaching the objective(s) of restrictive measures since these criteria may be too broad, thus watering down the quality of 'targeted' measures, or they may be deprived of a sufficient link or connection with the purpose of those measures.

[286] Recital 17 of COM (2025) 3501.

the ARSIWA[287] against third countries which, by actively supporting the circumvention of sanctions—measures themselves designed to bring to an end breaches of *erga omnes* obligations—aid or assist Russia in the commission (including the continuation) of an internationally wrongful act. An alternative justification for the EU trade restrictions could be to qualify them as a reaction to the failure of third States to comply with the obligation of cooperation stemming from Article 41(1) ARSIWA.

With regard to the risks associated with the confiscation of private assets, the Union lacks a direct competence to confiscate such assets. Nevertheless, since the violation of restrictive measures has been criminalised,[288] Member States may confiscate assets as a criminal penalty for sanctions evasion and may, on a voluntary basis, decide to channel them to Ukraine. In practice, however, the Union has focused on the revenues generated by the freezing of the CBR's assets and reserves, thereby refraining from 'touching' the principal, in light of the protection afforded to those assets under the law of international immunity. As this chapter has shown, the use of the revenues generated by the immobilisation of those funds is compatible with international law; this innovative solution, taken to ensure the resilience of the victim of an aggression, contributes to the progressive development of international law. The Union has strengthened Ukraine's financial resilience through the ULCM, in cooperation with several G7 members; in doing so, each participating country has also cooperated with Ukraine in order to ensure 'budgetary, military and reconstruction assistance.[289]

To date, the Union has refrained from making use of the total amount of the CBR's assets and reserves, thereby demonstrating respect for the special protection afforded to such funds by the law of immunities. Should Russia fail to comply with its international obligations, the Union may nonetheless decide to seize to those assets as a measure of last resort.

In principle, the immobilisation of Russian sovereign assets could be seen as a lawful countermeasure which the EU Member States take collectively through the Union. On this view, the legal basis for EU action could be found in Articles 48(1)(b) and 48(2)(b) of the ARSIWA. These provisions allow non-injured States to invoke the responsibility of a State that has breached an obligation owed to the international community as a whole—most notably the prohibition of aggression—and to seek performance of the obligation of reparation in the interest of the injured State. Article 48(2) ARSIWA could therefore provide the legal basis for the EU to confiscate Russian assets in the interest of Ukraine, with a view to ensuring cessation

---

287 'A State which aids or assists another State in the commission of an internationally wrongful act by the latter is internationally responsible for doing so if:

(a) that State does so with knowledge of the circumstances of the internationally wrongful act; and

(b) the act would be internationally wrongful if committed by that State.'

288 Chapter 7 in this book.

289 G7 Leaders' Statement on Extraordinary Revenue Acceleration (ERA) Loans, https://www.g7italy.it/wp-content/uploads/G7-Leaders-Statement-on-Extraordinary-Revenue-Acceleration-ERA-Loans.pdf [accessed on 12 December 2025].

of the breach and compliance with the obligation to repair the damage caused by the war. Nonetheless, EU Member States remain cautious about openly supporting confiscation. A more viable alternative may lie in transferring the sovereign assets to an internationally established compensation mechanism.

A significant legal development occurred once it became apparent that the Union needed to neutralise the risk that the freezing of Russia's sovereign assets might be lifted as a result of a possible failure by the Council to renew the restrictive measures. Unlike the United Kingdom and other jurisdictions, the Union is required to renew its sanctions on an annual basis, and Hungary has repeatedly opposed such renewal. This internal constraint, combined with Ukraine's request for further financial assistance for the period 2026–2027, led to the adoption of Regulation (EU) 2025/2600. That Regulation transformed the temporary freezing of the assets for CFSP purposes into a conditional freezing order also designed to ensure the Union's economic stability. This measure constitutes a truly exceptional legal instrument, as it is hybrid in nature: for the first time, an EU measure combines an internal dimension with objectives linked to the Union's external action. This hybrid character explains why the Regulation was adopted within the TFEU framework, thereby entrusting the Commission with responsibility for its implementation and review. Since the prohibition on returning the funds to the CBR remains temporary and reversible, the measure continues to qualify as a lawful countermeasure, adopted by the Union in support of Ukraine in order to ensure reparation for war-related damage and to safeguard Ukraine's financial resilience. The novelty of Regulation (EU) 2025/2600 further lies in its objective of safeguarding the Union's internal economic and security interests, in light of the deterioration of the Union's economy after four years of war and the threats posed by Russia to the territorial integrity of the Member States. There is little doubt that both the Union and its Member States may adopt emergency measures aimed, *inter alia*, at countering existential threats to the Union. In sum, by enacting this Regulation, the Union is cooperating with Ukraine to bring to an end serious breaches of obligations arising under *jus cogens* norms by the aggressor State. At the same time, Regulation (EU) 2025/2600 may also be characterised as a countermeasure adopted by the Union pursuant to Article 42 ARSIWA, in response to the deterioration of the Union's economic situation caused by Russia's aggression against Ukraine. It is not surprising that the CBR has sought to challenge this measure before the GC. It remains to be seen whether the GC will validate the legal basis of the contested measure.[290]

References

Abely C (2023) The Russia Sanctions: the Economic Response to Russia's Invasion of Ukraine. Cambridge University Press, Cambridge.

---

[290] https://www.themoscowtimes.com/2026/03/03/russian-central-bank-challenges-eus-indefinite-asset-freeze-in-european-court-a92100 [accessed on 4 March 2026].

Akande D et al. (2024) On Proposed Countermeasures Against Russia to Compensate Injured States for Losses Caused by Russia's War of Aggression Against Ukraine, https://www.iiss.org/globalassets/media-library---content--migration/files/research-papers/2024/05-new/iiss_on-proposed-countermeasures-against-russia-to-compensate-injured-states-for-losses-caused-by-russias-war-of-aggression-aga.pdf, accessed 20 May 2024.
Asada M (2024) The War in Ukraine under International Law: Its Use of Force and Armed Conflict Aspects. International Community Law Review 26: 5-38.
Beaucillon C (2021) The European Union's Position and Practice with Regard to Unilateral and Extraterritorial Sanctions. In: Beaucillon C (ed) Research Handbook on Unilateral and Extraterritorial Sanctions. Edward Elgar, Cheltenham, pp. 110–129.
Bogdanova I (2022) Unilateral Sanctions in International Law and the Enforcement of Human Rights. Nijhoff, Brill, Leiden/Boston
Brunk I (2023), Central Bank Immunity, Sanctions, and Sovereign Wealth Funds. The George Washington Law Review: 91, pp. 1647–1648.
Butchard P (2024) Sanctions, International Law and Seizing Russian Assets. Research briefing. House of Commons Library, https://researchbriefings.files.parliament.uk/documents/CBP-10034/CBP-10034.pdf.
Caprile A, Peters T (2025) Confiscation of Immobilised Russian Sovereign Assets- State of play, arguments and scenarios, EPRS, 2025, https://www.europarl.europa.eu/RegData/etudes/BRIE/2025/775908/EPRS_BRI(2025)775908_EN.pdf.
Cinelli F (2024) Le Contromisure di Stati terzi nella Guerra di Aggressione della Federazione Russa: Evoluzioni in Atto per Garantire la Riparazione nell'Interesse dell'Ucraina. Ordine Internazionale e Diritto Umani 841–868.
Darvas Z, Demertzis M et al. (2023) EU trade and investment following Russia's illegal invasion of Ukraine, July 2023, https://www.europarl.europa.eu/RegData/etudes/STUD/2023/702591/EXPO_STU(2023)702591_EN.pdf.
Dawidowicz M (2010) The Obligation of Non-recognition of an Unlawful Situation. In: Crawford J (ed) The Law of International Responsibility. Oxford University Press, Oxford, pp. 677–696.
De Sadeleer N, Damjanovic I (2024) The Rule of Law Between National and International Contexts: Introduction to the Special Issue on International Economic Law and the Rule of Law. European Journal of Risk Regulation 15: 477–484. https://doi.org/10.1017/err.2024.39.
Dunbar R (2021) Article 3(5) TEU a Decade on: Revisiting 'Strict Observance of International Law' in the Text and Context of Other EU Values. Maastricht Journal of European and Comparative Law 28: 479–497.
Fabbrini F (2024) "To Establish Justice": The EU Response to the War in Ukraine in the Field of Justice and Home Affairs. E.L. Rev. 49: 359–376.
Finelli F (2025) Countering the Circumvention of Targeted Sanctions. Legal Challenges in the EU, US and UK, PhD thesis (discussed June 2025).
Gallo D (2025) Direct Effects in EU Law. Oxford University Press, Oxford.
Gestri M (2022) Sanctions, Collective Countermeasures and the EU. Italian Yearbook of International Law 32: 67–92.
Goldmann M (2022) Hot War and Cold Freezes: Targeting Russian Central Bank Assets. VerfBlog, 2022/2/28, https://verfassungsblog.de/hot-war-and-cold-freezes/, https://doi.org/10.17176/20220301-001108-0.
Gordon J (2024) Extraterritorial and secondary sanctions and the problem of overcompliance. In: Sean Morris P (ed) Economic Sanctions under International Law: Trade Continuity with Special Purpose Vehicles. Taylor and Francis, pp. 259-277.
Grant T (2022) Multilateral Action Model for Reparation. https://newlinesinstitute.org/wp-content/uploads/20221031-MAMOR-Doc-w-toc-NLISP.pdf.
Hoffmeister, F. (2023) Strategic autonomy in the European Union's external relations law. Common Market Law Review 60, 667–699.
Hoffmeister F, Köppen A (2026) Protecting and Developing International law as EU foreign policy objective (on file with the author).

Jackson M, Paddeu F (2024) The countermeasures of others: when can states collaborate in the taking of countermeasures? American Journal of International Law 118: 231–274.

Kamminga M T (2023) Confiscating Russia's Frozen Central Bank Assets: A Permissible Third-Party Countermeasure? Netherlands International Law Review 70:1–17, https://doi.org/10.1007/s40802-023-00231-7.

Kassoti E (2024) Beyond Collective Countermeasures and Towards an Autonomous External Sanctioning Power? The General Court's Judgment in Case T-65/18 RENV, Venezuela v Council. European Papers, European Forum 9: 247–259, Insight of 3 July 2024.

Kerbrat Y (2021) Unilateral/extraterritorial sanctions as a challenge to the theory of jurisdiction. In: Beaucillon C (ed) Research Handbook on Unilateral and Extraterritorial Sanctions. Edward Elgar, Cheltenham, pp. 165–185.

Kotanidis S (2024) Legal options for confiscation of Russian state assets to support the reconstruction of Ukraine, EPRS, PE 759.602, https://www.europarl.europa.eu/RegData/etudes/STUD/2024/759602/EPRS_STU(2024)759602_EN.pdf.

Krisch N (2022) Jurisdiction Unbound: (Extra)territorial Regulation as Global Governance. European Journal of International Law 33, 481–514, https://doi.org/10.1093/ejil/chac028.

Moseienko A (2023) Legal: The Freezing of the Russian Central Bank's Assets. European Journal of International Law 34: 1007–1020.

Nakatani K (2024) Freezing, confiscation and management of the assets of the Russian Central Bank and the oligarchs: Legality and possibility under international law. In: Asada M, Tamada D (eds) The War in Ukraine and International Law. Springer, Singapore, 137–156, https://doi.org/10.1007/978-981-97-2504-5_6.

Leichsenring T, Popp J (2025) From Security to Economics: Freezing Russian Assets under Article 122(1) TFEU Violates the Treaties. VerfBlog, 2025/12/23, https://verfassungsblog.de/from-security-to-economics/, https://doi.org/10.59704/a3f9198e9a2473e8.

McCorquodale R (2016) Defining the International Rule of Law: Defying Gravity? ICLQ 65(2): 277-305, https://doi.org/10.1017/S0020589316000026.

Poli S (2025) The EU's contribution to Ukraine's reconstruction: the legality of the windfall tax on the extraordinary revenue generated by the immobilised assets and reserves of the Russian Central Bank. In: Pantaleo L, Siddi M (eds) The rule of law crisis and democratic backsliding in the EU—Open questions and outstanding challenges. Giappichelli, Turin, pp. 97–113, https://www.giappichelli.it/media/catalog/product/openaccess/9791221162134.pdf.

Poli S, Finelli F (2023) Context specific and structural changes in EU restrictive measures adopted in reaction to Russia's aggression to Ukraine. In: rivista.eurojus.it n. 3/2023, pp. 19–49, https://rivista.eurojus.it/wp-content/uploads/pdf/Qui-13.pdf.

Quaglia L, Verdun A (2023) Weaponisation of finance: the role of European central banks and financial sanctions against. West European Politics 46: pp. 872–895. https://doi.org/10.1080/01402382.2022.2155906.

Reinisch A (2006) State Immunity From Enforcement Measures. In: Hafner G, Kohen M G, Breau S (eds) State Practice Regarding State Immunities. Leiden/Boston, pp. 155–166.

Rosas A (2023) From Freezing to Confiscating Russian Assets? European Law Review 48: 337–347.

Ruys T, Rodríguez Silvestre F (2024) Secondary Sanctions after Russia's Invasion of Ukraine - A Whole New World. In: Ruys T, Ryngaert C, Rodríguez Silvestre F (eds) The Cambridge Handbook of Secondary Sanctions and International Law. Cambridge University Press, Cambridge, pp. 463–499.

Ruys T, Ryngaert C (2020) Secondary Sanctions: A Weapon Out of Control? The International Legality of, and European Responses to, US Secondary Sanctions. British Yearbook of International Law 89: pp. 1–116, https://doi.org/10.1093/bybil/braa007.

Ryngaert C et al. (2024) Introduction: Secondary Sanctions in the International Legal Order. In: Ruys T, Ryngaert C, Rodríguez Silvestre F (eds) The Cambridge Handbook of Secondary Sanctions and International Law. Cambridge University Press, Cambridge, pp. 1–10.

Sexton J P (2022) The European Union's Sanctioning of Russian Military Officers: An Urge for Caution, 5 August 2022, https://www.ejiltalk.org/the-european-unions-sanctioning-of-russian-military-officers-an-urge-for-caution/.
Silingardi S (2024) Unilateral Sanctions Before the General Court: Venezuela v. Council. Common Market Law Review 61: 1123–1142. https://doi-org.peacepalace.idm.oclc.org/10.54648/cola2024071.
Sossai M (2020) Legality of Extraterritorial Sanctions. In: Asada M (ed) Economic Sanctions in International Law and Practice. Routledge, London, pp. 62–79. https://doi.org/10.4324/97804290.
Terlinden M (2024) Recent Developments in the Sanctions Practice of the European Union: A Proportionality Review. Leuven Centre for Global Studies, Working paper 244, June 2024.
Van Damme I, Matthaiou A (2025) The administration and enforcement of EU sanctions revisited. In: Govaere I, Garben S, Spaventa E (eds) The Impact of War (in Ukraine) on the EU. Hart Publishing, pp. 185–214.
Van der Horst R (2023) Illegal, Unless: Freezing the Assets of Russia's Central Bank. European Journal of International Law 34: 1021-1031.
Van Elwuwege P (2025) Walking a Tightrope: On the Legal Stakes of the EU's Proposed Reparations Loan for Ukraine. VerfBlog, 2025/12/08, https://verfassungsblog.de/on-the-legal-stakes-of-the-eus-proposed-reparations-loan-for-ukraine/, https://doi.org/10.17176/20251208-172127-0.
Veber M (2025) EU sanctions and Russia's frozen assets, November 2025, PE 754.487, https://www.europarl.europa.eu/RegData/etudes/STUD/2025/754487/EXPO_STU(2025)754487_EN.pdf.
Veber M (2026) The Making of Custom Through Sanctions of International Organisations. In: Droubi S, d'Aspremont J (eds) International Organisations, Non-State Actors, and the Formation of Customary International Law. Manchester University Press, Manchester, pp. 284-305.
Wuert I (2024) The Controversial REPO Act Is Now Law. Lawfare: 25 April 2024. https://www.lawfaremedia.org/article/the-controversial-repo-act-is-now-law.
Wuerth I (2019) Immunity from Execution of Central Bank Assets. In: Ruys T, Angelet N, Ferro L (eds) The Cambridge Handbook of Immunities and International Law. Cambridge University Press, Cambridge, UK, pp. 266–284.

EU Secondary Law

CFSP Decision (CFSP) 2023/191 of 27 January 2023 amending Decision 2014/512 CFSP decision concerning restrictive measures in view of Russia's actions destabilising the situation in Ukraine, OJ L 26, 30.01.2023, p. 44.
Council Decision 2014/145/CFSP of 17 March 2014 concerning restrictive measures in respect of actions undermining or threatening the territorial integrity, sovereignty and independence of Ukraine, OJ L 78, p. 16.
Council Decision (CFSP) 2021/509 of 22 March 2021 establishing a European Peace Facility, and repealing Decision (CFSP) 2015/528, OJ L 102, 24.3.2021, p. 14.
Council Decision (CFSP) 2022/335 amending Decision 2014/512/CFSP, which prohibited any transactions related to the management of reserves of, as well as of assets of, the Central Bank of Russia, including transactions with any legal person, entity or body acting on behalf of, or at the direction of, the Central Bank of Russia, OJ L 57, 28.03.2022, p. 4.
Council Decision (CFSP) 2022/883 of 3 June 2022 amending Decision 2014/145/CFSP concerning restrictive measures in respect of actions undermining or threatening the territorial integrity, sovereignty and independence of Ukraine, OJ L 153, 3.06.2022, p. 92.
Council Decision (CFSP) 2023/501 of 7 March 2023 amending Decision (CFSP) 2020/1999 concerning restrictive measures against serious human rights violations and abuses, OJ L 69I, 7.03.2023.

Council Decision (CFSP) 2023/1094 of 5 June 2023 amending Decision 2014/145/CFSP concerning restrictive measures in respect of actions undermining or threatening the territorial integrity, sovereignty and independence of Ukraine, OJ L 146, 6.6.2023, p. 20.

Council implementing Decision (CFSP) 2024/2760 of 24 October 2024 implementing Decision 2014/512/CFSP concerning restrictive measures in view of Russia's actions destabilising the situation in Ukraine, OJ L, 2024/2760, 28.10.2024.

Council Decision (CFSP) 2024/577 of 12 February 2024 amending Decision 2014/512/CFSP concerning restrictive measures in view of Russia's actions destabilising the situation in Ukraine, OJ L, 2024/577, 14.2.2024.

Council Decision (CFSP) 2024/1470 of 21 May 2024 amending Decision 2014/512/CFSP concerning restrictive measures in view of Russia's actions destabilising the situation in Ukraine, OJ L, 2024/1470, 22.5.2024.

Council Decision (CFSP) 2025/388 of 24 February 2025 amending Decision 2014/145/CFSP concerning restrictive measures in respect of actions undermining or threatening the territorial integrity, sovereignty and independence of Ukraine, OJ L, 2025/388, 24.2.2025.

Council Decision (CFSP) 2025/397 of 24 February 2025 amending Decision 2014/386/CFSP concerning restrictive measures in response to the illegal annexation of Crimea and Sevastopol, OJ L, 2025/397, 24.2.2025.

Council Decision (CFSP) 2025/1204 of 16 June 2025 amending Decision 2014/386/CFSP concerning restrictive measures in response to the illegal annexation of Crimea and Sevastopol, ST/9244/2025/INIT, OJ L, 2025/1204, 17.6.2025.

Council, Guidelines on Implementation and Evaluation of Restrictive Measures (Sanctions) in the Framework of the EU Common Foreign and Security Policy' (Annex to Doc n. 5664/ 18, 4 May 2018).

Council Implementing Regulation (EU) 2023/429 of 25 February 2023 implementing Regulation (EU) No 269/2014 concerning restrictive measures in respect of actions undermining or threatening the territorial integrity, sovereignty and independence of Ukraine, OJ L 59I, 25.2.2023, p. 278.

Council Regulation (EU) 267/2012 of 23 March 2012 concerning restrictive measures against Iran and repealing Regulation (EU) No 961/2010, OJ L 88, p. 1.

Council Regulation (EU) 269/2014 of 17 March 2014 concerning restrictive measures in respect of actions undermining or threatening the territorial integrity, sovereignty and independence of Ukraine, OJ L 78, p. 6.

Council Regulation (EU) 2017/1509 of 30 August 2017 concerning restrictive measures against the Democratic People's Republic of Korea and repealing Regulation (EC) No 329/2007, OJ L 224, 31.8.2017, p. 1.

Council Regulation (EU) 2022/334 of 28 February 2022 amending Council Regulation (EU) No 833/2014 concerning restrictive measures in view of Russia's actions destabilising the situation in Ukraine, OJ L 57, p. 3.

Council Regulation (EU) 2022/838 of the European Parliament and of the Council of 30 May 2022 amending Regulation (EU) 2018/1727 as regards the preservation, analysis and storage at Eurojust of evidence relating to genocide, crimes against humanity, war crimes and related criminal offences, OJ L 148, 31.05.2022, p. 1.

Council Regulation (EU) 2023/2675 of the European Parliament and of the Council of 22 November 2023 on the Protection of the Union and Its Member States from Economic Coercion by Third Countries, OJ L, 2023/2675, 7.12.2023.

Council Regulation (EU) 2023/2878 of 18 December 2023 amending Regulation (EU) No 833/2014 concerning restrictive measures in view of Russia's actions destabilising the situation in Ukraine, OJ L, 2023/2878, 18.12.2023.

Council Regulation (EU) 2024/792 of the European Parliament and of the Council of 29 February 2024 establishing the Ukraine Facility, OJ L, 2024/792, 29.2.2024.

Council Regulation (EU) 2024/2773 of the European Parliament and of the Council of 24 October 2024 establishing the Ukraine Loan Cooperation Mechanism and providing exceptional macro-financial assistance to Ukraine, OJ L, 2024/2773, 28.10.2024.
Council Regulation (EU) 2024/1745 of 24 June 2024, amending Regulation (EU) No 833/2014 concerning restrictive measures in view of Russia's actions destabilising the situation in Ukraine, OJ L, 2024/1745, 24.6.2024.
Council Regulation (EU) 2025/395 of 24 February 2025 Council Regulation (EU) 2025/395 of 24 February 2025 amending Regulation (EU) No 833/2014 concerning restrictive measures in view of Russia's actions destabilising the situation in Ukraine, OJ L, 2025/395, 24.2.2025.
Council Regulation (EU) 2025/1106 of 27 May 2025 establishing the Security Action for Europe (SAFE) through the Reinforcement of the European Defence Industry Instrument, OJ L, 2025/1106, 28.5.2025.
Council Regulation (EU) 2025/1470 of July 18, 2025 (amending Regulation (EU) No 833/2014), OJ L, 2025/1494, 19.7.2025, ELI: http://data.europa.eu/eli/reg/2025/1494/oj
Council Regulation (EU) 2025/1975 of 29 September 2025 amending Regulation (EU) No 267/2012 concerning restrictive measures against Iran, OJ L, 2025/1975, 29.9.2025.
Council Regulation (EU) 2025/2033 of 23 October 2025 amending Regulation (EU) No 833/2014 concerning restrictive measures in view of Russia's actions destabilising the situation in Ukraine, OJ L, 2025/2033, 23.10.2025.
Council Regulation (EU) 2025/2600 of 12 December 2025 on emergency measures addressing the serious economic difficulties caused by Russia's actions in the context of the war of aggression against Ukraine, OJ L, 2025/2600, 13.12.2025.
Directive (EU) 2024/1226 of the European Parliament and of the Council of 24 April 2024 on the definition of criminal offences and penalties for the violation of Union restrictive measures and amending Directive (EU) 2018/1673, *OJ L, 2024/1226, 29.4.2024, ELI:* http://data.europa.eu/eli/dir/2024/1226/oj.
Directive (EU) 2024/1260 of the European Parliament and of the Council of 24 April 2024 on asset recovery and confiscation, *OJ L, 2024/1260, 2.5.2024, ELI:* http://data.europa.eu/eli/dir/2024/1260/oj.
European Commission, Proposal for a Council decision on the position to be taken on behalf of the Union in the Council of Europe bodies on the change of status of the European Union from Associate Member to Participant in the Enlarged Partial Agreement on the Register of Damage caused by the Aggression of the Russian Federation against Ukraine, COM (2024) 224.
European Commission, Proposal for a Council Decision authorising enhanced cooperation on the establishment of a Loan for Ukraine, COM/2025/806 final.
European Commission, Proposal for a Council Regulation amending Council Regulation (EU, Euratom) 2020/2093 of 17 December 2020 laying down the multiannual financial framework for the years 2021 to 2027, COM/2025/3500 final.
European Commission, Proposal for a Council Regulation on emergency measures addressing the serious economic difficulties caused by Russia's actions in the context of the war in Ukraine, COM (2025) 3501.
European Commission, Proposal for a Regulation of the European Parliament and of the Council establishing the Reparations Loan to Ukraine and amending Regulation (EU) 2024/792 of the European Parliament and of the Council of 29 February 2024 establishing the Ukraine Facility, COM (2025) 3502.
European Parliament, Resolution on continuing the unwavering EU support for Ukraine, after three years of Russia's war of aggression, 2025/2528(RSP), P10_TA (2025)0033, 12 March 2025.
ILC, Articles on State Responsibility of States for Internationally Wrongful Act, annex to General Assembly resolution 56/83 of 12 December 2001, and corrected by document A/56/49(Vol. I)/Corr.4.
ILC, Draft conclusions on the identification and legal consequences of peremptory norms of general international law (jus cogens) peremptory norms 2022.

List of Cases

GC, Case T-65/18 RENV, *Bolivarian Republic of Venezuela v Council*, EU:T:2019:649.
GC, Case T-125/22, *Russia Today France v Council*, ECLI:EU:T:2022:483.
GC, Case T-737/14, *Bank for Development and Foreign Economic Affairs (Vnesheconombank) v Council of the European Union*, ECLI:EU:T:2018:543.
GC, Case T-102/23, *SBK Art OOO*, ECLI:EU:T:2025:416.
GC, Case T-193/22, *OT v Council*, http://data.europa.eu/eli/C/2024/729/oj
GC Case T-271/22, *Melnichenko* v *Council*, ECLI:EU:T:2025:47.
GC, Case T-741/22, *Ezuvov v Council*, ECLI:EU:T:2024:605.
CJEU, C-380/09 P, *Melli Bank v Council*, ECLI:EU:C:2012:137.
CJEU, C-595/15 P, *NIOC v Council*, ECLI:EU:C:2016:721.
CJEU, Opinion n. 2/2013, *Accession of the European Union to the European Convention for the Protection of Human Rights and Fundamental Freedoms*, ECLI:EU:C:2014:2454.
CJEU, C-72/15 *Rosneft*, ECLI:EU:C:2017:236.
CJEU, C-703/23 P, *Elena Petrovna Timchenko*, ECLI:EU:C:2025:608
CJEU, C-124/20, *Bank Melli Iran v Telekom Deutschland GmbH*, ECLI:EU:C:2021:1035
CJEU, C-413/14 P Intel v. Commission, ECLI:EU:C:2017:632.
CJEU, C-72/11, *Afrasiabi and Others*, EU:C:2011:874.

Opinions of AG

AG's Medina Opinion of 26 June 2025 in Cases C-313/24 (*Opera Laboratori Fiorentini*).

Part II
The Impact of the War in Ukraine on the EU Legal Order: Selected Legal Issues

Chapter 7
In the Name of the Effectiveness of Restrictive Measures: The War in Ukraine as the Driver for an Expansion of the EU Competence in the Field of Criminal Law

Sara Poli

Contents

Abstract This chapter examines two Directives that were adopted after the EU has acquired the competence to lay down minimum rules on the criminalization of the violation of restrictive measures. The effectiveness of these measures was the justification put forward by the EU institutions to adopt Directive 2024/1226 and Directive 2024/1260. The confiscation of assets related to criminal activities, including the violation of restrictive measures, can hardly be justified by the need to ensure their effectiveness. The chapter argues that the EU has taken advantage of the conflict in Ukraine to harmonise domestic laws on confiscation of assets of criminal activities which only include, amongst other things, the violation of restrictive measures. We conclude that Directive 2024/1260 may be considered an

S. Poli et al., *The EU's Response to the War in Ukraine and Its Impact on the EU Legal Order*, Global Europe: Legal and Policy Issues of the EU's External Action 7,
https://doi.org/10.1007/978-94-6265-767-0_7

example of "harmonization by stealth," which was adopted taking the effectiveness of restrictive measures as a pretext to expand the EU competences. The only link with the CFSP is represented by a provision that makes it possible to use the proceeds of the confiscation to support Ukraine's reconstruction.

Keywords EU competence · Effectiveness · Restrictive measures · Harmonisation of criminal law · Confiscation · Article 83 TFEU · Harmonisation by stealth

7.1 Introduction

The outbreak of the conflict in Ukraine has caused a series of consequences for the European Union (EU) and its Member States, which do not only affect the Common Foreign and Security Policy (CFSP), the enlargement of the Union or other EU policies but also the division of competences between the EU and its Member States in the area of criminal law.[1] Indeed, in late November 2022 the EU has acquired a competence to address a new euro-crime: the violation of Union restrictive measures.[2]

The new prerogative, which was attributed to the EU on the basis of Decision (EU) 2022/2332,[3] was exercised in April 2024, when the Council adopted two Directives: the first on the definition of criminal offences and penalties for the violation of Union restrictive measures[4] and the second one on asset recovery and confiscation in the context of criminal proceedings.[5] The main reason put forward by the EU institutions to justify the expansion of EU competences is the need to ensure the effective implementation of restrictive measures.

The EU has triggered Article 83(1) TFEU, third indent[6] to acquire the mentioned new competence in the field of criminal law. The aim of this chapter is to understand whether the adoption of the two abovementioned Directives meets the conditions laid down by this provision or whether the EU institutions have taken advantage of the conflict in Ukraine to expand the EU competences in criminal law[7] in areas in

---

[1] Poli and Pau 2024.

[2] Council Decision (EU) 2022/2332 of 28 November 2022 on identifying the violation of Union restrictive measures as an area of crime that meets the criteria specified in Article 83(1) of the TFEU, https://eur-lex.europa.eu/eli/dec/2022/2332/oj.

[3] See Council Decision (EU) 2022/2332, above n. 2.

[4] See Directive (EU) 2024/1226 of the European Parliament and of the Council of 24 April 2024 on the definition of criminal offences and penalties for the violation of Union restrictive measures and amending Directive (EU) 2018/1673, https://eur-lex.europa.eu/eli/dir/2024/1226/oj.

[5] See Directive (EU) 2024/1260 of the European Parliament and of the Council of 24 April 2024 on asset recovery and confiscation, https://eur-lex.europa.eu/eli/dir/2024/1260/oj.

[6] This provision states: 'On the basis of developments in crime, the Council may adopt a decision identifying other areas of crime that meet the criteria specified in this paragraph. It shall act unanimously after obtaining the consent of the European Parliament.'

[7] See European Commission 2011, p. 7.

which the adoption of new legislation was not strictly necessary to strengthen the effectiveness of CFSP measures.[8]

The chapter is divided into six sections. After briefly explaining the technique used by Article 83 TFEU to expand EU competences in Sect. 7.2, Sects. 7.3 and 7.4 will examine the procedure leading to add a new area of crime to the existing list of crimes included in the Treaty and the reasons put forward by the EU institutions to establish minimum rules on the violation of restrictive measures. Section 7.4.1 will dwell on the definition of the criminal offense consisting in the violation of restrictive measures. Section 7.5 will show that the adoption of rules concerning asset recovery and confiscation does not seem to fully meet the conditions provided for in Article 83 (2) TFUE to adopt harmonisation measures since the connection between Directive 2024/1260 and the need to ensure the effective implementation of the CFSP is too tenuous. In Sect. 7.5.2, it is stressed that during the legislative procedure, leading to the adoption of Directive 2024/1260, a provision aimed at facilitating the achievement of a CFSP objective was eventually added. As a result, the link between the harmonisation of rules concerning asset confiscation and the objective of ensuring 'the effective implementation of a Union policy' (in this case, the CFSP), as set out in the Commission proposal for the Directive, was strengthened during the legislative procedure. Yet, this act remains centred on fighting organised crime. Section 7.6 provides some thoughts on the broader implications for the European integration process that are attached to the expansion of the EU competence in the field of substantive criminal law through Article 83 TFEU in a situation in which the trigger of the widening of the EU competence was the war in Ukraine.

7.2 The Dynamic Mechanism to Expand EU Competences in the Field of Criminal Law

Article 83(1) TFEU enables the EU to establish minimum rules concerning the definition of criminal offences and sanctions 'in areas of particularly serious crime' laid down in the Treaty.[9] However, it is possible to expand the list of 'EU crimes' on the basis of developments in crime by adopting a Council Decision (Article 83(1) TFEU, third indent).[10] The condition to add a new crime to the existing list is that the former has a cross-border dimension, which may result either from the impact of

[8] Moreover, it is necessary to establish whether criminal law is required to achieve the objectives of the action (principle of necessity) and define the criminal offences and penalties. On the problem of using criminal law to reinforce the effectiveness of restrictive measures, see Finelli 2023b, p. 726.

[9] These areas include terrorism, trafficking in human beings and sexual exploitation of women and children, illicit drug trafficking, illicit arms trafficking, money laundering, corruption, counterfeiting of means of payment, computer crime and organised crime. See Article 83(1) TFEU, second indent.

[10] This Decision must be approved by all EU Member States within the Council after obtaining the consent of the European Parliament. The requirement of unanimity is justified by the importance of the matter which is decided: an expansion of EU competence in areas at the heart of sovereignty: criminal law.

such an offence on different Member States or from the particular need to combat it on a common basis.

The mechanism under analysis injects flexibility to the EU's action in the area of freedom, security and justice, which is an area of shared competence. Indeed, EU competences may be expanded in domains that are reserved to Member States, without amending the Treaties. In addition, the mentioned mechanism is preferable in terms of transparency than that consisting in expanding EU competence as a result of the progressive 'occupation' of a given field.

As mentioned in the introduction, Council Decision 2022/2332 has laid the ground for the adoption of subsequent 'minimum' harmonisation measures. Directive 2024/1226 has harmonised the definition of violation of restrictive measures while Directive 2024/1260 is concerned with assets recovery and confiscation. The latter piece of legislation is based on Article 83(1), Article 83(2) TFEU and on other provisions.[11] Under Article 83(2) TFEU, the EU institutions are empowered to adopt Directives[12] to approximate criminal laws and regulations of the Member States if this 'proves essential to ensure the *effective implementation of a Union policy* in an area which has been subject to harmonisation measures' (emphasis added).

7.3 The Violation of Union Restrictive Measures Becomes a New Area of Crime: The Justifications Provided by Council Decision 2022/2332

A few months following Russia's war of aggression in February 2022, the Commission adopted a Communication entitled 'Towards a Directive on criminal penalties for the violation of Union restrictive measures,'[13] which advocated for the need to trigger Article 83(1) TFEU, third indent.[14]

In this document, the Commission outlined the reasons why adding the violation of restrictive measures to the list provided for in Article 83(1) TFEU, second indent, would be appropriate. In the same Communication, this institution announced the submission of a proposal for a Council Decision on adding the violation of Union restrictive measures to the 'EU crimes' and of a proposal for a Directive on asset recovery and confiscation. It is explained that the *status quo* with regard to enforcement of restrictive measures was not satisfactory. It is noteworthy that the EU had already imposed important obligations concerning substantive criminal law

[11] These are Articles 82(2) and 87(2) TFEU.

[12] The Directive is adopted following the ordinary legislative procedure.

[13] European Commission (2022c).

[14] 'On the basis of developments in crime, the Council may adopt a decision identifying other areas of crime that meet the criteria specified in this paragraph. It shall act unanimously after obtaining the consent of the European Parliament.'

in the EU restrictive measures adopted in reaction to Russia's aggression. In particular, in June 2022 a Regulation[15] had tasked Member States to lay down rules on penalties, 'including as appropriate criminal penalties.' This provision went beyond the standard clause of all sanction regimes whereby Member States are under an obligation to adopt 'effective, proportionate and dissuasive[16]' sanctions to be applied on a case-by-case basis in case restrictive measures are breached.

In addition, national authorities were also asked to counter the violation of Union restrictive measures by, *among other things*, providing for 'appropriate measures of confiscation of the proceeds of such infringements.'[17] The possibility to impose the confiscation of the proceeds of criminal activity was even challenged in Court, with no success.[18]

This context shows that the Union had already de facto constrained Member States' sovereignty with the concerned restrictive measures. Indeed, the choice on the *nature* of these measures adopted to ensure that sanctions are respected is usually left to national authorities.

Yet, the Commission stresses that obliging Member States to lay down penalties, including criminal ones, is not enough. This is the crucial passage:

---

[15] Council Regulation (EU) 2022/880. See, in particular, recital 2, stressing the need to clarify and strengthen the provisions on national penalties for the breach of the measures set out in Regulation 269/2014.

[16] The principle whereby 'infringements of Community law are penalized under conditions, both procedural and substantive, which are analogous to those applicable to infringements of national law of a similar nature and importance and which, in any event, make the penalty effective, proportionate and dissuasive' was laid down in the so-called 'Greek maize' case: C-68/88 *Commission v Greece*, EU:C:1989:339, para 24.

[17] Article 15(1) of Regulation 269/2014 as modified.

[18] It is noteworthy that the possibility to confiscate the proceeds of the violation of restrictive measures was introduced in EU restrictive measures before the violation of Union restrictive measures was included among the areas of crime referred to Article 83(1) TFEU, second indent. This is one of the grounds that was invoked by an applicant who had sought the annulment of its inclusion in the black-list before the GC. See CJEU, Case T-644/22 *Timchenko* v. *Council*, Judgement, 11 September 2024, ECLI:EU:T:2024:621, para 104. The applicant had also challenged the obligation to declare the assets and economic resources located in the Member States (Article 9(2) of Regulation 269/2014 as modified). More precisely, the applicant had also questioned the change of the nature of the measures that Member States could rely upon to enforce the mentioned obligation: Article 15(1) required national authorities to punish the violation of the mentioned obligation with confiscation orders. Therefore, they no longer enjoyed discretion in defining the type of measures to be adopted in case individuals did not comply with the obligation to declare; in any case the confiscation of the assets was a disproportionate measure. The Court did not uphold these arguments and stated: 'By referring [...] to 'appropriate measures' of confiscation of the proceeds of infringements of Regulation No 269/2014, the Council left a measure of discretion to the national authorities as regards the definition, nature and scope of that confiscation. Ibid., para 104. In a later ruling, the Court of Justice has confirmed that national competent authorities had broad discretion in imposing confiscation measures; such measures could be applied in a situation in which the violation of restrictive measures (i.e. prohibition to provide intermediary services in the case referred to by a Romanian court) was carried out outside the territory of a Member State. See C-351/22, *Neves 77 Solutions SRL*, ECLI:EU:C:2024:723. For a comment of the case see Poli, Finelli 2025.

> 'While these provisions serve as a legal basis for obliging Member States to lay down penalties, including criminal penalties, neither can be used for defining the exact types and levels of criminal penalties. The limited impact of obliging Member States to have criminal penalties in place, without approximating criminal definitions and penalties by a Directive based on Article 83 TFEU, means that Member States would still not have a harmonised approach towards confiscation measures, relative to the violation of Union restrictive measures, as well as freezing, management, and confiscation measures as provided for in the current and future Union acquis on asset recovery and confiscation would not apply to the violation of Union restrictive measures. Even if in several Member States the violation of Union restrictive measures has already been criminalised, differences among Member States can lead to a fragmented approach in cross-border cases.[19]'

This paragraph is remarkable since the Commission conflates the need to lay down common rules on the criminalisation of violation of restrictive measures with that of harmonising the law on assets confiscation; yet, the interconnection between the two harmonising measures is not self-evident.

Coming back to the procedure leading to the acquisition of a new competence to regulate an area of crime, on 7 July 2022, the European Parliament gave its consent to add the violation of Union restrictive measures to the list provided for in Article 83(1) TFEU, second indent, and, in November of the same year, the Council unanimously adopted the cited Decision 2022/2332.[20]

The speediness of this process cannot be overlooked and, indeed, is not accidental. The European Parliament gave its consent to the Council Decision by using the urgent procedure,[21] and the final act entered into force on the day following its publication in the Official Journal of the European Union.[22]

The fact that the EU competence was expanded in the span of a few months[23] proves that there was a wide consensus amongst Member States as to the transfer of new competences to the Union in concerned area. The procedure that allowed the violation of Union restrictive measures to be added to the list of 'EU crimes' was concluded before other previous initiatives taken by the Commission to criminalise *hate speech*.[24] Thus, the outbreak of the conflict at the Union's borders and the need

---

[19] European Commission 2022c, p. 2.

[20] The Council Decision is an example of the phenomenon of 'securitised criminalisation' whereby the use of criminalisation is aimed at reinforcing the security of the Union. See Mitsilegas 2016, pp. 54–62. See also Wieczorek 2020, pp. 96–97 and Kärner 2022, pp. 42 ff.

[21] European Parliament legislative resolution of 7 July 2022 on the draft Council decision on identifying the violation of Union restrictive measures as an area of crime that meets the criteria specified in Article 83(1) of the Treaty on the Functioning of the European Union.

[22] Council Decision 2022/2332, recital n 24.

[23] The adoption process relating to this Council Decision came to an end between May and November 2022 and was not hindered by any reasoned opinions by national parliaments in the context of the control mechanism provided for by Article 7(1) second indent of Protocol n. 2 on the application of the principles of subsidiarity and proportionality.

[24] The Commission has tabled a proposal to add *hate speech* and *hate crime* to the list of 'EU crimes' referred to in Article 83(1) TFEU since December 2021. See European Commission (2021b). However, at the time of writing, the Council Decision proposing to add this new area of crime to the existing list of Article 83(1) TFUE has not been adopted yet. For a critical commentary on the proposal, see Anrò 2023, pp. 35–37.

to address the crisis that originated from the war paved the way to an expansion of EU competence in substantive criminal law. In a similar fashion, Member States gave up their sovereignty and accepted to harmonise national law as far as the confiscation of assets is concerned. Without the conflict, Member States would probably have been far slower or even reluctant to take these steps. Therefore, the attribution of new competences to the EU occurred in the framework of an emergency or in exceptional circumstances with the consent of all the Member States.

This is not the first time an internal or external crisis has led the EU to adopt rules addressing new forms of crime emerging during such a crisis or emergency hindering EU security or other fundamental interests.[25]

It is now necessary to examine whether the violation of Union restrictive measures can be considered an area of particularly serious crime with a cross-border dimension, as required by the black letter of Article 83(1)TFEU. The reasons laid down in Council Decision 2022/2332 to justify the EU's intervention essentially refer to the need to ensure the effective implementation of restrictive measures and the links with other forms of crime.[26] The Decision also refers to an increase in crime rates because of the war in Ukraine.[27] In particular, there is a high risk of circumvention of Union restrictive measures considering that individual sanctions target prominent businessmen, who can take advantage of professional support granted by 'facilitators' (lawyers, notaries, etc.) and/or resort to complex legal tools (i.e. trust or shell companies) to avoid being subject to asset freezes.[28]

The Council underlines the cross-border dimension of the new form of crime, that is inherent to the violation of the restrictive measures[29] and claims that the envisaged Directive ensures an 'effective implementation of the Union's policy on restrictive measures.'[30] The idea is conveyed that in case the EU does not intervene to lay down uniform principles concerning the violation of restrictive measures,[31] the achievement of CFSP objectives is jeopardised. Restrictive measures are seen as an essential instrument to promote Union objectives, such as peace and EU security.[32]

---

[25] For instance, secondary law was adopted to harmonise criminal law of Member States in areas in which the EU enjoys shared competence in cases of terrorist attacks or to tackle human trafficking or even to react to oil spills at sea. For some examples, see Franssen and Weyembergh 2021, pp. 368–377 (esp p. 371).

[26] For instance, the Council highlights the possible correlation between the violation of the restrictive measures and some of the existing areas of crime listed in Article 83(1) TFEU, such as money laundering and terrorism. See Council Decision 2022/2332, recital n 6.

[27] Ibid., recitals nn 5 and 7.

[28] European Commission 2022b, p. 3 and Directive 2024/1226, recital n 8.

[29] For instance, see recitals nn 6, 10 and 13 of Council Decision 2022/2332. The Council also makes explicit reference to developments in crime witnessed following Russia's war of aggression against Ukraine (recital n 7).

[30] Ibid., recital n 9.

[31] Ibid., recital n 12.

[32] Ibid., recital n 10. The Council is not always convincing in listing the reasons justifying the expansion of the EU competence in order to protect peace and international security. One of this reason is that goods and natural resources traded in violation of the restrictive measures are used

The need to ensure *uniformity* in countering the violation of the restrictive measures is a further reason justifying the adoption of the Decision. Common definitions on what a violation of an EU sanction is and what are the sanctions may indeed safeguard the effectiveness of the restrictive measures by guaranteeing uniform implementation of sanctions throughout the Union.[33] The Council also emphasises that preserving the effectiveness of certain sanctions is also required by the United Nations Security Council.[34]

In conclusion, the reasons provided for the Europeanisation of Member States' criminal law[35] in order to ensure the effectiveness of restrictive measures are undoubtedly convincing. The conditions laid down in Article 83(1) TFEU, second indent, which must be met in order to harmonise the violation of restrictive measures, are satisfied. It is actually undeniable that there is a common interest at EU level in tackling the violation of restrictive measures. It is noteworthy a debate is open[36] on whether the competence of EPPO should be extended to the violation of restrictive measures, considering that it is legally possible to do so for any areas of serious crime having a cross-border dimension.[37]

The following paragraph will delve into the reasons justifying the adoption of Directive 2024/1226, in light of the subsidiarity principle.

7.4 The Justifications to Criminalise the Violation of the Restrictive Measures in Light of the Subsidiarity Principle

The reasons justifying the adoption of Directive 2024/1226, which in part overlap with those at the basis of Decision 2022/2332, are first, that the enforcement of restrictive measures, which are often circumvented, is inconsistent in the Member States.[38] Second, the legal basis for the adoption of restrictive measures does not provide for the approximation of criminal law definitions and the types and levels of criminal penalties.

to purchase arms and weapons. It is submitted that the link between the violation of the mentioned restrictions and the breach of peace and international security is not sufficient to justify the expansion of the EU competence to harmonise at EU level the violation of restrictive measures.

[33] Ibid., recital n 12.

[34] Council Decision 2022/2332 also refers to the United Nations Security Council Resolution (UNSCR) 1196 (1998) to underline the importance of strengthening the effectiveness of arms embargoes, encouraging States to consider the adoption of legislation or other legal measures making the violation of arms embargoes a criminal offence (see Ibid., recital n 11).

[35] This expression is borrowed from Sicurella 2024, p. 64.

[36] Csonka and Zoli 2024, p. 79.

[37] Article 86(4) TFEU.

[38] European Commission 2022d, p. 1.

Third, national systems do not uniformly criminalize the violation of these CFSP measures: not all the Member States, including Italy,[39] qualify the violation of the restrictive measures as a criminal offence[40]; moreover, they have adopted very different definitions and penalties.[41] Fourthly, there is a low number of proceedings initiated at the national level for the violation of Union restrictive measures. The lack of judicial proceedings is considered as an indication that in many Member States insufficient priority is given to investigating and prosecuting the violation of the restrictive measures.[42] The risk is that persons targeted by the restrictive measures may nullify the '*effet utile*' of sanctions since they continue to be able to access their frozen assets.[43]

In sum, the main reason advanced to criminalise the violation of the restrictive measures is connected to the need to ensure the effectiveness of sanction regimes. This argument is a powerful one and has been invoked by the same Court of Justice to uphold the EU competence to approximate national criminal measures to counter environmental crime since 2005 when the ruling in *Commission v. Council* was delivered.[44]

It is noteworthy that an unusually long space is dedicated to the reasons justifying the Union's action in light of the subsidiarity principle. In the context of this analysis, the Commission mostly reiterates the reasons why the proposed Directive is in line with the conditions laid down by Article 83 par. 1, second indent TFEU. The specific reason to support the common action concerns the scale and effects of the conduct at stake (i.e. violation of restrictive measures), 'which is of an inherent crossborder nature and which potentially undermines the achievement of EU objectives to safeguard international peace and security, and to uphold EU common values.[45]' As the Commission underlines, the cross-border response at EU level is necessary given that natural persons and legal entities that are affected by the Union's prohibitions operate on a global scale and that Union restrictive measures, such as restrictions on banking services, even forbid cross-border operations.[46] The Commission further argues that

---

[39] Alagia 2024, p. 22.

[40] In 12 Member States, the violation of Union restrictive measures always constitutes a criminal offence. In 13 Member States, the violation of such measures can amount to an administrative or criminal offence. See European Commission 2022b, pp. 4–6 and European Commission 2022d, pp. 2–3. Prison sentences and maximum fines vary greatly across Member States; see European Commission 2022b, pp. 4–6.

[41] European Commission 2022d, pp. 2–3.

[42] Ibid., p. 3.

[43] Ibid., p. 4.

[44] The Court of Justice justifies the competence of the Union to adopt 'measures which relate to the criminal law of the Member States which it considers necessary in order to ensure that the rules which it lays down on environmental protection are fully effective'. CJEU, Case C-176/03 *Commission* v. *Council*, 13 September 2005, ECLI:EU:C:2005:542, para 48.

[45] European Commission 2022b, p. 8. See, along the same lines, Decision 2022/2332, recital n 41.

[46] European Commission 2022b, p. 8.

the harmonisation of national rules increases the deterrent effect of penalties for the violation of Union restrictive measures.[47]

Overall, the reasons advanced by the EU institutions to harmonise substantive criminal law, as far as the violation of restrictive measures is concerned, are convincing.[48] The proximity of the war in Ukraine to the EU has made the effectiveness of the numerous prohibitions, enacted by the EU in response to Russia's aggression, a priority for the Union. The EU institutions trust that the criminalisation of the violation of restrictive measures is a means to achieve the objective of preserving effectiveness. Only time will tell whether this trust is well placed.

7.4.1 The Definition of a Criminal Offence Consisting in the Violation of Restrictive Measures in Directive 2024/1226 and the Possibility of Confiscating the Economic Resources and the Assets of Those Who Circumvent the Sanctions

The main objective enshrined in Directive 2024/1226, which was adopted under Article 83(1) TFEU, is to guarantee the effectiveness of the restrictive measures, as it comes out from the numerous references to this principle in the preamble of this act.[49]

The Directive lays down a broad definition of (criminal offence) consisting in the violation of Union restrictive measures.[50] These include, *among others*, making funds or economic resources available directly or indirectly to, or for the benefit of, a designated person, entity or body, breaching the prohibition of entry, failing to freeze funds or economic resources of designated persons, entering into or continuing transactions with a third State, bodies of a third State or entities or bodies directly or indirectly owned or controlled by a third State, the provision of services of various kinds, including financial services in violation of the related prohibition. Circumventing restrictive measures also qualifies as a criminal offence.[51] Although the owner of the frozen assets or economic resources or the members of his/her

[47] Ibid.

[48] Yet, there is at least one scholar who has contested the adoption of this Directive insofar as the EU institutions have not shown that the principle of 'last resort' of the criminalisation of a certain conduct was satisfied (Finelli 2023b).

[49] Directive 2024/1226, recitals nn 1, 3, 4, 6 and 14.

[50] For reasons of space, it is not possible to provide the full definition of what is a criminal offence consisting in the violation of Union restrictive measures in the Directive under exam. For more details see Article 3(1) of Directive 2024/1226. Given that the act is a minimum harmonisation measure Member States are left free to decide that activities falling within the definition of criminal offenses may be excluded in case they concern funds or transactions under the value of 10.000 euro (Article 3 (2), ibid.).

[51] Article 3(1) h of Directive 2024/1226.

family are the primary subjects engaging in circumvention, banks or consultants or professionals may also seek to support the owner of the funds to avoid the EU restrictions.[52]

The mentioned circumvention consists in a wide range of conducts held not only by the designated persons but also by third parties. Examples of prohibited behaviours are the following ones: (a) using or transferring frozen funds (b) providing false or misleading information to conceal the fact that a designated person, entity or body is the ultimate owner or beneficiary of funds or economic resources which are to be frozen pursuant to a Union restrictive measure, (c) violating the obligation to report to the competent administrative authorities funds or economic resources within the jurisdiction of a Member State, (d) failing to provide information about funds or economic resources belonging to, owned, held or controlled by designated persons, entities or bodies and which have not been frozen, where such information was obtained in the performance of a professional duty. All these violations entail serious consequences for the transgressors, including asset confiscation.[53]

Finally, the circumvention of restrictive measures also concerns derogations granted by Member States and therefore may include the breach or failing to fulfil conditions under authorisations granted by competent authorities to conduct certain activities.

Next, Directive 2024/1226 qualifies inciting, aiding and abetting, as well as attempting to commit the violation of the restrictive measures as a criminal offence.[54] Member States are required to punish the commission of criminal offences referred to in Article 3 by a maximum penalty of imprisonment and accessory criminal penalties. These can consist, among others, in fines, the withdrawal of authorisation to pursue commercial activities or the disqualification from holding a specific position within a legal entity.[55]

An important provision of the Directive under exam concerns legal professionals: Article 3(4) specifies that the latter are not required to report information that they receive from, or obtain on, one of their clients in the course of ascertaining the legal position of that client or performing the task of defending or representing that client in, or concerning, judicial proceedings, including providing advice on instituting or avoiding such proceedings. Yet, in case legal advice is granted to persons subject to restrictive measures for the purpose of violating Union restrictive measures,[56] the concerned legal professional may commit a criminal offense under the terms of the Directive.[57]

---

[52] Banks are affected by financial sanctions. See Cameron 2024, p. 394.

[53] This definition is consistent with the interpretation given by the Court to the concept of 'circumvention' of the sanctions. See CJEU, Case C-72/11, *Afrasiabi and others*, 21 December 2011, ECLI:EU:C:2011:874 and Finelli 2023a, pp. 734–735.

[54] Directive 2024/1226, Article 4.

[55] Ibid., Article 5.

[56] Ibid., Recital 18.

[57] In particular, if the legal professional fails to communicate information on frozen funds or economic resources to national competent authorities, this integrates a criminal offence, under Article 3(1)(h, iv).

Article 6 of Directive 2024/1226 also lays down minimum harmonisation rules for legal persons. They may be considered liable for violating Union restrictive measures 'when such an offence has been committed for the benefit of those legal persons by any person who has a leading position within the same legal person.[58]' The related penalties are detailed in Article 7.[59]

Finally, Articles 13 and 15 list a series of measures to ensure that the perpetrators of the criminal offences defined by the text of this act are brought to justice.[60]

Considering that the assets of prominent businessmen have been frozen in the EU member States, a particularly interesting provision of the Directive is Article 10, devoted to the enforcement of restrictive measures. The EU is not a State and therefore it has to rely on Member States to carry out this task. The mentioned provision imposes on national authorities to take the necessary measures to freeze and confiscate instrumentalities and proceeds from criminal offenses amounting to violation of restrictive measures. Member States are required to respect the provisions enshrined in Directive 2014/42, which establishes rules on freezing and confiscation in relation to criminal conduct and provides for a series of safeguards.[61] In case the designated natural person, or the representative of a designated entity or body, commits or participates in an offense which is defined as circumvention of restrictive measures under the terms of the Directive, Member States may also *confiscate* the frozen funds or economic resources subject to Union restrictive measures. While the freezing of funds are administrative measures, when a crime is committed by a given person, his/her assets may be confiscated. It is therefore possible that Russian nationals whose assets are frozen may be subject to confiscation measures in case their conduct falls within the definition of Article 3(1) h of the Directive. The frozen assets will never be sufficient to cover the damages caused by Russia's aggression. Yet, Member States may decide to use confiscated assets for the benefit of Ukraine for political reasons.

---

[58] Ibid., Article 6(1).

[59] See Articles 8 and 9 for rules on aggravating and mitigating circumstances.

[60] Where appropriate, Member States can use special investigative tools, such as those used in fighting organised crime or in other serious crime cases (ibid., Article 13). They shall also designate a unit or body for ensuring coordination and cooperation between law enforcement authorities and authorities in charge of implementing Union restrictive measures (ibid., Article 15).

[61] Directive 2014/42/EU of the European Parliament and of the Council of 3 April 2014 on the freezing and confiscation of instrumentalities and proceeds of crime in the European Union, https://eur-lex.europa.eu/eli/dir/2014/42/oj.

7.5 The Harmonisation of National Law on Asset Recovery and Confiscation: The Justifications Put Forward by the European Commission

Let us now turn to the reasons at the basis of the adoption of Directive 2024/1260 on asset recovery and confiscation.

In its Communication of May 2022, the Commission advocates for a common approach in defining the criminal offence for the violation of the restrictive measures and in relation to the confiscation of assets belonging to the perpetrators of such criminal offence.[62]

In addressing the reasons why harmonising rules on asset recovery is necessary, the Commission highlights that the proposed Directive 'significantly reinforces the current EU asset recovery framework, composed of the Confiscation Directive and the Council Decision on asset recovery offices.'[63] This appears to be the main objective of the new EU measure and it is confirmed by the proposed Directive on assets recovery in which the Commission highlights that 'fighting organised crime is the primary reason put forward to adopt the proposed harmonising measure.'[64]

Yet, since the Commission needs to link the proposed harmonization measure with the conditions of Article 83(2) TFEU and with the context of the war in Ukraine, it resorts to the argument of effectiveness. The wording of Article 83(2) TFEU is rather precise in requiring that the Commission proves that the envisaged Directive is designed to ensure the 'effective implementation of a Union policy' in an area which has been subject to harmonisation measures[65]; yet, the Commission justifies the harmonisation of the national law on assets confiscation with the need to ensure

[62] The Commission argues that: '[t]he limited impact of obliging Member States to have criminal penalties in place, without approximating criminal definitions and penalties by a Directive based on Article 83 TFEU, means that Member States would still not have a harmonised approach towards confiscation measures, relative to the violation of Union restrictive measures, as well as freezing, management, and confiscation measures as provided for in the current and future Union acquis on asset recovery and confiscation would not apply to the violation of Union restrictive measures.' European Commission 2022c, p. 3.

[63] European Commission 2022c, p. 4.

[64] The objective of the measure is to 'strengthen the capabilities of competent authorities to identify, freeze and manage assets, and reinforce and extend confiscation capabilities so as to cover all relevant criminal activities carried out by organised crime groups, thereby enabling confiscation for all relevant assets. Lastly, the Directive shall improve the cooperation between all authorities involved in asset recovery and promote a more strategic approach to asset recovery through a greater commitment from these authorities to the achievement of common goals in this area. European Commission 2022a, p. 2.

[65] The Commission's concern is to prove that the requirements referred to in Article 83(2) TFEU are fully met and, in particular, that it is necessary to harmonise the internal rules of the Member States because this is 'essential to ensure the effective implementation of a Union policy in an area which has been subject to harmonisation measures.' European Commission 2022a, p. 4. It is assumed that the area that has been subject to harmonisation measures is the one related to the definition of the criminal offence consisting in the violation of restrictive measures, even though this is not specified in the proposal for the Directive.

the *effective application of Union restrictive measures*,'[66] with particular reference to the ones adopted in response to the Russian aggression.

The proposed Directive identifies, among its objectives, the subsequent recovery of assets where necessary to prevent, detect or investigate criminal offences related to the violation of the restrictive measures.[67] Therefore, the proposed act is presented as a complementary measure to the Directive on the definition of the violation of Union restrictive measures. As will be discussed in the following paragraph, Directive 2024/1260 presents in reality a tenuous connection with Directive 2024/1226 and with the need to ensure the effectiveness of the restrictive measures. Therefore, the war in Ukraine was used as pretext to further harmonise national law; the adoption of the new act does not seem to respect the principle of subsidiarity laid down by Article 5(3) TUE.

7.5.1 Directive 2024/1260 on Asset Recovery and Confiscation: What Are the Connections with the Effectiveness of Union Restrictive Measures?

Two years after the publication of the May 2022 Communication by the Commission, the new rules on asset recovery and confiscation entered into force; Member States had 2 years to adopt implementing measures.[68]

At the time Directive 2024/1260 was proposed by the Commission, Directive 2014/42, laying down minimum harmonisation rules on freezing and confiscation, was already in place[69]; however, it had a limited scope insofar as it could be applied only to the criminal offences listed in its Article 3. The new act, which modifies this

[66] The Commission states that: 'The proposed Directive on asset recovery and confiscation contributes to the *effective application of Union restrictive measures* (emphasis added) in two ways. Firstly, it requires Member States to launch asset tracking and identification investigations where necessary to prevent, detect or investigate criminal offences related to the violation of Union restrictive measures, and to extend the mandate of asset recovery offices to swiftly trace and identify property of individuals and entities subject to EU targeted financial sanctions, and urgently freeze it whenever necessary to prevent its removal from the jurisdiction. Secondly, by making the enhanced rules on asset recovery and confiscation applicable to the criminal offence of violation of Union restrictive measures, the proposal would ensure the effective tracing, freezing, management and confiscation of proceeds derived from the violation of Union restrictive measures, pending the approximation of criminal definitions and penalties for the violation of Union restrictive measures.' Ibid.

[67] European Commission 2022a, p. 3. The Commission refers to this aspect also in the section devoted to the choice of the legal base. Ibid., p. 4.

[68] Member States must transpose the Directive by 20 May 2025 (Article 20).

[69] Directive 2014/42 also regulated the so-called 'extended confiscation' and the confiscation of properties transferred to or acquired by a third party.

Directive, is applicable to criminal offences regulated by provisions adopted at the EU level after 2014,[70] including Directive 2024/1226.[71]

The Directive under analysis in this paragraph is adopted pursuant to Articles 82(2), 83(1) and (2) as well as 87(2) TFEU. As it is stressed by Sicurella, a Directive which is based upon Article 83(2) TFEU can only be adopted strictly in connection with existing EU rules and never as an autonomous act (as considered able to improve the effectiveness of an EU policy as a matter of principle).[72] The adoption of Directive 2024/1260 was possible since Directive 2024/1226 laid the ground for it by criminalising the violation of restrictive measures. Yet, Directive 2024/1260 has as its primary objective the enhancement of Member States' operational capacity and the necessary means to effectively trace and identify, freeze, confiscate and manage the instrumentalities and proceeds of crime or property that stem from criminal activities. Existing confiscation tools employed by the Member States are not considered to be sufficiently efficient by the EU institutions.[73] For instance, 'overall results in terms of assets confiscated are not satisfactory and the confiscation rates in the EU remain very low.'[74] Directive 2024/1260 also pursues the objective of fighting organised crime by recovering related profits and improving the cooperation between all the authorities involved in asset recovery; the main aim is to reinforce and broaden confiscation capabilities, so as to cover all relevant criminal activities carried out by organised crime groups, both during investigations and in the recovery and confiscation phases.

In contrast, the mentioned Directive has a limited application in relation to the violation of the restrictive measures. Article 5(4) of the Directive empowers asset recovery offices to trace and identify properties belonging to persons and entities subject to Union restrictive measures, when necessary, to facilitate the detection of criminal offences laid down in Directive 2024/1226. The mentioned offices operate at the request of national competent authorities when there are reasonable grounds for believing that a criminal offence, consisting in the violation of Union restrictive measures, was committed.

An examination of the content of the act under consideration reveals that it is mainly aimed at implementing the 2021 EU strategy to tackle organised crime.[75]

[70] Following to the adoption of Directive 2014/42, frauds and counterfeiting of non-cash means of payment, money laundering and specific crypto assets are among the criminal offences regulated by Directives adopted after 2014.

[71] Directive 2024/1260, Article 2 (1)(p).

[72] Sicurella 2024, p. 74.

[73] European Commission 2022a, pp. 1–2 and 4.

[74] European Commission 2020, p. 17.

[75] European Commission 2021a. Recital n. 3 of Directive 2024/1260 refers to the capacity of criminal organisations to adversely affect the freedom of competition, or influence decisions of public authorities, threatening the rule of law and democracy.

This is confirmed by the preamble stressing that the objective of this Directive essentially consists in facilitating the confiscation of property in proceedings in criminal matters.[76] The violation of Union restrictive measures is only one of the many criminal offences subject to the provisions enshrined in Directive 2024/1260.

Therefore, it appears that this Directive presents limited connections with Directive 2024/1226 and with the objective of enhancing the effectiveness of the restrictive measures, contrary to what the European Commission argued in its Communication of May 2022. This is criticisable insofar as Article 83(2) TFEU requires that the approximation of criminal laws and regulations must be *essential* to ensure the effective implementation of a Union policy. The new rules on asset recovery are undoubtedly set to reinforce the capacity of national authorities to counter organised crime and therefore to strengthen security; the improvement of the effectiveness of Union restrictive measures remains a secondary objective.

7.5.2 Directive 2024/1260 Contributes to Supporting Ukraine's Reconstruction as an Ancillary CFSP Objective

In the previous paragraph, Directive 2024/1260 was criticised since its contribution to the enhancement of restrictive measures is limited. It is noteworthy that, thanks to the amendments of the European Parliament at the first reading,[77] the text eventually approved lays down a provision contributing to achieving a Union CFSP objective: Ukraine's reconstruction. In particular, Article 19(2) of the Directive[78] establishes that confiscated economic resources can be used 'to contribute to mechanisms to support third countries affected by situations in response to which Union restrictive measures have been adopted, in particular in cases of war of aggression.'[79] This is a clear reference to the situation in Ukraine. The Union's objective is to contribute to the reconstruction of this country with assets and resources belonging to persons

[76] Recital n. 61 of Directive 2024/1260.

[77] European Parliament legislative resolution of 13 March 2024 on the proposal for a Directive of the European Parliament and of the Council on asset recovery and confiscation, OJ C, C/2024/6571.

[78] This provision was not present in the original proposal for a Directive adopted by the Commission in May 2022.

[79] It is noteworthy the proposal of a scholar who has speculated on adding the international crime of aggression to the list on existing areas of crime defined by Article 83(1) TFEU; see Rosas A 2023, p. 337 ff, esp p. 346. Adding the crime of aggression to the mentioned list could have created the legal basis for the confiscation of Russian assets to be used for Ukraine's reconstruction. To the author's knowledge, there are no proposals in the pipeline to rely on Article 83(1) TFEU to make the crime of aggression a new euro crime. In the meantime, in February 2023 the EU has set up an International Centre for the Prosecution of the Crime of Aggression Against Ukraine at Eurojust and the latter has launched the Core International Crimes Evidence Database (CICED), following an extension of the competence of Europol to facilitate investigations into core international crimes allegedly committed in Ukraine, as well as other conflicts where these offences would occur.

violating the restrictive measures adopted against Russia, in full respect of international law.[80] Considering that it is not possible to confiscate assets and economic resources belonging to Russian citizens that have been frozen in the framework of Union restrictive measures,[81] Article 19(2) of Directive 2024/1260 provides for the use of assets confiscated from persons violating the Union restrictive measures to support the reconstruction of Ukraine. The same provision bestows upon the Commission, which is progressively gaining powers in CFSP matters,[82] the task of 'provid[ing] guidance on the arrangements for such contributions.' By so doing, Directive 224/1260 has the effect of contributing to Ukraine's reconstruction as an ancillary objective while the main aim of this act is fighting organised crime and this is reflected in the obligations imposed on Member States in the content of the Directive.

7.6 Conclusions: Directive 2024/1260 as an Example of 'Harmonization by Stealth'

The conflict in Ukraine offered the EU the opportunity to expand its competences in criminal law.[83] The enactment of Directive 2024/1226 is justified in the light of the principle of subsidiarity to the extent that this act establishes minimum rules concerning the definition of the violation of Union restrictive measures, thus making the latter more effective. In contrast, the adoption of Directive 2024/1260 raises doubts as to its compliance with Article 5(2) of the TEU. The Commission has taken

[80] On this topic, see Chap. 6.

[81] Since being owned by private citizens, these assets and economic funds can be subject to administrative freezing but not to seizure and confiscation. See Council of the European Union 2022, para 29.

[82] The European Commission can establish a network of experts and practitioners to share best practices and has to be informed by national authorities on practical issues on patterns of circumvention (see Articles 16(2) and 16(4) of Directive 2024/1226). This proves that the Commission is stepping into a role of coordinator in this field.

[83] It is noteworthy that the EU has also relied on Eurojust to support Ukraine in bringing Russian perpetrators of international crimes to criminal justice. The mentioned Agency has supported the establishment of a Joint Investigation Team (JIT) on alleged core international crimes committed in Ukraine since the beginning of the war. Estonia, Latvia, Slovakia and Romania became members of the JIT and were later joined by Europol. Further information is available on https://www.eurojust.europa.eu/joint-investigation-team-alleged-crimes-committed-ukraine [Accessed 11 February 2025]. Even more importantly, the competences of Europol have been expanded as a result of the conflict in order to make easier for Ukraine and Member States to start cases against authors of crimes. For example, the Agency was enshrined the task of supporting Member States' action in combating genocide, crimes against humanity, war crimes and related criminal offences, including by preserving, analysing and storing evidence related to those crimes and related criminal offences and enabling the exchange of such evidence with, or otherwise making it directly available to, competent national authorities and international judicial authorities, in particular the International Criminal Court.' See Article 1(1) of European Parliament, Council (2022) Regulation (EU) 2022/838.

the conflict in Ukraine and the need to ensure the effectiveness of restrictive measures as a pretext to regulate asset confiscation connected to criminal activities; overall, the adoption of this measure was not strictly necessary to make sanctions and, more generally, the CFSP more effective.

As stressed by Wieczorek, 'The EU, as a non-state entity, is in need of community building factors. Criminal law is particularly appealing in this respect, since the monopoly on the use of force and the administration of criminal justice is one of the sovereign functions of the state (*jura regalia*). As a consequence, acquiring competence in this policy area and adopting autonomous policy decisions therein has a specific symbolic significance for a supranational organisation. Indeed, it might work as a legitimising factor for the EU project and move it towards being a state-like entity.[84]'

The harmonisation of national law as far as confiscation of assets is concerned is an example of the phenomenon described by the Wieczorek.

Yet, a practice whereby Article 83(2) TFEU may be easily triggered to enact new EU legislation, in the absence of a clear basis for the EU to harmonise substantive criminal law, is risky. Indeed, for instance, the German Federal Constitutional Court established that reliance on such a provision is possible only if there is 'a serious enforcement *deficit* that can only be eliminated through penalties (emphasis added).'[85]

The Commission could have confined itself to propose Directive 2024/1226 and to add in this act obligations of collaboration and information-sharing on Member States designed to identify the assets belonging to the persons targeted by the restrictive measures. This would have been sufficient to enhance the cooperation in identifying and recovering properties owned or controlled by the targeted persons and entities, an objective which is at the basis of Directive 2024/1260.[86] It should also be stressed that the latter does not seem to add much to the rules on freezing and confiscation in relation to the violation of restrictive measures. Indeed, Article 10 of Directive 2024/1226 regulates the freezing and confiscation of instrumentalities and proceeds originating from criminal offences, as well as of funds and economic resources attributable to designated individuals carrying out circumvention activities. It is not clear what is added value of Directive 2024/1260 for the purpose of regulating this area.[87]

Considering the reasons that led the EU to trigger Article 83 TFEU and to adopt Directives 2024/1226 and 2024/1260, the question arises as to whether there is a risk that this Treaty provision will be used and interpreted in the same way as Article 114 TFEU. More precisely, it is necessary to understand whether Article 83 TFEU has been used to considerably expand the scope of EU rules that harmonise substantive criminal law beyond what the letter or spirit of this legal basis allows the Union to

[84] Wieczorek 2020, pp. 91–92.

[85] BVerfG, Case 2/08, Judgement 30 June 2009, ECLI:DE:BVerfG:2009:es20090630.2bve000208, para 362.

[86] Article 29.

[87] European Commission 2022a, p. 3.

do. Article 114 TFEU enables, in practice, to approximate national provisions laid down by law or regulation with the objective of ensuring the proper functioning of the internal market. Nevertheless, this legal basis has been used *ultra vires* to harmonise internal rules in areas that fall within national competence,[88] or in policy domains in which the EU enjoys mere complementary competences, such as, for instance, in the education sector. Sacha Garben has called this phenomenon 'harmonization by stealth'[89] and has identified several tools and techniques allowing the EU to make inroads in areas of national competence 'in a hidden manner.'

Applying by analogy the principles relating to the application of Article 114 TFEU to the legislative developments regarding the criminalization of the violation of Union restrictive measures, the view is taken that the expansion of EU competences in this area meets the conditions referred to in Article 83(1) TFEU, second indent. Therefore, there is no risk of abuse of such a provision in the wake of the crisis stemming from the Russo-Ukrainian conflict. In contrast, Directive 2024/1260, which was adopted to harmonise the rules on asset confiscation applying to a wider list of criminal activities compared to the ones laid down in Directive 2014/42, which established minimum rules in this sector, seems to be an example of 'harmonisation by stealth'.

References

Alagia E (2024) La direttiva (UE) n. 2024/1226 relativa alla definizione dei reati e delle sanzioni per la violazione delle misure restrittive dell'Unione: qualche prima (e minima) riflessione sul futuribile enforcement europeo del "nuovo FCPA." [Directive (EU) 2024/1226 on the definition of criminal offences and penalties for the violation of Union restrictive measures: some initial (and limited) reflections on the prospective European enforcement of a "new FCPA"]. Giurisprudenza Penale web 7: 1–22.

Anrò A (2023) Online hate speech: la prospettiva dell'Unione europea tra regolamentazione della condotta dei prestatori di servizi intermediari e ricorso al diritto penale. [Online hate speech: the European Union's perspective between the regulation of intermediary service providers' conduct and recourse to criminal law]. Osservatorio sulle fonti 1: 13–39.

Csonka P, Zoli L (2024), The New Directive on the Violation of Union Restrictive Measures in the Context of the EPPO. EUCRIM 1: 75–80.

Cameron (2024) EU sanctions. In: Valsamis M, Bergström M, Quintel T (eds) Research Handbook on EU Criminal Law, 2nd edn. Edward Elgar, Cheltenham, pp. 392–407.

Council of the European Union (2022) Update of the EU Best Practices for the effective implementation of restrictive measures, 10572/22, 27 June 2022.

Council Regulation (EU) 2022/880 of 3 June 2022 amending Regulation (EU) No 269/2014 concerning restrictive measures in respect of actions undermining or threatening the territorial integrity, sovereignty and independence of Ukraine, https://eur-lex.europa.eu/eli/reg/2022/880/oj?utm_source=chatgpt.com.

---

[88] The first example is represented by CJEU, Case C-376/98, *Germany v. European Parliament and Council* (Advertising and sponsorship of tobacco products), 12 December 2006, ECLI:EU:C:2000:544. In this context, the provision under analysis was Article 100 A of the EC Treaty. For a study on the unlimited scope of Article 114 TFUE, see Schütze 2014, pp. 215–233.

[89] Garben 2017, p. 303.

European Commission (2011) Communication from the Commission to the European Parliament, the Council, the European Economic and Social Committee and the Committee of the Regions Towards an EU Criminal Policy: Ensuring the effective implementation of EU policies through criminal law, COM(2011) 573 final.

European Commission (2020) Report from the Commission to the European Parliament and the Council—Asset recovery and confiscation: Ensuring that crime does not pay, COM(2020) 217 final.

European Commission (2021a) Communication from the Commission to the European Parliament, the Council, the European Economic and Social Committee and the Committee of the Regions on the EU Strategy to tackle Organised Crime 2021–2025, COM(2021) 170 final.

European Commission (2021b) Communication from the Commission to the European Parliament and the Council—A more inclusive and protective Europe: Extending the list of EU crimes to hate speech and hate crime, COM(2021) 777 final.

European Commission (2022a) Proposal for a Directive of the European Parliament and of the Council on asset recovery and confiscation, COM(2022) 245 final.

European Commission (2022b) Proposal for a Council Decision on adding the violation of Union restrictive measures to the areas of crime laid down in Article 83(1) of the Treaty on the Functioning of the European Union, COM(2022) 247 final.

European Commission (2022c) Communication from the Commission to the European Parliament and the Council. Towards a Directive on criminal penalties for the violation of Union restrictive measures, COM(2022) 249 final.

European Commission (2022d) Proposal for a Directive of the European Parliament and of the Council on the definition of criminal offences and penalties for the violation of Union restrictive measures, COM(2022) 684 final.

European Parliament legislative resolution of 7 July 2022 on the draft Council decision on identifying the violation of Union restrictive measures as an area of crime that meets the criteria specified in Article 83(1) of the Treaty on the Functioning of the European Union (10287/1/2022—C9-0219/2022—2022/0176(NLE)), OJ C 47.

European Parliament, Council (2022) Regulation (EU) 2022/838 of the European Parliament and of the Council of 30 May 2022 amending Regulation (EU) 2018/1727 as regards the preservation, analysis and storage at Eurojust of evidence relating to genocide, crimes against humanity, war crimes and related criminal offences, OJ 2022, L 148/1.

Finelli F (2023a) Countering Circumvention of Restrictive Measures: The EU Response. Common Market Law Review 60: 723–762.

Finelli F (2023b) Principio di effettività e misure restrittive UE: la lotta all'elusione nel contesto della guerra in Ucraina [The principle of effectiveness and EU restrictive measures: combating circumvention in the context of the war in Ukraine]. I Post di AISDUE IV, Atti Convegni AISDUE: 32, 7 July 2023: 723–743.

Franssen N, Weyembergh A (2021) From facts and political objectives to legal bases and legal provisions: Incremental European integration in the criminal law field. European Law Journal 27: 368–377.

Garben S (2017) Restating the problem of competence creep, tackling harmonization by stealth and reinstating the legislator. In: Govaere I, Garben S (eds) The division of competences between the EU and the Member States, 1st edn. Bloomsbury Publishing, Oxford, pp. 300–336.

Kärner M (2022) Interplay between European Union criminal law and administrative sanctions: Constituent elements of transposing punitive administrative sanctions into national law. New Journal of European Criminal Law 13: 42–68.

Mitsilegas V (2016) EU Criminal Law after Lisbon. Rights, Trust and the Transformation of Justice in Europe. Hart Publishing, Oxford.

Poli S, Pau A (2024) La nuova competenza dell'Unione europea ad armonizzare le norme interne in materia di violazione di misure restrittive e quelle relative alla confisca: quali connessioni con l'effettività delle misure restrittive? [The new competence of the European Union to harmonise

domestic rules on the violation of restrictive measures and on confiscation: links with the effectiveness of restrictive measures]. In: Daniele L, Simone P, Venturini C, Di Marco R (eds) L'Unione europea e la crisi del mondo contemporaneo. Tra 'valorizzazione' delle competenze e prospettive di riforma [The European Union and the crisis of today's world: between the "enhancement" of competences and prospects for reform]. Wolters Kluwer, pp. 145–167.
Poli S, Finelli F (2025) La Corte di Giustizia dell'Unione Europea e le tendenze giurisprudenziali emergenti in materia di misure restrittive adottate in relazione all'aggressione russa all'Ucraina [The Court of Justice of the European Union and emerging trends in the case law on restrictive measures adopted in response to Russia's aggression against Ukraine]. In: Alì A (ed) Le sanzioni dell'U.E. nei confronti della Russa tra sicurezza internazionale e diritti umani [EU sanctions against Russia between international security and human rights]. Giappichelli/Nomos, Baden-Baden/Turin.
Rosas A (2023) From freezing to confiscating Russian assets? European Law Review 48: 337–347.
Schütze R (2014) Limits to the Union's "Internal Market" Competences: Constitutional Comparisons. In: Azoulai L (ed) The Question of Competence in the European Union. Oxford University Press, Oxford, pp. 215–233.
Sicurella R (2024) EU competence in criminal matters. In: Valsamis M, Bergström M, Quintel T (eds) Research Handbook on EU criminal law, 2nd edn. Cheltenham, pp. 61–89.
Wieczorek I (2020) The Legitimacy of EU Criminal Law. Hart Publishing, Oxford.

Chapter 8
The Impact of the War in Ukraine on the Enlargement of the European Union

Madalina Moraru

Contents

Abstract The European Union's enlargement policy has undergone a significant revival in the aftermath of Russia's invasion of Ukraine in 2022. Enlargement, long associated with conditionality and normative integration, has increasingly been reframed in strategic and geopolitical terms. This chapter examines how Ukraine's application for membership brings into focus both the strengths and the limitations of the EU's institutional architecture as regards the enlargement process, where the Council retains decisive control through unanimity, the Commission provides technical and legal assessments without binding force, and the European Parliament contributes to political legitimacy and agenda-setting despite limited formal powers. Drawing on the Copenhagen criteria, Article 49 TEU, and recent reform debates, the chapter traces the evolution of conditionality from its classical compliance-for-reward logic towards more flexible and strategic applications. The Ukrainian case is analysed in depth, with attention to the Association Agreement, rule-of-law challenges, the July 2025 anti-corruption controversy, and proposals for phased integration. It concludes by presenting proposals for reform in order to ensure that EU enlargement is a more resilient, credible, and geopolitically responsive enlargement framework.

S. Poli et al., *The EU's Response to the War in Ukraine and Its Impact on the EU Legal Order*, Global Europe: Legal and Policy Issues of the EU's External Action 7,
https://doi.org/10.1007/978-94-6265-767-0_8

Keywords Enlargement · Decision-making in the Council · Unanimity · Copenhagen criteria · Conditionality · EU security

8.1 Introduction

The Russian Federation's invasion of Ukraine in February 2022 represents a watershed moment in the history of the European Union. Beyond the immediate military and humanitarian crisis, the war has fundamentally altered the EU's external and internal priorities, and most significantly, its enlargement policy.[1] In contrast to a decade of inertia in the EU's enlargement following Croatia's accession in 2013, the EU has responded to the war by, *inter alia*, granting candidate status to Ukraine and Moldova in 4 months from their application to the Council, and providing Georgia with a European perspective.[2] These decisions were unprecedented in their speed and of great political significance, reflecting the EU's recalibrated role as a geopolitical actor in a dramatically altered security environment.

Nowhere in the Treaties is enlargement set out expressly as an end goal of the European Union. Nevertheless, enlargement has been approached by the EU as necessary in order to ensure the security and stability of Europe. The geopolitical element has been recognised by the Council and the Commission long before the war in Ukraine, for instance, it was a factor to ensure that the accession of Romania will not be postponed, in spite of the lacking behind certain accession chapters.[3] However, the Russian war against Ukraine has recalibrated the Union's enlargement rationale, elevating geopolitical considerations, such as the region's security, to a central determinant and thereby reinforcing the imperative to expedite the initiation of accession processes.

Historically, the EU enlargement has been governed by legal and political frameworks established in the Copenhagen criteria (1993), Articles 49 and 2 TEU, in the European Council's shaping of additional conditions for accession[4] and soft law guidance issued by the European Commission under its monitoring role. These criteria condition accession on the candidate's adherence to the EU's foundational values: democracy, the rule of law, respect for human rights, and the acceptance of the *acquis communautaire*. In practice, accession has required extensive legal harmonisation and institutional reforms in candidate countries, monitored through

[1] Orenstein 2023.

[2] European Commission Opinion on Ukraine 2022c; European Commission Opinion on Moldova 2022b; European Commission Opinion on Georgia 2022a. Georgia's accession process came to a halt in 2024 by both decision of the EU and Georgian's government, see more at: https://www.consilium.europa.eu/en/policies/georgia/ [last accessed on 25 August 2025].

[3] See Article 39 pf the Act of Accession of the Republic of Bulgaria and Romania.

[4] In June 2024 the European Council has stated that the pace of the enlargement must take Union's absorption capacity into account. This is the so-called 'fourth Copenhagen criteria.' See European Council conclusions 2006, para 53 and Inglis 2006, p. 64.

an incremental and heavily bureaucratised process structured around the negotiation of 35 acquis chapters.[5]

However, the practical implementation of this framework has faced growing criticism. From a legal-political perspective, scholars and practitioners alike have identified systemic obstacles to enlargement, especially towards the Western Balkans. A key criticism has been voiced against the requirement for unanimous decision-making in the Council, which empowers individual Member States to block accession steps on grounds often unrelated to EU conditionality. For example, France's veto in 2019 over Albania and North Macedonia, ostensibly justified by concerns over methodology, masked deeper political hesitation. Similarly, Greece and Bulgaria have delayed North Macedonia's accession over historical and linguistic disputes.[6] More recently, Hungary has been an obstacle to the progress of Ukraine's application for membership.[7] These actions demonstrate the tension between legal conditionality and political discretion.

This paralysis in the EU enlargement since 2013 has led to an erosion of the EU's credibility as a transformative actor.[8] Countries like Albania and North Macedonia have waited for a prolonged timeline between the application and the actual negotiation phase in their EU accession processes.[9] Bosnia and Herzegovina, despite applying for EU membership in February 2016, was only granted candidate status in December 2022—following a Commission recommendation in October 2022.[10] The resulting prolonged time between the application of EU membership and the start of the accession negotiations, as well as the time variability between the various Western Balkans states and the EU's reply to Moldova and Ukraine, has been what many scholars describe as a "credibility gap," where the EU's conditionality lacks both predictability and enforcement.[11]

The war in Ukraine, however, has served as a catalyst for rethinking these dynamics. It is not by chance if Kosovo, which is not recognised by five Member States, submitted its application for membership to the Council of Europe (May

[5] Inglis 2010; European Commission glossary of terms for the enlargement procedure, available at: https://enlargement.ec.europa.eu/enlargement-policy/glossary-old/chapters-acquis-negotiating-chapters_en.

[6] Dionysiou 2023; Anghel and Džankić 2023; Hoxhaj 2025; Fabbrini 2025; Hillion 2025.

[7] In June 2025 the conclusions of the European Council giving the green light to the Council to take the next steps in the accession process of Ukraine (i.e. the opening of the accession negotiation) were supported by 26 Heads of State or Government. See President of the European Council, European Council meeting 2025, para 14.

[8] On the transformative role of the EU, see Manners 2002.

[9] For Albania, five years passed between the application for EU membership and being granted EU candidate status, and six more years passed until the opening of accession negotiations. While for North Macedonia 18 years passed from applying for EU membership and opening of accession negotiations. See more on the historical evolution in Dionysiou 2023.

[10] That means six years, whereas Moldova and Ukraine received a reply in four months. See more on the accession process of Bosnia and Herzegovina in Nielsen 2023.

[11] Dionysiou 2023; Anghel and Džankić 2023; Hoxhaj 2025; Kochenov and Basheska 2025.

2022)[12] and to the EU (December 2022)[13] and that Bosnia Herzegovina was recognised as a candidate country in December 2022. But the most formidable change provoked by the war concerns selected Eastern neighbours. Within days of the invasion, Ukraine, Moldova, and Georgia submitted their membership applications. The European Council's swift response—granting candidate status to Ukraine and Moldova in June 2022—departed from precedent and suggested a move towards strategic conditionality, where geopolitical urgency supersedes procedural modus operandi. This shift aligns with scholars' argument that enlargement has transitioned from a tool of normative transformation to one of geopolitical consolidation.[14] Scholars similarly note that the war has forced the EU to adopt a more assertive foreign policy stance, using enlargement to anchor vulnerable states in the EU's legal and institutional order.[15]

The legal implications of this acceleration are profound. While Article 49 TEU sets the formal legal basis for accession, the speed and symbolism of Ukraine's candidacy raise questions about the flexibility of conditionality and the evolving function of enlargement law. Scholars such as Nádasi and Trón argue that while the Copenhagen criteria remain legally binding, the exigencies of war and geopolitics may require a pragmatic application that balances formal compliance with strategic interest.[16] This implies a reconceptualization of conditionality from a rigid, rule-based model to a more context-sensitive approach.

The transformation of EU–Ukraine relations must also be understood in light of the Europeanization theory, defined as the diffusion of EU norms and practices through legal and institutional alignment.[17] Since the 2014 Association Agreement and the Deep and Comprehensive Free Trade Area (DCFTA), Ukraine has embarked on an ambitious process of aligning its legislation with EU standards. While the DCFTA has led to some regulatory convergence, the institutional capacity to implement and sustain reforms remains challenged by corruption, judicial dysfunction, and now, wartime disruption. These obstacles illustrate the dual challenge of legal approximation and governance resilience under conflict conditions.

From a legal-economic standpoint, Ukraine's integration into the EU's single market has been partial but symbolically significant. The DCFTA has fostered trade liberalisation and institutional reform, but the economic transformation necessary for full membership remains incomplete. Structural issues in public finance, property rights, and industrial policy continue to impede convergence with EU economic

---

[12] Kosovo's application for membership is directly related to the withdrawal of Russia from the Council of Europe which in its turn is due to the outbreak of the war. Russia ceased to be a member of the Council of Europe as of 16 March 2022.

[13] It is noteworthy that the Council remains seized of Kosovo's application for membership. COM 2024a, p. 17. This implies that the Council has not yet decided whether to continue the accession procedure.

[14] Fabbrini 2025; Anghel and Jones 2024; Anghel and Džankić 2023.

[15] Kaveshnikov 2022; Maurer et al. 2023.

[16] See Nádasi and Trón 2023.

[17] Radaelli 2003, p. 30.

norms.[18] Furthermore, the war has severely impacted Ukraine's infrastructure, investment environment, and administrative capacity—raising legal questions about how candidate countries at war can be assessed under traditional accession metrics. But most importantly, the rule of law conditionality criteria, such as judicial independence and anti-corruption, are chapters on which Ukraine faces difficulty to advance within the current war climate.[19]

In response to these challenges, the EU has signalled its willingness to adopt a phased accession model, as proposed in the Franco-German initiative of September 2023. This model envisions gradual integration, reversibility in case of backsliding, and the progressive extension of rights and responsibilities.[20] Legally, this could entail an intermediate status below full membership, coupled with sectoral participation in EU programmes, including the Single Market, Digital Europe, and Erasmus+. The viability of this approach will depend on the EU's capacity to institutionalise flexibility within its legal framework, without undermining the acquis or the integrity of the Union.

Against this backdrop, this chapter investigates how the war in Ukraine has impacted the EU's enlargement process and reshaped its relationship with Ukraine. It argues that the war in Ukraine has fundamentally re-legitimized EU enlargement as a geopolitical and legal tool. It has also exposed the need to reform internal EU mechanisms—particularly unanimity in the Council for all intermediary steps during accession, and the rigidity of accession conditionality—to ensure that enlargement remains credible, effective, and aligned with the Union's strategic interests. Ukraine's candidacy represents both an opportunity and a test case for a new, more resilient model of enlargement.

To that end, the chapter proceeds as follows. Section 8.2 critically evaluates the evolution of the enlargement process, focusing on the Copenhagen Criteria, the institutional structure of accession negotiations, and the tension between normative and strategic conditionality. Section 8.3 explores the trajectory of EU–Ukraine relations, distinguishing between pre-war legal integration and post-war strategic alignment. Section 8.4 concludes by identifying the legal, institutional, and political implications of Ukraine's accession process and offering reflections on the future of EU enlargement in the context of a changing geopolitical order.

---

[18] Rabinovych 2022; and Commission Ukraine 2024b.

[19] Commission Ukraine 2024b.

[20] Franco-German Working Group of Twelve 2023.

8.2 Evolution of the EU Enlargement Process: From Normative Conditionality to Strategic Imperatives

8.2.1 Legal Framework and Conditions for Membership

The legal basis for enlargement is found in Article 49 TEU, which stipulates that any European state that respects and is committed to promoting the values enshrined in Article 2 TEU—including democracy, the rule of law, human rights, and respect for minorities—may apply for EU membership. These foundational provisions are operationalised through the Copenhagen criteria, adopted by the European Council in 1993, which set out three principal requirements: (i) stable institutions guaranteeing democracy and the rule of law, (ii) a functioning market economy, and (iii) the capacity to adopt and implement the *acquis communautaire*, which is the comprehensive body of EU law.[21]

EU conditionality is a core mechanism through which the Union influences external actors, particularly candidate countries, by linking specific reforms to rewards like membership or financial aid. This operates through what scholars call the "external incentives model", where countries adopt reforms if the benefits outweigh the costs.[22] The Copenhagen criteria serve as the legal framework, requiring stability in democratic governance, a functioning market economy, and the ability to adopt the EU acquis.

Conditionality was highly effective in Central and Eastern European countries due to a strong and credible membership perspective.[23] However, after the 2004/2007 enlargement, its effectiveness has been uneven, as proven by the accession process of Turkey and Western Balkans, with the EU's inconsistent application of conditions and political obstacles—like blocked negotiation chapters and France's veto—undermining credibility. Scholars refer to this as "selective conditionality", weakening the EU's transformative power.[24]

The success of conditionality also depends on domestic political will. In Turkey's case, reforms stalled post-2005, with increasing authoritarianism and diminished alignment with EU values, especially after the 2016 coup attempt. As scholars have emphasized, local actors' normative commitment is crucial.[25] Thus, while conditionality remains central to EU enlargement policy, its effectiveness is highly contingent on both internal EU consistency and the domestic political context of candidate states.

The EU enlargement process is a legally structured yet politically driven procedure. When a European state applies for membership under Article 49 TEU, the

---

[21] European Council 1993, p. 13. For an analysis, see Hillion 2004.

[22] Schimmelfennig and Sedelmeier 2004.

[23] In contrast, the presumption of the effectiveness of value-based conditionality in the context of the EU neighbourhood policy is contested. See Kochenov and Basheska 2016, pp. 154–155.

[24] Bartlett et al. 2016; Grabbe 2006.

[25] Dimitrova 2010.

application is formally submitted to the Council of the European Union, which transmits it to the European Commission for an opinion on the applicant's readiness and compliance with the Copenhagen criteria. On the basis of that opinion, it is the European Council—composed of the Heads of State or Government—that decides, as a matter of political discretion and by unanimity, whether to grant candidate status and to open accession negotiations. Although this decision is not expressly foreseen in Article 49 TEU, it has become established institutional practice since the 1993 Copenhagen criteria. The European Parliament does not play a formal role at this stage, though it frequently adopts resolutions shaping the political discourse on enlargement and conditionality. Its legally binding consent is required only at the final stage of the process, when the Council of the European Union concludes the Accession Treaty with the applicant state, following unanimous agreement among the Member States.[26]

Critically, the Parliament has often positioned itself as a stronger advocate of enlargement than the Council. It has repeatedly pressed Member States to move forward with negotiations for the Western Balkans, and it has consistently urged respect for the rule of law, democracy, and fundamental rights as indispensable conditions for accession. This dual role—championing enlargement while upholding strict conditionality—illustrates both the Parliament's political weight and its institutional limitations. Unlike the Council, which operates on the unanimity rule, the Parliament's positions are non-binding until the final consent vote. This institutional asymmetry has raised concerns about the democratic legitimacy of enlargement policy, given that the only directly elected EU institution exercises relatively limited influence over the pace and content of negotiations.[27]

Historical examples demonstrate both the potential and limits of the Parliament's role. In the case of Turkey, the Parliament's critical resolutions on human rights and democratic backsliding significantly shaped the political climate around accession, contributing to the effective freezing of negotiations.[28] Conversely, in the Western Balkans, the Parliament has acted as an enlargement entrepreneur, advocating for progress when the Council was reluctant. Its role has been particularly visible in debates on North Macedonia, where the Parliament repeatedly endorsed accession despite bilateral blockages in the Council.[29] These instances underline the Parliament's function as a political guardian of EU values, even if it lacks binding powers at intermediate stages of the accession process.

The Ukrainian case illustrates the Parliament's proactive influence in times of crisis. In March 2022, only days after Russia's full-scale invasion, the Parliament adopted a resolution calling for Ukraine to be granted candidate status, anticipating and arguably shaping the subsequent Commission Opinion and European Council decision in June 2022.[30] This demonstrated the Parliament's ability to act as a political

[26] Cremona 2003; Inglis 2006.

[27] Hillion 2004; Schimmelfennig and Sedelmeier 2004.

[28] European Parliament 2019.

[29] Anghel and Džankić 2023.

[30] Maurer et al. 2023

frontrunner, reinforcing the Union's geopolitical narrative of anchoring Ukraine to the European project. Yet, its influence remained limited to agenda-setting and signalling, since the decisive steps rested with the Council.[31]

Accession negotiations begin with a screening process (explanatory and bilateral) assessing the candidate's legal framework. Traditionally, negotiations have been conducted across 35 chapters, each corresponding to specific areas of the acquis.[32] Each chapter requires unanimous approval by the Council for both opening and closing. This unanimity rule is embedded in the intergovernmental nature of EU enlargement, which, while preserving Member State sovereignty, allows national vetoes to be deployed for reasons unrelated to the applicant's formal compliance with EU law. This has been a persistent source of legal inconsistency and procedural opacity. For instance, France blocked Albania and North Macedonia in 2019, citing the need for procedural reforms rather than non-compliance. Similarly, Greece and Bulgaria vetoed North Macedonia over historical and linguistic disputes.[33]

Scholars have pointed out that the accession process, while legally formalised, remains politically opaque and highly discretionary.[34] Although the criteria for membership are detailed and grounded in the Copenhagen framework, the procedural implementation is vulnerable to bilateral grievances and political obstruction. Notably, the European Commission's role is primarily advisory, with its opinions lacking binding legal force. Final decisions rest with the Council of the European Union, where unanimity is required, and outcomes are often shaped by non-legal considerations. As a result, the Commission's monitoring lacks enforceability and is contingent on the political will of Member States, who may arbitrarily withhold support. Moreover, there are no formal judicial remedies or appeal mechanisms available to candidate countries when decisions are delayed or vetoed, reinforcing the legal asymmetry and discretionary character of the enlargement framework.[35]

A key innovation came in 2020, when the Commission revised the enlargement methodology in response to mounting criticism.[36] Rather than following the traditional chapter-by-chapter format, the new methodology groups the acquis into six thematic clusters:

1. Fundamentals (rule of law, public administration, economic criteria);
2. Internal Market;
3. Competitiveness and inclusive growth;
4. Green agenda and sustainable connectivity;
5. Resources, agriculture, and cohesion;
6. External relations.

---

[31] Kochenov and Basheska 2025.

[32] Dionysiou 2023.

[33] Hoxhaj 2025.

[34] Kochenov and Basheska 2025; Cremona 2003.

[35] Kochenov 2008.

[36] Commission 2020.

This thematic approach was designed to allow for more structured negotiations, better monitoring, and the early delivery of benefits to reforming countries. The methodology also introduced the possibility of reversibility, whereby negotiations can be frozen or chapters re-closed in cases of backsliding. This new architecture strengthens the political conditionality but does not eliminate the legal opacity and the reliance on Council unanimity.

Both legal and political scholars have criticised that the process remains non-transparent and procedurally rigid. Negotiations are conducted in diplomatic secrecy, with no fixed timeline, and limited input from the European Parliament or national parliaments of candidate states. There is also no formalised legal pathway for judicial review of Council decisions, leaving no option to the candidate states than comply with the political requirements, regardless of whether connected or not to the Copenhagen criteria or its implementation guidelines.

8.2.2 Evolving Conditionality: From Normative Power to Strategic Discretion

The EU's enlargement policy has long been rooted in its identity as a normative power—an actor that shapes its neighbourhood through the export of democratic values, the rule of law, and human rights.[37] This approach, underpinned by the Copenhagen criteria and formalised through Article 49 TEU, formed the legal and normative foundation of the Central and Eastern enlargement. The success of the 2004 and 2007 enlargement waves is often attributed to the credibility and coherence of this conditionality model: candidate countries implemented sweeping legal and institutional reforms in exchange for a clear and attainable promise of membership. However, while the 2004 and 2007 enlargement waves were initially seen as emblematic of the EU's transformative power, subsequent developments have revealed limitations in the conditionality model. Although candidate countries undertook significant legal and institutional reforms during the accession process, the durability of these reforms has proven uneven, with post-accession backsliding—particularly in areas such as judicial independence, media freedom, and the rule of law—raising questions about the long-term effectiveness of EU conditionality in ensuring democratic consolidation.[38]

At the core of the Central and Eastern Europe enlargement was the compliance-for-reward logic. The EU linked benefits such as financial aid, market access, and eventual membership to measurable progress in adopting the *acquis communautaire* and aligning domestic institutions with European standards. The legal clarity of accession benchmarks and the perceived reliability of EU commitments ensured the model's effectiveness.

However, this normative paradigm began to erode in the post-2007 period. A series of internal and external developments—including enlargement fatigue, the

[37] Radaelli 2003; Sedelmeier 2011.

[38] Anghel and Džankić 2023.

Eurozone crisis, Brexit, and rule-of-law backsliding within existing member states from the 2004/2007 enlargement waves—undermined the EU's credibility as an anchor of democratic reform. In parallel, the accession process itself became increasingly politicised and protracted. Candidate countries such as Albania, Serbia, and Montenegro, despite formal progress, faced extensive delays due to both their own democratic shortcomings and external vetoes by Member States over issues unrelated to the acquis, such as bilateral disputes or identity politics.

The case of North Macedonia epitomises this tension. After applying in 2004 and receiving candidate status in 2005, it waited nearly two decades before accession negotiations began in 2022. This delay was not due to failure to meet EU legal benchmarks, but to successive political blockades—first by Greece (resolved through the Prespa Agreement), then France (demanding a new methodology), and later Bulgaria (over linguistic and historical disputes).[39] These obstructions, falling outside the EU's formal legal framework, highlight the increasing divergence between legal norms and political practice in the enlargement process.

Compounding this problem are domestic constraints in many candidate countries. In Turkey, initial reforms following the 1999 Helsinki Summit eventually gave way to authoritarian regression, weakened judicial independence, and the curtailment of fundamental freedoms. In the Western Balkans, entrenched corruption, state capture, and limited progress on judicial reform continue to hinder genuine alignment with EU standards.[40] Some states -particularly Serbia—have also maintained strategic partnerships with actors such as Russia and China, often diverging from the EU's Common Foreign and Security Policy (CFSP) and raising questions about their long-term alignment with the Union.[41] This begs the question as to whether, in a situation of war, the Union should impose on candidate countries to make the alignment with the CFSP a priority for them.

In response to these challenges, the EU has progressively moved towards a more flexible and geopolitical application of conditionality.[42] The emergence of strategic conditionality represents a recalibration of the accession process: instead of rigid adherence to technical benchmarks, the Union increasingly prioritises geopolitical stability, regional security, and strategic alignment. This shift became most apparent following Russia's full-scale invasion of Ukraine in February 2022.

After the invasion, Ukraine, Moldova, and Georgia submitted formal applications for EU membership.[43] While the possibility of immediate accession of Ukraine to the EU because of the war was discarded,[44] the first procedural steps of Article 49 TEU were greatly accelerated. By June 2022, Ukraine and Moldova were granted

[39] Dionysiou 2023.

[40] Hoxhaj 2025.

[41] Commission Serbia Report 2023a.

[42] The Commission refers for the first time in relation to the EU enlargement process to 'geopolitical context', and priorities in its Communication to the Parliament from 2024, see Commission Communication 2024a.

[43] European Council 2022.

[44] Petrov 2023.

candidate status, and Georgia followed in December 2023 based on the positive European Commission opinions.[45] While these decisions acknowledged progress made under Association Agreements and Deep and Comprehensive Free Trade Areas (DCFTAs)—particularly in regulatory approximation—they were also driven by the urgent need to anchor these states within the EU's normative and security space. These accelerated candidacies occurred despite unresolved rule-of-law and governance challenges, raising legitimate legal and institutional questions about the consistency of conditionality application.

This approach reveals the strategic discretion now shaping enlargement. Although the Copenhagen criteria remain formally intact, their interpretation has become more context-dependent. For Ukraine and Moldova, the EU demonstrated a willingness to proceed with candidate status even amid incomplete reforms and ongoing conflict, relying instead on political signalling and symbolic alignment. In contrast, Western Balkan states, which have engaged in the accession process for over a decade, remain stalled—partly due to their own failings, but also due to an accession framework increasingly susceptible to vetoes and inconsistent application.

The result is a process characterised by institutional inconsistency. The lack of judicial remedies or appeal mechanisms for candidate states, the advisory (rather than binding) nature of the Commission's monitoring reports, and the requirement of unanimity within the Council collectively render the process opaque and discretionary. Strategic conditionality thus enables the EU to act with agility in moments of crisis but also introduces risks: if not carefully managed, it may undermine the rule-based nature of the enlargement acquis, foster perceptions of unequal treatment, and weaken the EU's long-term transformative credibility.[46]

Going forward, the challenge for the EU is twofold: to adapt its conditionality instruments to contemporary geopolitical realities, while reinforcing the legal predictability, transparency, and normative coherence of the accession process. Balancing strategic responsiveness with legal rigour will be critical to the Union's ability to retain legitimacy as both a geopolitical actor and a community of law.

8.2.3 Institutional Reform and the Role of Qualified Majority Voting

Given the procedural fragility and political volatility of the enlargement framework, proposals for institutional reform have gained traction.[47] Key among these is the potential extension of Qualified Majority Voting (QMV) to certain stages of the enlargement process, such as:

45 Ibid.

46 Coli 2025.

47 Anghel and Džankić 2023; Dionysiou 2023; Hoxhaj 2025.

- The opening and closing of negotiation clusters;
- Approval of interim benchmarks;
- Assessing compliance with the rule of law and economic criteria.

Any formal stage of enlargement, such as the decision to open accession negotiations, their formal conclusion, or the granting of full membership, necessarily requires unanimity among the Member States. The simplified amendment procedure of Article 48(7) TEU cannot apply in this context, as Article 48(7) TEU is limited to Title V TEU, whereas Article 49 TEU—governing accession—falls under Title VI TEU. However, it remains open to discussion whether the Treaties would also need to be amended to cover certain intermediate steps within the negotiation process itself. While these stages are not expressly regulated by Article 49 TEU, they play a decisive role in shaping the path to membership, and the question arises whether the current unanimity requirement extends to them as well.

In parallel, proposals such as the Franco-German "regatta" model envision a phased, reversible accession process. Under this model, candidate countries could integrate into certain EU policies or institutions prior to full membership, contingent on reform progress. This would operationalise a graduated system of rights and obligations, where benefits accrue over time, and regression can be sanctioned.

Legally, such models raise questions about the allocation of rights without membership, the applicability of EU law to non-members, and the design of enforcement mechanisms. Without a formal status in the Treaties, such intermediate frameworks risk generating legal uncertainty and democratic deficits.

Overall, the evolution of the enlargement process reflects a complex interplay of law and politics. While the EU continues to present enlargement as a rule-based, merit-driven enterprise, the realities of geopolitical urgency, institutional resistance, and bilateral disputes have eroded its normative coherence. Reconciling the EU's foundational values with its strategic interests will require a recalibration of legal mechanisms, transparency norms, and institutional procedures.

8.3 EU–Ukraine Relations: From Association to Accession

8.3.1 Pre-War Relations: The Association Agreement and DCFTA

The legal and institutional foundations of EU–Ukraine relations were laid well before the outbreak of the 2022 war. The key turning point was the 2014 Association Agreement,[48] including the Deep and Comprehensive Free Trade Area (DCFTA), which replaced the 1998 Partnership and Cooperation Agreement. This agreement has been

---

[48] The Association Agreement between the European Union and Ukraine was signed on 27 June 2014; DCFTA provisionally applied from 1 January 2016 and fully entered into force 1 September 2017.

widely acknowledged as the EU's most ambitious legal integration framework with a non-member state at the time—so much so that scholars have described it as a model of "integration without membership"[49] or, in other cases, integration-oriented agreements.[50]

Legally, the Association Agreement is based on Article 217 of the Treaty on the Functioning of the European Union (TFEU), which authorizes the Union to conclude association agreements involving reciprocal rights and obligations, common actions, and special procedures. The Association Agreement with Ukraine spans more than 1,000 pages and includes both political and economic dimensions, ranging from sectoral cooperation to trade liberalisation, competition policy, and regulatory approximation.

The DCFTA component provides for far-reaching integration of Ukraine into the EU single market. It mandates the alignment of Ukrainian legislation with substantial parts of the EU acquis, particularly in areas like technical standards, sanitary and phytosanitary measures, public procurement, intellectual property, and competition policy. In this sense, it operates as a de facto legal approximation mechanism, without explicitly offering membership to Ukraine.

Critically, Article 475 of the Association Agreement introduces binding obligations for Ukraine to ensure that national legislation gradually conforms to EU law. The Agreement also includes "evolutionary" clauses that permit dynamic adaptation and deepening of integration, conditional on Ukraine's compliance with EU standards and values. This conditionality-based model mirrors elements of the pre-accession frameworks used with Central and Eastern European countries, particularly the Europe Agreements of the 1990s.[51]

However, despite its legal sophistication, implementation has been uneven. European Commission implementation reports highlight deficiencies in critical reform areas such as the judiciary, anti-corruption mechanisms, and public administration.[52] While institutions like National Anti-Corruption Bureau of Ukraine and the High Anti-Corruption Court have been established, their effectiveness has been undermined by political interference and systemic oligarchic resistance.

The Venice Commission has issued multiple legal opinions and technical recommendations, especially regarding judicial reform. Persistent issues include poor vetting procedures for judges, weak prosecutorial oversight, and fragmented institutional frameworks—factors that compromise rule-of-law benchmarks embedded in the Association Agreement.[53]

Moreover, the EU's enforcement tools under the Association Agreement lacked the coercive edge of pre-accession instruments. The "more-for-more" approach, tied to incremental rewards like market access or funding, lacked the symbolic and political force of full membership conditionality. Consequently, while Ukraine achieved

[49] Van Elsuwege 2025.

[50] See, in particular, Petrov 2016, p. 101 and Poli and Bartoloni 2021, p. 194.

[51] Van Elsuwege and Chamon 2019.

[52] Commission 2021, 2023b.

[53] Venice Commission 2019, 2020, 2021.

substantial regulatory convergence in areas like customs, energy, and food safety, structural governance reforms remained fragile.[54]

Economically, the DCFTA has yielded clear results. The EU became Ukraine's largest trading partner, and bilateral trade volumes rose significantly. Nevertheless, trade liberalization was asymmetrical. Market access remained constrained by tariff-rate quotas and transitional periods, particularly in sensitive sectors like agriculture—highlighting the limits of the agreement's market-opening promises.[55]

Politically, the Association Agreement became a geopolitical flashpoint. President Yanukovych's decision to suspend its signature in late 2013 triggered the Euromaidan protests, resulting in regime change. Russia's annexation of Crimea and destabilization of Donbas were, in part, reactions to Ukraine's alignment with the EU's normative and economic space. Thus, the Association Agreement transcended its legal character to become a symbol of Ukraine's geopolitical reorientation.

8.3.2 Post-War Transformation: Ukraine as a Geopolitical Partner

Russia's full-scale invasion of Ukraine in February 2022 marked a watershed moment in EU–Ukraine relations. Within days, Ukraine submitted its formal application for EU membership under Article 49 TEU. In a striking departure from precedent, the European Commission issued its Opinion within months, and the European Council granted Ukraine candidate status in June 2022—a process that typically unfolds over years.

This acceleration signalled a paradigm shift in the EU's external action. Ukraine was no longer viewed merely as a neighbour under the European Neighbourhood Policy (ENP), but rather as an integral component of the EU's strategic and normative space. While the Commission acknowledged Ukraine's notable reform achievements—particularly in anti-corruption and public administration—it also recognized the adverse impact of war on institutional resilience. Nonetheless, the symbolic and geopolitical weight of Ukraine's candidacy prevailed.

Ukraine's military resilience, active civil society, and unwavering commitment to European values played a decisive role in catalyzing this shift. Legally, however, the Copenhagen criteria remain the central benchmark for accession. The 2023 enlargement package reaffirmed this, while also suggesting greater flexibility in adapting to the evolving geopolitical environment.[56]

Three complex legal questions emerge in this context:

---

[54] See Van Elsuwege 2025.

[55] European Commission, *EU-Ukraine Deep and Comprehensive Free Trade Area: Yearly Report* (Various years), available at: https://policy.trade.ec.europa.eu/eu-trade-relationships-country-and-region/countries-and-regions/ukraine_en.

[56] Commission 2024b; and Commission 2023b.

1. Wartime Accession: Can a country in active conflict meet the institutional and legal criteria for accession? While Article 49 TEU does not explicitly require peace or full territorial control, functional compliance with EU law assumes a minimum level of effective governance and territorial integrity.
2. Territorial Integrity: The EU has no definitive legal stance on whether full territorial control is a precondition for accession. Precedents like Cyprus's 2004 accession, despite its territorial division, suggest that exceptions are possible, though not without legal complications or opt-outs.
3. Rule of Law under Emergency: Wartime governance, including martial law and emergency powers, may constrain civil liberties in ways that challenge EU rule-of-law standards. These derogations must be evaluated under the EU Charter of Fundamental Rights, particularly as Ukraine moves through the accession process.

Despite these challenges, Ukraine has demonstrated continuity in its reform agenda. Efforts such as the establishment of a new judicial selection council, progress on vetting procedures, and legislative initiatives to combat oligarchic influence were highlighted in the 2023 Commission report.[57] In spite of the welcomed institutional reforms, in July 2025, a law stripped Ukraine's anti-corruption watchdogs (NABU and SAPO) of their autonomous status by transferring key functions to the presidentially-appointed Prosecutor General, prompting the largest domestic protests of the wartime period. The backlash—from civil society, the public, and European partners—highlighted the intrinsic link between anti-corruption institutions and EU accession credibility.[58] President Zelenskyy responded just days later, pledging to reverse the reforms and submitting a bill to restore institutional independence, a move endorsed by Brussels as essential for maintaining financial support and accession momentum.[59] By the end of July, parliament passed the corrective legislation, reinstating the agencies' autonomy—an outcome hailed by EU officials as vital for upholding rule-of-law norms and democratic legitimacy in the enlargement process.[60] Still, the war continues to limit Ukraine's institutional reform, making full and sustained implementation a major hurdle.

---

[57] Commission 2023b.

[58] See Dan Peleschuk, Ukraine curbs autonomy of anti-corruption agencies, Reuters 23 July 2025, https://www.reuters.com/en/ukraine-curbs-autonomy-anti-corruption-agencies-2025-07-22/.

[59] Olena Harmash and Dan Peleschuk, Zelenskiy vows to protect Ukraine's anti-corruption agencies, bows to protests, Reuters, 24 July 2025, https://www.reuters.com/world/zelenskiy-vows-protect-ukraines-anti-corruption-agencies-bows-protests-2025-07-23/.

[60] Illia Novikov, Ukraine's Parliament approves law restoring independence of anti-graft watchdogs following backlash, https://www.pbs.org/newshour/world/ukraines-parliament-approves-law-restoring-independence-of-anti-graft-watchdogs-following-backlash.

8.3.3 Accession Prospects and Conditional Integration

Given the magnitude of Ukraine's challenges, full EU accession remains a medium- to long-term objective. In the interim, the EU has adopted a phased integration strategy, reflecting proposals such as the Franco-German "regatta model" introduced in September 2023. This model envisions candidate states progressively integrating into select EU institutions and benefiting from legal and financial frameworks—without immediate full membership.

This emerging phased accession model raises important legal considerations. While the EU Treaties do not currently provide for an explicit "associate membership," Article 8 TEU allows for "special relationships" with neighboring countries, which could serve as a legal foundation. Existing frameworks like the EEA or Stabilisation and Association Process offer further precedents for incremental institutional and legal convergence.

The phased model features:

- Selective participation in EU programs and agencies (e.g. Horizon Europe, Erasmus+, Digital Europe);
- Sectoral legal integration into specific areas of the EU internal market;
- Performance-based benchmarks, with funding or access conditional on reform progress;
- Reversibility clauses, aligning with the 2020 revised Enlargement Methodology, to manage backsliding risks.

This reflects a move from classical merit-based conditionality to strategic conditionality, where geopolitical stability influences the sequencing of integration. As Schimmelfennig and Sedelmeier[61] argue, EU conditionality has always carried strategic undertones, but Ukraine's case amplifies this, aligning enlargement with geopolitical deterrence and normative projection.

Legally, this transition has multiple implications:

- The potential need for a new legal category or framework that defines intermediate membership statuses;
- Possible Treaty amendments to accommodate a more flexible and layered enlargement policy;
- The clarification of legal rights and obligations attached to each phase of integration.

This recalibrated approach also introduces normative tensions. How far can the EU stretch its standards to respond to geopolitical urgency without undermining its credibility? Some scholars warn that relaxing objective accession criteria risks delegitimizing the enlargement process, while others argue that strategic enlargement is essential in today's security architecture.

Finally, internal EU reforms will be crucial for phased integration to work. These include:

---

[61] Schimmelfennig and Sedelmeier 2004.

- Qualified Majority Voting (QMV) for intermediate decisions in regard to closing chapters in the accession negotiations[62];
- Institutional adjustments, particularly in the European Parliament and Council;
- Budgetary reform, to ensure sustainable enlargement without diluting cohesion policy or straining the EU budget.

In sum, Ukraine's trajectory has transformed EU–Ukraine relations from contractual legal alignment under the Association Agreement to a strategically driven path to membership. This transformation is testing the limits of the EU's legal framework and conditionality paradigm, demanding innovative tools and sustained political commitment.

8.4 Conclusion: Institutions, Conditionality, and the Future of Enlargement

The war in Ukraine has revived EU enlargement as a central policy, but it has also exposed the complex EU institutional interplay that shapes the process. Legally, Article 49 TEU and the Copenhagen criteria remain the formal anchors, yet their application has become increasingly mediated by institutional discretion and geopolitical urgency.

The European Council and the Council of the EU continue to hold the decisive power, as unanimity is required for every major step of accession. This institutional design preserves Member State sovereignty but also creates recurring blockages, often based on bilateral disputes or broader political considerations. In Ukraine's case, the Council's capacity to act swiftly in June 2022 demonstrated how unanimity can, under geopolitical pressure, accelerate enlargement. Yet, subsequent delays and the risk of vetoes illustrate how fragile this consensus remains.

The European Commission plays the monitoring role, issuing opinions and progress reports that provide the legal and technical foundation of conditionality. Its monitoring of Ukraine's judicial and anti-corruption reforms—as seen in the July 2025 controversy and subsequent legislative reversal—underscores both the value of its expertise and the limits of its enforcement powers.[63] Without a binding authority, the Commission relies on political backing from the Council and the Parliament to give weight to its assessments.

The European Parliament, by contrast, embodies the democratic dimension of enlargement. While its consent is formally required only at the final stage, the Parliament has consistently acted as an enlargement entrepreneur. Its resolutions on Turkey and the Western Balkans have shown how it can both constrain and advance the process, and in the case of Ukraine, the Parliament's early call in March 2022

[62] See also Petrov and Hillion 2022.

[63] Human Rights Watch 2025.

for candidate status signalled political momentum that shaped subsequent institutional decisions. This underlines the paradox of an institution with high democratic legitimacy but limited procedural power.

Taken together, the Ukraine case highlights both the potential and the shortcomings of the EU's institutional architecture. The Council dominates the enlargement process but is prone to paralysis; the Commission provides expertise but lacks coercive tools; the Parliament offers legitimacy but remains marginal in negotiations. Reconciling these asymmetries is crucial if enlargement is to remain credible. Proposals for phased accession, qualified majority voting on intermediate steps, and clearer parliamentary involvement all point toward a model where institutions share responsibility in a more balanced and transparent way.

If successfully reformed, enlargement could once again serve as both a legal instrument of transformation and a geopolitical tool of consolidation. Ukraine's candidacy, therefore, should not be seen solely as a response to war but as a test case for building a more resilient and institutionally coherent enlargement framework—one capable of delivering both credibility to candidates and legitimacy to the Union itself.

This chapter is funded by the European Research Council 2022 Starting Grant *Gatekeepers to International Refugee Law – The Role of Courts in Shaping Access to Asylum* [101078683].

References

Anghel V, Džankić J (2023) Wartime EU: Consequences of the Russia–Ukraine War on the Enlargement Process. Journal of European Integration 45(3): 487–501.

Anghel V, Jones E (2024) The Enlargement of International Organisations. West European Politics 48(1): 1–28.

Bartlett W et al. (2016) A Comparative Perspective on Institutional Quality in Countries at Different Stages of European Integration. Tijdschrift voor Economische en Sociale Geografie 108(1): 92–108.

Coli M (2025) La tutela dei valori fondanti dell'unione alla prova delle recenti domande di adesione: alla ricerca della coerenza perduta? [Protecting the Union's founding values under the test of recent membership applications: in search of lost coherence?] In: Poli S, Marinai S (eds) L'Unione europea sulla scena internazionale: sfide a trasformazioni sul piano interno ed esterno, Atti del VI° Convegno AISDUE, Pisa 24–25 October 2024. [Poli S, Marinai S (eds) The European Union on the international scene: challenges to internal and external transformations, Proceedings of the VI AISDUE Conference, Pisa 24–25 October 2024] Editoriale Scientifica, Naples, pp. 171–201.

Cremona M (2003) The Enlargement of the European Union. European Foreign Affairs Review 8(1): 75–101.

Dimitrova AL (2010) The New Member States of the EU in the Aftermath of Enlargement: Do New European Rules Remain Empty Shells? Journal of European Public Policy 17(1): 137–148.

Dionysiou E (2023) Building a Geopolitical European Union after Russia's Attack on Ukraine: The Valuable Tool of Enlargement. Studia Europejskie 27(2): 7–26.

European Commission (2020) Enhancing the accession process—A credible EU perspective for the Western Balkans. COM(2020) 57 final, 5 February 2020.

European Commission (2021) Association implementation report on Ukraine. SWD(2021) 307 final, 1 December 2021.

European Commission (2022a) Opinion on Georgia's application for membership of the European Union. COM(2022) 405 final, 17 June 2022.
European Commission (2022b) Opinion on Moldova's application for membership of the European Union. COM(2022) 406 final, 17 June 2022.
European Commission (2022c) Opinion on Ukraine's application for membership of the European Union. COM(2022) 407 final, 17 June 2022.
European Commission (2023a) Serbia 2023 report. SWD(2023) 640 final, 8 November 2023.
European Commission (2023b) Albania 2023 report. SWD(2023) 641 final, 8 November 2023.
European Commission (2023c) Ukraine 2023 report. SWD(2023) 662 final, 8 November 2023.
European Commission (2024a) 2024 communication on EU enlargement policy. COM(2024) 690 final.
European Commission (2024b) Ukraine 2024 report: Enlargement and Eastern Neighbourhood. SWD(2024) 699 final.
European Council (1993) Conclusions of the Presidency—Copenhagen European Council, 21–22 June 1993. SN 180/1/93 REV 1.
European Council (2006) European Council conclusions of 15–16 June 2006. Doc. 10633/1/06 REV 1.
European Council (2022) Conclusions on enlargement and Ukraine, Moldova and Georgia, 23 June 2022.
European Parliament (2019) European Parliament resolution of 13 March 2019 on the 2018 Commission Report on Turkey (2018/2150(INI))
Fabbrini F (2025) The Impact of the War in Ukraine on the Enlargement of the European Union: "Securing the Blessings of Liberty" and its Challenges. International & Comparative Law Quarterly 74(1): 123–146.
Franco-German Working Group of Twelve 2023, Sailing on High Seas: Reforming and Enlarging the EU for the 21st Century. Paris–Berlin, 18 September 2023. Presented at the General Affairs Council meeting, 19 September 2023.
Grabbe H (2006) The EU's Transformative Power: Europeanization through Conditionality in Central and Eastern Europe. Palgrave Macmillan, Basingstoke.
Hillion C (2004) The Copenhagen Criteria and Their Progeny. In: EU Enlargement. Hart Publishing, Oxford.
Hillion C (2025) Making a Success of EU Enlargement: Three Proposals. Swedish Institute for European Policy Studies, Working Paper, January 2025.
Hoxhaj A (2025) How to Make EU Enlargement a Fairer and Merit Based Process: A Legal and Policy Analysis. European Law Journal 30(1): 1–23.
Human Rights Watch (2025) Ukraine: New Law Undercuts Independence of Anti-Corruption Bodies, 24 July 2025, https://www.hrw.org/news/2025/07/24/ukraine-new-law-undercuts-independence-of-anti-corruption-bodies.
Inglis K (2006) Enlargement: Membership Conditions Applied to the Future and Potential Member States. In: Blockmans S, Lazowski A (eds) The European Union and Its Neighbours—A Legal Appraisal of the EU's Policies of Stabilisation, Partnership and Integration. T.M.C. Asser Press, The Hague, pp. 61–92.
Inglis K (2010) Eligible Candidates and Procedural Steps to Accession. In: Evolving Practice in EU Enlargement with Case Studies in Agri-Food and Environment Law. Martinus Nijhoff Publishers (Studies in EU External Relations), pp. 19–55.
Kaveshnikov N (2022) Ukraine's Membership Application as a Trigger to Reform the EU Enlargement Policy. Herald of the Russian Academy of Sciences 92(S7): S651–S659.
Kochenov D (2008) EU Enlargement and the Failure of Conditionality: Pre-Accession Conditionality in the Fields of Democracy and the Rule of Law. Kluwer Law International.
Kochenov D, Basheska E (2016) The European Neighbourhood Policy's Value Conditionality: From Enlargements to Post-Crimea. In: Poli S (ed) The European Neighbourhood Policy: Values and Principles. Routledge, pp. 143–166.

Kochenov D, Basheska E (2025) Ukraine and the EU Enlargement: What Is the Law and Which Is the Way Forward? European Journal of Risk Regulation 16(2): 233–249. https://doi.org/10.1017/err.2025.23.

Manners I (2002) Normative Power Europe: A Contradiction in Terms? Journal of Common Market Studies 40(2): 235–258.

Maurer H et al. (2023) The EU and the Invasion of Ukraine: A Collective Responsibility to Act? International Affairs 99(1): 219–238.

Nádasi L, Trón Z (2023) How Decisive Are the Copenhagen Criteria for EU Enlargement? European Mirror 26(2): 49–71.

Nielsen KL (2023) EU Candidate Status for Bosnia and Herzegovina: A Meaningful Step Forward? Geneva Graduate Institute, Working Paper, 11 July 2023. https://www.graduateinstitute.ch/communications/news/eu-candidate-status-bosnia-and-herzegovina-meaningful-step-forward-0. Accessed 29 July 2025.

Orenstein M (2023) Transformation of Europe after Russia's Attack on Ukraine. Journal of European Integration 45: 333–575 (special issue).

Petrov R (2016) EU Values in Integration Oriented Agreements with Ukraine, Georgia and Moldova. In: Poli S (ed) The European Neighbourhood Policy: Values and Principles. Routledge, pp. 99–111.

Petrov R (2023) Applying for EU Membership in Time of War: "Accession through War" of Ukraine. IAI Working Paper. https://www.iai.it/en/pubblicazioni/c03/applying-eu-membership-time-war-accession-through-war-ukraine. Accessed 29 July 2025.

Petrov R, Hillion C (2022) Accession through War—Ukraine's Road to the EU. Common Market Law Review 59(5): 1289–1300.

Petti A (2024) EU Neighbourhood Law: Wider Europe and the Extended EU's Legal Space. Hart Publishing, Oxford.

Poli S, Bartoloni ME (2021) L'azione esterna dell'Unione europea. [The European Union's external action]. Editoriale Scientifica, Naples.

President of the European Council (2025) European Council meeting 2025. EUCO 16/25, 26 June 2025.

Rabinovych M (2022) EU–Ukraine "Deep" Trade Agenda: The Effectiveness and Impact Perspectives. International Politics 61(6): 1078–1096.

Radaelli CM (2003) The Europeanization of Public Policy. In: Featherstone K, Radaelli CM (eds) The Politics of Europeanization. Oxford University Press, Oxford, pp. 27–56.

Schimmelfennig F, Sedelmeier U (2004) Governance by Conditionality: EU Rule Transfer to the Candidate Countries of Central and Eastern Europe. Journal of European Public Policy 11(4): 661–679.

Sedelmeier U (2011) Europeanisation in New Member and Candidate States. Living Reviews in European Governance 6(1): 1–52.

Van Elsuwege P (2025) Revisiting the EU–Ukraine Association Agreement: A Crucial Instrument on the Road to Membership. In: Rabinovych M, Pintsch A (eds) Ukraine's Thorny Path to the EU. Palgrave Studies in European Union Politics. Palgrave Macmillan, Cham. https://doi.org/10.1007/978-3-031-69154-6_4.

Van Elsuwege P, Chamon M (2019) The Meaning of "Association" under EU Law: A Study on the Law and Practice of EU Association Agreements. European Parliament. https://doi.org/10.2861/53571.

Venice Commission 2019, Opinion on the Law on the Judiciary and the Status of Judges of Ukraine. CDL-AD(2019)020, 16 March 2019.

Venice Commission 2020, Opinion on the Draft Law on the Constitutional Court of Ukraine. CDL-AD(2020)022.

Venice Commission 2021, Urgent Opinion on the Reform of the Supreme Council of Justice of Ukraine. CDL-PI(2021)029, 5 July 2021.

Chapter 9
Managing Mass Influx in the EU: The New Pact on Asylum and Migration and the War in Ukraine

Luisa Chaloub and Madalina Moraru

Contents

Abstract This chapter analyses the European Union's use of temporary protection as a response to mass influx, situating the Temporary Protection Directive (2001/55/EC) within the broader context of the New Pact on Asylum and Migration and the displacement triggered by Russia's invasion of Ukraine. It explores the conceptual evolution of temporary protection in refugee law, the Directive's legal design and political activation, and its implementation during the Ukrainian crisis. The chapter argues that the Directive's first activation exposed both its potential as a solidarity tool and its fragility as a rights instrument, given the fragmented application across Member States and its reliance on political framing. By linking EU law with UNHCR guidelines and global practice, the analysis highlights tensions between protection and containment, temporariness and permanence, and solidarity and discretion. The conclusion situates temporary protection within EU crisis governance, identifying reforms necessary to ensure durable solutions and consistency in future displacement scenarios.

Keywords Temporary protection · EU asylum law · Ukraine · New pact on migration and asylum · Mass influx · Solidarity

S. Poli et al., *The EU's Response to the War in Ukraine and Its Impact on the EU Legal Order*, Global Europe: Legal and Policy Issues of the EU's External Action 7,
https://doi.org/10.1007/978-94-6265-767-0_9

9.1 Introduction

The increasing prominence of migration as a key governance issue at the international, regional, national, and local levels, along with the growing recognition of the need for international cooperation, has brought the migration governance framework into focus.[1] This movement was especially triggered by the recognition of the importance of international cooperation to ensure that states can collectively maximise the benefits and minimise the costs associated with migration while simultaneously meeting human rights obligations. This framework gains even more relevance when refugees arrive in large numbers, and states' absorption capacity becomes a severe issue. Within this socio-legal context, the basic standards of international refugee law appear terribly expensive and generous, and the idea of "more refugees, less asylum" is increasingly presented as an inescapable equation.[2]

The mass influx of migrants in the EU is framed under the so-called "crisis rhetoric"[3] or "crisis thinking",[4] anchored in the sense of emergency, which prevents long-term solutions from emerging, reinforcing the focus on a security-based approach guided by the pretended need to fight against "irregular migration". On the one hand, this approach obscures the lack of anticipation by European countries—which would have had time to prepare to welcome people with dignity—by putting in place the necessary systems and structures in situations of "permanent emergency" or "permanent crisis".[5] This type of discourse reflects the lack of political will of the EU and its Member States to properly address this matter, creating the imaginary of migratory invasion[6] and trumpeting the novelty of mass-influx situations, as it was not an age-old phenomenon.[7] On the other hand, the "crisis rhetoric" or "crisis thinking" legitimises the political choices of tightening controls, one of the central goals of which is to keep foreigners who attempt to come to Europe at a distance. Therefore, "migration crisis" has constituted the basis for new restrictive migration policies, establishing dysfunctional and many times unethical solutions, based on the "crisification"[8] of mass influxes and effectively turning crisis into a mode of governance.[9]

In this context, the notion that the "common immigration policy and the efficient management of current migration flows to European countries belong to the most sensitive areas of EU law"[10] gained even more importance since the beginning of the Ukrainian war. The Russian invasion of Ukraine in February 2022 did not just trigger

[1] Betts and Kainz 2017.

[2] Durieux 2021.

[3] Imbert 2022, p. 95.

[4] Moreno-Lax 2024.

[5] Trauner and Wolff 2024.

[6] Imbert 2022 p. 89.

[7] Greenhill 2022.

[8] Moreno-Lax 2024.

[9] Ibid.; Imbert 2022, p. 99.

[10] Scheu 2014, p. 195.

the largest displacement crisis in Europe since World War II, but also underscored the deeply geopolitical nature of mass-influx situations. As Trauner argues,[11] Russia has deliberately used migration and forced displacement as a geopolitical weapon—pushing migrants towards European borders to destabilise neighbouring states, test the EU's unity, and exacerbate societal tensions around migration. This practice, known in policy discourse as "instrumentalisation" or "weaponisation" of migration,[12] illustrates how migration is increasingly entangled with security discourses and strategic geopolitical calculations.

Therefore, the political and strategic use of mass-influxes unfolds into two different situations: the first, based on the "crisification" with the incremental normalisation of exceptions[13] and security-driven responses, which can serve to host countries' interest in imposing new restrictive migration policies by overlooking the credibility of those situations and consequently undermining human rights; and the second with the "weaponisation" of migrants, which serves the interests of the origin country to destabilise the target countries. It is then a geopolitical phenomenon exploited by different actors who try to take advantage of the palpable anxieties permeating mass-influx situations.[14]

The Ukrainian war thus reinforced the securitisation of migration within EU policymaking, where refugees are not solely viewed as rights-holders but also as potential vectors of instability. The activation of the Temporary Protection Directive (TPD) and its implementation in response to the Ukrainian mass influx were influenced by this duality: on the one hand, it reflected solidarity and an unprecedented protection-oriented approach; on the other, it took place against a backdrop of heightened security concerns and fears of further manipulation of migration flows by hostile actors. This raises critical questions about the extent to which crisis-driven mechanisms in migration—originally designed to uphold protection standards—might become subordinated to security logics, particularly when facing complex geopolitical threats.

At the time, as stated in the Treaty on the Functioning of the European Union (TFEU) in Article 78,[15] two forms of international protection can be found at the European Union (EU) level, based on the Qualification Directive,[16] which implements the 1951 Convention.[17] While there is an exhaustive list of grounds to define

---

[11] Trauner 2024.

[12] Greenhill 2022

[13] Moreno-Lax 2024.

[14] Imbert 2022, p. 82.

[15] EU (2008) Treaty on the Functioning of the European Union (Consolidated Version), opened for signature 13 December 2007, OJ C 115/47 (9 May 2008) (entered into force 1 December 2009).

[16] European Parliament and Council (2011) Directive 2011/95/EU of 13 December 2011 on standards for the qualification of third-country nationals or stateless persons as beneficiaries of international protection, for a uniform status for refugees or for persons eligible for subsidiary protection, and for the content of the protection granted OJ L337/9.

[17] UN (1951) Convention Relating to the Status of Refugees (adopted 28 July 1951, entered into force 22 April 1954) 189 UNTS 137.

who would fall under the scope of international protection of the Refugee Convention, the subsidiary protection encompasses categories that go beyond the refugee definition, based on Member States' obligations under international and European human rights law. Additionally, the TPD[18] stipulates conditions for granting protection status in cases of mass or imminent influx, guaranteeing a minimum level of rights and containing arrangements for accessing asylum determination procedures and incorporating provisions on solidarity and balancing of integration efforts.[19] However, it is important to clarify that the Temporary Protection Directive does not constitute a third form of international protection in itself. Rather, it functions as an emergency mechanism designed to provide immediate and temporary protection in situations of mass influx, while ensuring that those benefiting from it retain access to the two main forms of international protection—refugee status and subsidiary protection—should they wish to apply for them.

Until recently, the TPD was the sole EU legal framework specifically aimed at responding to mass influx situations.[20] However, on 14 May 2024, as part of the New Pact on Migration and Asylum, the Council enacted Regulation 2024/1359[21] (referred to as the Crisis Regulation[22] or Exceptions Regulation[23]), addressing situations of crisis and force majeure[24] in the field of migration and asylum and amending Regulation (EU) 2021/1147,[25] and the Asylum and Migration Management Regulation 2024/1351 providing the Annual Solidarity Pool under Articles 58 and 59. Therefore, the EU crisis framework has expanded to include two additional tools to address the complexities of mass-influx situations and create four possible response scenarios.[26] These instruments can be applied independently, offering three distinct approaches: as stated in the TPD, the Exceptions Regulation, and the Solidarity Pool, respectively. Additionally, a fourth scenario allows for the simultaneous application of both the TPD and the Exceptions Regulation.[27]

[18] European Council Directive 2001.

[19] Tsourdi 2021.

[20] Other than that, Article 78(3)TFEU foresees that provisional measures can be adopted specifically related to a Member State "In the event of one or more Member States being confronted by an emergency situation characterised by a sudden inflow of nationals of third countries, the Council, on a proposal from the Commission, may adopt provisional measures for the benefit of the Member State(s) concerned. It shall act after consulting the European Parliament."

[21] European Parliament and Council (2024) Regulation (EU) 2024/1359 of 14 May 2024 addressing situations of crisis and force majeure in the field of migration and asylum, amending Regulation (EU) 2021/1147. OJ L1359/1.

[22] İneli-Ciğer M 2024a.

[23] Peers 2024a.

[24] Because it refers to two different categories of exceptions (crisis and force majeure) this chapter opted to refer to this regulation as the Exceptions Regulation.

[25] European Parliament and Council (2021) Regulation (EU) 2021/1147 of 7 July 2021 establishing the Asylum, Migration and Integration Fund. OJ L248/1.

[26] İnel-Ciğer M 2024a.

[27] European Parliament and Council 2024.

Even though the EU toolkit for dealing with mass influx situations has expanded from one to three different and complementary frameworks, concerns have been raised by numerous lead institutions involved in refugee protection, as reflected by the Human Rights Watch statement.[28] This gathered a total of 163 signatures, and organisations such as the International Rescue Committee, which have warned that the Exceptions Regulation could be "exploited as a legal loophole to bypass established rules and diminish refugee protection".[29] The consolidation of "exceptional" measures into the New Pact—through widespread derogations, legal fictions, and the erosion of rights—is steadily institutionalising limited access to international protection in the EU.[30] This development might not only endanger the rights of asylum seekers but also undermine the EU's legal order and fundamental rights framework and it raises questions about whether the enlarged EU crisis architecture is compatible with the legal human rights and refugee protection standards, and the political commitments enshrined in the ideals of orderly, safe, and regular migration governance, as particularly stated in the UN Global Compacts on Refugees (GCR) and Migration (GCM).

Much has already been written about the TPD and its (in)adequacy to the global migration governance standards (Gluns & Wessels,[31] Durieux,[32] Koo,[33] among others). Many analyses of the TPD's first activation and comparisons between the TPD and the Implementing Decision[34] (Carrera & Meltem,[35] Schutz[36]) have been produced as well. The study of the New Pact and its implications for crisis management has also been discussed (Meltem,[37] Peers[38]) and whether these new crisis tools provide a valuable addition to the existing European legal framework governing mass influx situations (Meltem, 2024[39]; Neidhardt[40]). Nevertheless, there has been limited

---

[28] Human Rights Watch (2024) Civil society organisations call on MEPs to vote down harmful EU migration pact. https://www.hrw.org/news/2024/04/15/civil-society-organisations-call-meps-vote-down-harmful-eu-migration-pact. Accessed 20 September 2025.

[29] Kaiser J (2024) Unpacking the most contested elements of the EU's new migration and asylum pact. https://www.theparliamentmagazine.eu/news/article/unpacking-the-most-contested-elements-of-the-eus-new-migration-and-asylum-pact. Accessed 20 September 2025.

[30] Moreno-Lax 2024.

[31] Gluns and Wessels 2017.

[32] Durieux 2021.

[33] Koo 2017.

[34] Council 2022.

[35] Carrera and İneli Ciğer 2023.

[36] Schultz J (2022) Collective protection as a short-term solution: European responses to the protection needs of refugees from the war in Ukraine. https://eumigrationlawblog.eu/collective-protection-as-a-short-term-solution-european-responses-to-the-protection-needs-of-refugees-from-the-war-in-ukraine/?print=print. Accessed 20 September 2025.

[37] İneli-Ciğer 2024.

[38] Peers 2024a.

[39] İneli-Ciğer 2024a

[40] Neidhardt 2024.

discussion so far on how the new EU crisis architecture aligns with the broader migration governance framework. This chapter aims to bridge that gap by analysing the compatibility of the EU's new legal crisis framework with global migration governance, focusing on the EU response to the Ukrainian crisis, the first-ever activation of the TPD, and the lessons learned, possibly guiding the implementation of the new measures.

It starts with a brief overview of mass influx management and the examination of the key elements of temporary protection mechanisms (TPMs), including its concept, minimum rights, and ending, to establishing its central role in the migration governance framework (Sect. 9.2). This analysis is followed by a discussion of the Temporary Protection Directive (Sect. 9.3.1), its first activation with the Ukrainian crisis (Sect. 9.3.2) and its main challenges (Sects. 9.3.2.1, 9.3.2.2 and 9.3.2.3). It will then explore the Exceptions Regulation and briefly the Annual Solidarity Pool (Sect. 9.4), followed by a comparative analysis of the TPD and the tools introduced under the New Pact on Migration and Asylum within the global governance framework (Sect. 9.5), and the conclusions (Sect. 9.6).

In this chapter, it is argued that while the New Pact on Migration introduces a broader set of crisis migration management tools, it might potentially weaken the system of international protection depending on its implementation. The isolated application of the derogation measures in the Exceptions Regulation, without its use alongside the TPD, can exacerbate the system's fragmentation, threaten basic rights, and undermine adherence to the international protection framework. Although the TPD has implementation shortcomings, it still remains more aligned with international protection standards, offering a structured response to mass influx situations, reducing precarity in exile, and prioritising durable solutions. Therefore, an integrated approach through which the new crisis management tools are used together with the TPD, ensuring its minimum rights framework remains intact, is arguably a more effective strategy than a purely one-instrument application.

9.2 The Origins of Temporary Protection Mechanisms as a Tool for Mass Influx Management

Mass influx situations strain even the most robust asylum systems, demanding rapid protection responses, support for overwhelmed host states, and temporary solutions to avoid collapsing reception and integration structures. Among these, TPMs have gained prominence as pragmatic, short-term tools intended to stabilise crises without fully activating individual asylum systems.[41] While the related solutions are complex and multifaceted, including an increasing focus on combating the root causes,[42] the TPMs can offer a temporary and fair solution, designed to provide a structured yet

[41] İneli-Ciğer 2024b.

[42] United Nations 2018.

flexible framework, ensuring at least a basic level of stability and protection in such crises.

Though lacking a universally accepted definition,[43] TPMs have a long-standing—if contested—history in refugee practice. Emerging prominently in the 1980s and 1990s, they were formalised as legal and operational responses to mass displacement from conflicts like those in Indochina, the Balkans[44] and Central America.[45] The UNHCR's 1981 Executive Committee Conclusion on large-scale influx, [46] recognised states' obligations to provide, at minimum, temporary refuge and basic protection, laying early groundwork for TPMs as emergency instruments balancing humanitarian obligations with states' security interests.[47] This framing was later echoed in the UNHCR's 2012 Guidelines,[48] which stressed TPMs' value in providing swift protection while deflecting pressure from asylum systems.

The UNHCR conceptualises TPMs as "practical devices for meeting urgent protection needs in situations of mass influx".[49] And clarifies that "its value in ensuring protection from *refoulement* and basic minimum treatment in accordance with human rights without overburdening individual status determination procedures has been demonstrated",[50] recommending an average of five years of duration.[51] This concept allows the incorporation of various forms of protection, such as temporary admission, temporary refuge, and temporary asylum, making it a recognised tool in the international protection framework[52] and is structured around three key pillars: temporality, mass-influx situations management and protection needs.

However, TPMs have always reflected the tension between protection and containment. Their appeal to states lies in their inherent temporariness, return orientation, and flexibility—allowing governments to manage large influxes without long-term

43 UNHCR 2012.

44 Chimni 2000.

45 The large-scale influx of refugees in Central America was also a key catalyst for the adoption of the Cartagena Declaration. Drawing on this experience, the Cartagena Declaration (Conclusions (II)(3)) recognises that the refugee definition in the 1951 Convention is insufficient to address mass influx situations in the region and advocates for an expanded refugee definition. This broader concept includes individuals fleeing generalised violence, foreign aggression, internal conflict, massive human rights violations, or other circumstances seriously disturbing public order. See Colloquium on the International Protection of Refugees in Central America, Mexico and Panama (1984) Cartagena Declaration on Refugees. Adopted on 22 November 1984 and Fitzpatrick 2000.

46 UNHCR 2009.

47 This document's significance is reflected in its explicit mention in the Cartagena Declaration (Conclusion (III)(8) The Declaration highlights the importance of establishing minimum standards of treatment for refugees in large-scale influx situations, drawing on the 1951 Refugee Convention, the 1967 Protocol, the American Convention on Human Rights, and key UNHCR guidance—particularly Conclusion No. 22.

48 UNHCR 2012.

49 UNHCR 2001.

50 UNHCR 2012.

51 Ibid.

52 Ibid.

legal commitments.[53] Yet, this very design risks institutionalising precariousness and "permanent temporariness",[54] trapping individuals in prolonged legal limbo, particularly when conflicts are protracted.

As the name implies, the temporal factor emerges as a pivotal consideration in the evaluation of temporary protection strategies. Therefore, it is generally deemed unsuitable for situations deeply rooted in longstanding conflicts or events, particularly when the prospect of a swift return to the country of origin or transition to alternative solutions is unlikely in the short term. Its continuing suitability as a protection tool in a particular situation calls for constant monitoring, and maximum limits should be set to ensure that persons can transition to other solutions.[55]

Even though temporary protection mechanisms are relevant tools to deal with migration crisis scenarios and hold appeal for governments due to their return-oriented nature and avoidance of a perceived long-term commitment, their implementation should reduce the precarity of life in exile or as a "returnee" in the country of origin. This is achieved by providing durable solutions with repatriation, resettlement or integration, which includes stable legal status, protection and opportunities for productive activity in the country of residence. After all, it is a temporary form of protection that must evolve into a lasting situation.

UNHCR guidelines propose an average duration of five years to avoid this, but in practice, TPMs often outlast the intended timelines. Their minimalist rights framework[56]—basic civil protections, access to courts, essential services—ensures survival but frequently falls short of the standards guaranteed under the 1951 Convention. As such, the extended use of TPM sits uneasily within the international protection regime, risking the erosion of durable solutions like integration or resettlement.

Generally, the ending of temporary protection involves two possibilities: expiration and/or termination. On the one hand, expiration means that temporary protection concludes when the predetermined period elapses. The UNHCR suggested that an average time of five years should be enough to support beneficiaries' minimum rights while searching avenues for long-lasting solutions without keeping them in a limbo situation for a prolonged time, the so-called "permanent temporariness".[57] On the other hand, termination links the conclusion of temporary protection with meeting specific criteria in the country of origin. A "maximalist approach" aligns

[53] Betts 2010.

[54] Durieux 2014.

[55] UNHCR 2012.

[56] UNHCR 2009.

[57] Schultz 2020.

these criteria with those in the "ceased circumstances" clauses of the 1951 Convention. [58] In contrast, a "minimalist approach" may only necessitate a change in conditions enabling a dignified and safe return or transition to alternative arrangements and solutions.[59]

Ending temporary protection presents further challenges. The UNHCR[60] recommends termination align with clear, objective conditions—ideally those in the "ceased circumstances" clause of the 1951 Convention. Yet, states often adopt more restrictive approaches, invoking even modest changes in country-of-origin conditions to justify return. This underscores the political utility of TPMs: while designed as humanitarian tools, they also serve as instruments of migration control, allowing states to calibrate their obligations amid securitised migration debates.

The TPD reflects this global evolution, codifying TPMs into EU law but activating them only once—during the Ukrainian crisis—highlighting the enduring ambivalence around their use. The TPD's activation, alongside new crisis tools under the EU New Pact, raises fresh questions about TPMs' place within a migration governance framework increasingly shaped by security logics and geopolitical instrumentalisation.

[58] UN 1951 Article 1 (c) "C. This Convention shall cease to apply to any person falling under the terms of section A if: (1) He has voluntarily re-availed himself of the protection of the country of his nationality; or (2) Having lost his nationality, he has voluntarily re-acquired it; or (3) He has acquired a new nationality, and enjoys the protection of the country of his new nationality; or (4) He has voluntarily re-established himself in the country which he left or outside which he remained owing to fear of persecution; or (5) He can no longer, because the circumstances in connection with which he has been recognized as a refugee have ceased to exist, continue to refuse to avail himself of the protection of the country of his nationality; Provided that this paragraph shall not apply to a refugee falling under section A(1) of this article who is able to invoke compelling reasons arising out of previous persecution for refusing to avail himself of the protection of the country of nationality; (6) Being a person who has no nationality he is, because of the circum- stances in connection with which he has been recognized as a refugee have ceased to exist, able to return to the country of his former habitual residence. Provided that this paragraph shall not apply to a refugee falling under section A (1) of this article who is able to invoke compelling reasons arising out of previous persecution for refusing to return to the country of his former habitual residence. Provided that this paragraph shall not apply to a refugee falling under section A (1) of this article who is able to invoke compelling reasons arising out of previous persecution for refusing to return to the country of his former habitual residence."

[59] UNHCR 2012.

[60] UNHCR 2005.

9.3 The Temporary Protection Directive

9.3.1 General Overview

For over two decades, the TPD remained dormant in the European Union's legal framework.[61] Despite repeated calls for its activation during major displacement crises—such as the Arab Spring, the Syrian conflict, or the fallout of wars in Afghanistan and Libya—the Council of the European Union never triggered the mechanism.[62] Its activation hinges on a qualified majority vote in the Council (Article 5(1)), a threshold that proved politically unattainable until 2022. Efforts by frontline states like Italy, Greece, and Malta to invoke the TPD during the so-called 2015 refugee crisis were blocked by a resistant coalition of Member States,[63] unwilling to commit to shared responsibility and wary of setting a precedent for large-scale, rights-based responses to asylum seekers from the Global South.[64]

This political impasse reflected not only divergent national interests but also deep-rooted tensions within the EU over solidarity and migration burden-sharing. The failure to activate the TPD in 2015, when over a million predominantly Syrian, Afghan, and Iraqi refugees arrived in Europe, exposed the instrument's vulnerability to geopolitical selectivity and internal divisions. Scholars (Carrera & Geddes[65]; Trauner[66]; Moreno-Lax[67]) have noted how the racialised and securitised framing of the 2015 influx—as a "crisis" or "threat"—clashed with the TPD's protection rationale, leading to its sidelining in favour of restrictive national and EU-level responses.

In stark contrast, the 2022 activation of the TPD in response to Russia's invasion of Ukraine and the mass displacement of millions of Ukrainians marked a historic first. This activation was not only unprecedented but politically telling. Ukrainians—mostly white, Christian, and geographically proximate—were quickly constructed as deserving beneficiaries of solidarity, while their displacement was framed through a geopolitical lens: an attack on European values and security. As Trauner[68] highlights, Russia's aggression redefined the migration influx as a security crisis with clear external aggressors, enabling unprecedented unity among EU Member States. This

[61] Nevertheless, member states used temporary mechanisms to deal with large influx of refugees, such as Germany dealing with the Syrian crisis and granting only temporary residency to part of this group.

[62] İneli-Ciğer 2016.

[63] Council Decision 2015.

[64] In the absence of triggering the TPM, the Member States of first entry of asylum seekers in the EU would remain responsible for asylum claims processing. N.B. that Poland asked for assurances that there would be no Dublin-like transfer mechanisms for Ukrainians entering the EU through Poland during the discussions to activate the TMP, see more in Trauner 2024.

[65] Carrera and Geddes 2021.

[66] Trauner 2024.

[67] Moreno-Lax 2024.

[68] Trauner F, Wolff S 2024.

reveals the TPD's latent role as a geopolitical tool, activated not solely by the scale of displacement but by the political context, perceived proximity, and identity of the displaced.

Legally, the TPD provides a group-based protection status (Article 5(1)), granting residence permits (Article 8) and basic rights (Articles 12–14), initially valid for one year and extendable up to three years (Article 4). It aims to bypass lengthy individual asylum procedures, easing pressure on national systems during mass influxes. While Member States retain the discretion to grant more favourable conditions (Article 3(5)), they are bound by minimum standards, including rights to education, work, and housing. After the first step of its activation, the EU needs to deal with the different phases of implementing the TPD and designing medium and long-term policy responses focusing on durable solutions, including an effective route for applying for asylum or regularisation, as well as socio-economic inclusion/integration, security of residency and family life of beneficiaries.[69] Thus, the "proper function" of this concept/practice in Europe is "*to facilitate admission and the obtaining of satisfactory durable solutions* in large-scale influx situations".[70] Therefore, the EU TPD outlines a temporary protection mechanism according to the UNHCR's definition and its three key elements (mass-influx situations management, protection needs and temporary measures).

The Directive also establishes a solidarity mechanism (Articles 24–26), allowing for the relocation of persons holding temporary protection between Member States, albeit on a voluntary basis and with the individuals' consent. Yet, the non-binding nature of this mechanism reflects ongoing EU struggles over mandatory responsibility-sharing, an issue left unresolved by the TPD's first activation.

Ultimately, the TPD mirrors the broader contradictions of EU migration governance: designed as a tool for protection, it has been repurposed by political contingencies and geopolitical interests. Its selective use raises critical questions about the consistency of European solidarity, the influence of racialised and geopolitical narratives, and the future of rights-based crisis responses within the Union.

9.3.2 The Ukrainian Crisis and the Temporary Protection Directive's First Activation

The Russian invasion of Ukraine in February 2022 triggered the largest refugee movement in Europe since World War II,[71] with millions fleeing primarily into neighbouring EU Member States such as Poland, Slovakia, Hungary, and Romania.[72]

---

[69] Carrera and İneli-Ciğer 2023.

[70] Durieux JF 2021.

[71] United Nations 2022.

[72] Czech Republic faces a particular situation, considering it is the country which has the most Ukrainian refugees per capita of all EU states.According to Eurostat data in 04 of March 2025. This is due to a few main factors, as the already large concentration of Ukrainians in the area (before the

In response, the European Commission took the unprecedented step of proposing the activation of the TPD[73]—a mechanism left untouched during previous crises, including the 2015 Syrian refugee influx.

The swift political consensus—formalised by the Council Implementing Decision (EU) 2022/382 on 4 March 2022,[74] adopted only one week after the start of the war—reflected not only the scale of displacement but also the geopolitical framing of the conflict: solidarity with Ukraine was quickly mobilised as a defence of European values against Russian aggression. Although the speed and scale of large-scale arrivals justified the activation of the TPD, and it was understood as the right move which provided many benefits to those seeking refuge and the Member States,[75] this activation also exposed the selective nature of EU solidarity, raising critical questions when contrasted with the refusal to apply the same mechanism during past displacements from Syria, Afghanistan, or Libya.[76]

While the TPD allowed rapid access to residence, work, and social rights for Ukrainians and eligible third-country nationals, its implementation revealed significant weaknesses. Wide discretion left to Member States led to fragmented application—varying eligibility criteria, differing rights access, and inconsistent procedural safeguards across jurisdictions. States like Denmark opted out, applying parallel national measures, further complicating coordination.[77]

Moreover, the temporary nature of the TPD raises longer-term concerns. Its design prioritises short-term protection and return, potentially delaying durable solutions like full refugee status, local integration, or resettlement. This risks creating legal uncertainty and prolonged precarity for beneficiaries, especially if conditions for safe return do not materialise swiftly.

These challenges underscore broader tensions within the EU's crisis response: while the TPD's activation marked a political success, its fragmented implementation tests the EU's commitment to consistent protection standards and the principles of the Global Compacts on Refugees and Migration. The following sections assess these issues through the lens of the TPM's three core elements: managing mass influx, ensuring protection, and safeguarding temporariness.

---

war, an estimated 140,000 to 200,000 Ukrainians were living and working in the Czech Republic), linguistic similarities (united by belonging to the Slavic family); and the geographical proximity to their country. For more information, see: Eurostat 2022.

[73] Commission 2022.

[74] Council Implementing Decision (2022) 2022/382 of 4 March 2022 establishing the existence of a mass influx of displaced persons from Ukraine within the meaning of Article 5 of Directive 2001/55/EC, and having the effect of introducing temporary protection. OJ L71/1.

[75] İneli Ciğer M 2022.

[76] Faiola A, Noack R, Adam K (2022) Suddenly welcoming, Europe opens the door to refugees fleeing Ukraine. https://www.washingtonpost.com/world/2022/02/28/ukraine-refugees-europe/. Accessed 20 September 2025.

[77] EUAA 2025a.

9.3.2.1 Personal Scope of Temporary Protection: Who Is Covered, Who Is Excluded, and Diverging National Practices

While the TPD and the Council Implementing Decision (EU) 2022/382 created an EU-wide framework to respond to the Ukrainian refugee influx, the personal scope of protection remains fragmented and contested. Despite claims of solidarity, strict temporal and personal-based eligibility criteria, discretionary provisions, and divergent Member State practices have generated legal uncertainty and unequal treatment. TPD's protection applies only to specific groups defined by political and legal criteria, meaning access is limited by design and shaped by state discretion.

The Temporary Protection Directive does not set clear limits on how many displaced persons each EU Member State must receive, leaving this to national discretion. While the Council's Decision briefly refers to "absorption capacity," no binding quotas were established.[78] Instead, there is a margin of discretion for the Member States, who must indicate their capacity to receive displaced persons in figures or general terms (Article 25 (1)).[79] Over time, it is possible to see the resumption of squabbles about where responsibility should lie and end. For example, Norway has announced that it will no longer grant automatic asylum to all refugees from Ukraine, as the absorption capacity has reached its limit.[80]

The personal scope of the temporary protection is also not completely defined at the EU level. The Council Decision[81] defined three core categories entitled to temporary protection: 1. Ukrainian nationals residing in Ukraine before 24 February 2022 (Article 2(1)(a)); 2. Stateless persons and third-country nationals granted international or equivalent protection in Ukraine (Article 2(1)(b)); 3. Close family members of the above (Article 2(1)(c))—spouses, unmarried partners (where recognised), minor children, and dependent relatives.

---

[78] Peers S (2022) Temporary Protection for Ukrainians in the EU? Q and A. EU Law Analysis. http://eulawanalysis.blogspot.com/2022/02/temporary-protection-for-ukrainians-in.html. Accessed 20 September 2025.

[79] Schultz J, Drangsland K A, Karlsen M A, Kienast J, Tan N F and Vedsted-Hansen J (2022) Collective Protection as a Short-Term Solution: European Responses to the Protection Needs of Refugees from the War in Ukraine. https://eumigrationlawblog.eu/collective-protection-as-a-short-term-solution-european-responses-to-the-protection-needs-of-refugees-from-the-war-in-ukraine/. Accessed 20 September 2025.

[80] Although Norway is not a member of the EU nor bound by the TPD, the situation raises concerns about how the Ukrainian crisis is overwhelming different protection systems, which may cause local setbacks in rights. See ECRE (2024a) Norway—Fence on Russian border under consideration—End to automatic asylum for refugees from Ukraine—NGOs express concern about proposed changes to migration law. https://ecre.org/norway-—-fence-on-russian-border-under-consideration-—-end-to-automatic-asylum-for-refugees-from-ukraine-—-ngos-express-concern-about-proposed-changes-to-migration-law/. Accessed 20 September 2025.

[81] Council 2022.

However, critical exclusions and discretionary elements emerged. For instance, Ukrainians who fled shortly before 24 February 2022—anticipating the invasion—fall outside automatic protection.[82] Some states, like Germany and Austria, extended protection to this group; others, such as the Czech Republic, did not.[83]

The definition of "family members" also sparked divergent interpretations. The TPD[84] offers in Article 15 a narrower definition than the Family Reunification Directive,[85] and courts in Austria and Germany excluded unmarried partners, while Lithuania granted protection, citing ECHR Article 8.[86] This reflects the broader tension between state sovereignty in migration control and respect for family rights under human rights law[87]—an area where the ECtHR's margin of appreciation often leads to inconsistent outcomes.[88]

A particularly contested group includes third-country nationals and stateless persons legally residing in Ukraine on the basis of permanent residence who cannot safely return home (Article 2(2)).[89] Those with temporary status—such as students or workers—were largely excluded if deemed able to return safely to their country of origin. Courts in Germany and Luxembourg upheld such exclusions, exacerbating protection gaps.[90]

Finally, Article 7 of the TPD[91] gives Member States broad discretion to extend temporary protection to "other displaced persons," but this is optional. Some countries (Germany, France, Italy) offered wider protection; others (Austria) did not, creating a patchwork of national responses.[92]

This fragmented implementation risks undermining the principle of equal treatment and creates legal uncertainty, particularly for border states facing the practical challenges of first reception. The Commission's March 2022 Communication,[93] rightly stressed the need for non-discriminatory treatment of all fleeing Ukraine, but the selective application of protection continues to expose racialised and geopolitical biases—particularly towards non-European third-country nationals.

Importantly, exclusion from temporary protection does not negate refugee rights under the 1951 Convention.[94] The TPD explicitly preserves access to individual asylum claims, ensuring that those outside its scope can seek protection based on

---

[82] Ibid. For further information, see recital 14 of the Decision.

[83] EUAA 2024a.

[84] Council 2001.

[85] Council 2015.

[86] EUAA 2024a.

[87] Edlund and Stehlík 2021.

[88] ECtHR. Greece V. The United Kingdom, 1956. (176/56)—Commission (Plenary)—Report (31).

[89] Council 2022.

[90] EUAA 2024a.

[91] Council 2001.

[92] EUAA 2025a.

[93] Commission 2022.

[94] The deliberate targeting of civilian infrastructure in Ukraine highlights the grave risks faced by Ukrainians and others within the country, who are subject to persecution and other human rights

their personal circumstances.[95] However, practice shows that access to asylum procedures for excluded groups remains inconsistent,[96] raising concerns about the EU's adherence to international protection standards and commitments under the Global Compacts.

9.3.2.2 Ensuring Protection: Gaps, Divergences, and Positive Outcomes in Medium- and Long-Term Solutions

A core challenge in the TPD implementation lies in the tension between its temporary nature and the long-term protection needs of displaced persons. While the TPD grants immediate access to rights such as residence, work, education, and healthcare (Articles 12–14), it does not create a clear pathway toward durable solutions like permanent residency or integration. In contrast, the 1951 Refugee Convention operates on a logic of progressive accrual of rights—refugees gain increasing rights as their connection to the host country deepens.[97] For example, certain rights (such as property ownership, wage-earning employment, or access to public relief) are granted depending on the refugee's duration of stay or level of attachment to the host society, reflecting the expectation that over time, refugees should be enabled to rebuild their lives and integrate. The TPD, however, lacks this rights progression and instead offers a fixed, temporary status designed primarily to provide immediate protection while facilitating eventual return. This design creates a structural challenge: while displaced persons' needs evolve over time, the TPD framework remains focused on short-term protection, often failing to provide clear pathways toward durable solutions like permanent residency or full integration.[98]

The EU Agency on Asylum argues[99] that the low number of court cases related to temporary protection reception further reflects its effectiveness and that overall, the TPD's implementation across EU+ countries followed a harmonised approach.

violations due to their nationality and falling under refugee categorisation. See Schultz, Drangsland, Karlsen, Kienast, Tan, and Vedsted-Hansen 2022.

[95] Preamble (10) and Article 3(1)).

[96] Some Member States argue that the existence of a safe third country of origin for a family member may justify the use of accelerated asylum procedures, potentially undermining the right to family unity under EU law. In contrast, France adopts a more inclusive approach by recognizing that family members of beneficiaries of temporary protection (TP) may also be eligible for TP, without requiring them to prove that return to their country of origin would be unsafe or unsustainable. Austria, however, takes a more restrictive stance: it excludes most third-country nationals (TCNs) from temporary protection unless they were beneficiaries of international protection (BIPs) in Ukraine or, in the case of stateless persons, held protection status there. All other TCNs—including family members of Ukrainians covered by TP—must instead rely on the regular asylum system. For further details, see: ECRE (2024b) AIDA Temporary Protection Compilation on 2023. Asylum Information Database. https://asylumineurope.org/wp-content/uploads/2024/11/Compilation-temporary-protection-2023-update.pdf. Accessed 20 September 2025.

[97] Hathaway 2007.

[98] Durieux 2014.

[99] See EUAA 2024a.

Nevertheless, the practical reality reveals considerable variation across Member States. This divergence stems from two main factors: (1) uneven distribution of refugees[100]—over 60% are concentrated in Germany, Poland, and Czechia—creating unequal pressure on national systems,[101] and; (2) lack of harmonised integration rights—the Council's Implementing Decision does not specify integration measures, leaving Member States to define the scope of protection in practice.

As a result, while the TPD framework guarantees basic access to services, long-term integration conditions vary significantly. Some states (Germany, France) have provided broader support, while others have narrower interpretations, limiting social benefits or imposing additional barriers. For example, in Czechia, by 2024, half of the Ukrainian refugees remained trapped in low-paid, unskilled jobs, with two-thirds working below their qualifications[102]—despite overall high employment rates among Ukrainians across the EU.[103]

Structural challenges further complicate integration. Many Member States' housing, education, and healthcare systems were already under strain before the war. This exacerbates unstable housing situations, childcare shortages, and limited school capacity, disproportionately affecting women and children. NGOs play a crucial role in filling these gaps, but reliance on civil society raises concerns about sustainability and unequal access.[104]

Nevertheless, the Ukrainian case also shows positive aspects of the TPD framework. Unlike past crises, the TPD facilitated rapid labour market access, leading to relatively high employment rates compared to other refugee groups. The recognition of professional qualifications and targeted support in some states—alongside widespread societal solidarity—has accelerated integration for many Ukrainians, especially those with existing social networks or skills in demand.[105]

Yet, the absence of binding integration obligations means the medium- and long-term future of Ukrainians in Europe remains uncertain. Without clearer pathways to permanent status, many risk being left in protracted legal limbo, dependent on repeated TPD extensions.

Research[106] shows that while the vast majority of displaced Ukrainians (88%) registered for temporary protection, only around 30% applied for international protection—despite their significantly higher recognition rates compared to the EU

[100] The TPD's free-choice model represents a significant shift in EU asylum policy, favouring applicants' preferences and freedom of movement over the traditional "costs-by-cause" approach embedded in the Dublin System. See Saracino 2024.

[101] Motivated by language and culture similarities, proximity to the Ukrainian border and previous concentration in the region, putting increased pressure on the protection systems of those countries. This uneven distribution reflects a broader challenge in the CEAS, where a few countries disproportionately shoulder responsibility, highlighting that solidarity does not occur automatically, even under temporary protection. See Eurofound 2024 and Saracino 2024.

[102] PAQ Research 2023.

[103] Eurofound 2024.

[104] Ibid.

[105] Ibid.

[106] EUAA 2024b.

average.[107] Nevertheless, in 2024, asylum applications by Ukrainians surged by 90% compared to 2023, reaching 27,000, largely due to ongoing war-related insecurity and economic uncertainty, as return intentions have declined sharply—from 52% in 2023 to 31% in 2024.[108]

In this regard, the following section examines the temporality-related aspects of the TPD, including potential exit strategies and their correlated possible consequences.

9.3.2.3 Temporality-Related Issues

Following the TPMs ending possibilities, Article 4 of the TPD foresees the same two main ways temporary protection ceases, that is, termination or expiration. In the first case, if safe and durable returns become possible, the Council can choose to terminate the temporary protection regime at any time (termination). In the second case, if safe and durable returns are not possible, the temporary protection regime must be terminated when the time limit is reached—which, according to the TPD, would be three years (expiration).[109] Nevertheless, the Commission proposed on 11 June 2024 to further extend temporary protection implemented for the protection of Ukrainians until March 2026, and the Council adopted this proposal.[110] Later, on 4 June 2025, the Commission proposed a further extension until 4 March 2027, which was adopted by the Council[111] on 13 June 2025, totalling now five years of temporary protection. In this sense, scholars seem to have opted for one of the two possibilities. Either disregard the time limit of three years and recognise that TP can be implemented for longer, as it has been undeniably enlarged.[112] Or a more "positivist" approach, understanding that TP ended when the three-year time limit expired, and that what has been implemented is now another tool.[113]

In any case, considering the extension to now five years of duration, if the first scenario happens and the war ends before March 2026, the temporary protection beneficiaries who still may have a well-founded fear could apply for international protection. At the same time, asylum applications of the temporary protection beneficiaries that were not considered until the end of the temporary protection regime

---

[107] Ibid.

[108] EUAA 2025b.

[109] The Council of the European Union has extended the TPD for those fleeing Russia's war against Ukraine—first to 4 March 2025, in June 2024, to 4 March 2026 and again in June 2025, to 4 March 2027. These extensions were made under Article 4(2) of the TPD, which allows annual renewals based on a Commission proposal. See: Commission 2022 and ECRE (2024c) Op-Ed: The EU is stretching the limits of the Temporary Protection Directive beyond 2025—but is it enough? https://ecre.org/op-ed-the-eu-is-stretching-the-limits-of-the-temporary-protection-directive-beyond-2025-but-is-it-enough/. Accessed 20 September 2025.

[110] Commission 2022.

[111] Council 2025.

[112] İneli-Ciğer 2024a.

[113] Víchová and Zaimović 2024.

must also be processed and decided by the Member States (Article 17). For those who have no interest in applying for international protection but nevertheless wish to stay in the EU, existing laws and policies on migration and Member State laws on aliens would apply (Article 20). If a previous temporary protection beneficiary has no legal reason to stay in the Member State territory, then he/she can be returned to Ukraine, given there is no risk of *refoulement*. In such cases, the TPD requires Member States to adopt measures to return the former temporarily protected persons. Exceptions for return should be given for humanitarian reasons and when someone's health prevents them from travelling (Articles 22–23).

If the second scenario happens and the TPD expires before the war ends, the Commission's proposal on a Coordinated Exit Strategy[114] and accompanying Communication on a Predictable and Common European Path[115] outline two main transition pillars: (1) integration through national channels, such as residence permits under domestic or EU legal migration frameworks, and (2) assisted voluntary return for those wishing to go back to Ukraine. However, most Ukrainians do not expect to return soon,[116] and involuntary returns are permissible only under restrictive conditions. With resettlement options limited, local integration remains the most realistic and durable solution.

The annual extensions of temporary protection—beyond the original scope of the TPD—have prolonged uncertainty, and despite March 2027 being the nominal end date, vague language in the Recommendation leaves open the possibility of further extensions without clear benchmarks.[117]

This situation reveals two key problems: the inadequacy of the TPD's time limits in addressing both the immediate and long-term dimensions of displacement, and the lack of coherence among Member States in managing the status or exit pathways of Ukrainians.

The Commission's call for transition to national migration regimes, without strong coordination, risks further fragmentation and "transition shopping," as Ukrainians move between countries with more favourable residence conditions. Divergent national approaches—such as Poland's three-year residence permits and Italy's work-based transitions—create inequalities and weaken harmonised protection standards.[118]

Finally, while the Commission's initiative aims to streamline migration management, its encouragement to prioritise national residence permits over asylum applications raises concerns about access to long-term international protection. Without stronger EU-level coordination, these trends risk undermining refugee safeguards,

[114] Commission 2025a.

[115] Commission 2025b.

[116] Sohst et al. 2025.

[117] İneli Ciğer M (2025) Towards Temporary (Prolonged) Protection? https://eumigrationlawblog.eu/towards-temporary-prolonged-protection/. Accessed 20 September 2025.

[118] Ibid.

eroding solidarity among Member States, and deepening protection gaps,[119] which would challenge the EU's commitment to sustainable refugee protection and durable solutions, as enshrined in international law and the Global Compact on Refugees.

9.4 The New Pact

9.4.1 General Overview

The reform of the European Union's migration and asylum policies has been a prolonged and contentious process,[120] largely due to persistent divisions among Member States on issues of solidarity and responsibility-sharing. [121] This section investigates how does the New Pact on Migration and Asylum reshape the EU's legal framework for managing migration crises, particularly in light of recent geopolitical upheavals such as the Russian aggression against Ukraine? This question situates the Pact within a socio-legal context shaped by competing national interests, increasing migratory pressures, and evolving security dynamics at Europe's borders.

In April 2024, after years of deadlock, the EU formally adopted the New Pact on Migration and Asylum. This package of legislative reforms seeks to harmonise asylum procedures, enhance burden-sharing, and bolster the EU's capacity to respond to migration crises. A key component of this reform is the introduction of new instruments explicitly designed to manage exceptional situations, many of them drawn from restrictive practices previously adopted during past "crises," particularly the Syrian displacement. This reflects a broader trend: once exceptional, crisis-driven measures are introduced, they tend to become embedded in the legal framework—a process described as "incremental normalisation." Over time, emergency measures risk becoming permanent features of asylum governance.[122]

On 14 May 2024, the Council enacted two significant regulations under the Pact: the Regulation on Crisis and Force Majeure in the field of Migration and Asylum and the Asylum and Migration Management Regulation (AMMR), which operationalises the *Annual Solidarity Pool* (Articles 58 and 59). These measures expand the EU's crisis-response toolkit beyond the previously existing Temporary Protection Directive,[123] which had not been activated until the Russian invasion of Ukraine triggered its use in 2022 to manage the unprecedented displacement of millions of Ukrainians.

---

[119] Ugolini E (2025) An unambitious exit from Temporary Protection? Fragmentation and risks ahead. https://www.epc.eu/publication/an-unambitious-exit-from-temporary-protection-fragmentation-and-risks-ahead/. Accessed 20 September 2025.

[120] The reform has spanned over 8 years (2016–2024) and two different mandates of the European Commission and Parliament.

[121] Moraru 2022.

[122] Moreno-Lax 2024.

[123] İneli-Ciğer 2024a.

Interestingly, the European Commission's original 2020 proposal for the Pact had questioned the relevance of the TPD, suggesting its repeal on the grounds that it no longer met Member States' needs.[124] The proposed *Crisis and Force Majeure Regulation* at the time envisioned replacing the TPD with an "immediate protection status" activated directly by the Commission,[125] thereby streamlining the response mechanism and minimising political delays inherent in requiring unanimous Council action.[126]

However, the actual course of events—notably the war in Ukraine—dramatically shifted this assessment. The successful and swift activation of the TPD in response to the Ukrainian displacement underscored its practical utility.[127] As reflected in the Preamble (Recital 3) of the 2024 Crisis Regulation, the TPD was ultimately preserved as part of the EU's crisis management architecture: "This Regulation sets out rules that are complementary to that approach as well as to the rules set out in Council Directive 2001/55/EC, which can be used at the same time."

This socio-legal evolution reflects the EU's attempt to balance flexibility and legal certainty while responding to complex geopolitical realities. The war in Ukraine served as a catalyst, not only demonstrating the necessity of the TPD but also influencing the broader direction of the Pact.[128] At the same time, the Pact introduces new instruments that intersect with—but do not supersede—existing frameworks.

The *Exceptions Regulation* and the *Solidarity Pool* under the AMMR are designed to handle different dimensions of crisis: while the TPD provides group-based temporary protection, the Crisis Regulation offers derogatory procedural rules during crises, and the Solidarity Pool operationalises responsibility-sharing among Member States. Furthermore, the Crisis Regulation also includes further derogations from the common asylum procedure when addressing the use of migrants by third countries as a political tool. The new rules represent the EU's effort to legally codify responses to external geopolitical pressures—such as those exerted by Russia or Belarus—that weaponise migration.

In sum, the reformed crisis framework now consists of three main tools—the TPD, the Crisis Regulation, and the Solidarity Pool—which may operate independently or concurrently.[129] This layered architecture reflects the EU's effort to create a more resilient and flexible system capable of responding to both humanitarian emergencies and geopolitical manipulation of migration flows.

---

[124] Commission 2020a.

[125] Commission 2020a.

[126] Carrera S, İneli-Ciğer M (eds) 2023.

[127] İneli-Ciğer 2024a, p.16.

[128] Trauner F, Wolff S 2024.

[129] Preamble (3) Regulation 2024/1359.

9.4.2 The Exceptions Regulation

The Exceptions Regulation creates a new crisis-response tool allowing Member States to derogate from EU asylum standards during situations of mass influx, force majeure, or instrumentalisation of migration. Unlike the TPD, which grants immediate protection, the Regulation primarily facilitates procedural derogations that risk undermining core asylum rights.[130] It is an overly complex and intricate framework.[131]

In contrast to the TPD, the Exceptions Regulation is not only applicable to mass influx situations, but it also foresees the application to other exception situations defined in Articles 1(4)—crisis, which, according to the Regulation, unfold in two different possibilities—mass arrivals or instrumentalisation[132] and; (5)—force majeure.[133] The Regulation brings broad and flexible definitions seeking to provide adaptability. Still, it risks legal uncertainty and inconsistent interpretation. This ambiguity may undermine the CEAS, affect humanitarian actors, and lead to ongoing institutional disagreements over the use of derogations and solidarity measures in crisis situations.[134]

While formally complementing the TPD, the Exceptions Regulation shifts the EU's crisis response towards a securitised, state-centric model. Its broader scope—covering not only mass influx but also geopolitical manipulation—reflects the EU's growing focus on migration as a threat rather than a humanitarian challenge.

This regulation seeks to improve crisis preparedness and strengthen the governance of the CEAS alongside the AMMR. However, its effectiveness is limited by persistent gaps and ambiguities. While Member States are expected to maintain resilient asylum and migration systems to access solidarity measures, the Regulation does not clearly link this to the use of existing support tools.[135] This dual-track framework raises fundamental questions: Is the Exceptions Regulation a protective tool or a legal avenue to restrict access to asylum? Academic critiques warn that it risks becoming a "loophole" enabling states to sideline international protection norms under the guise of crisis,[136] and affirm that while it does not eliminate the right to asylum, there is a risk that Member States "given an inch, will take a mile" to

130 İneli-Ciğer 2024a.

131 İneli-Ciğer 2024b.

132 The Regulation classifies "instrumentalisation" of migrants as a form of crisis, contrary to the Commission's initial plan for a separate instrument. Some Member States continue to seek special treatment of such situations and for further targeted measures, prompting calls for further reforms, including a joint letter from 15 Member States in May 2024 See A H Neidhardt, 2024.

133 Understood as abnormal, unforeseeable events that prevent a Member State from meeting its obligations under EU Regulations 2024/1351 and 2024/1348, despite all efforts to comply.

134 İneli-Ciğer, 2024a.

135 Ibid.

136 Kaiser J and Schug S (2024) Unpacking the most contested elements of the EU's new migration and asylum pact. https://www.theparliamentmagazine.eu/news/article/unpacking-the-most-contested-elements-of-the-eus-new-migration-and-asylum-pact. Accessed 20 September 2025..

further restrict asylum rights in practice, with the Commission potentially facilitating this trend.[137]

Unlike the TPD's automatic rights-based protection, the Exceptions Regulation offers no mandatory prima facie status.[138] Instead, it provides states with extensive discretion to delay registrations, prolong border procedures, and derogate responsibility-sharing rules, which might effectively limit access to protection rather than expanding it.

9.4.2.1 Triggering

For all scenarios, the triggering mechanisms are the same. A Member State facing a crisis or force majeure can request solidarity measures and limited derogations from asylum procedures, provided fundamental rights are respected (Article 2(1)). The Commission then assesses the request and, if conditions under Article 1 are met, adopts an implementing decision within two weeks (Article 3(1)). The Council must then assess the Commission's proposal, when appropriate, and adopt its own decision—also within two weeks—authorizing derogations (Articles 10–13) and establishing a Solidarity Response Plan foreseen in Article 4(2)(b) (Article 4(3)). Additionally, the Commission may recommend expedited protection procedures for certain applicant groups (Article 14).

Although designed to strengthen migration governance, this procedure continues to present gaps, raising potential sources of tension and legal uncertainty. For example, the procedure's tight deadlines for issuing the implementing decisions, combined with the complexity of potential crisis scenarios, pose a significant challenge.[139]

Other than that, the limited duration of the measures under the Exceptions Regulation raises further concerns. The Council's implementing decision is time-limited,[140] with measures lasting a maximum of 12 months—initially set for three months and extendable up to three additional times (Article 5(3)).[141] These measures can also be terminated earlier if the crisis or force majeure ends (Article 6(3)). However, it remains unclear what happens if the situation persists beyond the 12-month limit,

---

[137] Peers 2024b).

[138] See Sect. 9.4.2.6 below.

[139] Neidhardt 2024.

[140] Peers 2024a, p. 59.

[141] Initially 3 months, with a 3-month extension confirmed by the Commission; then another Council decision amending it or prolonging it for 3 months, again with a possible 3-month extension if the Commission agrees, according to Articles 5 and 6.

how soon a Member State could request a new decision[142] or and how the simultaneous management of multiple crises (as allowed in Preamble (25)) would be coordinated.[143] This limited timeframe raises concerns, especially given the Commission's past willingness to extend legal interpretations—as seen with Article 4(2) of the TPD[144]—which can lead to extended use of derogations, increasing the risk of fragmentation within the CEAS.

There are three different categories of measures that can be taken under the Exceptions Regulations and analysed below: derogation measures, expedited asylum procedures and solidarity measures. According to the Preamble (25), the Member States can apply or benefit from those measures simultaneously, as they are designed to work complementarily.

9.4.2.2 Derogation Measures

The Exceptions Regulation introduces multiple derogations from existing EU asylum and migration frameworks to address crisis situations. There are three primary exceptions and special provisions, which include extended registration deadlines for asylum applications, border procedure expansions, and Dublin procedures derogations (soon to be Asylum and Migration Management).

The Regulation does not allow Member States to suspend the right to asylum in situations of crisis or force majeure. The permitted derogations are strictly time-limited and procedural, allowing only for delays in registration, extended deadlines, or longer border procedures—none of which revoke the fundamental right to seek asylum. These measures must still comply with EU law and human rights obligations, including the principle of non-refoulement.[145]

Although those measures should be tailored to a specific Member State situation, given the interconnectedness of national asylum and reception systems, poorly balanced derogations could lead to negative spill-over effects and risk turning a national emergency into an EU-wide crisis. It is therefore crucial that the Commission and Council ensure affected Member States receive adequate support while continuing to meet their broader obligations. Derogations should only be authorised when strictly necessary to address the specific crisis or force majeure situation.[146]

9.4.2.3 Extended Registration Deadlines for Asylum Applications

Article 10(1) extends the deadlines to register applications from five days according to Article 27(1) of Regulation (EU) 2024/1348 or eight days under Article 27(3), up

---

[142] Peers 2024a, p. 59.

[143] Neidhardt 2024.

[144] İneli-Ciğer 2024a.

[145] Peers 2024b.

[146] Neidhardt 2024.

to four weeks. As stated in Preamble (24), this derogation may be applied immediately—up to 10 days after the request is submitted to the Commission—even before formal Council approval. If the Council later authorises it under Article 4(3), the derogation can continue beyond that initial period (Article 10(6)). In this matter, the Regulation presents some inconsistency: while it urges the Commission to assess requests quickly to minimise the gap between the immediate application of registration delays and the Council's decision, the derogation lasts only 10 days, yet the Council's decision may take up to two weeks after the Commission's proposal—potentially leaving a procedural gap.[147]

Article 10(4) further clarifies that the extended registration deadline in crisis situations can only be applied during the initial three-month period set by the Council implementing decision under Article 4(3), as outlined in Article 5(1). It cannot be used during any subsequent extensions mentioned in Article 5(1) or (2).

This derogation still imposes certain obligations on Member States. They must prioritise applicants with special reception needs, minors and their families (as defined in Directive 2024/1346), and those likely to have well-founded claims (Article 10(2)–(3)). Member States must also guarantee effective access to rights from the moment an application is made, including clear, accessible information about the process (Article 10(5)). Crucially, the extension does not affect the obligation to transmit biometric data to Eurodac within 72 h for applicants at borders or transit zones who do not meet entry conditions (Article 10(7)). Nonetheless, scholars[148] have raised concerns about this measure, arguing that allowing delayed registrations—and consequently delaying the issuance of documents confirming applicants' status and providing essential information about their application—may create practical barriers that hinder applicants' ability to access their rights for a protracted period.

9.4.2.4 Border Procedure Expansions

Article 11 sets out exceptional measures for the asylum border procedure during crises or force majeure. Under Article 11(1), Member States may extend the border procedure by six weeks, up to a maximum of 18 weeks. Article 11(2) allows them to suspend examining certain applications if national contingency plans are insufficient, excluding cases of instrumentalisation. In mass influx situations, Article 11(3) permits lowering the threshold for accelerated procedures from 20 to 5%, while Article 11(4) allows merit-based decisions for applicants from countries with EU-wide protection rates below 50%. These two measures must prioritise vulnerable groups, including those with special needs, minors, and likely well-founded claims (Article 11(5)). Nevertheless, as more applicants may be channelled into border

---

147 Neidhardt 2024.

148 Neidhardt 2024.

procedures, national authorities could face difficulties in managing their responsibilities effectively while ensuring the timely and accurate identification of individuals with special needs.[149]

Overall, those measures allow the personal scope of border procedures to be tailored to the specific characteristics of each situation. While this flexibility may help ease pressure on national authorities, scholars[150] argue that it can also, paradoxically, lead to increased administrative burdens, depending on how the measures are implemented.

Crucially, Articles 11(10)–(11) ensure that these derogations uphold fundamental rights, including the right to asylum, non-refoulement, and the guarantees set out in Regulation (EU) 2024/1348—such as access to an effective remedy. Yet, this situation raises concerns among experts[151] and advocacy organisations, as Member States may impose certain limitations on these activities for reasons of public order, security, or administrative necessity, as long as such restrictions do not unduly hinder access, possibly undermining human rights. The CJEU already ruled[152] that in situations of instrumentalisation, Member States could not detain asylum seekers solely for irregular entry or refuse to process their applications. Nevertheless, these derogations might open the room for Member States to attempt similar measures indirectly, such as by detaining people on border procedure grounds, and by closing border posts.[153]

Lastly, these derogations should not affect the responsibility determination process under Regulation 2024/1351, which must continue, and if it exceeds time limits, the determining Member State must finalise the procedure under Article 51 of Regulation 2024/1348.

9.4.2.5 Dublin Procedures Derogations

Articles 12 and 13 of the Exceptions Regulation introduce flexibility within the Dublin system (soon to be the Asylum and Migration Management System) to support Member States in mass influx or force majeure situations under exceptional pressure. Article 12 allows Member States facing mass influx or force majeure to derogate from key procedural deadlines (Articles 39, 40, 41, and 46 of Regulation 2024/1351) if timely actions are taken. In such cases, transfers to the responsible Member State may be suspended unless that state explicitly agrees to receive the applicant and depending on the case, the Member State may retain or receive responsibility for examining the application under Regulation (EU) 2024/1351 (Article 12(3)).

---

149 Neidhardt 2024.

150 Neidhardt 2024.

151 Tan and İneli Ciğer 2024; Neidhardt 2024.

152 CJEU, Staatssecretaris van Justitie en Veiligheid v. X. Judgment of 30 June 2022. Case C-72/22 ECLI:EU:C:2022:505.

153 Peers 2024b.

Although Article 12 does not explicitly mention it, Recital 52 clarifies that the extension and possible transfer of responsibility is without prejudice to the option of prolonging transfer deadlines under Article 46(2) RAMM. This could, in practice, cancel the benefit to the affected Member State as it allows transfer deadlines to be extended up to three years in cases where the applicant absconds, resists transfer, or fails to comply with medical requirements. Such grounds are already frequently invoked by Member States under the current Dublin system.[154]

It should be noted that, delaying a transfer up to one year will lead to uncertainty, stress and anxiety for asylum applicants which should be considered regarding both outgoing and incoming transfers. In this sense, the ECRE[155] recommends that when this derogation is applied, Member States should promptly assess whether a transfer is feasible and, if not, immediately apply discretionary clauses. Prolonging applicants' uncertainty until the one-year deadline expires contradicts the purpose of the responsibility rules, which seek to ensure a fair and efficient asylum system across the EU.

Article 13 goes further by enabling a Member State under severe strain from mass arrivals to be temporarily relieved of its obligation to take back asylum seekers. Responsibility may shift to another Member State—typically where the second application was lodged—or, if no other responsible state is identified, the latter becomes responsible for examining the claim.

This measure is considered by experts[156] to be one of the few that offers concrete and immediate relief to Member States facing a crisis, while also respecting applicants' autonomy by avoiding forced transfers and allowing their claims to be examined in the country they moved to. However, it remains unclear when this derogation can be triggered, as mass arrivals already imply serious consequences under Article 1(4)(a) of the Crisis Regulation and the additional requirements to meet the threshold for activation of the derogation are not set out.

9.4.2.6 Expedited Asylum Procedures

The second measure introduced by the Exceptions Regulation is the welcomed use of expedited asylum procedures for likely well-founded applications, as outlined in Article 14, covering all grounds for international protection, beyond only situations of armed conflict—as initially foreseen in the Commission's proposal.[157] Although Member States are not required to apply this procedure, once they choose to do so, they are bound by the provisions of Article 14 of the Crisis Regulation. In such

---

[154] ECRE (2024d) 'Comments on the Regulation of the European Parliament and of the Council Addressing Situations of Crisis and Force Majeure in the Field of Migration and Asylum and Amending Regulation (EU) 2021/1147' https://ecre.org/wp-content/uploads/2024/05/ECRE_Comments_Crisis-and-Force-Majeure-Regulation.pdf. Accessed 20 September 2025.

[155] Ibid.

[156] Ibid.

[157] Ibid.

cases, the Commission may issue a recommendation—after consulting the High-Level EU Solidarity Forum and relevant actors such as UNHCR—to support the use of accelerated processing. This may include omitting the personal interview (Article 13(12)(a), Regulation 2024/1348) and prioritising the application (Article 34(5)(a), Regulation 2024/1348). The examination of the claim must then be completed within four weeks of lodging, rather than the standard six-month timeframe set in Article 35(4) of Regulation 2024/1348.

Scholars[158] argue that this expedited procedure falls under the definition of *prima facie* procedures[159] and that the option to grant prima facie international protection to groups with likely well-founded claims is a positive step aligned with the Refugee Convention. However, its practical use is uncertain, as Member States may prefer to apply the Temporary Protection Directive instead—allowing them to offer temporary status while deferring longer-term obligations linked to refugee recognition. Other than that, it is also possible to find contrary opinions[160] affirming that the expedited procedure does not go as far as *prima facie* recognition as recommended by UNHCR.

Nevertheless, if considered a *prima facie* procedure, there are three possible scenarios for using expedited asylum procedures during crisis situations: group-based determination, legislative individual fast-track procedure and administrative individual fast-track procedure. The first one is inspired by the TPD[161] and the recognition of entire groups as eligible for protection based on nationality or prior status in the country of origin. On the second approach, refugee status is granted based on 'file review' only, without an interview, under a formal fast-track process in national law for certain asylum profiles deemed "less complex." Lastly, the third this model would expedite cases at the administrative level, guided by national asylum authorities' precedents.

Overall, the targeted use of expedited procedures—particularly when based on nationality or country of origin—could provide a practical and legally sound alternative to the TPD, enhancing the Crisis Regulation's ability to respond effectively to emergencies.[162] Still, it remains uncertain whether these procedures will ensure immediate protection or simply fast-track processing at the expense of procedural safeguards (Preamble 56),[163] with past practice suggesting that the latter—a more restrictive interpretation—is the most likely outcome.

---

158 Tan and İneli Ciğer 2024.

159 Understood as the "approach as processes that recognize asylum seekers as in need of international protection on a group basis, based on a common risk of harm arising from circumstances in the country of origin." Ibid.

160 ECRE, 2024a.

161 With the TPD activation, individuals seeking protection were granted immediate access to EU territory. In many Member States, their temporary protection status was registered either on the same day or within a few days. This illustrates how group-based recognition can serve as an effective and protective tool in crisis situations. See N F Tan and İneli Ciğer 2024.

162 Ibid.

163 İneli-Ciğer M 2024a.

9.4.2.7 Solidarity Measures

The lack of an effective solidarity mechanism, as acknowledged by the Commission in 2020,[164] has led some Member States to disengage from their responsibilities—at times resorting to practices such as "waving through" migrants or conducting illegal pushbacks.[165]

In response to these shortcomings, Article 8 of the Exceptions Regulation introduces structured solidarity and support measures in crisis situations. These include relocation, financial contributions, and alternative solidarity actions (Article 8(1)), with a clear emphasis on prioritising vulnerable groups during relocation (Article 8(2)). Nevertheless, concerns have been raised[166] about the compatibility of these measures with broader human rights standards, particularly regarding the potential use of strategies to prevent onward movement from third countries, which may risk undermining the principle of non-refoulement.

Article 9 of the Exceptions Regulation establishes responsibility offset measures, allowing up to 100% of unmet relocation needs to be redistributed to contributing Member States when initial pledges fall short. However, these offsets cannot be applied if a Member State opts out of the take-back obligation under Article 11 of the TPD or if Article 13 of the Exceptions Regulation is triggered. If relocation needs remain unmet, the High-Level EU Solidarity Forum must be reconvened (Article 9(2)). Additionally, Articles 9(3)–(5) enable a Member State receiving solidarity support to request other Member States to assume responsibility for certain asylum claims, with contributing States permitted to reduce future solidarity contributions in return, under specific conditions. Finally, Articles 9(7)–(8) allow contributing Member States to request support or reduced contributions if they become overwhelmed, ensuring that both the Solidarity Pool and additional support measures can operate simultaneously in crisis situations. Although responsibility offsets are advantageous to Member States and applicants alike, they might have their value reduced, considering it was designed as a last resort solidarity measure.[167]

While solidarity measures can support Member States during crises, they further complicate the already complex solidarity framework under the RAMM once the mechanism introduces adjustment scenarios for increased support or exemptions, adding to the system's overall complexity. In this context, scholars[168] affirm that the effectiveness of those measures will depend on clever and targeted choices, for example, through the use of relocations as they—together with responsibility offsets—represent the most effective forms of solidarity support for overburdened Member States compared to the other available options.

[164] Commission 2020b.

[165] Maiani F 2024.

[166] ECRE 2024a.

[167] Ibid.

[168] Ibid.

9.4.3 *Solidarity Pool*

Similar to the Exceptions Regulation, the Solidarity Pool under the Asylum and Migration Management Regulation (EU) 2024/1351 offers three types of solidarity contributions: relocations, financial support, and alternative measures (Article 56(2)).[169] In crisis situations, Member States can access a broader range of measures compared to when facing high migration flows, including the Annual Solidarity Pool and potential reductions in contributions, as determined by the Commission and the Council (Articles 10 and 12).[170]

In line with concerns raised in relation to other measures, questions likewise arise regarding this provision, particularly with respect to its practical implementation and overall effectiveness, notwithstanding the introduction of innovative mechanisms intended to address emerging needs. For instance, when the Solidarity Pool falls short, the Council is expected to seek additional pledges in its Implementing Decision, yet there is no assurance that these needs will be fully met. Moreover, if the Pool is fully used during a prolonged crisis, the Regulation offers no clear process for its replenishment to address ongoing or future demands.[171]

9.5 Comparative Analysis of the Temporary Protection Directive and the Exceptions Regulation: Scope, Activation, and Protection Frameworks

In terms of scope, the Temporary Protection Directive (TPD) was designed exclusively to address mass-influx situations. By contrast, the Exceptions Regulation extends beyond mass influx, encompassing two additional exceptional scenarios: instrumentalisation and force majeure, as outlined in Article 1(4). This broader scope introduces new dimensions to the EU's crisis response toolkit.

Regarding activation, the TPD is triggered by two cumulative conditions: the occurrence of a mass influx of displaced persons, as defined in Article 2(d), and the risk of overwhelming a Member State's asylum system. The Exceptions Regulation, however, permits the invocation of derogation and solidarity measures when a "crisis" is formally declared. Specifically, this occurs when the asylum, reception (including child protection), or return system of a Member State is rendered non-functional due to a large-scale influx, as detailed in Article 1(4)(a). Crucially, the Commission is tasked with assessing whether the affected Member State—even if adequately prepared—has been overwhelmed by such an influx, thereby jeopardising the functioning of the Common European Asylum System (CEAS). Notably, the European Parliament introduced the "well-prepared" requirement in Article 1(4)(a), ensuring

[169] Maiani 2024.

[170] İnel-Ciğer 2024a.

[171] Neidhardt 2024.

that pre-existing structural deficiencies cannot be mischaracterised as crisis-induced failures.

In comparison, the TPD leaves "mass influx" vaguely defined, whereas the Exceptions Regulation provides more precise indicators (Article 3(6)) for triggering derogations. Nevertheless, scholars[172] still argue that the Regulation's broad and flexible definitions—though intended to ensure adaptability—risk generating legal uncertainty and inconsistent interpretation. This ambiguity may undermine the coherence of the CEAS, fuel institutional disagreements over the application of derogations and solidarity measures, and leave significant discretion to Member States in determining whether exceptional migratory movements constitute a mass influx or a crisis.[173]

Procedurally, both instruments require a qualified majority of the Council upon a proposal by the Commission. Yet, their activation mechanisms diverge. The TPD employs a two-step process whereby the Commission may act *ex officio* (Article 5). In contrast, the Exceptions Regulation follows a three-step process initiated by a Member State's request. It further mandates consultations post-crisis declaration (Preamble 27), with strict procedural timelines: the Commission must assess the request within two weeks, after which the Council has an additional two weeks to decide on the proposal for an implementing decision (Articles 3(8) and 4(3)).

With regard to protection, scholars[174] observe that the TPD operates on a *quid pro quo* basis: it guarantees immediate access to temporary protection status and specific rights for those fleeing mass-influx situations, in exchange for certain derogations. The Exceptions Regulation departs from this approach, potentially restricting core rights—such as the right to seek asylum, liberty and security, effective remedy, and humane treatment—depending on the scope and application of the derogations.[175]

The TPD thus prioritises a rights-based framework, ensuring immediate protection and minimum rights. Conversely, the Exceptions Regulation lacks explicit provisions for automatic protection. The closest equivalent is found in Article 14, which allows a Member State—at its discretion—to adopt the Commission's recommendation to apply expedited procedures to certain third-country nationals and stateless persons. However, it remains unclear whether such expedited procedures imply prima facie recognition or merely the acceleration of asylum processing at the expense of procedural safeguards (Preamble 56).[176] Moreover, minimum rights are ambiguously addressed in the Exceptions Regulation. Article 2(1) references general respect for fundamental rights, while Article 10(5) includes limited safeguards for applicants with special needs. Other than that, the Regulation does not establish a specific, mandatory, or independent monitoring mechanism for fundamental rights in crisis or force majeure situations. Although the Commission may request the EUAA to carry out targeted monitoring exercises and oversight mechanisms provided under

[172] Neidhardt 2024.

[173] İneli-Ciğer 2024a.

[174] Ibid.

[175] Ibid.

[176] İneli-Ciğer 2024a.

other legal instruments remain applicable, questions remain whether those measures would effectively address potential gaps in accountability and protection.[177]

The temporal scope of these instruments also diverges significantly. The TPD, initially limited, now extends up to four years, reflecting the protracted nature of certain displacement situations. By contrast, measures under the Exceptions Regulation are capped at one year. Although formally limited, critics warn of potential repeated extensions or renewed requests, risking an "emergency creep" that normalises exceptional measures. This temporal fragility contrasts sharply with the TPD's longer-term horizon, which fosters greater stability.

Ultimately, these differences create a two-speed protection system. Beneficiaries of the TPD—currently including Ukrainians—enjoy clearer, though unevenly implemented, rights. In contrast, other groups—or potentially Ukrainians in future geopolitical shifts—may fall under the Exceptions Regulation's framework, facing reduced protections and heightened precarity.

Setting reasonable temporal limits for emergency mechanisms is essential to enable transitions toward durable solutions.[178] UNHCR suggests that five years is an average duration for temporary protection. The implementation of the TPD has demonstrated that three years is insufficient for effective transitions, and the legal contortions required to extend it raise concerns about the credibility and coherence of time limits within the broader protection framework.

On one hand, the TPD aligns with the EU's human rights obligations, offering practical tools for urgent protection during mass influxes.[179] Despite persistent implementation gaps that demand redress, the TPD's design has largely succeeded. However, fragmented implementation undermines long-term solutions, emphasising the need for stronger EU-level coordination as several Member States continue to struggle with ensuring basic rights and facilitating durable solutions within national frameworks.[180] This necessity grows increasingly apparent as the war in Ukraine illustrates the importance of transforming emergency responses into medium- and long-term integration strategies—a task that must respect national competencies while improving collective coherence.[181]

On the other hand, the New Pact on Migration and Asylum and the Global Compacts adopt fundamentally divergent approaches. While the New Pact emphasises border management and security-driven policies, the Global Compact for Migration (GCM) and the Global Compact on Refugees (GCR) prioritise human rights, due process, and access to justice,[182] reaffirming state sovereignty alongside the rule of law. Scholars[183] argue that the New Pact missed an opportunity to

177 Neidhardt 2024.

178 Ibid.

179 Näre and Tkach 2024.

180 Neidhardt 2024.

181 Kvorning Lassen C (2022) and İneli Ciğer M (2022).

182 Trauner F, Wolff S 2024.

183 Kvorning 2022.

leverage crisis-forged structures to move beyond temporary political compromises, advocating instead for tangible incentives to enhance Member State cooperation.

The Exceptions Regulation exemplifies this tension. By offering greater flexibility for derogations, it grants governments broad discretion, potentially facilitating restrictive and fragmented responses that risk violating fundamental rights.[184] This shift underscores a broader trend within EU asylum policy—privileging securitization over protection—with profound implications for the future of the CEAS.

9.6 Conclusions: Lessons Learned and Prospects for the Future

The global migration framework, particularly the principles enshrined in the two global compacts, is rooted in a human-rights-based approach. In mass influx situations, this approach would rely on three key pillars: effective crisis management, ensuring timely and coordinated responses to displacement; temporality, with a clear and limited timeframe for temporary protection and a focus on identifying durable solutions; and the safeguarding of protection needs, guaranteeing that asylum seekers have access to rights and essential services from the outset. This perspective recognises the complexity of crisis scenarios and the need for adaptable emergency measures, while emphasising that such flexibility must not compromise legal certainty or the protection of fundamental rights.

On the one hand, the TPD prioritises a rights-based framework, guaranteeing immediate protection and minimum rights and aligning with a global protection framework. While the shortcomings in the implementation do not undermine its success, it calls out urgent attention to the fragmentation of the system and the need to address it swiftly and effectively. The resulting picture of the exacerbated focus on the margin of discretion is a high degree of legal uncertainty concerning the obligations of relevant Member States, which leads to inconsistent and potentially discriminatory and insufficient national approaches, raising concerns about adequate coverage and long-term sustainability. This issue has become even more relevant with the Commission's recent proposal on the exit strategy, which emphasises transition to national migration statuses instead of pursuing a common EU-wide approach, risking further fragmentation in dealing with mass-influx situations. At the same time, these challenges could offer guidance for future displacement crises and migrant protection policy design and implementation.

On the other hand, while the Exceptions Regulation introduces measures to help Member States handle large-scale arrivals, its derogations risk compromising international and EU law obligations rather than significantly easing the burden on states.[185] Other than that, derogations might not address the root causes of a crisis,

[184] Neidhardt 2024.

[185] İneli Ciğer 2024b.

only treating the symptoms, if not coupled with further concerted actions—including diplomatic, political, and policy initiatives—which go beyond the means foreseen by the Exceptions Regulation.[186] The uncertain access to protection for asylum seekers and the security-driven approach adopted by the Exception Regulation do not align with the broader international protection framework. The lessons from the TPD implementation, particularly the fragmentation it caused, appear to have been overlooked. The EU missed a crucial opportunity to establish a cohesive mass-influx framework with a robust crisis management structure and has instead reinforced legal uncertainties and disjointed national responses.

This chapter argues that while the New Pact on Migration introduces a broader set of crisis management tools within the EU, it might weaken the system depending on the implementation. The isolated application of the derogation measures in the Exceptions Regulation, without its use alongside the TPD, can exacerbate the system fragmentation, threaten basic rights and undermine adherence to the international protection framework. Although the TPD has implementation shortcomings, it remains more aligned with international protection standards, offering a structured response to mass influx situations, reducing precarity in exile, and prioritising durable solutions. Therefore, an integrated approach, where the new crisis management tools are used in tandem with the TPD, ensuring its minimum rights framework remains intact, would be a more effective strategy than a purely complementary application.

This chapter is funded by the European Research Council 2022 Starting Grant *Gatekeepers to International Refugee Law—The Role of Courts in Shaping Access to Asylum* [101078683].

References

Articles, Books and Other Documents

Betts A (2010) Soft Law and the Protection of Vulnerable Migrants. Georgetown Immigration Law Journal 24(3): 533–552. Accessed 8 September 2025.

Betts A, Kainz L (2017) The History of Global Migration Governance. Refugee Studies Centre Working Paper No. 122. https://www.rsc.ox.ac.uk/publications/the-history-of-global-migration-governance. Accessed 8 September 2025.

Carrera S, Geddes A (eds) (2021) The EU Pact on Migration and Asylum in Light of the United Nations Global Compact on Refugees: International Experiences on Containment and Mobility and Their Impacts on Trust and Rights. European University Institute. https://hdl.handle.net/1814/70600. Accessed 8 September 2025.

Carrera S, İneli-Ciğer M (eds) (2023) EU Responses to the Large-Scale Refugee Displacement from Ukraine: An Analysis of the Temporary Protection Directive and Its Implications for the Future EU Asylum Policy. European University Institute. https://cadmus.eui.eu/handle/1814/75377. Accessed 8 September 2025.

Chimni BS (2000) Globalization, Humanitarianism and the Erosion of Refugee Protection. Journal of Refugee Studies 13(3): 243–263. https://doi.org/10.1093/jrs/13.3.243. Accessed 8 September 2025.

[186] Neidhardt 2024.

Council Directive (2001) Directive 2001/55/EC of 20 July 2001 on minimum standards for giving temporary protection in the event of a mass influx of displaced persons and on measures promoting a balance of efforts between Member States in receiving such persons and bearing the consequences thereof OJ L212/12.

Council Decision (2015) Decision 2015/1601 of 22 September 2015 establishing provisional measures in the area of international protection for the benefit of Italy and Greece OJ L248/80.

Council Implementing Decision (2025) Implementing Decision 2025/1460 of 15 July 2025 extending the temporary protection introduced by Implementing Decision (EU) 2022/382 *OJ L, 2025/1460*

Durieux JF (2014) Temporary Protection: Hovering at the Edges of Refugee Law. Netherlands Yearbook of International Law 45: 221–253. https://doi.org/10.1007/978-94-6265-060-2_9. Accessed 8 September 2025.

Durieux JF (2021) Temporary Protection and Temporary Refuge. In: Costello C, Foster M, McAdam J (eds) The Oxford Handbook of International Refugee Law. Oxford University Press, Oxford. Accessed 8 September 2025.

Edlund J, Stehlík V (2021) A Migrant's Right to Respect for Family Life—The Problematic Developments of the European Court of Human Rights' Case Law. International and Comparative Law Review 21(2): 116–137. https://doi.org/10.2478/iclr-2021-0021. Accessed 8 September 2025.

Eurofound (2024) Social Impact of Migration: Addressing the Challenges of Receiving and Integrating Ukrainian Refugees. Publications Office of the European Union. Accessed 8 September 2025.

European Commission (2020a) Proposal for a Regulation Addressing Situations of Crisis and Force Majeure in Migration and Asylum. COM(2020) 613 final. https://eur-lex.europa.eu/legal-content/EN/TXT/?uri=CELEX:52020PC0613. Accessed 8 September 2025.

European Commission (2020b) Communication on a New Pact on Migration and Asylum. COM(2020) 609 final. https://eur-lex.europa.eu/legal-content/EN/TXT/?uri=CELEX:52020DC0609. Accessed 8 September 2025.

European Commission (2020c) Communication to the European Parliament, the Council, the EESC and the CoR on a New Pact on Migration and Asylum. COM(2020) 610 final. https://eur-lex.europa.eu/legal-content/EN/TXT/?uri=COM:2020:610:FIN. Accessed 8 September 2025.

European Commission (2022) Communication on Operational Guidelines for the Implementation of Council Implementing Decision (EU) 2022/382 of 8 March 2022. [Online]. https://eur-lex.europa.eu/legal-content/EN/TXT/?uri=oj:JOC_2022_126_I_0001. Accessed 8 September 2025.

European Commission (2022) Proposal for a Council Implementing Decision establishing the existence of a mass influx of displaced persons from Ukraine within the meaning of Article 5 of Council Directive 2001/55/EC COM 91 final. https://eur-lex.europa.eu/legal-content/EN/TXT/?uri=celex:52022PC0091. Accessed 8 September 2025.

European Commission (2023) Proposal for a Council Implementing Decision Extending Temporary Protection as Introduced by Implementing Decision (EU) 2022/382. COM(2023) 546 final. https://eur-lex.europa.eu/legal-content/EN/TXT/?uri=COM:2023:546:FIN. Accessed 8 September 2025.

European Commission (2025a) Proposal for a Council Recommendation on a coordinated approach to the transition out of temporary protection for displaced persons from Ukraine. COM (2025) 651 final. https://eur-lex.europa.eu/legal-content/EN/TXT/?uri=COM:2025:651:FIN. Accessed 8 September 2025.

European Commission (2025b) Communication from the Commission to the European Parliament, the Council, the European Economic and Social Committee and the Committee of the Regions—A predictable and common European way forward for Ukrainians in the EU. COM (2025) 649 final. https://eur-lex.europa.eu/legal-content/EN/TXT/HTML/?uri=CELEX:52025DC0649. Accessed 8 September 2025.

European Union Agency for Asylum (EUAA) (2024a) Jurisprudence on the Application of the Temporary Protection Directive: Analysis of Case Law from 2022–2024. https://euaa.europa.eu/sites/default/files/publications/2024-10/2024_jurisprudence_Temporary_Protection_Directive_EN.pdf. Accessed 8 September 2025.
European Union Agency for Asylum (EUAA) (2024b) Surveys of Arriving Migrants from Ukraine: Movements and Returns Report. https://euaa.europa.eu/publications/surveys-arriving-migrants-ukraine-movements-and-returns-report. Accessed 8 September 2025.
European Union Agency for Asylum (EUAA) (2025a) Temporary Protection. EUAA Who's Who. https://whoiswho.euaa.europa.eu/temporary-protection. Accessed 8 September 2025.
European Union Agency for Asylum (EUAA) (2025b) Latest Asylum Trends 2024: Annual Analysis. https://euaa.europa.eu/sites/default/files/publications/2025-02/EUAA_Latest_Asylum_Trends_2024.pdf. Accessed 8 September 2025.
Eurostat (2022) Temporary Protection for Persons Fleeing Ukraine—Monthly Statistics. https://ec.europa.eu/eurostat/statistics-explained/index.php?title=Temporary_protection_for_persons_fleeing_Ukraine_-_monthly_statistics. Accessed 8 September 2025.
Feith Tan N, İneli-Ciğer M (2024) Beyond Derogations in the EU Crisis Regulation: Making Expedited Procedures for Manifestly Well-Founded Asylum Claims Work in Practice. European Journal of Migration and Law 26(4): 421–445. Accessed 8 September 2025.
Fitzpatrick J (2000) Temporary Protection of Refugees: Elements of a Formalized Regime. American Journal of International Law 94(2): 279–306. https://doi.org/10.2307/2555293. Accessed 8 September 2025.
Gluns D, Wessels J (2017) Waste of Paper or Useful Tool? The Potential of the Temporary Protection Directive in the Current "Refugee Crisis". Refugee Survey Quarterly 36(2): 57–83. https://doi.org/10.1093/rsq/hdx001. Accessed 8 September 2025.
Greenhill KM (2022) When Migrants Become Weapons. Foreign Affairs 101(2): 130–142.
Hathaway JC (2007) The Rights of Refugees under International Law. Cambridge University Press, Cambridge. Accessed 8 September 2025.
Imbert L (2022) Immigration: fabrique d'un discours de crise. [Immigration: the making of a crisis narrative] Éditions du Cerf, Paris.
İneli-Ciğer M (2016) Time to Activate the Temporary Protection Directive. European Journal of Migration and Law 18(1): 1–26. https://brill.com/view/journals/emil/18/1/article-p1_1.xml. Accessed 8 September 2025.
İneli Ciğer M (2022) 5 Reasons Why: Understanding the reasons behind the activation of the Temporary Protection Directive in 2022. https://eumigrationlawblog.eu/5-reasons-why-understanding-the-reasons-behind-the-activation-of-the-temporary-protection-directive-in-2022/. Accessed 20 September 2025.
İneli-Ciğer M (2024a) Navigating the labyrinth of derogations: A critical look at the Crisis Regulation. https://eumigrationlawblog.eu/navigating-the-labyrinth-of-derogations-a-critical-look-at-the-crisis-regulation/. Accessed 15 September 2025.
İneli-Ciğer M (2024b) Unpacking the Crisis Regulation: A Valuable Addition to the European Legal Framework Governing Mass Influx Situations? RSC Working Paper No. 2024/40. European University Institute. https://hdl.handle.net/1814/77282. Accessed 8 September 2025.
Koo J (2017) The European Union Temporary Protection Directive: An Example of Solidarity in Law but Not in Practice. Refugee Law Initiative Working Papers (Special Edition, 1st Annual Conference): 176–205. https://openresearch.lsbu.ac.uk/item/8701v. Accessed 8 September 2025.
Kvorning Lassen C (2022) The New Pact on Migration and Asylum and the War in Ukraine: Time for a Paradigm Shift? EUROPEUM Institute for European Policy (Policy Paper). https://www.europeum.org/wp-content/uploads/ckl-intempl-final-edit.pdf. Accessed 8 September 2025.
Maiani F (2024) The new solidarity mechanism: The right "insurance scheme" for the CEAS? EU Immigration and Asylum Law and Policy. https://eumigrationlawblog.eu/the-new-solidarity-mechanism-the-right-insurance-scheme-for-the-ceas/. Accessed 15 September 2025

Moraru M (2022) The Future Architecture of the EU's Return System. In: Thym D, Odysseus Academic Network (eds) Reforming the Common European Asylum System. Nomos, Baden-Baden, pp. 187–208. Accessed 8 September 2025.
Moreno-Lax V (2024) Crisis as (Asylum) Governance: The Evolving Normalisation of Non-Access to Protection in the EU. European Papers 9(1): 179–208. Accessed 8 September 2025.
Näre L, Tkach O (2024) The Temporary Protection of Ukrainian Refugees: A Model for the Future or a Case of Discriminatory Exceptionalism? Mixed Migration Centre. https://mixedmigration.org/temporary-protection-ukrainian-refugees/. Accessed 8 September 2025.
Neidhardt AH (2024) The Crisis and Force Majeure Regulation: Towards Future-Proof Crisis Management and Responses? FEPS / Friedrich-Ebert-Stiftung / European Policy Centre. https://www.epc.eu/content/FEPS-Policy_Study_-_Migration.pdf. Accessed 8 September 2025.
PAQ Research (2023) Voice of Ukrainians. https://www.paqresearch.cz/post/voice-of-ukrainians. Accessed 8 September 2025.
Peers S (2024a) The New EU Asylum Laws: Taking Rights Half-Seriously. Yearbook of European Law. https://doi.org/10.1093/yel/yeae003. Accessed 20 September 2025.
Peers S (2024b) The New EU Asylum Laws (part 8): The 'crisis' regulation—and conclusions. EU Law Analysis. Accessed 20 September 2025.
Saracino D (2024) The European Union's Response to the Refugee Movements from Ukraine: The End of the Solidarity Crisis? Central and Eastern European Migration Review 13(2): 1–20. Accessed 8 September 2025.
Scheu HC (2014) Citizenship, Migration and Anti-Discrimination Law. The Lawyer Quarterly 3: 195–202. Accessed 8 September 2025.
Schultz J (2020) An End to Asylum? Temporary Protection and the Erosion of Refugee Status. In: Jacobsen CM, Karlsen MA, Khosravi S (eds) Waiting and the Temporalities of Irregular Migration. Routledge, London/New York, pp. 169–170. Accessed 8 September 2025.
Sohst R et al. (2025) Exploring Refugees' Intentions to Return to Ukraine: Data Insights and Policy Responses. Migration Policy Institute Europe & International Organization for Migration. https://www.migrationpolicy.org/sites/default/files/publications/mpie-iom_ukraine-return-intentions-2024-final.pdf. Accessed 20 October 2025.
Trauner F, Wolff S (2024) The Impact of the Russian War Against Ukraine on the Reform of the Common European Asylum System. European Politics and Society. https://doi.org/10.1080/23745118.2024.2435401. Accessed 8 September 2025.
Tsourdi EL (2021) Regional Refugee Regimes: Europe. In: Costello C, Foster M, McAdam J (eds) The Oxford Handbook of International Refugee Law. Oxford University Press, Oxford.
UNHCR (2001) Protection of Refugees in Mass Influx Situations: Overall Protection Framework. EC/GC/01/4. http://www.unhcr.org/3ae68f3c24.html. Accessed 8 September 2025.
UNHCR (2005) Executive Committee Conclusion No. 103 (LVI): Provision of International Protection, Including Through Complementary Forms of Protection. https://www.refworld.org/policy/exconc/excom/2005/en/114516. Accessed 8 September 2025.
UNHCR (2009) Conclusions Adopted by the Executive Committee on the International Protection of Refugees: 1975–2009 (Conclusion Nos 1–109). https://www.unhcr.org/sites/default/files/legacy-pdf/578371524.pdf. Accessed 8 September 2025.
UNHCR (2012) Roundtable on Temporary Protection. International Institute of Humanitarian Law (IIHL). https://www.unhcr.org/media/discussion-paper-temporary-protection-roundtable-temporary-protection. Accessed 8 September 2025.
United Nations (2018) Global Compact for Safe, Orderly and Regular Migration. https://www.un.org/en/ga/search/view_doc.asp?symbol=A/RES/73/195. Accessed 8 September 2025.
United Nations (2022) Ukraine: The War Has Caused the Fastest and Largest Displacement of People in Europe Since World War II. https://ukraine.un.org/en/175836-war-has-caused-fastest-and-largest-displacement-people-europe-world-war-ii. Accessed 8 September 2025.
Víchová V, Zaimović E (2024) Beyond the Temporary: Extension of Temporary Protection and "Special Long-Term Stay" for Its Holders. Paper presented at the Scientific Conference on

Current Issues in Refugee and Alien Law, Office of the Ombudsman, Brno, 14–15 November 2024.

Cases

Court of Justice of the European Union (2022) Staatssecretaris van Justitie en Veiligheid v. X. Judgment of 30 June 2022. Case C-72/22 ECLI:EU:C:2022:505.
European Court of Human Rights (1956) Greece V. The United Kingdom, 1956. (176/56)—Commission (Plenary)—Report (31).

Treaties

EU— Treaty on the Functioning of the European Union (Consolidated Version), opened for signature 13 December 2007, OJ C 115/47 (9 May 2008) (entered into force 1 December 2009).
UN. Convention Relating to the Status of Refugees (adopted 28 July 1951, entered into force 22 April 1954) 189 UNTS 137.

Chapter 10
The Limited Role of the War in Ukraine in the Development of the European Defence Policy

Luca Paladini

Contents

Abstract Among the initiatives launched by the EU in response to Russia's aggression against Ukraine, some have been undertaken within the framework of the Common Security and Defence Policy. These concern both support for the attacked country and, at the institutional level, the development of the European Defence Policy. This chapter focuses on the latter, arguing that while the outbreak of the Ukraine war had a limited impact on defence developments, the so-called 'Trump Effect' has been considerably more influential. Indeed, the chapter points out that the recently announced U.S. disengagement from NATO sparked the start of 'European rearmament'—an expression that has gained currency in the public debate since the adoption of the Joint White Paper for European Defence (Readiness 2030) of March 2025. A discussion of Readiness 2030 and its implementation shows that the driving forces behind European defence developments are now financial resources and the limited time available to establish the necessary industrial and technological base to achieve 'genuine strategic autonomy'. The chapter concludes by offering some considerations on the contents of Readiness 2030, as well as a brief overview of the latest developments of the European Defence Policy and their short-term implications.

S. Poli et al., *The EU's Response to the War in Ukraine and Its Impact on the EU Legal Order*, Global Europe: Legal and Policy Issues of the EU's External Action 7,
https://doi.org/10.1007/978-94-6265-767-0_10

Keywords War in Ukraine · European Union · European defence policy · Strategic compass · Readiness 2030 · NATO · Article 41 TEU

10.1 Introduction

As we all know, the European Union (EU or Union) reacted to the war in Ukraine by implementing a series of actions based on the policies outlined in the Treaty on European Union (TEU) and the Treaty on the Functioning of the European Union (TFEU). With regard to the latter, the EU exercised its competence to address the migration crisis caused by the partial evacuation from the country under attack—which led the Council to grant temporary protection to Ukraine's displaced persons[1]—as well as to contain the economic impact of the war on the EU's internal market and its consumers.[2] In addition, the so-called 'Team Europe' (i.e., the Union and its Member States) mobilised significant financial resources to support Ukraine, including a dedicated macro-financial assistance programme in the form of highly concessional loans.[3]

With respect to the TEU, the Union rapidly initiated Ukraine's EU accession process—a step that has raised quite a few doubts among legal scholars.[4] Furthermore, the Union imposed a massive package of restrictive measures on Russia and Belarus within the framework of its Common Foreign and Security Policy (CFSP), measures that it has since continued to update (so far, it has adopted a total of 18 sanctions packages against Moscow).[5] Other CFSP actions thus far implemented have also had implications for the Common Security and Defence Policy (CSDP). First, the Union has financially supported (and is still supporting) Ukraine's defence capabilities through the European Peace Facility,[6] providing for the supply of both non-lethal and—amidst a mixture of consensus and dissent[7]—lethal military equipment. Moreover, in October 2022, it established the EU Military Assistance Mission in support of Ukraine (EUMAM Ukraine)[8] to provide training to the Ukrainian

---

[1] See Chap. 9 in this book.

[2] E.g., see Regulation (EU) 2022/2560 of the European Parliament and of the Council of 14 December 2022 on foreign subsidies distorting the internal market, in OJ L 330/2022.

[3] Regulation (EU) 2024/2773 of the European Parliament and of the Council of 24 October 2024 establishing the Ukraine Loan Cooperation Mechanism and providing exceptional macro-financial assistance to Ukraine, in OJ L, 2024/2773.

[4] See Chap. 8 in this book.

[5] See Chaps. 2, 3, and 4 in this book.

[6] Council Decision (CFSP) 2021/509 of 22 March 2021 establishing a European Peace Facility, and repealing Decision (CFSP) 2015/528, in OJ L 102/2021.

[7] The provision of lethal military equipment has led to an increased use of constructive abstention under Article 31 TEU. See Chap. 5 in this book.

[8] Council Decision (CFSP) 2022/1968 of 17 October 2022 on a European Union Military Assistance Mission in support of Ukraine (EUMAM Ukraine), in OJ L 270/2022.

Armed Forces (UAF) within the territory of certain Member States,[9] thus enabling the UAF to develop the necessary skills to defend their country's territorial integrity and protect civilians.

The war's outbreak also led to institutional developments within the CSPD, specifically with regard to the European Defence Policy (EDP)—that is, the progressive framing of a common defence policy, and potentially a common defence, as envisaged in Article 42(2) TEU.[10] In response to Russia's aggression against Ukraine and the broader rise in international aggression, the Council of 21 March 2022 and the subsequent European Council of 24 and 25 March 2022 adopted the Strategic Compass for Security and Defence,[11] a policy document that sets out a goal for the EU to achieve strategic and military autonomy by 2030, while still maintaining close cooperation with NATO.[12] At the same time, two other events from 2022 are noteworthy as factors likely to influence the developments of the EDP. Firstly, Denmark officially ended the EU security and defence opt-out it had held since 1993,[13] and, secondly, Finland and Sweden, two Member States located quite close to Russian borders, applied to join NATO.

While the EU's support for Ukraine was virtually unanimous and unconditional[14]—and fully backed by NATO partners—throughout 2022–2024, the scenario has now changed. 2025 has been a tempestuous year since day one, due to heightened international tension,[15] as well as the US's shift in position not only on Ukraine support, but also on its own role within NATO. As is well known, the alliance's effectiveness has so far largely depended on direct US involvement. However, 2025 has

---

[9] Namely, Poland and Germany. In this regard, Hoffmeister 2024, p. 35, notes that this is an exception due to Ukraine's state of belligerency, whereas normally EU peace missions are carried out in the territory of the inviting Third State. On this point, see Recital 10 of Council Decision (CFSP) 2022/1968, under which training outside of the territory of the inviting Third State is a temporary measure in line with Article 42(1) TEU. On the conformity of EUMAM's activities with international law, see Council of the EU (2022b).

[10] See Sect. 10.2.

[11] Council of the EU 2022a.

[12] It is worth recalling that EU-NATO cooperation was formalised in the Berlin Plus Agreement of 16 December 2002 and has undergone periodic updates, most recently with the Joint Declaration on EU-NATO Cooperation of 10 January 2023. In line with the Strategic Compass and the 2022 NATO Strategic Concept, this declaration further strengthens the Euro-Atlantic cooperation to address more effectively the growing threats and challenges posed by aggressive actors on the international scene. On the EU-NATO strategic partnership, see Blockmans et al. 2019 and Duff 2024.

[13] Ministry of Foreign Affairs of Denmark, Danes vote yes to abolish EU defence opt-out—here are the next steps, 2 June 2022.

[14] As is well known, Budapest has on several occasions hindered support for Ukraine, both by making explicit political statements and by resorting to legal forms of dissent (abstentions, leaving Council sessions, etc.).

[15] The press has reported on a turbulent international context not only in terms of warfare but also with regard to non-traditional conflicts, which typically take place in less tangible realms, such as trade wars and malicious activities in the cyberspace. For more on the latter, see Insolia 2025, p. 957 ff.

seen the US shift from involvement to non-involvement, and then again to involvement but on condition that the EU make a greater contribution to the alliance's operations.[16] Faced with this uncertain international scenario and Washington's shifting stance, Brussels recognised the need to renew its full support for Kyiv and emancipate the Union on the defence front with a sort of 'Declaration of European Independence' in the military sphere.[17]

In light of the above background, my aim in this chapter is to report on the recent developments of the EDP. To do so, I will first examine the fragmented nature of EDP cooperation leading up to Russia's aggression on Ukraine. I will then discuss the change of pace triggered by the outbreak of the Russo-Ukrainian war, with a focus on the adoption of the Strategic Compass. Next, I will turn to the acceleration that was brought about by the swift adoption of the Joint White Paper for European Defence (Readiness 2030)[18] in March 2025, in the days immediately following the meeting between Zelensky and Trump at the White House. I will then focus on the implementation of Readiness 2030, covering the adoption of the SAFE regulation, the recent activation of the National Escape Clause of the Stability and Growth Pact for 15 Member States and, finally, the progress made so far in finding new financial resources to allocate to defence. Since these are financial measures, they do not in and of themselves bring about 'European rearmament'—to use an expression that has entered the European public debate following the adoption of Readiness 2030—but they can enable the technological and industrial base that will allow the EU to develop the military capabilities necessary to defend itself from external threats. Based on this observation, the final section of this chapter will seek to establish an operational link between Readiness 2030 and the Strategic Compass, and to provide an overview of the latest developments of the EDP and their short-term implications.

10.2 Fragmented Cooperation: The Norm in European Defence Before the Outbreak of the War in Ukraine

Under Article 42(2) TEU, the CSDP includes the progressive framing of a common defence policy, which "will lead to a common defence, when the European Council, acting unanimously, so decides." In the latter case, the European Council will "recommend to the Member States the adoption of such a decision in accordance with their respective constitutional requirements." Thus, this provision envisages the incremental achievement of a goal: first, bringing about a common defence policy, and then (potentially) creating a common defence.

---

[16] See Missiroli 2025.

[17] See Goldhammer 2025.

[18] European Commission, High Representative of the Union for Foreign Affairs and Security Policy/Vice-President of the European Commission 2025.

At present, the EU has neither a common defence policy nor, clearly, a common defence. But let us clarify an essential point: in this context, defence must be understood as a deterrent. Indeed, we can assume that if the Union ever succeeds in establishing a common defence policy, or a common defence, its resulting military capabilities will be employed to deter, or at worst respond to, armed attacks, but certainly not to infringe upon the freedom and integrity of Third States. This assumption has a solid basis not only in Article 2 TEU, which outlines the Union's founding values, but also Article 3 and Article 21 TEU. These provisions set out, respectively, the Union's aims and the objectives of its external action. Moreover, they both make reference to strict observance of international law, including the principles of the United Nations Charter (UN Charter), and, therefore, the prohibition on the threat or use of force in international relations.[19] The aforesaid assumption seems confirmed also by the so-called 'mutual aid and assistance clause' or 'mutual defence clause' contained in Article 42(7) TEU (one of the new features added to the CSDP by the Treaty of Lisbon), whose operation is tied to compliance with Article 51 of the UN Charter, which concerns the right of individual or collective self-defence.

Turning now to cooperation among Member States within the framework of the EDP, it is important to understand the current state of play. To this end, I will first try to clarify what that cooperation consists of. Since the treaties are silent on this matter, an indication can be drawn from a 2017 document[20] where the Commission addressed the subject of security and defence within the broader debate on the post-Brexit EU. The Commission envisaged three possible future scenarios: (1) voluntary, non-binding cooperation; (2) cooperation as the norm rather than the exception; and, finally, (3) the development of a common defence. In the opinion of this writer, scenario 2 corresponds to the common defence policy, given that scenario 1 refers to voluntary cooperation, without necessarily a common EU element, while scenario 3 refers to the second objective outlined in Article 42(2) TEU. According to the Commission, in scenario 2 cooperation between Member States would become systematic, with greater alignment in terms of defence planning and on the acquisition and maintenance of military capabilities. This, in turn, would improve the interoperability of national armed forces and reduce duplications. The Member States that are so coordinated would receive financial contributions from the EU budget to develop defence capabilities. At present, however, cooperation in the area of defence cannot be said to be entirely systematic, and, therefore, we must conclude that the Member States have not yet reached scenario 2.

Naturally, some initiatives have been undertaken in recent years to move beyond the stage of purely voluntary and non-binding cooperation, but the variable geometry of Member State participation continues to hinder the achievement of the common defence policy.

One example is the European Defence Agency (EDA), which has progressively taken on a significant role in defence matters. Although the agency was established to support Member States in their efforts to improve European crisis management

[19] Article 2, para 4, UN Charter.

[20] European Commission 2017.

capabilities and to sustain defence cooperation without prejudice to national competences, it has taken on new duties over time. It has become a venue for the conduct of defence-related projects and programmes, as well as research activities in synergy with the military industry, and has been tasked with coordinating, evaluating, and monitoring the achievement of objectives related to the development of the EU's military capabilities and the promotion of cooperation among Member States.[21] Worthy of mention among EDA-run programmes is the Coordinated Annual Review On Defence (CARD), whose purpose is, on one hand, to achieve the greatest possible alignment between national defence budgets and, on the other, to make them converge towards spending choices that contribute to the development of the CSDP. The EDA has done a commendable job in stimulating integration among Member States, but several factors suggest it may not be a reliable indicator of systematic defence cooperation. First and foremost, the fact that the Agency has no operational tasks means its results have been limited, including with regard to CARD. Moreover, membership of the EDA is still voluntary.[22] It should be recalled that it was only in 2023, following the outbreak of the Russo-Ukrainian war, that Denmark ended its opting-out from the CSDP and joined the EDA,[23] which has only since then included all the Member States. In any case, participation in EDA projects remains on a voluntary basis.

Another example is the Permanent Structured Cooperation (PESCO).[24] Introduced by the Treaty of Lisbon and launched in 2017, PESCO binds the Member States that participate in it on an operational and financial level,[25] but still does not include all EU Member States, thus remaining a form of differentiated integration. From an initial 23 members, it soon grew to include 25 Member States, excluding Denmark and Malta. The accession of Denmark in 2023[26] raised the number of participating Member States to 26, but as yet Malta has not joined.[27] These initial considerations alone already suggest that PESCO cannot currently be regarded as an indicator of systematic defence cooperation. The results obtained since its establishment in 2017 seem to confirm this. While over 70 operational projects have been

---

21 Article 42, paras 1 and 3, TEU. In the literature, see Terpan 2013, p. 1624 ff.

22 Article 45, para 2, TEU.

23 European Defence Agency, Denmark joins the European Defence Agency, Brussels, 23 March 2023.

24 Article 42, para 6, and Article 46 TEU. In literature, see Fiott et al. 2017.

25 Article 42, para 6, and Article 46 TEU. See also Council decision (CFSP) 2017/2315 of 11 December 2017 establishing permanent structured cooperation (PESCO) and determining the list of participating Member States, in OJ L 331/2017.

26 Council decision (CFSP) 2023/1015 of 23 May 2023 confirming the participation of Denmark in PESCO, and amending Decision (CFSP) 2017/2315 establishing permanent structured cooperation (PESCO) and determining the list of participating Member States, in OJ L 136/2023.

27 As reported by the local press, Malta's accession to PESCO can be considered on hold, although, contrary to the past, some recent political developments suggest greater favour towards the initiative. See Maltatoday.com.mt 2025.

launched within PESCO,[28] only a few have been completed, and the most significant ones are still underway. A case in point is the "Military Mobility" project, which has a very broad membership.[29] Its purpose is to standardise the procedures for moving military forces among participating States, thereby enabling the rapid mobilisation of military capabilities both inside and outside the EU, including, if necessary, for defence purposes. Launched in 2017, this project is still under implementation, despite repeated calls for its completion, especially since the outbreak of the war in Ukraine. In light of all this, it is my view that the limited outcomes achieved under PESCO, like other factors previously discussed, do not support the conclusion that EU defence cooperation has become systematic.

Next, we need to turn again to Article 42(7) TEU. The EU mutual defence clause certainly represents a form of cooperation, since it provides that in the event of armed aggression on the territory of a Member State, the other Member States shall provide aid and assistance by all means in their power. At present, however, this clause cannot yet be applied. This is because, in the event of an armed attack against a Member State that is also a NATO member,[30] the question would arise of whether Article 42(7) TEU, or Article 5 of the North Atlantic Treaty—which would trigger NATO's defence protection—could be invoked. While formally both Articles could be invoked and contribute to the defence of the same territory, in practice only NATO's Article 5 can be activated, given that joint exercises aimed at making Article 42(7) TEU operational are still underway. If and when the two provisions become equally operational, the question will arise as to which should be activated or, perhaps, how to coordinate them on a practical level. In any case, the EU mutual defence clause does not currently translate into a concrete form of systematic cooperation. This conclusion is further corroborated by the lack of a common position among Member States on Article 42(7) TEU and the operation of NATO's Article 5. In fact, not all Member States are in favour of the EU clause, and some—such as Poland and the Baltic States—have shown a preference for the well-established NATO clause.[31]

Despite being fragmented, cooperation between Member States has benefited from several financial levers, namely funding programmes whose disbursements from the EU budget have been used to support military capability development projects. An example is the well-known European Defence Fund,[32] which, for the 2021–2027 period, co-finances investment projects that contribute to a strong,

---

[28] The complete list of PESCO projects is available at this link: https://www.pesco.europa.eu/#projects.

[29] The 26 Member States that have joined PESCO and three Third States—namely, Norway, Canada and the USA—are participating in this project. See https://www.pesco.europa.eu/project/military-mobility/.

[30] As of the time of this writing, of the 27 EU Member States, 23 are also NATO members. Of the remaining four, Cyprus has no relationship with the alliance, while Austria, Ireland and Malta are NATO partners.

[31] See Clapp 2022, p. 18 ff.

[32] Regulation (EU) 2021/697 of the European Parliament and of the Council of 29 April 2021 establishing the European Defence Fund and repealing Regulation (EU) 2018/1092, in OJ L 170/2021.

competitive, and innovative defence industrial and technological base, or the Connecting Europe Facility,[33] which, for the same period, supports the development of transport and mobility, including in the military field. Also worthy of mention are ASAP[34] and EDIRPA,[35] the two programmes launched in 2023 to support the production of ammunition and foster the common procurement of defence products, respectively. Both temporary instruments (in fact, ASAP has already expired), they will be replaced by the EU Defence Industrial Programme (EDIP) that is currently undergoing approval.[36] In terms of legal bases, it is important to note that the regulations establishing these funding programmes were adopted under the EU's TFEU competences (industry, research and technological development and space policies, and trans-European network) and not under the CSDP. This is because, given the rule governing defence expenditures under Article 41 TEU,[37] it would have been impossible otherwise to charge the relevant disbursements to the EU budget. Therefore, these funding programmes demonstrate the *pro-quota* nature of the EU budget's contribution to the EDP.

10.3 The Outbreak of the War in Ukraine and the Adoption of the Strategic Compass

The cooperation between Member States remained slow and fragmented until February 2022, when Russia's invasion of Ukraine prompted a greater demand for security within the EU, which in turn led to a boost in the development of the EDP.[38]

Thus, in late March 2022, the Council and the European Council adopted the Strategic Compass, which sets out a concrete plan of action not only to provide the broadest possible support to Ukraine, but also to ensure the EU achieves strategic autonomy by 2030. The Strategic Compass identifies 81 objectives for strengthening security and defence, along with the instruments to achieve them and their respective deadlines. These objectives are divided into four work strands: "Act", "Secure", "Invest", and "Partner". The first, "Act", aims to make the mutual defence clause operational and to implement the "Military Mobility" project by 2025. The second,

---

[33] Regulation (EU) 2021/1153 of the European Parliament and of the Council of 7 July 2021 establishing the Connecting Europe Facility and repealing Regulations (EU) No 1316/2013 and (EU) No 283/2014, in OJ L 249/ 2021.

[34] Regulation (EU) 2023/1525 of the European Parliament and of the Council of 20 July 2023 on supporting ammunition production (ASAP), in OJ L 185/2023. ASAP ended last 25 June. On this regulation, see Fabbrini (2025).

[35] Regulation (EU) 2023/2418 of the European Parliament and of the Council of 18 October 2023 on establishing an instrument for the reinforcement of the European defence industry through common procurement (EDIRPA), in OJ L, 2023/2418.

[36] See Sect. 10.5.

[37] Ibidem.

[38] See Flash Eurobarometer survey EU's response to the war in Ukraine, May 2022, https://europa.eu/eurobarometer/surveys/detail/2772.

"Secure", has a more miscellaneous content and aims to bolster the Union's resilience in facing various types of threats (including, for example, cyber defence), as well as to ensure its presence in non-terrestrial domains (such as the high seas and airspace). The third work strand, «Invest», aims to increase defence expenditures and, at the same time, reduce financial fragmentation, all of which is to be achieved through the joint procurement of defence capabilities. Finally, «Partner» focuses on the need to strengthen the EU's cooperation with Third States and International Organizations (primarily NATO) to address common global security challenges.[39] All these objectives are subject to adjustment, since the Strategic Compass itself is subject to annual progress reports, as well as to reviews and updates. Indeed, based on the threat analysis review scheduled for 2025, the High Representative of the Union for Foreign Affairs and Security Policy (HR), who is responsible for the annual progress reports, will present proposals for a possible revision of the document.

The HR presented the first progress report on the implementation of the Strategic Compass in March 2023,[40] and a second progress report followed in 2024.[41] The reports provide a comprehensive overview of achievements, as well as remaining objectives and critical issues that emerged during their respective years. While emphasizing the achievements reached across the four work strands, the HR acknowledges that «more remains to be done to reach all the objectives set in the Strategic Compass and much depends on Member States to provide necessary resources, forces and capabilities. There is no other choice for the EU and its Member States to invest in their Defence Readiness».[42] Of the 81 total objectives, the deadline for implementation of 51 was 2022, but since only about half of those objectives were met, the deadline has been postponed.[43] More specifically, while appreciable results have been achieved in the "Secure" and "Partner" work strands,[44] there are significant gaps between objectives and actual results with respect to "Act" and "Invest". On the one hand, the mutual defence clause is not yet operational, and the "Military Mobility" project has not yet been implemented; on the other, the gap is even more pronounced in the financial area. While Member States' defence spending has increased, it still varies from state to state, has not yet reached the 2% GDP threshold, and is still not fully coordinated with the EDP. As for the budgets used to buy defence equipment, the level of cooperation among the Member States is still too low, so much so that the HR states: «We are mobilising EU tools to spend better together».[45]

---

[39] For a discussion of these objectives, see Hoffmeister 2024.

[40] Annual Progress Report on the Implementation of the Strategic Compass for Security and Defence 2023.

[41] Annual Progress Report on the Implementation of the Strategic Compass for Security and Defence 2024.

[42] Ibidem, p. 30.

[43] See Clapp 2022, p. 1 ss.

[44] See Anderson 2023.

[45] Annual Progress Report on the Implementation of the Strategic Compass for Security and Defence 2023 p. 15.

The state of implementation of the Strategic Compass shows just how slow and faltering the journey is towards greater strategic autonomy. Fewer objectives have been achieved than scheduled, and the achievement of those still being pursued (or still to be pursued) is now expected only in the medium-to-long term, which means that the progressive framing of a common defence policy will have a longer timeline. The HR was supposed to present the third annual progress report and the threat analysis review in March 2025, but, as of this writing, these documents have not yet been released. In my view, that is because the tumultuous events of March 2025 forced the EU to put the Strategic Compass on hold to make way for Readiness 2030.

10.4 The 'Trump Effect' and Readiness 2030: A Turning Point on the Path Towards a Common Defence?

After the acrimonious meeting between Ukrainian President Zelenskyy and U.S. President Trump at the end of February 2025, Brussels recognised the need to accelerate the process towards a common defence policy. This was seen as necessary regardless of potential policy reversals by Washington—not an uncommon occurrence[46]—and of the potential unavailability of NATO protection, despite maintaining collaborative relations with the alliance. Consequently, on March 4, in her press statement on the nascent ReArm Europe plan,[47] European Commission President Ursula von der Leyen noted that «(w)e are in an era of rearmament. [...] Europe is ready to assume its responsibilities» and, importantly, that «(w)e will continue working closely with our partners in NATO. This is a moment for Europe. And we are ready to step up».[48]

In the weeks that followed, events unfolded rapidly.

The special European Council meeting held on 6 March established that, in light of the current challenges and of the Strategic Compass, the EU should assume greater responsibilities for its own defence. In its conclusions, the European Council stated that: «In this context, the European Union will accelerate the mobilisation of the necessary instruments and financing in order to bolster the security of the European Union and the protection of our citizens. In doing so, the Union will reinforce its overall defence readiness, reduce its strategic dependencies, address its critical capability gaps and strengthen the European defence technological and industrial base accordingly across the Union so that it is in a position to better supply equipment

---

[46] For example, the widely-circulated photo from 26 April 2025, taken in St. Peter's Basilica on the solemn occasion of Pope Francis's funeral, shows President Zelenskyy and President Trump engaged in a one-on-one conversation. International press reports indicated that the Ukrainian leader called it a 'Good meeting,' while the White House described it as "a very productive discussion." See Politico.eu 2025.

[47] The very first version of Readiness 2030.

[48] See Press Statement by President von der Leyen on the defence package, Brussels, 4 March 2025.

in the quantities and at the accelerated pace needed. This will also contribute to boosting European industrial and technological competitiveness».[49] And it is worth noting that this passage not only effectively describes the European Council's treaty-based task to provide the EU with political impetus, as laid down in Article 15 TEU, but also identifies speed of action and the availability of financial resources as the two key factors for achieving the stated objective of better supplying defence equipment rapidly. Furthermore, the European Council stressed the need to substantially increase expenditure on security and defence and called on the Commission to propose additional funding sources.[50] It also urged «the Commission and the co-legislators to swiftly take work forward on simplifying the legal and administrative framework» in sectors of practical importance for bolstering the defence industry (for example, public procurement and industry cooperation), and invited the Commission to prioritise the EDP.[51] Finally, the European Council identified a first list of priority areas for action[52]—air and missile defence; artillery systems; missiles and ammunition; drones and anti-drone systems; strategic enablers; military mobility; cyber; artificial intelligence and electronic warfare—and underlined «the importance of working together with like-minded non-EU partners».[53] The European Council also reaffirmed its full support for Ukraine, but had to do so in a separate statement endorsed by 26 of its 27 members, due to Hungary's refusal to agree to joint conclusions on Ukraine.[54]

Less than two weeks later, on 19 March, the European Commission presented Readiness 2030, which lays out a plan for developing the European defence industry by 2030 through substantial funding. The plan aims to close the gap created in recent decades by under-investment in defence (a gap also emphasised in the Strategic Compass reports discussed above) and establish the technological and industrial base necessary to ensure the Union's strategic defence autonomy in deterring armed aggression. Emphasising that the 'rearmament' that is necessary to protect Europe «requires, as a starting point, a massive investment over a sustained period»,[55] the document identifies both immediate, short-term actions and mid-to-long term projects.[56] While the former entail the adoption of measures to relaunch the EU's financial support through existing instruments (such as PESCO), the latter focus on the development of the defence industry. The Commission, which in effect assumes the role of directing the implementation of Readiness 2030, including through legislative initiative, proposes that, in the short term, the Council should "adopt the [proposed draft] Regulation on Security and Action For Europe (SAFE) [as a matter of urgency]" and Member States should promptly "request the activation of the National Escape Clause" under the Stability and Growth Pact. The Commission

[49] European Council (6 March 2025), conclusions, EUCO 6/25, Brussels, point 5.

[50] Ibidem, point 6.

[51] Ibidem, letter (m).

[52] Ibidem, letter (f).

[53] Ibidem, point 4.

[54] European Council (6 March 2025), conclusions, EUCO 10/25, Brussels.

[55] Readiness 2030, p. 2.

[56] For an effective summary, see Clapp et al. 2025.

also invites the co-legislators to approve as soon as possible the European Defence Industry Programme (EDIP)[57] (whose adoption process is currently underway) and to prioritise the proposal for amendment of the European Regional Development Fund to include defence objectives.[58] Moreover, the Commission encourages Member States to swiftly step up collaborative defence procurement, including by accessing funding under the SAFE instrument, and calls on the European Investment Bank to increase financial support to the European defence industry.

On 20 and 21 March, the European Council accepted these points and called for «an acceleration of work on all strands to decisively ramp up Europe's defence readiness», inviting the Council and the Parliament to «swiftly take work forward on the recent Commission proposals» and requesting the prompt «implementation of the actions identified in its conclusions of 6 March 2025 in the field of capabilities to start as a matter of urgency and for continued work on the relevant financing options».[59] In the months that followed, the meeting schedule of the European institutions became even more crowded and work proceeded swiftly, including within the Parliament, which not only endorsed Readiness 2030 and its planned roadmap,[60] but also invited the institutions concerned to implement it quickly.[61]

10.5 The Security Action for Europe Regulation

The SAFE regulation[62] establishes a financial assistance fund for Member States that, upon request, can disburse long-term subsidised-rate loans (with a maximum maturity of 45 years), to be used for common procurements and joint defence projects. The regulation was approved in record time.

With regard to common procurements, purchases must concern some of the capabilities identified by the European Council of 6 March (ammunitions, missiles, drones, etc.), so SAFE will not cover the acquisition of other military equipment, which will therefore remain fragmented. Regarding the projects that can be financed, they must be transnational, involving at least one EU Member State and a Third State from among Iceland, Liechtenstein, Norway and Switzerland (which belong to the European Economic Area) and Ukraine. On 18 September 2025, the Council adopted a decision authorising the Commission to open negotiations with the UK and with Canada to allow to British and Canadian companies and products to be involved in

---

[57] Proposal for a Regulation of the European Parliament and of the Council establishing the European Defence Industry Programme and a framework of measures to ensure the timely availability and supply of defence products ('EDIP'), COM/2024/150 final.

[58] See Sect. 10.7.

[59] European Council (20 March 2025), conclusions, EUCO 1/25, Brussels, point 21.

[60] European Parliament 2025a, points 76 and 22, and European Parliament 2025b, point 5.

[61] European Parliament 2025a, point 15.

[62] Council Regulation (EU) 2025/1106 of 27 May 2025 establishing the Security Action for Europe (SAFE) through the Reinforcement of the European Defence Industry Instrument, in OJ L 2025/1106.

procurements under SAFE.[63] In addition, negotiations are reportedly underway to open SAFE projects to Turkey as well.[64] The SAFE Regulation thus has a broad range of beneficiaries, including the partnerships whose development has been prompted under the Strategic Compass, and is in line with the EU's full support for its neighbour Ukraine.

While SAFE essentially complements other EU financial levers, it is a new instrument that differs from them. Rather than being a fund paid out of the EU budget, such as the European Defence Fund, it provides loans with favourable terms. To date, 19 Member States have requested access to these loans, for a total estimated credit of €150 billion. The programme is already at full capacity.[65]

The SAFE regulation has attracted criticism since the very idea of its creation was first proposed, mainly about its operation and its impact on national economies. Some have pointed out that a number of Member States will be unable to manage an increase in defence spending over the medium and long term, including with regard to their ability to secure financing at certain interest rates. Others have argued that SAFE will only benefit Member States with a spread of more than 10 or 20 basis points, who thus borrow at higher rates than those available to the EU and which are applied to SAFE loans. Yet others have noted that, for any Member State, the decision on whether to request a SAFE loan is complicated by the need to balance increased defence spending with other major areas of expenditure, such as social policies, which may face sharp cutbacks.

In addition to the above criticisms, the choice of Article 122 TFEU as the legal basis for SAFE has been controversial. Article 122 TFEU is a provision of primary legislation that falls outside the legal framework of the CSDP and aims to address emergency situations. It provides that the Council may, on a proposal from the Commission, decide upon the measures appropriate to the economic situation, in particular if severe difficulties arise in the supply of certain products, or if a Member State is in difficulties or is seriously threatened with severe difficulties caused by natural disasters or exceptional occurrences beyond its control. In this context, it is worth noting that, when it proposed the establishment of SAFE, the Commission justified the proposal by arguing that «(t)he brutal deterioration of the Union's security context since the beginning of 2025 is a sudden and exceptional event entailing a massive and potentially disruptive impact on the supply of defence products essential for the defence and security interests of the Union and its Member States».[66] In other words, the use of Article 122 TFEU as a legal basis was justified by the rapid turn of events in early 2025 and, in particular, the fact that «(a)t the same time, the United States, traditionally a strong ally, is clear that it believes it is over-committed

63 See Council of the EU, Defence investment: Council authorises negotiations with UK and Canada on their participation in SAFE, Brussels, 18 September 2025.

64 On the requirements for, and advisability of, extending the scope of SAFE, see Momtaz 2025.

65 President of the Commission 2025.

66 Proposal for a Council Regulation establishing the Security Action for Europe (SAFE) through the reinforcement of European defence industry Instrument, COM/2025/122 final, p. 4.

in Europe and needs to rebalance, reducing its historical role as a primary security guarantor».[67]

However, legal scholars have deemed Article 122 TFEU an inadequate legal basis, also in light of the fact that the Member States' defence shortfalls are neither exceptional in nature, nor in any way a 'novelty'—the United States has been asking its NATO European partners to increase military spending for quite some time now. In addition, the question of the democratic legitimacy of the decisions taken (and measures adopted) under Article 122 TFEU has also been raised,[68] which in this case is clearly problematic. Indeed, Article 122 TFEU provides for a special—rather than ordinary—legislative procedure that does not involve the European Parliament in any way (not even through a requirement for its consultation or consent), but only requires that, once the procedure is completed, the Parliament be informed of the decision taken.[69] While this simplified procedure certainly has the advantage of allowing for the swift adoption of emergency measures, the complete exclusion of the Parliament from important decisions in the economic and industrial spheres has raised understandable concerns. Furthermore, it has been noted that relying on Article 122 TFEU made it possible to speed up the adoption process for SAFE, overcoming potential obstacles within the Council itself,[70] since decisions on emergency measures are taken by qualified majority.

Critical stances have been taken also within EU institutions. Based on European parliamentary reports, the Committee on Legal Affairs (JURI) expressed a position against the use of Article 122 TFEU on two occasions. At the session of 23 April 2025, it examined and unanimously rejected the provision as an inappropriate legal basis for the SAFE regulation.[71] On the second occasion, the JURI Committee reportedly recommended to President Metsola that the Parliament appeal to the EU Court of Justice to have the regulation annulled,[72] more specifically by bringing a legal action under Article 263 TFEU for the adoption of the wrong legal basis. These negative reactions did not, however, sway the Commission, which, pending the adoption of SAFE, confirmed its position that the choice of Article 122 TFEU was fully justified in light of the deteriorating international situation.

On 20 August 2025, the Parliament took up the recommendation of the JURI Committee and lodged an application with the Court of Justice, initiating proceedings for the annulment of the SAFE regulation.[73] The Parliament is challenging the emergency decision-making procedure under Article 122 TFEU, which bypasses the Parliament and, therefore, undermines democratic legitimacy. The Parliament does

---

[67] Ibidem, p. 1.

[68] See Chamon 2023, p. 34 ss, and Clapp et al. 2025, p. 5.

[69] Article 122, para 2, TFEU.

[70] See Dermine 2025.

[71] Minutes, Meeting of 23 April 2025, Brussels, JURIPV(2025)04231, point 17. See also Article 138, para 2, of the European Parliament's Rules of Procedure.

[72] Euronews.com 2025.

[73] Case C-560/25, *European Parliament v Council of the European Union*, action brought on 20 August 2025, in OJ C 2025/5209.

not question the merits of the regulation, which has its full support, but, rather, the choice of Article 122 TFEU as a legal basis and the procedure thereunder for adopting urgent measures. Approval of the merits of the regulation seems confirmed by the Parliament's positive remarks on the many loan requests received by the Commission, as well as by the fact that it did not request immediate annulment with *ex tunc* effects, but, rather, annulment upon the adoption of a new legislative act replacing SAFE. In its application to the Court, the Parliament submits that the content of the SAFE regulation pertains to the development of the Union's industrial policy in the defence sector and should therefore be based on Article 173 TFEU. This Article stipulates the adoption of support measures for Member States according to the ordinary (formerly "co-decision") legislative procedure, thereby requiring the participation of the Parliament in the deliberative stage. Secondly, the Parliament submits that the Council has failed to adequately state the reasons justifying the choice of the legal basis for the regulation, in particular with regard to whether it met Article 122 requirements. The Parliament's second plea reinforces its position regarding the inadequacy of the justification for the emergency decision, with regard to both the grounds contained in the Commission's proposal and those set out in the recitals of the contested regulation. Since an action under Article 263 TFEU has no suspensive effects, the legal effects produced up to that point will be preserved, including procurements and projects undertaken or concluded under SAFE.

While we share the concerns about democratic legitimacy, we cannot help but wonder how else the adoption process for the SAFE regulation could have been carried out as swiftly as requested by the Council and endorsed by the Parliament itself.[74] Given that the average duration of the ordinary legislative procedure is around 20–24 months,[75] another option could have been to rely on the special procedures envisaged under the Parliament's Rules of Procedure to shorten the legislative process, such as the urgent procedure (Rule 170) or the simplified procedure (Rule 52).[76] In that way, the regulation would have certainly been approved more rapidly than under the ordinary procedure, but perhaps not as rapidly as just two and a half months—the time it took using the procedure under Article 122 TFEU.[77]

However, since this is a very recent case (with details not yet fully made public), we will have to wait for further developments to get a clearer picture. It will be interesting to see whether other institutions intervene in the case (for example, the Commission in support of the Council) and to read the conclusions of the Advocate General. Certainly, the Court of Justice will have an opportunity to re-examine whether the use of Article 122 TFEU is legitimate in emergency situations, which might lead to

---

[74] European Parliament 2025b, point 15.

[75] European Parliament 2024, p. 27.

[76] Ibidem, p. 7 ff.

[77] It has been observed that recourse to Article 122 TFEU enabled a faster adoption of SAFE, as emergency measures are passed by qualified majority, bypassing potential Council obstacles. See Dermine 2025.

having to find an alternative legal basis for SAFE, with all the difficulties that would entail.[78]

10.6 The Activation of the National Escape Clause

The second action implemented under Readiness 2030 was the coordinated activation for Member States of the National Escape Clause under the Stability and Growth Pact (SGP). The clause covers a period of four years from 2025 (subject to extension) and a maximum of 1.5% of GDP in fiscal flexibility.[79] Its activation means that the Member States concerned may legitimately exceed the budget deficit ceiling and increase defence spending within the prescribed limits.

The activation of the National Escape Clause is governed by Article 26 of Regulation 2024/1263 on the coordination of economic policies and surveillance of budgetary policies (the SGP's 'preventive arm'),[80] which together with Regulation 2024/1264 on the excessive deficit procedure (the 'corrective arm')[81] and Directive 2024/1265 on the requirements for budgetary frameworks of the Member States,[82] constitutes the SGP as reformed in 2024, now an integral part of EU Economic Policy. Article 26 lays down three conditions for the activation of the National Escape Clause, which allows a Member State to deviate from its net expenditure path as set by the Council. Firstly, there must be exceptional circumstances outside the control of the Member State; secondly, those circumstances must have a major impact on the Member State's public finances; and, thirdly, that deviation must not endanger fiscal sustainability over the medium term. Once the National Escape Clause is activated, the Member States concerned can derogate from SGP rules and be exempted from the Excessive Deficit Procedure[83] regulated by the SGP's 'corrective arm', but only for the expenditure items authorised under the clause's activation.

On 8 July 2025, the Council activated the National Escape Clause for 15 Member States[84]—a number only slightly lower than the loan requests made under SAFE. The Council's assessment on Germany's request for the clause's activation, however,

[78] See Grossio 2025.

[79] Press release Council activates flexibility in EU fiscal rules for 15 member states to increase defence spending, Council of the EU, 8 July 2025.

[80] Regulation (EU) 2024/1263 of the European Parliament and of the Council of 29 April 2024 on the effective coordination of economic policies and on multilateral budgetary surveillance and repealing Council Regulation (EC) No 1466/97, in OJ L 2024/1263.

[81] Council Regulation (EU) 2024/1264 of 29 April 2024 amending Regulation (EC) No 1467/97 on speeding up and clarifying the implementation of the excessive deficit procedure, in OJ L 2024/1264.

[82] Council Directive (EU) 2024/1265 of 29 April 2024 amending Directive 2011/85/EU on requirements for budgetary frameworks of the Member States, in OJ L 2024/1265.

[83] See Article 126 TFEU.

[84] Belgium, Bulgaria, Czech Republic, Croatia, Denmark, Estonia, Finland, Greece, Latvia, Lithuania, Poland, Portugal, Slovakia, Slovenia and Hungary.

is still pending, as that Member State has yet to submit its 2025–2029 medium-term fiscal-structural plan to the Commission (as required under the 'preventive arm'), for which it has requested a deadline extension.[85] As for the remaining Member States,[86] while the Council makes clear in its press release of 8 July 2025 that it stands ready to act on possible additional requests, it also seems to imply that their failure to request the activation of the flexibility is justified by the fact that «already planned build-up of defence capabilities is also underway».[87] Aside from the Council's official statements, it seems likely to this writer that, in the remaining Member States, either no political consensus has fully formed on the decision to go into debt for defence by taking out the EU-backed loans, or that decision is hindered by constitutional constraints.[88]

Like in the case of SAFE, the official justification for the flexibility provided under the National Escape Clause is the existence of exceptional circumstances. However, this justification has given rise to some doubts, for two reasons. Firstly, the envisaged significant increase in defence spending would not be in response to emergency needs but to structural ones. Secondly, the implications of the resulting budget overruns for the national economies of the 15 Member States that activated the clause remain unclear, considering their different financial situations with respect to the varied landscape of defence investments. Indeed, while several EU Members already spend over 2% of GDP in defence, many others remain below that threshold,[89] which—it must be recalled—corresponds to the standard set by NATO as far back as 2014.[90] In this regard, it is worth noting that at the recent NATO summit in The Hague, the 23 EU Members that are part of NATO committed to invest 5% of GDP on defence expenditures by 2035.[91] Given that the clause activated by the Council will be effective until expiry of its prescribed term, I believe that the increase in defence spending will have to be re-planned in light of this rather burdensome 5% commitment taken by NATO Allies, with all the financial and political consequences that this adjustment will have on the national economies concerned.

[85] See Sole24ore.com 2024.

[86] Austria, Cyprus, France, Ireland, Italy, Luxembourg, Malta, Netherlands, Romania, Spain, and Sweden.

[87] Press release Council activates flexibility in EU fiscal rules for 15 member states to increase defence spending, Council of the EU, 8 July 2025.

[88] As is the case in Spain. See López 2025.

[89] See Cottarelli and Virgadamo 2024, and Clapp et al. 2025, p. 2.

[90] See Wales Summit Declaration, 5 September 2014, point 14.

[91] See the recent The Hague Summit Declaration, 25 June 2025, points 2 and 3.

10.7 The Mobilisation of Additional Financial Resources

Readiness 2030 also provides for measures where additional investment, both public and private, is channelled towards EU defence. Unlike the SAFE instrument and the activation of the National Escape Clause, these measures do not entail going into debt on the part of the Member States. Instead, they involve either adjusting the spending priorities already set within the EU budget, or relying on private capital.

The first measure concerns the European Investments Bank (EIB), which will not only continue to increase its defence-related investments but will eventually replace its previous initiatives with «a dedicated transversal public policy goal to contribute to Europe's peace and security, with an ambitious financial and capital allocation».[92] It will thereby take on a structural role in the funding of European defence and, most importantly, will operate in line with the EDP. The systematic involvement of the EIB in this ongoing financial effort to support the development of European defence is, therefore, to be achieved by expanding the Bank's activities, a process for which there are precedents in other policy areas.[93] To this end, on 21 March 2025, the EIB's Board of Governors moved swiftly to adjust its funding eligibility criteria, thereby allowing access to funds for projects concerning common defence.[94] In line with Readiness 2030, these funds were tripled in June 2025, reaching the considerable amount of over €3 billion.[95]

The second measure concerns the Savings and Investments Union—a project presented by the Commission alongside Readiness 2030—and, within the framework of EU competence on financial services, aims to mobilise private capital to supplement the banking system. This is intended to fill the credit needs of companies, in particular small and medium enterprises and innovative companies involved in the defence sector (among others). In this regard, the Commission intends to promote private investment in the Union's new strategic objectives, which demand significant sums—the Draghi report estimates «an additional €750–800 billion per year by 2030», a figure that is «further impacted by increased defence needs».[96] To this end, the Commission is expected to exercise its initiative to adopt measures in the sectors most directly connected to promoting competitiveness within the priorities set for 2025, one of which is the creation of a technological and industrial base for defence. At the time of this writing, no legislative proposal has been adopted. However, an impact assessment was launched not too long ago for the Sustainable

[92] Readiness 2030, cit., p. 20.

[93] E.g., see Bougrea 2024.

[94] See European Investments Bank, EIB steps up financing for European security and defence and critical raw materials, Press release, 21 March 2025.

[95] See European Investments Bank, EIB Group increases 2025 financing ceiling to record €100 billion to step up investments in security and defence, energy grids and Europe's tech leadership, Press release, 20 June 2025, and Eunews.com 2025.

[96] European Commission 2025a.

Finance Disclosures Regulation (SFDR),[97] which applies to all industries including the defence sector. It therefore seems at least probable that the adoption process for relevant proposals will be accelerated.

Finally, a proposal has been made to source additional defence funding from the EU budget as part of a revision of the EU's Cohesion Policy, with new priorities for the European Regional Development Fund, the Cohesion Fund, and the Just Transition Fund,[98] including support for the military industry. Nevertheless, the reallocation of these European funds remains uncertain. Under the proposed revision, Member States will be granted a degree of flexibility in deciding how to use the structural funds available in the 2021–2027 Multiannual Financial Framework, which means they may use them to strengthen defence capabilities, in particular military mobility. It is, however, by no means a given that all EU Members will avail themselves of this flexibility, as their choice will depend on the national political debates over which priorities to finance with European funds. Moreover, even where structural funds are used for defence, the allocation is unlikely to be uniform, with the amount being high in some Member States (e.g., the Baltic States) and more modest in others. Consequently, the implementation of this measure will result in a fragmented scenario, which will only partially contribute to the financial effort envisaged by Readiness 2030.

In connection with the above, we should also mention the Recovery and Resilience Facility (RRF), a financial instrument that has comparable effects and also falls under the EU Economic, Social and Territorial Cohesion Policy, especially with regard to the coordination of Member States' economic policies. In a recent Communication[99] on the status of NextGenerationEU (NGEU), which is set to expire in 2026, the Commission emphasised the need to accelerate implementation. It encouraged Member States to amend their national plans based on a number of options, including that of redirecting unused RRF funds to defence. The Parliament, a co-legislator for the NextGenerationEU revision, supported this approach in its resolution of 18 June 2025,[100] thus paving the way for the revision of the RRF.

---

[97] Regulation (EU) 2019/2088 of the European Parliament and of the Council of 27 November 2019 on sustainability-related disclosures in the financial services sector, in OJ L 317/2019.

[98] Proposal for a Regulation of the European Parliament and of the Council amending Regulations (EU) 2021/1058 and (EU) 2021/1056 as regards specific measures to address strategic challenges in the context of the mid-term review, COM/2025/123 final.

[99] European Commission 2025b.

[100] European Parliament 2025c.

10.8 Concluding Remarks: The War in Ukraine as an Important But Not Decisive Factor in Strengthening EU Defence Cooperation

Since March 2025, the EU has developed substantial financial packages aimed at building an adequate defence technological and industrial base by 2030—a necessary prerequisite for achieving 'genuine strategic autonomy'.

What has happened in 2025 is unprecedented in the previous decades of European defence cooperation. Not even with the outbreak of the war in Ukraine and the adoption of the Strategic Compass in its aftermath did we see the level of concreteness that now characterises Readiness 2030 and its implementation. As discussed above, the Strategic Compass progress reports emphasised that only limited results were obtained, especially in terms of defence investment and procurement, whereas the ultimate objective is to achieve systematic defence collaboration among Member States by 2030. While some progress was made in the 2022–2024 period, the work on developing defence capabilities was still proceeding too slowly, to the point where a revision of the Strategic Compass seemed inevitable. As noted by the HR: «Thus far, the Compass has served its goal of pointing the direction of our travel. In a difficult year for European security, the Compass provided much needed vision and guidance. The rapidly changing geostrategic environment may require a possible revision of the Strategic Compass based on a revised threat analysis in 2025. The EU's security and defence deserve our constant attention. We thus expect this to be high on the next Strategic Agenda for the EU».[101] In light of all this, we must conclude that the war in Ukraine was an important, but not decisive, factor in strengthening EU defence cooperation, whereas the "Trump effect" of this tumultuous 2025 has had far more impact in terms of prompting concrete developments within the EDP.

In this scenario, it appears to me that Readiness 2030 has picked up the baton, so to speak, from the Strategic Compass, removing from the latter some defence capability objectives[102] and providing that they be achieved by 2030, first through joint procurement, and then hopefully via direct production. The focus of Readiness 2030 on investment is, therefore, no coincidence, as this was the most neglected area in the implementation of the Strategic Compass during the 2022–2024 period. Thus, in March 2025, no roadmap was laid out for the creation of a European army or any form of common defence by 2030. In this sense, speaking of 'European rearmament' makes very little sense—in my view, the expression is unhelpful, since, at best, it can only refer to a greater focus of the European economy on military production. On the other hand, I believe that in March 2025 a decision was made in Brussels to provide a massive financial injection into some re-selected priorities, with the aim of launching the autonomous production of defence capabilities by 2030.

---

[101] Annual Progress Report on the Implementation of the Strategic Compass for Security and Defence 2024, p. 30.

[102] See Dermine 2025.

Assuming the full and correct implementation of Readiness 2030, the progressive framing of the EU's common defence policy called for by Article 42(2) TEU will be quite well underway. This, of course, remains subject to many different variables, especially political and economic, both internal and international. However, it is possible that tangible results will be achieved in defence domains in the short term. To this end, current EU financial levers (the European Defence Fund in particular) will need to be effectively coordinated with the measures set out in Readiness 2030 to boost defence investment—and the European Commissioner for Defence and Space and the HR will have to oversee the management of this patchwork of initiatives.

It seems, therefore, that the most reasonable solution for addressing the current emergency is a complex financial framework that combines existing EU financial levers with Readiness 2030 measures, and which—based on a now well-tested practice—identifies additional defence funding by relying on the EU's competences under the TFEU. This is a solution imposed by necessity, adopted on the basis of established law, and which aims to overcome the limits of the general rule governing military or defence expenditure in the EU. But this rule, which is contained in Article 41 TEU and places the burden of that expenditure on the Member States, is no longer suited to the current needs of European defence. As shown by recent developments, the time is ripe for the Union to finance its own defence directly, and thus move beyond the *pro quota* approach applied so far to the EU budget. It is therefore indirectly and from a long-term perspective that Readiness 2030 provides a point of reflection on the future of European defence funding and on the limits of Article 41 TEU—a primary provision that will likely be reconsidered when the treaties are eventually revised. Just to give an example, a possible revision of Article 41 TEU could consist in changing the current rule on defence expenditure so that use of the EU budget to fund the development of the EDP becomes the norm. In this way, the current wording—«Operating expenditure to which the implementation of this Chapter gives rise shall also be charged to the Union budget, except for such expenditure arising from operations having military or defence implications and cases where the Council acting unanimously decides otherwise»—would be streamlined into the following provision: «Operating expenditure to which the implementation of this Chapter gives rise shall also be charged to the Union budget, except cases where the Council acting unanimously decides otherwise».

In conclusion, I will briefly examine the European Council's agenda for the coming months to highlight the steps likely to be taken in the implementation of Readiness 2030. Inevitably, these steps will be influenced by the US' latest policy reversal on support for Ukraine, which occurred during the summit between the US and Russian presidents in Alaska on 15 August 2025. Shortly after the summit, several European leaders, the President of the European Council and the President of the Commission released a joint statement: «Our support to Ukraine will continue. We are determined to do more to keep Ukraine strong in order to achieve an end to the fighting and a just and lasting peace. As long as the killing in Ukraine continues, we stand ready to uphold the pressure on Russia. We will continue to strengthen sanctions and wider economic measures to put pressure on Russia's war economy until there is a just and lasting peace».[103]

The statement above was echoed by an informal meeting of Member States' foreign and defence ministers held in Copenhagen on 28 and 29 August. Despite the meeting taking place outside the EU institutional framework, a number of proposals were formulated ahead of the European Council of October 2025. In particular, the defence ministers took the decision to identify 'lead nations' from among the Member States to ensure that the objectives set by the European Council of 6 March 2025 for priority defence areas (such as air and missile defence, drones, ammunition, etc.)[104] are implemented within the expected timelines, which are tighter than ever. As emphasized by the President of the Commission in her 2025 State of the Union Address before the Parliament on 10 September 2025: "In every country I visited, I heard the same message: there is no time to waste. At the next European Council, we will therefore present a clear roadmap. For getting new common defence projects off the ground. For setting clear goals for 2030. And for creating a European Defence Semester. 2030 is tomorrow. So Europe must get ready today".[105]

As for the months to come, aside from various Council sessions already on schedule, two European Council meetings will be of particular relevance. On 23 and 24 October 2025, the European Council is expected to review progress and examine the next steps for the implementation of Readiness 2030.[106] It is also reasonable to presume that it will discuss ongoing legislative work—in particular, the adoption of EDIP and the revision of the Cohesion policy, both of which are currently undergoing their first reading in the Parliament[107]—as well as future Commission proposals on new or amended legislation to support the development of defence capabilities (for example, military mobility). Finally, the European Council of 18 and 19 December 2025 will prepare the first annual assessment of the implementation of Readiness 2030 and conclude this eventful 2025 with new policy guidelines for the development of the EDP.

---

[103] Statement by President Macron, Prime Minister Meloni, Chancellor Merz, Prime Minister Starmer, President Stubb, Prime Minister Tusk, President Costa, President von der Leyen, Brussels, 16 August 2025.

[104] Informal meeting of defence ministers: press remarks by High Representative Kaja Kallas after the meeting, Copenhagen, 29 August 2025.

[105] See President of the Commission 2025 and Chap. 11 of this book.

[106] European Council (26 June 2025), conclusions, EUCO 12/25, Brussels, point 22.

[107] The Council already adopted its position at first reading in July 2024 for EDIP and in July 2025 for the revision of the Cohesion Policy.

References

Anderson J J (2023) European Defence Partnerships. European Union Institute for Security Studies, Luxembourg.

Annual Progress Report on the Implementation of the Strategic Compass for Security and Defence (2023) Report of the High Representative of the Union for Foreign Affairs and Security Policy to the Council. Brussels, March.

Annual Progress Report on the Implementation of the Strategic Compass for Security and Defence (2024) Report of the High Representative of the Union for Foreign Affairs and Security Policy to the Council. Brussels, March.

Blockmans S et al. (2019) North Atlantic Treaty Organization (NATO) Reinforcing EU-NATO Cooperation—Walking the Talk? In: Wessel R A, Odermatt J (eds) Research Handbook on the European Union and International Organizations. Cheltenham/Northampton, pp. 411–428.

Bougrea A (2024) The European Investment Bank in Sub-Saharan Africa: constrained expansion. In Journal of Economic Policy Reform, 28(1):12–36.

Chamon M (2023) The use of Article 122 TFEU. Institutional implications and impact on democratic accountability. Brussels.

Clapp S (2022) Implementation of the Strategic Compass. Opportunities, challenges and timelines. European Parliament Research Service. Brussels, December.

Clapp S et al. (2025) ReArm Europe Plan/Readiness 2030: Financing EU Defence. European Parliamentary Research Service, Brussels.

Cottarelli C, Virgadamo L (2024) Spesa per la difesa nell'UE—Paesi. Institute for European Policymaking—Università Bocconi, Milan/Luglio.

Council of the EU (2022a) A Strategic Compass for Security and Defence—For a European Union that protects its citizens, values and interests and contributes to international peace and security. 7371/22, Brussels, 21 March.

Council of the EU (2022b) Revised paper on third-party countermeasures under international law. 15858/2022, Brussels, 17 November.

Dermine P (2025) A First Take On the Commission's ReArm Europe Plan. InVerfassungsblog.de, 5 March.

Duff A (2024) NATO and the European Union: Bridging the gap. European Policy Centre, Brussels, 13 May.

Eunews.com (2025) EIB raises 2025 defense financing to a record of up to 3.5 billion. 20 June. https://www.eunews.it/en.

Euronews.com (2025) Metsola threatens to sue Commission over plan to bypass MEPs to set up €150 bn defence loan plan. 7 July. https://euronews.com.

European Commission (2017) Reflection Paper on the Future of European Defence. COM/2017/0315 final, Brussels, 7 June.

European Commission (2025a) Strategy for the Savings and Investments Union (SIU). Brussels, 19 March 2025.

European Commission (2025b) Communication to the European Parliament and the Council, NextGenerationEU—The road to 2026. COM/2025/310 final, Brussels, 4 June.

European Commission, High Representative of the Union for Foreign Affairs and Security Policy/Vice-President of the European Commission (2025) Joint White Paper for European Defence Readiness 2030. JOIN/2025/120 final, Brussels, 19 March.

European Parliament (2024) The Activity Report. Developments and trends in the ordinary legislative procedure. 9th legislature (2019–2024), Brussels.

European Parliament (2025a) Resolution of 12 March 2025 on the white paper on the future of European defence.

European Parliament (2025b) Resolution of 2 April 2025 on the implementation of the common foreign and security policy—annual report 2024.

European Parliament (2025c) Resolution of 18 June 2025 on the implementation of the Recovery and Resilience Facility.

Fabbrini F (2025) EU Defence Capabilities after the War in Ukraine: The Act in Support of Ammunition Production and the Development of an EU Defence Industrial Policy. In: Govaere I, Garben S, Spaventa E (eds) Impact of War (in Ukraine) on the EU. Bloomsbury Publishing, pp. 167–186

Fiott D et al. (2017) Permanent Structured Cooperation: What's in a Name? EUISS, Paris.

Goldhammer A (2025) Toward a Declaration of European Independence. The Tocqueville Review, 46:91–108.

Grossio L (2025) Il Parlamento adisce la Corte di giustizia contestando il ricorso all'art. 122 TFUE per l'istituzione dello strumento di azione per la sicurezza dell'Europa (SAFE). Eurojus, 1 September.

Hoffmeister F (2024) Higher, faster, further: Recent legal developments in the European Union's Common Security and Defence Policy under the 2022 Strategic Compass. In: Kadelbach S, Hofmann R (eds.) The Common Security and Defence Policy of the EU. Perspectives from Member States. Nomos, Baden-Baden, pp. 55–72.

Insolia A (2025) The impact of the practice of international organizations on the United Nations recent works on cybersecurity. In DPCE Online 70(2):957–974.

López I (2025) Sobre el Plan ReArm Europe/Readiness 2030: (I) la activación de la cláusula de escape nacional. Apuntes Fedea 2025/17, April.

Maltatoday.com.mt (2025) Malta needs more defence engagement at EU level. 5 February. https://maltatoday.com.mt.

Missiroli A (2025) NATO: Il vertice del 5% e l'ombra lunga del disimpegno americano. ISPI, 25 June, www.ispionline.it.

Momtaz R (2025) Taking the Pulse: Should "Buy European" in Defense Spending Include the UK and Turkey? Carnegie Europe, Brussels, 20 March.

Politico.eu (2025) Zelensky, Trump speak in Rome in first meeting since Oval Office bust-up. 26 April. https://politico.eu.

President of the Commission (2025) State of the Union Address. Strasbourg, 10 September.

Sole24ore.com (2024) La Germania ha chiesto a Bruxelles una proroga sul Psb. 17 ottobre. https://sole24ore.com.

Terpan F (2013) Article 45 [Tasks and Powers of the European Defence Agency]. In: Blanke H-J, Mangiameli S (eds) The Treaty on European Union (TEU). A Commentary. Springer-Verlag Berlin/Heidelberg, pp. 1261–1274.

Chapter 11
The Transformation of the EU and of EU Governance as a Result of the War in Ukraine

Sara Poli, Madalina Moraru, Luca Paladini and Clara Portela

Contents

Abstract Our final chapter assesses how the EU was changed by the aggression of Ukraine in February 2022; the transformative effects of this event on the division of competences between the EU and its Member States and across several EU policy fields are scrutinised. We provide an overview of the findings yielded by our exploration of each of these policy fields, accompanied by a determination of the magnitude of their impact on EU governance and the institutional balance between the Commission and the Council. The contribution of the Court of Justice to preserving the effectiveness of restrictive measures while respecting the rule of law is also highlighted. The analysis demonstrates that, while effects were invariably far-reaching

Although the conclusions of the volume are the result of a collective effort by the authors, Sara Poli wrote Sects. 11.3 and 11.6.1; Madalina Moraru wrote Sects. 11.4, 11.5, 11.6.6 and 11.6.7; Luca Paladini wrote Sects. 11.6.3, 11.6.4 and 11.6.5; and Clara Portela wrote Sects. 11.1, 11.2 and 11.6.2.

S. Poli et al., *The EU's Response to the War in Ukraine and Its Impact on the EU Legal Order*, Global Europe: Legal and Policy Issues of the EU's External Action 7,
https://doi.org/10.1007/978-94-6265-767-0_11

in most policy fields (CFSP, the EU enlargement and crisis management), this was not the case in the CSDP. The chapter examines the practice of restrictive measures in the light of international law and identifies on the one hand, tensions between this practice and respect of international law and on the other hand, the EU's contribution to the development of international law when a State with veto power in the UN Security Council carries out an aggression. The EU's complex response to the war in Ukraine through restrictive measures is overall lawful.

Keywords CFSP · Sanctions · Competence · Migration · EU governance · Defence · Enlargement · Judicial review

11.1 The EU's Response Across Key Policy Fields and the Impact on the EU Legal Order

Our volume opened with the question as to whether the response to the Russian aggression against Ukraine had elicited not only major changes in EU policies, but also a transformation in the governance or character of the organisation. In order to answer this question, we explored a number of key policy fields such as CFSP, CSDP, enlargement and migration in-depth. Having reviewed innovations in all of them, we devote our final chapter to summarising and consolidating our findings. First, we focus on the response to the war in Ukraine and then on the impact that the EU's response has had on the policy fields examined in the volume.

11.2 The EU's Response Within the Framework of the CFSP

Within the framework of the CFSP, the EU has responded to the war in Ukraine by enacting an unprecedented range of restrictive measures against the Russian Federation and providing substantial support to Ukraine through CSDP initiatives, notably the European Peace Facility (EPF) and the launch of the EUMAM Ukraine training mission. The use of sanctions has taken centre stage in the EU response to Russian aggression, which justifies a thorough analysis of these measures. A first aspect that deserves mention is the broadening of designation criteria in sanctions regimes.[1] The definition of the designation criteria of individual restrictive measures has experienced a remarkable expansion. The possibility of inclusion in an EU blacklist affects not only those directly responsible for the condemned actions, but also individuals facilitating, supporting or benefiting from them, in addition to persons who are linked to these categories of individuals. Moreover, in addition to the condemned actions, such as the annexation and destabilisation efforts in our case, the inclusion in the

[1] See Chaps. 2 and 6.

list threatens notably those engaging in sanctions circumvention. These designation criteria are considerably broader than those applicable to other EU sanctions regimes. Their breath puts into question the traditionally targeted approach that characterised EU sanctions. Indeed, restrictive measures are increasingly employed to undermine the economic foundations of Russia, marking a shift away from the original objective of stigmatising individuals directly responsible for acts of aggression, annexation, destabilisation, and other violations of the sovereignty, territorial integrity, and independence of the affected state. Overall, the approach to sanctions has suffered alterations of such magnitude that they modify the character of the EU as a sender. Although it is still unknown whether the innovations identified will outlive the sanctions package against Russia, a line has been crossed that positions the EU as a bolder and more assertive sanctions sender than it used to be.

11.3 The EU's Response in the Context of the CFSP, the Impact on International Law and the Role of the Court of Justice

The EU's response to Russia's aggression through restrictive measures is impressive in terms of the number and variety of prohibitions or restrictions. The seriousness of the illegal activities carried out by Russia, which is a State with a veto power in the UNSC and the damages caused in Ukraine, in addition to the EU's proximity to the conflict, have made it necessary to display an intense legal and political effort to cease the aggression. International law obligations represent the outer limits for the EU. Support to Ukraine must be provided, ensuring full respect for international law. This was not without challenges. The EU has enacted very broad designation criteria in individual restrictive measures, and at times, the nexus with the primary targets was tenuous.[2] The General Court has ensured full respect of the designation criteria and, in some cases, for example, in *Tokareva*[3] or in cases involving family members, has annulled the impugned Council decision. Yet, the judiciary has overall shown particular attention to ensuring the effectiveness of sanctions, especially in litigation involving prominent business figures and their relatives.

The EU also responded to Russia's illegal activities through numerous sector-related restrictive measures. Some of them were innovative, as in the case of the broadcasting ban, which was considered lawful in the case of *Russia Today France*. Others, such as the freezing of the assets and reserves of the Russian Central Bank, were used in other contexts but were unprecedented for the potential impact on EU Member States: most of the Russian Central Bank's assets are in Belgium. This has placed the EU in a very difficult position: on the one hand, the need to support Ukraine's reconstruction and on the other hand, the need to protect the credibility of

---

[2] See Chap. 6.

[3] See Chap. 3.

the EU financial sector. The wide use of sector-related measures is in line with international law, considering the objective of the EU was to weaken the war machine. The case-law on sector-related restrictive measures is relatively modest compared to the challenges of individual sanctions by oligarchs and family members. It is noteworthy that the General Court has generally adopted a deferential stance towards the Council, prioritising the effectiveness of sanctions. This approach is evident in the rejection of annulment actions in *Russia Today France* and the *Ordre néerlandais des avocats du barreau de Bruxelles*.[4] This is in contrast to *Jemerak*, where the CJEU permitted Russian nationals to access notarial services for the purpose of divesting property within the Union, thereby introducing a pragmatic exception to the prohibition to provide legal advisory services. A special problem posed by sector-related measures concerns the progressive expansion of their global reach, in particular in 2024–2025. Those who support Russia's shadow fleet may be subject to sanctions. But these are not the only cases. Some of the most recent restrictions of July 2025 target operators in third countries and may be difficult to reconcile with the principle of prescriptive jurisdiction in selected cases. The justification for these measures is that they were enacted in a context of repeated violations of Member States' airspace by Russia's drones. The EU security was therefore directly undermined by the incursions of drones. A geographic amplification of the reach of restrictive measures has thus become necessary to protect the essential security interests of the EU Member States.

A truly innovative instrument concerns the exploitation of the revenues resulting from the reinvestment of the cash flow generated by the frozen assets of the Central Bank of Russia. In this case, the EU has devised a mechanism to provide a modest financial support to Ukraine, leaving sovereign assets intact in full respect of international law. A far more difficult challenge is represented by the confiscation of those assets which may be necessary in case Russia does not pay for the war damages after the cessation of the hostilities; it is not sure that the EU is willing to take these measures. Yet, the EU will have to play a crucial role in supporting Ukraine's requests for reparation of the war damages in order not to lose its credibility.

11.4 The Revitalisation of the Enlargement Policy

The EU institutions responded to the war in Ukraine by revitalising the enlargement policy. The conflict has fundamentally reconfigured the status of the enlargement within EU governance. This is also evident from the designation of a commissioner for enlargement within the *collège* of 2024. Once a stalled policy field beset by "enlargement fatigue," it has been transformed into a geopolitical tool, most visibly through the rapid granting of candidate status to Ukraine and Moldova in June 2022.[5] What had long been framed primarily as a conditionality-driven process of normative

---

[4] Ibid.

[5] See Chap. 8.

convergence has been recast as a strategic instrument of security and geopolitical consolidation. The swift granting of candidate status to Ukraine and Moldova, and the renewed attention to the Western Balkans, illustrate how enlargement now functions not only as a mechanism of legal approximation but also as a means to stabilise the Union's neighbourhood in the face of Russian aggression.

11.5 Solidarity in Action: The Activation of the Temporary Protection Directive ('TPD')

The Russian invasion of Ukraine in February 2022 triggered the largest displacement crisis in Europe since World War II. The Commission proposed to trigger the Temporary Protection Directive for the first time.[6] This act ('TPD'), which is a crisis instrument, had remained dormant in the European Union's legal framework since 2001; in practice, reliance on this Directive has exposed both its potential as a solidarity tool and its fragility as a rights instrument, given the fragmented application across Member States and its reliance on political framing. By linking EU law with UNHCR guidelines and global practice, Chap. 10 highlights tensions between protection and containment, temporariness and permanence, and solidarity and discretion. The Directive under exam mirrors the broader contradictions of EU migration governance: designed as a tool for protection, it has been repurposed by political contingencies and geopolitical interests.

Its asymmetrical implementation, combined with unequal refugee distribution and different national capacities, has resulted in a fragmented system where protection standards and long-term opportunities vary significantly among Member States. The successive extensions—now reaching five years—expose its structural limits. The absence of coordinated EU exit strategies and the shift toward national migration regimes risk deepening the fragmentation of responses and unequal protection standards, leaving many Ukrainians in protracted uncertainty. Without stronger coordination and clearer pathways to permanent status, the EU's temporary protection framework raises critical questions about the consistency of European solidarity, the influence of racialised and geopolitical narratives, and the future of rights-based crisis responses within the Union. It is noteworthy that solidarity also emerged in other policy areas, which were not explored in this book. The adoption of an EU-wide windfall tax on energy companies, justified by the extraordinary profits generated during the energy crisis provoked by Russia's aggression, is an example. Although formally based on internal market competencies, this initiative was politically framed as an act of solidarity, redistributing unexpected revenues to mitigate the social costs of soaring energy prices. It illustrates how emergency fiscal tools, typically reserved for national governments, were Europeanised under conditions of geopolitical strain.

[6] See Chap. 9.

11.6 The Impact of the War on the EU Legal Order

11.6.1 The War in Ukraine and Its Impact on EU Competences

The war in Ukraine has been the driver for an expansion of the EU's competence in the field of criminal law. This conflict has affected the division of competences between the EU and its Member States.[7] The effectiveness of restrictive measures was the justification put forward by the EU institutions to adopt Directive 2024/1226 and Directive 2024/1260. The former act imposes on Member States to criminalise the violation of restrictive measures, and its adoption is justified in the light of the principle of subsidiarity to the extent that this act establishes minimum rules concerning the definition of the violation of Union restrictive measures, thus making the latter more effective. The latter act concerns the confiscation of assets related to criminal activities, including the violation of restrictive measures; the adoption of this measure raises doubts as to its compliance with Article 5(2) of the TEU. The Commission seems to have taken the conflict in Ukraine and the need to ensure the effectiveness of restrictive measures as a pretext to regulate asset confiscation connected to criminal activities; overall, the adoption of this measure was not strictly necessary to make sanctions and, more generally, the CFSP more effective. The only link with the CFSP is represented by a provision that makes it possible to use the proceeds of the confiscation to support Ukraine's reconstruction. The link between the harmonisation of rules concerning asset confiscation and the objective of ensuring 'the effective implementation of a Union policy' (in this case, the CFSP) as set out in the Commission proposal for the Directive was strengthened during the legislative procedure. Yet, the Directive remains centred on fighting organised crime. Therefore, Directive 2024/1260 may be considered an example of 'harmonisation by stealth.' The Commission could have confined itself to proposing Directive 2024/1226 and to add in this act obligations of collaboration and information-sharing on Member States designed to identify the assets belonging to the persons targeted by the restrictive measures. This would have been sufficient to enhance the cooperation in identifying and recovering properties owned or controlled by the targeted persons and entities, an objective which is at the basis of Directive 2024/1260.[8]

---

[7] See Chap. 7.

[8] Article 29 TEU.

11.6.2 Institutional Developments: The Institutional Balance Between the Commission and the Council and the Role of the European Parliament as an Advocate of Solidarity

The new centrality of economic sanctions in EU foreign policy has allowed the European Commission to increase both its political influence and, to some extent, its formal powers. This was particularly thanks to its new role in the preparation of sanctions and especially in their implementation.[9] By the time the Ukraine war of 2022 erupted, an agenda prepared by the Commission to improve implementation and enforcement across the EU was already in place. The response to the war delivered a powerful impulse to a goal that had started to gather steam after the annexation of Crimea. Since 2014, the Commission had been gradually developing its role in sanctions implementation and enforcement, in a bid to increase the stringency and homogeneity of the EU's decentralised approach to ensuring the application of sanctions. Internally, EU exporters are now obliged to include an anti-circumvention clause in their commercial contracts. But the main innovations are visible externally, in sanctions legislation: participation by third-country actors in circumvention attempts can give rise to designations under EU sanctions regimes. Even third countries, different from Russia, face the prospect of being blacklisted for failing to adopt the necessary regulatory framework to avoid circumvention. This may give the EU's restrictive measures a global reach that exposes these measures to criticism for being extraterritorial in nature. Benefiting from the political impulse of the Ukraine war, the Commission enhanced its influence in sanctions implementation thanks to the establishment of an EU Sanctions Envoy under its remit. This is a *sui generis* figure in the EU external relations construct, different from the Special Representatives who report directly to the HR/VP, and who remain under the Council's remit. While efforts to combat circumvention are still ongoing and data on the effectiveness of the new measures is missing, the new legal arrangements to counter circumvention and the post of Special Envoy for the implementation of sanctions are designed to complement each other remarkably well. The Commission also spearheaded the criminalisation of sanctions violations,[10] a move that situates sanctions enforcement within the realm of EU criminal law, expanding the competences of the Union in an area traditionally reserved for Member States. Together, these initiatives highlight how the war prompted innovative uses of EU competences that may outlive the crisis, embedding solidarity and enforcement in the Union's constitutional practice. The European Parliament emerged as an important actor in shaping the political narrative of solidarity. Its resolutions in the early days of the war not only called for Ukraine's candidate status but also legitimised the activation of the Temporary Protection Directive as an expression of pan-European unity.[11] While the Parliament

---

[9] See Chap. 4.

[10] See Chap. 7.

[11] See Chap. 10.

lacks formal powers in the design of restrictive measures or in the activation of protection instruments, it has consistently pressed for robust humanitarian responses and a principled approach to solidarity. In the migration field, it has acted as a counterweight to the Council's preference for discretionary burden-sharing, insisting on stronger rights guarantees for displaced persons. In the enlargement debate, it has functioned as an agenda-setter and norm entrepreneur, advocating for swift progress and anchoring enlargement within a rule-of-law and values-based framework.[12] The Parliament's interventions thus underscore the significance of symbolic authority and democratic legitimacy in crisis governance, complementing the executive-driven measures of the Commission and the Council.

11.6.3 Consensus Building Within the CFSP and the Reliance on Flexible Mechanisms

The adoption of CFSP measures in reaction to the war has revealed tensions in consensus-building.[13] While unanimity remains the formal rule for the Council, Member States have relied on flexible mechanisms such as temporary derogations to accommodate their specific energy security concerns. In the context of the CFSP, constructive abstention (under Article 31(1) second paragraph TEU) was relied upon on several occasions. The war in Ukraine provided the opportunity to test the effects of this mechanism designed to facilitate the achievement of consensus-building. As it is known, a dissenting Member State is not obliged to implement the CFSP decision; therefore, a redistribution of operational burdens among supporting Member States is necessary. In practice, compensatory measures undertaken by dissenting States—especially neutral ones in relation to the EPF—have emerged as tangible expressions of the duty to actively and unreservedly support the CFSP in a spirit of loyalty and mutual solidarity, as enshrined in Article 24(3) TEU. These voluntary commitments may be understood as derivative obligations stemming from the general duty to support CFSP. More broadly, the level of flexibility within the CFSP decision-making architecture has increased. The persistent tension between the imperative of unity in EU external action—championed by the European Parliament, the Council, and many Member States—and the divergent national interests pursued by others has led to adaptive shifts in the institutional practice. These adjustments may, in the future, give rise to procedural innovations aimed at overcoming systematic or obstructive decision-making deadlocks.

[12] See Chap. 8.

[13] See Chap. 5.

11.6.4 The Comparatively Limited Impact of the War on the Defence Policy

The impact of the war has been comparatively limited on the 'defence component' of the CFSP—understood as the protection of European borders and territory rather than support for third countries.[14] Although the Strategic Compass was adopted in March 2022, its implementation has been slow and only partially satisfactory. Progress has been incremental, and the sense of urgency required to accelerate the construction of a European defence architecture has not materialised. This inertia was compounded by the continued reliability of NATO's security guarantee, which remained unquestioned during President Biden's administration. A substantive shift occurred with Presidency Trump and the developments of early 2025. Following the meeting between Trump and Zelenskyy on 28 February 2025, and the announcement of a US disengagement from NATO, momentum towards European defence integration intensified. The Readiness 2030 initiative was swiftly approved, and its implementation—though ongoing—has proceeded at an accelerated pace. This shift reflects what may be termed the 'Trump effect': a strategic recalibration prompted by the perceived erosion of transatlantic guarantees. In parallel, the so-called 'Putin effect'—if one may adopt such a term—has served to further intensify momentum behind European defence initiatives. This refers to the European response to armed incursions involving violations of Polish and Romanian airspace by Russian drones, widely interpreted as tests of European resolve. In her State of the Union speech on 10 September 2025, the President of the European Commission explicitly linked these developments to new defence initiatives, stating: "This is why I can also announce that Europe will frontload EUR 6 billion from the ERA loan and enter into a Drone Alliance with Ukraine. Ukraine has the ingenuity. What it needs now is scale." She also announced the creation of a European Defence Semester, modelled on the European Semester for economic policy, intended to support the EU's efforts to coordinate defence planning and expenditure across Member States by synchronising national defence strategies with EU-level priorities. The Trump and Putin effects have also instilled renewed vigour in European support for Ukraine, as it clearly emerges from the Commission President's remarks in the mentioned speech: "The images in Alaska were not easy to digest. But just a few days later, Europe's Leaders came to Washington to support President Zelenskyy and secure commitments." This statement reflects a turning point in the EU posture: Ukraine's exclusion from direct negotiations between Washington and Moscow in the Alaska summit catalysed a collective reaffirmation of solidarity. The swift mobilisation of European leaders in Washington signalled not only diplomatic alignment but a renewed commitment to defending Ukraine's sovereignty.

[14] See Chap. 5.

11.6.5 *The Role of the CJEU Within the CFSP*

The role of the Court of Justice in the CFSP has been crucial to ensuring the effectiveness of restrictive measures while respecting the rule of law. The Court's position in pending cases will be no less important. A particularly significant development is the Parliament's challenge—for the first time—to a CFSP decision adopted by the Council (C-883/24).[15] The contested decision provides for the adoption of implementing acts by unanimity, contrary to Article 31(2), third indent, TEU, which prescribes qualified majority voting for decisions implementing a Union action or position. The case might prompt a reconfiguration of the CFSP decision-making process. Its importance is underscored by the intervention of the High Representative/Vice-President of the Commission in the proceedings, advocating for a broader application of qualified majority voting—a position reiterated by the Commission President in her 2025 address before the European Parliament. Equally noteworthy is Hungary's action for annulment in T-457/24, challenging a decision of the EPF Committee. The case concerns the so-called 'domino effect' of constructive abstention, whereby a Member State—having abstained constructively—is excluded from subsequent decision-making and financial obligations. Should the General Court deem the action admissible, it will be instructive to observe its interpretation of the legal consequences of constructive abstention, which are not explicitly regulated by the Treaties. Finally, in the context of the TFEU, attention must be given to the Parliament's action for annulment of the SAFE regulation adopted under Article 122 TFEU (C-560/25). The Parliament contests the use of the emergency procedure, arguing that it bypasses the ordinary legislative process and undermines institutional balance. While the Court's prior jurisprudence may lend support to the Parliament's claims, it is worth noting that the SAFE regulation may nonetheless be 'safe'. The Parliament did not seek its immediate annulment, but rather its replacement upon the adoption of a new legislative act. Given that 19 Member States have already submitted loan requests under the €150 billion programme, and implementation is imminent, it is likely that by the time the Court delivers its judgment—should it favour the Parliament—the SAFE regulation will have already produced its intended effects. This could pave the way for a successor regulation, adopted under a non-emergency legal basis, with full parliamentary involvement.

[15] Ibid.

11.6.6 The Transformation of Enlargement into a Geopolitical Priority

Enlargement has thus become embedded in the EU's security rationale: by anchoring vulnerable states within the Union's legal and institutional orbit, it reduces their exposure to external coercion and reinforces the EU's collective security. Yet this geopolitical turn also magnifies tensions within the enlargement framework. The unanimity requirement in the Council continues to expose the process to political blockages unrelated to legal conditionality, while the flexibility introduced to advance Ukraine's candidacy risks eroding the credibility of the Copenhagen criteria. Enlargement now serves as a dual instrument: a security measure to anchor vulnerable states within the EU's normative and institutional order, and a constitutional challenge that tests the Union's capacity to adapt its decision-making procedures. The Ukrainian case illustrates both dimensions: while accession conditionality has been formally preserved, its application has become more flexible, infused with strategic considerations of security and resilience. The implications are twofold. On the one hand, enlargement has regained centrality as an external policy instrument of the Union in times of conflict. On the other hand, it exposes institutional fragilities, from unanimity in the Council to rule of law backsliding within the Union itself. Whether enlargement consolidates into a credible, reformed policy framework or reverts to past inertia will be decisive for the EU's long-term character as both a legal order and a geopolitical union. Building on this shift, Chap. 8 has argued that the credibility and resilience of enlargement will depend on institutional reform, including the introduction of qualified majority voting for intermediary steps of the accession process, in order to limit political blockages and align enlargement more closely with the Union's strategic and security interests.

11.6.7 Uncertainties in the Reformed Crisis Framework

The successful and swift activation of the Temporary Protection Directive (TPD) in response to the mass influx of Ukrainians ultimately preserved this instrument as part of the EU's crisis management architecture under the New Pact on Migration and Asylum. The reformed framework now comprises three main tools—the TPD, the Crisis (or Exceptions) Regulation, and the Solidarity Pool—which may operate independently or concurrently. This layered architecture reflects the EU's attempt to build a more resilient and flexible system capable of addressing both humanitarian emergencies and the geopolitical manipulation of migration flows. However, the Ukrainian war also reinforced the securitisation of migration within EU policymaking, where refugees are increasingly viewed not solely as rights-holders but as potential vectors of instability. Migration thus appears ever more entangled with security discourses and strategic geopolitical calculations, raising concerns that crisis-driven mechanisms—originally designed to uphold protection standards—risk becoming subordinated to security logics. While the New Pact introduces a broader array of crisis management instruments, their fragmented application risks weakening the system of international protection. The isolated use of derogation measures under the Exceptions Regulation, without the balancing function of the TPD, can exacerbate institutional incoherence, erode basic rights, and undermine adherence to international and EU protection obligations. Although the TPD's implementation has revealed several shortcomings, it remains the instrument most aligned with international protection standards, providing a structured and rights-based response to mass influx situations. By contrast, the Exceptions Regulation's security-driven approach and extensive derogations risk addressing only the symptoms of a crisis rather than its root causes, unless complemented by broader political and diplomatic measures. The EU has therefore missed a critical opportunity to establish a cohesive, rights-centred crisis framework. An integrated approach—ensuring that the TPD's minimum protection guarantees remain intact when applied alongside the new crisis tools—would offer a more coherent, humane, and effective response to large-scale displacement within an increasingly securitised migration governance landscape.

Index

S. Poli et al., *The EU's Response to the War in Ukraine and Its Impact on the EU Legal Order*, Global Europe: Legal and Policy Issues of the EU's External Action 7,
https://doi.org/10.1007/978-94-6265-767-0

F

G

H

I

P

R

S

T

U

V

W

FSC
www.fsc.org
MIX
Papier | Fördert gute Waldnutzung
FSC® C083411

Kolibri 360 GmbH
Ferdinand-Jühlke-Straße 7
99095 Erfurt, Deutschland
produktsicherheit@kolibri360.de